Navigating Historical Crosscurrents in the Irish Atlantic:
Essays for Catherine B. Shannon

Catherine B. Shannon; Glucksman Ireland House-NYU, 2018
(Image courtesy of Glucksman Ireland House, New York University)

Navigating Historical Crosscurrents in the Irish Atlantic
Essays for Catherine B. Shannon

MARY C. KELLY

EDITOR

First published in 2022 by
Cork University Press
Boole Library
University College Cork
CORK
T12 ND89
Ireland

© the author, 2022

Library of Congress Control Number: 2022932546
Distribution in the USA: Longleaf Services, Chapel Hill, NC, USA

All rights reserved. No part of this book may be reprinted or reproduced or utilised
in any electronic, mechanical or other means, now known or hereafter invented,
including photocopying and recording or otherwise, without either the prior written
permission of the publishers or a licence permitting restricted copying in Ireland
issued by the Irish Copyright Licensing Agency Ltd., 25 Denzille Lane, Dublin 2.

British Library Cataloguing in Publication Data
A CIP record for this book is available from the British Library.

ISBN 978-1-78205-499-3

Printed by BZ Graf in Poland.
Print origination & design by Carrigboy Typesetting Services
www.carrigboy.co.uk

COVER IMAGE – courtesy of Shutterstock.com
Front flap: Celtic Cross erected in Cohasset Central Cemetery, Massachusetts,
by AOH in 1914 to honour those lost in the 1849 *Brig St. John* shipwreck.
Photo by Kjeld Mahoney, Kjeld Mahoney Gallery, Scituate, Massachusetts.

www.corkuniversitypress.com

Contents

LIST OF FIGURES	vii
NOTES ON CONTRIBUTORS	viii
ACKNOWLEDGEMENTS	xi

PREFACE: CATHERINE B. SHANNON: HAPPY RECOLLECTIONS
Nicholas Canny xiii

INTRODUCTION
Mary C. Kelly 1

PART 1: FRAMING THE IRISH ATLANTIC

1 The 'Kingdom of God' and the 'kingdom of Ireland': the life, work and politics of hymnist Cecil Frances Alexander (1818–95)
Mary M. Burke and Rachael Sealy Lynch 13

2 Shovelling out Ireland's permanent deadweight during the Great Famine: the Cork workhouse paupers sent to New Brunswick in 1850
Gerard Moran 25

3 Ireland, America and transnational radicalism
David M. Doolin 44

4 When history and hope rhymed: Fanny Parnell – nationalist, feminist and patriot poet
Christine Kinealy 61

5 'I cannot banish the thought of home': young Irish women's responses to urban-industrial America
Kerby A. Miller 74

6 The Balfour war mission to America in 1917 and the Irish problem
Francis M. Carroll 88

PART 2: CROSSCURRENTS: IDENTITIES AND INCARNATIONS

7 'Ireland's family re-union': the 1932 Eucharistic Congress
Mary E. Daly 105

8	Differing with the American cousins: the Irish Catholics of Canada fight the Great War, 1914–18 *Mark G. McGowan*	120
9	The *Gaelic American*, 1921–8: reporting on the Anglo-Irish Treaty and the Irish Free State *Michael Doorley*	137
10	Duelling mythologies of James Michael Curley *Suzann Buckley*	152
11	John McGahern and the historian of modern Ireland *Diarmaid Ferriter*	166
12	Wild Atlantic Ways *Gearóid Ó Tuathaigh*	184
13	John Hume and the evolution of power-sharing in Northern Ireland *Seán Farren*	197
14	Boston's three Irelands: busing, class and Irish ethnic identity, 1970–2015 *Matthew O'Brien*	211

PART 3: BRIDGING ATLANTIC WORLDS

15	'forever one and the same person' *Thomas E. Hachey*	229
16	Charting a course: framing scholarship and practical politics in the work of Catherine B. Shannon *Maureen O'Rourke Murphy*	236
17	Catherine B. Shannon: in her own words *Edited by Miriam Nyhan Grey*	244
18	Catherine B. Shannon and the role of women in the Northern Ireland peace process *Monica McWilliams*	262
19	Safe spaces on the Falls *Margaret MacCurtain*	267

NOTES	275
SELECT BIBLIOGRAPHY	319
INDEX	331

List of figures

1.1 Window in north vestibule commemorating poet and hymn-writer Cecil Frances Alexander, St Columb's Cathedral, Derry, Northern Ireland.   8

5.1 Mary Ann Rowe.   77

5.2 Mary Ann Rowe Sutton, 1897.   77

5.3 James Rowe Sutton, 6 months, 1898.   77

6.1 Robert Lansing, secretary of state (1915–20), greeting A.J. Balfour, Washington, DC, 1917.   92

17.1 Catherine B. Shannon's maternal grandparents, Bridget (neé Tonra) Cannon (1867–1942) and Thomas Cannon (1863–1940), both from County Mayo.   245

17.2 Cork-born New York businessman David J. Shannon (1842–1908), paternal grandfather of Catherine B. Shannon, undated.   246

17.3 Catherine B. Shannon with her maternal grandmother, Bridget Cannon, Hingham, Massachusetts, *c.*1941.   251

17.4 Catherine B. Shannon in November 2019, receiving a doctorate of sacred letters (*honoris causa*) from the University of St Michael's College, University of Toronto.   260

Notes on contributors

GENERAL EDITOR: Mary C. Kelly is professor of history at Franklin Pierce University. Her research interests include Irish-American Famine memory, political and intellectual cultures, and the historical relationship with Ireland. She is a native of Westport, County Mayo.

PREFACE: Nicholas Canny is an emeritus professor of history at NUI Galway and a former president of the Royal Irish Academy. His most recent book, *Imagining Ireland's Pasts*, was published by Oxford University Press in 2021.

CONTRIBUTORS

Suzann Buckley (1943–2021) held several academic roles, including provost and professor of history. Her research encompassed twentieth-century Canadian history, women's history, and Irish-American history.

Mary M. Burke is a professor of English at the University of Connecticut, where she directs the Irish Literature Concentration. She has published widely on Irish and Irish-American culture and identities.

Francis M. Carroll is professor emeritus at St John's College, University of Manitoba. His most recent book is *America and the Making of an Independent Ireland*.

Mary E. Daly is professor emerita in Irish history at University College Dublin. She has published widely on the history of nineteenth- and twentieth-century Ireland.

David M. Doolin is Newman Fellow at the School of History, University College Dublin. His teaching and research cover nineteenth- and twentieth-century American and Irish history topics.

Michael Doorley is associate lecturer in history in the Open University in Ireland. His research and publications focus on Irish-American nationalism in Irish revolutionary years 1912–22.

Notes on contributors

Seán Farren is a visiting professor at Ulster University's School of Education and former minister of further and higher education in Northern Ireland. He is author-editor of *John Hume in His Own Words* (2018).

Diarmaid Ferriter is professor of modern Irish history at UCD. A member of the Royal Irish Academy, he has published extensively on the social, political and cultural history of twentieth-century Ireland.

Miriam Nyhan Grey is associate director and the global coordinator for Irish studies at New York University. She specialises in the intersections of migration, race and ethnicity.

Thomas E. Hachey is university professor of history emeritus, Boston College, who specialises in twentieth-century Anglo-Irish relations and Irish-American history.

Christine Kinealy is a graduate of Trinity College in Dublin and is author of many books on nineteenth-century Ireland, with a focus on the Famine and the abolition movement. In 2013, she was appointed founding director of Ireland's Great Hunger Institute at Quinnipiac University.

Rachael Sealy Lynch is emerita professor of English at the University of Connecticut, and specialises in recent and contemporary Irish women's fiction.

Margaret MacCurtain, OP (1929–2020), retired from the History Department of University College Dublin, where she introduced women's history during her forty years of teaching there. Prioress of Sion Hill convent, she was the recipient of six honorary degrees.

Mark G. McGowan is professor of history at the University of Toronto and principal and vice-president of the University of St Michael's College. He is an award-winning author of books and articles on the Catholic Church in Canada, Irish migration to North America, and the Great Famine.

Monica McWilliams is emerita professor in women's studies at Ulster University and led the Northern Ireland Women's Coalition's negotiating team in the multi-party peace talks leading up to the 1998 Good Friday Agreement.

Notes on contributors

Kerby A. Miller is curators' professor emeritus of history at the University of Missouri and author of several books about Ireland and Irish emigration, including the prize-winning *Emigrants and Exiles* (1985).

Gerard Moran is a researcher at the Social Science Research Centre at NUI Galway and has lectured in the Department of History, NUI Galway, and Maynooth University. His research interests include Irish emigration and the diaspora, and famines and subsistence in Ireland.

Matthew O'Brien is a professor of history at Franciscan University in Steubenville, Ohio. He specialises in twentieth-century Irish migration and ethnicity.

Maureen O'Rourke Murphy is professor emerita at Hofstra University and the former co-director of the university's Irish Studies programme.

Gearóid Ó Tuathaigh is professor emeritus in history at the National University of Ireland, Galway, and was a member of the Irish Council of State 2011–18.

Acknowledgements

The title of this book and the cover image evoke a centuries-long history of Irish Atlantic migration that shaped both native home and adopted North American homelands. They also reference the transatlantic scholarship and advocacy of the book's honouree, Professor Catherine B. Shannon. Likewise well-represented is my own experience as enduringly Irish, together with newer American roots – cultural navigations familiar to several contributors to this volume. Collectively, these meanings inform the efforts of all involved in bringing this book to fruition. It is a pleasure to thank each and every one of the contributors for their careful scholarship and their collegial cooperation throughout the book's preparation. I am privileged to have worked with such eminent historians, Irish Studies scholars, and public leaders to honour our friend and colleague, Professor Shannon. I further appreciate the inclusion of the essays of Professors Margaret MacCurtain, OP, and Suzann Buckley here, following their sad passing in 2020 and 2021, respectively. Suzann's assistance and support in the preparation of this book are deeply appreciated. She will be missed.

Several individuals assisted with specific tasks in the book's development. I am grateful to Nicholas Canny for his luminous preface and helpful involvement throughout. I thank Kieran Hoare, archivist at James Hardiman Library, NUI Galway, for his efforts to secure permission to publish the Mary Ann Rowe photographs, and Kate Manning, principal archivist at UCD Archives, for her help in tracking down permissions. Thanks to the honouree for the personal photographs appearing in the book, and to Glucksman Ireland House, New York University, for the frontispiece image. I also credit the Library of Congress, Prints and Photographs Division, for the Balfour photograph by Harris & Ewing (repr. no. LC-DIG-hec-08329), and Andreas F. Borchert for the Cecil Frances Alexander window photograph. I am indebted to Kjeld Mahoney and the Kjeld Mahoney Gallery, Scituate, Massachusetts, for permission to reproduce his photograph of the Cohasset Cross on the book jacket, and to John Sullivan, Esq., also of Scituate, for his kind assistance and interest in the book. To James S. Donnelly Jr for early encouragement, and the input and support of American Conference for Irish Studies friends, particularly E. Moore Quinn, Beth Anish O'Leary, Margaret Lasch Carroll, David Brundage and (Westport-area native) Mary Madec – thank you indeed. I am grateful to New Hampshire Humanities lecture audiences who refresh and refine my thinking on Irish-American history. I thank Margaret Susan Thompson at Syracuse University for valuable lessons on writing history. Many of them find reflection in this volume. I also would like to acknowledge here the professionalism and guidance of all involved with this book's preparation at Cork University Press, particularly the judicious manuscript readers, editor Maria O'Donovan, publication director Mike Collins, the design team, and copy-editor Aonghus Meaney.

At Franklin Pierce University, my History Department colleagues Douglas A. Ley (1958–2021) and Melinda M. Jetté provided support and encouragement throughout this process. Doug's sad passing in June 2021 renders all the more meaningful his assistance in helping me navigate converging realms of teaching, writing and labour organising with characteristic resourcefulness and humour. I am grateful to other colleagues who enriched this book's evolution: Donna Decker, Frank Cohen, Séamus Pender, Jed Donelan, Jessica Landis, Zan Walker-Goncalves, John Lund, library director Paul Jenkins, librarians Jill Wixom and Amy Horton, and former dean Kerry McKeever (d. 2021) – thank you all. I also express gratitude to current and former students who provided research assistance: Adam Carman, Abigail Purches, Cameron Supple, Shinel Nicholas and Alexa M. Harrington.

Finally, thanks, as always, to my Barrett family in-laws, and Catherine Roddy, Michele King-Harrington, and my cousin Aedamar Kirrane for the right words at the right times. Warm thanks to Sean Tierney, Frances Tierney and Frank Steffens, to my Ruane relatives, and especially to my sisters Eileen Kelly, Jane Tierney and Susan Kelly for consistent support and input, and my brother James Kelly for all of the above and guidance to obscure sources. Boundless thanks to my husband Mike Barrett and daughter Eileen Barrett for the myriad ways they supported me on this book's voyage – your loving support is everything. Lastly, it is a pleasure to present this volume to Catherine, in thanks and in appreciation for her exceptional contributions in spheres of Irish history, politics, and culture on both sides of the Atlantic.

MK
NH, 2021

PREFACE

Catherine B. Shannon: happy recollections

Nicholas Canny

My first meeting with Catherine B. Shannon, or the first I can recall, was in November or early December 1974 at a dinner party in the Brookline apartment of her friend Donald Logan. I can remember the time with precision because I was spending that semester as a visiting Fulbright Fellow at Harvard without my wife, Morwena Denis, who, in my absence, had given birth to our daughter on 2 November in her home city of Rennes in Brittany, and was prohibited from travelling to join me in the United States for the six weeks it took to recover from a caesarean section. These circumstances had brought me back to being a bachelor in a strange city, and Donald Logan, whom I had known from days we had spent together as researchers at the old Public Record Office in London, had generously called on me to join his party at dinner.

Besides Catherine and Donald, the other diner, whose name I do not recall, was an Irish woman attached to the Irish consulate in Boston. It soon became clear in conversation that Catherine, who at this point held an established faculty position in history at Westfield State College, Massachusetts, had become an unofficial liaison officer between Ireland and the Irish-American community in Boston. Her self-defined duty at the local level was to explain to people of Irish birth and descent how the Ireland they had known or imagined was being transformed and challenged both by its membership, since May 1973, of the European Economic Community (now the European Union), and by the ongoing 'Troubles' in Northern Ireland that had erupted in 1969. Then on her

xiii

xiv *Preface*

travels to the other side of the Atlantic, Catherine had taken to explaining to relatives, friends and the wider community how Irish America, or at least Irish Boston, was responding to developments at 'home'.

Another matter that I can recall from that evening is the enthusiasm Catherine expressed for the interlude she had spent at University College Dublin, where in 1963 she had completed an MA by research in history mentored by Professors T. Desmond Williams and Kevin B. Nowlan. She spoke with warm affection of both men (now sadly no longer with us), while making it clear that her moral supporter in those UCD days had been Margaret MacCurtain, or Sister Benvenuta as she would certainly still have been known in 1963. It was clear from conversation with Catherine on that evening that it was her two academic mentors who had kindled her interest in Arthur, Lord Balfour – nephew of Lord Salisbury – whose involvement with Ireland would preoccupy Catherine for many years, but that it was Margaret MacCurtain (happily able to receive visits from Catherine whenever she passed through Dublin) who had raised her awareness of women's rights (or rather the suppression of them) in Ireland, the United States and internationally – an issue that has preoccupied Catherine Shannon ever since.

I doubt that I was able on that evening to enlighten Catherine on either one of her two academic interests. Despite this we remained in touch and, when I next visited the United States for an academic year in 1979–80, Catherine arranged to have me speak to an academic/community group at Westfield State College. On this occasion my wife, and now two children, accompanied me, and we all stayed over in Catherine's house. I recall that she had arranged a reception with lots of people, but I have no idea on what subject I spoke since for me and Morwena the abiding memory of that visit was that our daughter spent her every waking moment in Westfield howling for a security toy that she had lost in the course of our car journey there. Because Catherine is a woman with a forgiving nature, she obliterated this disruption of a cherished academic/social event from her memory and remained in touch and has visited us in Galway on her intermittent expeditions to Ireland.

Such visits were, in the early years, primarily academic, because Catherine was working on what is known as 'constructive unionism', which culminated in the book that has become the standard work of reference on the subject: *Arthur J. Balfour and Ireland, 1874–1922* (Washington, DC, 1988). The publication of this excellent study marked the completion of an odyssey that had begun with Catherine's UCD MA thesis on the

Preface   xv

Irish Local Government Act of 1898, and that had persisted through her preparation of a PhD degree at the University of Massachusetts, Amherst, which she conducted simultaneously with her teaching at Westfield. The subject of Catherine's PhD dissertation was Balfour and Ireland, and once Catherine was conferred with her doctorate in 1975, she continued to work on the subject until she published it in book form thirteen years later.

Many seemed to think that Catherine had chosen to write on Balfour because he was considered the villain who had proposed the partition of Ireland and the creation of a twenty-six-county Free State as a Tory solution to the Irish problem. However, while Catherine did nothing to hide her disdain for the sometimes shady understandings that Balfour and his Tory associates engaged upon with the more intransigent unionists, she was generally sympathetic towards Balfour, who she portrayed as an honourable man who, with his brother Gerald and George Wyndham, successively chief secretaries for Ireland, believed that the demand of home rule for Ireland, and the consequent break-up of the United Kingdom, could be averted if a Tory government pursued ameliorative policies for Ireland. Their only caveat was that these had to be policies of Tory devising, and based on some 'scientific' evidence, rather than surrenders to extra-legal pressures in Ireland.

Once Catherine's book was published and her reputation established as a leading authority on British/Irish relations in the late nineteenth and early twentieth centuries, I noted that whenever she dropped by on her ever more regular visits to Ireland, her end purpose seemed invariably to be conferences and seminars, usually in Northern Ireland locations, dedicated to considering and seeking solutions for what seemed the increasingly intractable problem of Northern Ireland with its escalating death toll. It was evident also that she still saw herself as a mediator between some in the Irish-American community, who favoured what she saw to be simplistic solutions to complex problems, and groups in Northern Ireland (particularly women's groups) who remained hopeful (even at the bleakest moments) that solutions could be found notwithstanding the complexity of the problems.

As Catherine spoke, always with enthusiasm, of this new transatlantic mission she was engaged upon, she also mentioned with admiration the new friends she had made among women peace-seekers, of both denominations and none, in Northern Ireland. At this stage she had moved into a realm of which I knew nothing. However, we can see with the benefit of hindsight how prescient Catherine was in recognising that it was women from both sides who had witnessed too much suffering who led the way to finding a solution by standing up to the hard men within their communities for whom violence had become their favoured way of life, and death. The phenomenon that Catherine came to understand from the connections she had established on the ground in Northern Ireland, and that she has explained in many of her presentations and published papers over the past three decades, has been described in graphic detail by the Belfast-born Anna Burns in *Milkman*, which, to date, has won more prizes than any of her other novels. Burns explains how those she describes as the 'issue women' succeeded in winning over the 'normal women' and the 'traditional women', including the narrator's own mother, to their point of view, as a preliminary to forcing the gunmen to desist from what she represents as bullying actions.[1]

This brief appraisal will, I trust, show how Catherine Shannon has become an authority on each of the two academic interests she developed during the years she spent as a student at UCD. However, as she won international recognition as an authority on these particular subjects, she continued to expand her interests in all aspects of Irish Studies and became ever more active in the several organisations in the United States, and particularly in Boston, that promoted these interests. I had an opportunity to witness this expanded interest and expertise at first hand when Catherine spent the year 2001–2 as the Irish-American Cultural Institute Research Fellow at NUI Galway. This has been made manifest also in her more recent involvement with promoting the study of the Great Irish Famine as a transatlantic phenomenon. My wife also, who, as I mentioned, was absent from that introductory dinner in Brookline, enjoyed many opportunities to bond with Catherine Shannon during the year she spent in Galway. For that reason also I consider it an honour and a privilege to introduce this richly deserved *festschrift* dedicated to Catherine B. Shannon – a committed, imaginative and talented transatlantic ambassador for Irish Studies.

Introduction

Mary C. Kelly

Historians crafting accounts of the past follow a familiar sequence of steps as they marshal evidence and create arguments. Employing the traditional tools of the historian's trade, they seek to construct meaningful understandings of past experiences. They also address gaps and shortcomings in their selected fields of historical inquiry, frequently accompanied by earnest promises to navigate ideological currents and depths, anchor or debunk arguments, plumb historiographical waves, nail interpretative colours to polemical masts, and chart new courses. Some topics lend themselves to such nautical-themed rhetorical devices more directly than others, of course, but the pages ahead provide a clear example of synchronicity between these lexical props and the book's historical content. As the title proclaims, and as the subject matter affirms, centuries of emigrant Irish passage across the Atlantic exerts enduring influence over Ireland's modern historical course. The present collection addresses a range of themes and experiences forged by these Atlantic movements or framed within their contexts. Honouring the scholarly achievements of Professor Catherine B. Shannon, the essays gathered here reflect major themes in her contributions to the modern history of Ireland and of Ireland's North American diaspora.

* * *

A century's worth of scholarship on emigrant Irish passage across the Atlantic evolved from pioneering accounts in the 1920s and 1930s, followed by Oscar Handlin's evocative narratives on immigrant Irish displacement and exile.[1] These studies emerged in years when negative perceptions of Roman Catholic Irish communities in the United States had still not entirely disappeared. Over those same years, furthermore, much of Ireland's social and cultural history had yet to be considered worthy of professional study. As Cold War tensions and social-justice movements informed and reconfigured the writing of history in the wake of the Second World War, however, both Irish and Irish-American topics gained increasing acceptability. By the time Handlin observed that '[t]he whole history of the peopling of the continent had been one of immigration',[2] scholarly engagement with Irish arrival and settlement had begun to formalise. In notable progressions over several decades in the later 1900s, Cecil Woodham-Smith's landmark study broadened academic and popular understandings of transatlantic Irish movement,[3] and Nicholas Canny and others developed Atlantic world theories that supplanted older accounts of population movement and labour supply and revealed transatlantic incubators of Irish identity.[4] Colonial American east coast ports and industrial centres took on new significance within these studies. Maurice Bric's revolutionary-era Philadelphia, for example, emerged as a dynamic internationalist locus visited by prominent United Irishmen (including Theobald Wolfe Tone in August 1795) who actively cultivated political operations on both sides of the Atlantic.[5]

The briny thoroughfare solidified as an Irish immigrant crucible by the end of the twentieth century, as concepts of representation, meaning and symbolism drew the interest of historians who embraced expanding social and cultural turns in those years.[6] Wrought in words and images, from shipping company advertisements to Famine-era emigration schemes, and dispatched in streams of handwritten correspondence from North American streetscapes to Ireland's rural townlands, the Atlantic world encompassed a rich historical storehouse.[7] Explorations of the 'truly transatlantic phenomenon' of Protestant Covenanters entered the narrative, alongside experiences of other Irish cohorts who negotiated the saltwater passage.[8]

Since then, themes of religious affiliation, political activism, educational advancement, immigrant labour and other ethnic identity markers have continued to inform transatlantic models.[9] Recent emphasis on economic exchange as crucial to Irish identity construction is further expanding the field.[10] As such, our understanding of ways in which the Atlantic both separated and homogenised the Irish, and established North American immigrant enclaves as wellsprings of connection with the native home, has grown more sophisticated. This is particularly true regarding quantitative and globalised interpretations.[11] Traditional focuses such as agricultural failure, the erosion of land-holding systems, transatlantic

Introduction 3

fares, and shipboard experiences may now be examined within new analytic frameworks.[12] Likewise, findings of gendered emigrant conditions and coded civil, labour, educational and legal restrictions recover the experience of women migrants and reconfigure the field accordingly.[13] Bronwen Walter's 'circulatory Transatlantic journeys' theory and Michèle Milan's 'translocal' and 'expatriate' models, for example, expose previously understudied exchange channels, as do new approaches to centuries of Ulster Scots movement to North America.[14] Building on these advancements, the essays that follow engage a number of these approaches and conceptual frameworks in making new contributions to the field.

* * *

No reflection on transatlantic history would be complete without addressing efforts to incorporate nationalist campaigns. Among many explorations of these political currents, Kerby A. Miller's study of emigration and *mentalité(s)* retains influence almost forty years on. His landmark book *Emigrants and Exiles* infiltrated inner sanctuaries of the emigrant experience, including the polarising theme of exile, and restored agency to anonymous souls whom a generation of historians had professed to study, but often ignored.[15] Historical accounts of North American communities within, from and to which nationalist leaders conducted transatlantic campaigns now incorporate the activism of John Mitchel, Charles Stewart Parnell, John Devoy and Éamon de Valera, to take prominent examples, as a matter of course.[16] A number of the essays in the present collection add to the scholarship in analysing the Atlantic passage from the perspective of political actors between the Famine and the treaty.[17] They affirm the crosscurrents navigated beneath Fenian, Land League and similar banners,[18] and consider the theme of Irishness within concepts of duality, ethnic identity and performativity.[19]

These explorations also shed new light on Irish–US foreign relations,[20] as transatlantic linkages involving Irish borders, the Northern Irish Troubles and the peace process receive expanded attention.[21] Globalised and diasporic methodologies trained on identity politics and sports are further reconfiguring Atlantic history models in the field;[22] as well they should, in light of persistent questions regarding future directions for Ireland's history and critiques of the 'remarkably insular lines' enveloping Irish historical themes.[23] In response, efforts to track religious influences between Ireland and North America are yielding views of Catholic exchange as 'objectively transnational',[24] and the same may be said of

Irish Protestant Atlantic worlds.[25] Recent ventures beyond Canada, Italy, New Zealand and Australia also contribute new perspectives; for example, links between Irish and African migratory passages align Daniel O'Connell's homegrown abolitionism and Frederick Douglass' work (his *Narrative* appearing in 1845, the same year as his visit to Ireland), and oblige historians to continue engaging these focuses on both sides of the Atlantic.[26]

Intersectional *histoire crosée* Atlantic models have also gained traction,[27] underscoring new sites of engagement and informing recent efforts to plumb these depths.[28] As several essays here illustrate, these concepts reinvigorate the Irish Atlantic field and remind us that older concepts and questions still retain value. A case in point is Irish Studies pioneer John V. Kelleher's 1961 observation that 'my father's generation is the only one to whom the term "Irish-American" can properly be applied'. In this view, the previous generation embraced those Irish who made their home in the United States, but who did not become American. In due course, their children 'led their parents out of the Patch, the Acre, the Shantytown, and into new two-apartment houses in the new streets'. Could Kelleher's generation, coming of age in the 1920s and '30s, retain the same Irishness?[29] Indeed, how did these generations preserve their ethnic identity? The same might be said of considerations of 'Irish-American' as disproportionately parochial.[30] Lawrence McCaffrey in 2004 asked, 'How much of Ireland has existed in the fiber of Irish America?' – to which he responded, elusively, 'Answers are a matter of time and place.'[31] And whither the creed D.H. Akenson abridged as 'Irish exceptionalism'?[32] Irish impact in the US must be contextualised beyond the merely familiar, Timothy J. Meagher noted, and contested meanings continually scrutinised.[33] Outgrowths of ethnic identity such as an 'Irish sense of belonging' or 'Ireland's other history' also merit debate in the diasporic context, and are engaged in the pages that follow.[34]

The quality of 'versatility' T.C. Barnard cited in reference to transnational history finds reflection in the essays making up this anthology.[35] Mindful of Braudel's caution that no conceptual structure can unilaterally contain a historical episode or a phase of history, these contributions embrace theoretical foundations and frameworks referenced above in one form or another.[36] They illuminate centuries of movement by native-born Irish or diaspora members with new meanings and associations, and affirm the land of Ireland as a foundation for the Irish transatlantic historical experience.[37] They do not propose to embrace every

Introduction   5

dimension of these focuses, but they deepen our understanding of worlds
within worlds, whose depths and currents, to evoke the title, continue to be
navigated. Writer Darryl Pinckney, whose work interrogates meanings of
African-American history and culture, has been described as unconcerned
with 'who is the "realest." His focus is black history, with all of its twists,
turns, triumphs and self-negations'.[38] Similarly, this anthology explores
concepts of Irishness and Irish identity on both sides of the Atlantic,
and affirms emigration, transition and change as crucial dimensions of a
modern shared history.

* * *

Dual qualifications of peerless contributions to Irish Atlantic history
and warm regard for Professor Shannon render Nicholas Canny an ideal
choice to pen the preface, which he records with characteristic élan. His
words combine a discerning review of Professor Shannon's scholarship
with esteem for the volume's honouree.[39] From there, four sections engage
distinct aspects of the book's major theme. Part One focuses on cultural
and political cornerstones in Irish Atlantic history, with essays addressing
topics from Ireland's politics of community and separation to the role
of the Great Famine in cementing the transatlantic passage in the heart
of Ireland's modern course. Mary M. Burke and Rachael Sealy Lynch
reflect Professor Shannon's intersecting interests in women's history,
nationalist political cultures, and the fate of Ulster, by means of an 1844
ballad, 'The Legend of Stumpie's Brae', by Cecil Frances Alexander. A
popular composer of hymns, including 'All Things Bright and Beautiful',
Alexander serves as a lens through which Burke and Lynch expose a fairy
tale functioning as both warning and illumination, and reveal cultural
sites where a woman once renowned could all but disappear. Gerard
Moran engages a similar theme from a different perspective in his study
of Cork workhouse indigents who moved to New Brunswick in 1850.
His essay strengthens our understanding of departure in illuminating
experiences of 'invisible emigrants' caught up in forces they could not
hope to control. Next, David M. Doolin, Christine Kinealy and Kerby
A. Miller tackle nationalist crosscurrents that spanned spectrums from
symbiotic to contradictory. Doolin's probing of radical nationalist activism
in post-Famine decades affirms the watery thoroughfare as a crucible of
incubation for nineteenth-century political energies. Miller's contribution
examines the movement of Irish women from one cosmos to another,

with the experiences of Clare-born Catherine Greene and Kilkenny's Mary Ann Rowe illustrating emigrant women's agency as independent wage-earners. Miller engages their stories to argue that, for many emigrant women in those times, home and adopted homeland diverged in meaningful ways. Fanny Parnell, on the other hand, as Christine Kinealy demonstrates, navigated the choppy waters of later 1800s political culture as a self-styled Irish Atlantic archetype. Kinealy analyses someone who should be remembered as a leader but is instead relegated to footnotes as a reflexive reminder of her famous brother, Charles Stewart Parnell, and sister, Anna Parnell. Kinealy's essay illuminates gendered aspects of contemporary political activism, and she draws on Parnell's campaigns to frame important questions about forces that determine who and what we commemorate. The section concludes with Francis M. Carroll's examination of the Balfour war mission – a topic that evolves organically from Professor Shannon's fêted study of British prime minister Arthur J. Balfour. Carroll deftly weaves elements of the fragile Irish republic proclaimed in 1916 and American support for Britain during the First World War in this captivating essay.[40]

Part Two engages Irish Atlantic themes from perspectives of place, pulpit, editorial desk and partisan stump. Between country lane and metropolitan streetscape, sites of significance for the Irish on both sides of the water rise within these essays. Mark G. McGowan's analysis of Canadian and American ethnic perspectives on the First World War spotlights fascinating issues of diversity among Catholics facing the Irish Atlantic from different vantage points. Likewise, Michael Doorley's study of the 1921 treaty and Free State formation broaches these topics from a North American standpoint. Doorley's essay exposes ethnic positions on Ireland's path to Free State status through *Gaelic American* newspaper coverage. Taking its cue from the paper's full title, *The Gaelic American: A journal devoted to the cause of Irish independence, Irish literature and the interests of the Irish race*, Doorley maps contemporary ideas of 'Irish race' in the evolution of ethnic Irishness. In Boston, meanwhile, populist politician James Michael Curley is seen to exemplify a number of these constructions in Suzann Buckley's 'Duelling Mythologies of James Michael Curley'. Here, Curley's contested legacy is evident in divergence over ethnic remembrance of his life today, and comprises one of several captivating focuses examined in her essay.

The twentieth century ushered in evident change on both sides of the Atlantic, and its course wrought new iterations in Irish identity and bonds

Introduction   7

between native and adopted homes. Simply put, the Irish Atlantic entered
a new phase, and several essays in this collection break new ground in
tackling its more recent course. Mary E. Daly, Gearóid Ó Tuathaigh and
Diarmaid Ferriter collectively remind us of Ireland's progress to modernity
from standpoints of church, landscape and literature. Mary E. Daly's
case study examines Free State aspirations to deepen connections with
Irish-American Catholics through the 1932 Eucharistic Congress. The
interactions she documents reveal important strands of the transatlantic
relationship between native home and ethnic homeland at a time of social
and political pressure. Advancing chronologically, Diarmaid Ferriter
engages literary and historical intersectionality in a provocative essay on
John McGahern and questions the limitations of sources in the writing of
history. How can we understand a particular moment in history, he asks,
without knowing the effects of the event or experience in question on
those who witnessed it? These essays reflect several of Catherine Shannon's
major research interests, as do other contributions in this section. Gearóid
Ó Tuathaigh beautifully engages some of the crosscurrents in the book's
title while drawing on Professor Shannon's research on Arthur Balfour
and his views on improving and 'saving' Ireland's western seaboard
counties. Here, Balfour's attitudes serve as a lens through which to
examine contemporary portrayals of the same landscape more recently
enshrined in Wild Atlantic Way promotional campaigns. Ó Tuathaigh's
framing of Ireland's western regions in cultural and political constructions
established a century apart, yet enduringly similar, raise intriguing
questions about perspective and environment. Seán Farren, meanwhile,
blends Catherine Shannon's scholarly and activist roles in another essay
with contemporary significance: this time John Hume's role in advancing
the cause of peace in Northern Ireland. Rooted in Professor Shannon's
research interests and contributions to the peace process, Farren's careful
consideration of Hume's faith in local and regional activism as a moral
foundation for his political agenda reiterates the centrality of community
for the Irish, both at home and across the Atlantic. Echoing Farren's
snapshot of Ireland's modern struggles over political and cultural identity,
Matthew O'Brien swings the pendulum back across the Atlantic to South
Boston in a nuanced exploration of ethnic Irish responses to court-ordered
desegregation of Boston schools and contested meanings of identity and
sanctuary. His research raises important new considerations for Irish-
American self-reflection and construction of the ethnic history.

1.1 Window in north vestibule commemorating poet and hymn-writer Cecil Frances Alexander, St Columb's Cathedral, Derry, Northern Ireland. (Photograph by Andreas F. Borchert)

Finally, Part Three engages the book's themes from the special perspective of Catherine Shannon's social and political activism within the Irish Atlantic world. Her historical scholarship and sustained contribution to the Northern Ireland peace process and the role of women therein is deliberated and memorialised here in the hands of colleagues and

Introduction   9

associates who have themselves traversed these pathways in noteworthy
ways. Bridging Ireland and North America through Professor Shannon's
transatlantic scholarship and civic engagement, Thomas E. Hachey and
Maureen O'Rourke Murphy reflect on a career where research, writing
and political community-organising dovetailed in the service of liberal
values of peace and freedom in Ireland and enduring connections with the
North American diaspora. Hachey's warmly wrought review of Professor
Shannon's scholarly pathways recognises the spectrum of historical
focuses she engaged with in her career. Documenting her accolades,
including Boston's Charitable Irish Society's John L. McDonough
Award in 2012 (the only woman to be so honoured by an august body
dating back to 1737), he reminds us that her long and successful teaching
career included the mentorship of generations of students at Westfield
State University. O'Rourke Murphy's essay affirms Professor Shannon's
particular capacity to not only produce high-quality historical scholarship
but inform partitioned cultural and political contexts with its lessons.
Miriam Nyhan Grey reveals the scholar-activist to be as deeply committed
to the principles of inclusion, equality, peace and freedom as ever in a
moving essay based on personal interviews. Finally, Monica McWilliams
and Margaret MacCurtain bring the volume to a close with appraisals of
Catherine Shannon's quiet pursuit of, and enduring commitment to, these
revered principles. McWilliams salutes Shannon's deep commitment to
peace in Ireland and the role of women in the struggle for its achievement.
Her absorbing essay reveals a transatlantic process of engagement
constructed on strong foundations in Irish and Irish-American history
and politics. The late Margaret MacCurtain, lastly, contemplates ideals
of perseverance and collaboration that she and Catherine Shannon
experienced and advocated for through historical scholarship and political
action. Her affecting essay serves as a fitting epilogue to this volume.

PART I

Framing the Irish Atlantic

CHAPTER ONE

The 'Kingdom of God' and the 'kingdom of Ireland':[1] The life, work and politics of hymnist Cecil Frances Alexander (1818–95)

Mary M. Burke and Rachael Sealy Lynch

An examination of the biography and output of Cecil Frances Alexander (1818–95) reveals far more than a superficial summary of the life of this poetically gifted clergy wife initially suggests. It grants us an understanding of the importance she placed not just on her Church of Ireland religion but also on writing both hymns and poems, place, Irish history, legend, and landscapes, and the lives of ordinary people. We begin to understand why she would have wanted to undertake a verse version of a local legend, a project that married all these interests except, arguably, the religious. In addition, we interrogate a vein of ambivalence running through her life and work. This bishop's wife identified as Anglo-Irish, and was deeply opposed to the disestablishment of the Church of Ireland, yet she was a key contributor to the hymnal of the disestablished church. She is never considered to be a nationalist writer, yet she shares more than a little with later revival writers. Not least, her work, with its close and loving focus on Irish landscapes and Ulster dialect, seems to prefigure both the early poetry of Yeats and post-partition Ulster regional literature. Her biographers and critics argue she is not a feminist, yet this Victorian woman is a stout supporter of many women's issues, and biographers cite a softening of her colonial stance as she grew in understanding throughout her life. In this essay we interrogate these seeming contradictions, in an attempt to do full justice to a complex and understudied writer, with a particular focus on two of her works, 'St Patrick's Breastplate' and 'The Legend of Stumpie's Brae'. In addition, we surmise that gender has played a particularly strong role in her critical neglect in the country of her birth.

During her lifetime Mrs Alexander was seen as a writer of great importance, even if her reputation has waned since her death in 1895. John Keble, professor of poetry at Oxford, was an admirer and mentor of her work, and wrote a prefatory 'Notice' to her *Hymns for Little Children* (first published in 1848), in which he predicted that the poems 'will win a high place for themselves in the estimation of all who know how to value true poetry'.[2] A review of her poems, edited by her husband, published in the *Ulster Journal of Archaeology* the year after her death, makes it clear that they did so: 'As a writer of sacred song, Mrs. Alexander stands in the first rank of modern poets.' The review continues, 'As a writer of secular pieces she is less known', but goes on to single out 'The Siege of Derry' and 'The Legend of Stumpie's Brae' for particularly high praise. Overall, the review concludes, 'Ireland has lost a true poet, and Derry its brightest ornament, in the death of Cecil Frances Alexander.'[3] The historian Gordon Lucy praises her as 'the celebrated hymn-writer and poetess',[4] while her biographer, Ernest Lovell, calls her 'queen' of the distinguished company of Irish hymn-writers, and compares her work very favourably to that of Christina Rossetti and contemporaneous British writers.[5] Such a comparison, while gratifying, also serves to draw attention to the fact that Alexander has never been assessed within the context of her contemporaneous Irish women peers to the extent that she is routinely identified today by careless commentators with labels such as 'one of England's finest hymn writers'.[6]

This neglect extends to the Irish locales with which she was associated. She was born Frances Humphreys on Eccles Street in Dublin city (also the location that Joyce imagined to be the home of his *Ulysses* hero, Leopold Bloom, of course), and lived also in Ballykeane, County Wicklow, as a child. However, she spent her most important years in Ulster, after her family's move from Wicklow to Strabane in 1833, and during the entirety of her subsequent marriage to Church of Ireland clergyman William Alexander.[7] Writing in 1970, Lovell notes that the 'several houses in which she spent her life are, for the most part, still standing, but none bears a

The life, work and politics of hymnist Cecil Frances Alexander

mark that a lady of gigantic stature passed that way'.[8] However, this has been partly remedied of late. Although, of course, Alexander was born in Dublin and later moved to Wicklow, she remains better remembered in Ulster than in Leinster. The not-for-profit heritage organisation Ulster History Circle, which erects blue plaques in Northern Ireland,[9] erected a plaque on Bishop Street, Derry, to commemorate Mrs Alexander in 1995,[10] the centenary of her death. Her religion and ostensible politics lend themselves better to being remembered in what became Northern Ireland, of course, but her unfashionable politics alone do not account fully for the manner in which her legacy remains underappreciated in the Republic of Ireland at present. One might argue that her association with Dublin was short-lived and that the bulk of her life and career played out elsewhere, of course, but this is also true of other Anglo-Irish writers who remain celebrated in present-day Ireland, such as Jonathan Swift, Oscar Wilde or George Bernard Shaw. In short, it becomes evident that gender seems to play a massive role in her critical neglect: according to Rose Novak's work on Catholic and Protestant Irish women poets who supported the radical nationalist Young Ireland and Fenian movements in the 1840s and 1860s respectively – Jane Wilde, Eva O'Doherty, Ellen O'Leary and Mary Jane O'Donovan Rossa – it appears to be the invariable fate of highly successful and influential Irish women writers of Alexander's generation to be neglected and underappreciated in the centuries that followed.[11]

William was born in Londonderry,[12] in the north of Ireland, and it was in that province that he and Fanny were married in 1850, beginning their life together in the diocese of Derry and Raphoe and living, variously, in Strabane, Castlederg, Upper Fahan and Derry between 1833 and 1895.[13] William's final appointment was to the see of Derry, and, as the bishop's wife, Mrs Alexander was in a position to perform admirable philanthropic work, with a particular focus on women. Indeed, Irish commentator Mary Kenny perceives a woman-centred tone in 'Once in Royal David's City', noting that it is a 'feminine' carol, 'with its emphasis on the central, maternal role of Mary in this miracle of birth'.[14] Moreover, and although it would be anachronistic to call her a 'feminist', circumstances render Alexander quite a contemporary figure in certain regards: she was six years older than her husband and also had access to her own money, since she earned income from her stories and verses. Her father had settled a trust of £3,000 on her, which produced a good annual income.[15] In addition, Katharine Brown notes Alexander's work in educating the deaf, in nurturing and providing role models for young women, finding 'socially

16   *Navigating Historical Crosscurrents in the Irish Atlantic*

useful ways for women to express themselves or to work with dignity in professions such as teaching and nursing', and in aid to the poor, sick and 'fallen'.[16] The Church of Ireland Derry and Raphoe School for the Deaf and Dumb was founded in 1846 in Strabane by Alexander, and the proceeds of some of her hymns went to the support of the institution. Kenny incisively muses that Alexander's work with the deaf 'may have trained her ear for metre and cadence in verse'.[17] Alexander grew to cherish the people in her husband's various parishes, and in return she was beloved, with a rare fervour, by those from all walks of life and across denominations.[18] And yet, as always with Alexander, there are darker undertones that cry out for further contextualisation: child inmates of the school burned to death in a fire under troubling circumstances in 1856,[19] a little-discussed story that should be integrated within the broader tragic history of child institutionalisation that is only now emerging in Irish Studies.

Primed by earlier circumstances and exposure, Alexander also thrilled to the Ulster landscapes and scenery, and started to write very young. Young Fanny was lucky in that her father attended to her education; while he 'could not send her to Oxford, as he did his two sons', he did provide her with 'intellectual stimulation through travel, reading, discussion, and friendships'.[20] Moreover, Alexander's family early noted and encouraged her 'poetic gifts'.[21] A closer look at Alexander's social status, religious affiliation and political thinking, including on topical colonial issues, is necessary for an understanding of the nature and relevance of what is perhaps surprising ambivalence in her work. Brown notes that 'Fanny grew up in privileged circumstances with limited contact with the native Irish, amidst a class and a family whose well-being was identified with British rule in Ireland'.[22] She therefore 'received a sound education in the established church and learned the social responsibilities and benevolent activities considered appropriate to pious gentry'.[23] Her belief in the rightness of empire, Christianity and the class system she knew is evidenced in her writing. At her most orthodox, her hymns are an expression of colonial certainty. For example, Hymn 22 in *Hymns for Little Children* offers a stark contrast:

> There are strange countries far away,
> Where God's name is unknown,
> Where children live who say their prayers
> To gods of wood and stone.

But Christian children go to church,
They kneel at home in prayer;
And God, Who is a Spirit, hears
And answers everywhere.[24]

Yet we must attend to both Alexander's allegiance to the status quo and also her departures from established thinking. Brown cites the young woman's feelings of 'kinship of generation and gender' with Queen Victoria in her first published poem, 'Verses Written on the Accession of Her Majesty the Queen',[25] which, as with her depiction of Mary, humanises an elevated woman by identifying with her in terms of gender. Brown also notes that Fanny experienced personally the high costs of colonisation and empire, through the losses of dear friends from 'such nineteenth-century Irish ravagers as consumption and famine fever' in 'Britain's incessant colonial wars in Africa and Asia'.[26] Indeed, typhus killed her first love, Archer Butler.[27] Although she did not herself go hungry, she addressed the suffering caused by famine and emigration in 'The Irish Mother's Lament', a dialogue between an elderly mother and her spinster daughter, over the mother's ritual lighting of a candle in the window at night in case one of her emigrant sons should return. Again, Alexander's woman-centred vision focuses the sense of tragic loss caused by emigration on the maternal body and its labours:

I nursed them at my yielding breast,
I rear'd them at my knee,
They left me for the golden West,
They left me for the sea.[28]

Furthermore, both Brown and Lovell take issue with facile assumptions, like those voiced by Sean McMahon, that 'Alexander's view of class was "simplistic and cosy"'.[29] For example, she has been condemned for this now-omitted third stanza in the hymn 'All Things Bright and Beautiful':

The rich man in his castle,
The poor man at his gate,
GOD made them, high and lowly,
And ordered their estate.[30]

However, both Brown and Lovell argue that what Alexander is here stressing is not that the 'rich man' is intrinsically superior but that we are all 'lowly' in the sight of God. As Lovell stresses, 'In the context of the hymn, these lines are surely intended to affirm the often neglected truth that men in all states, the poor no less than the rich, are God's children. The verse also contradicts the notion that poverty is a consequence of God's disfavour.'[31]

Alexander was a loyal colonial subject and Brown suggests that Alexander 'could not comprehend the democratic and nationalistic drive',[32] but close attention to her works suggest that this view is too simple. Moreover, as we initially contend, her writing, so admired by her contemporaries, does not now receive the attention it deserves. Frances Cecil Alexander is far more than a good poet and female hymn-writer; it would be more correct to honour her as one of Ireland's earliest and best regional writers and even as a forerunner of the revival. To make this argument, we now direct our attention to a representative selection of her work, spotlighting in particular a pair of hymns and a pair of ballads.

We have already stressed Alexander's reputation during her lifetime. Her hymn output is magisterial, magnificent and diverse, and she is still admired for the best-known of these works. She composed at least one hundred and fifty,[33] fourteen of which are contained in the Church of Ireland's 1960 *Church Hymnal*.[34] Seven can also be found in the US *Hymnal 1982: According to the use of the Episcopal church*.[35] All are regularly sung during services. Brown stresses the ubiquity and enduring nature of Alexander's most famous compositions, including 'All Things Bright and Beautiful', 'Once in Royal David's City', 'There Is a Green Hill Far Away' and 'St Patrick's Breastplate'.[36] Many of these hymns are used in a wide variety of Christian denominations and remain particular to central celebrations in the western Christian liturgical calendar such as Christmas and Easter. Extraordinarily, 'All Things Bright and Beautiful' 'was included in Jewish hymnals produced during the Victorian period of Jewish reform, which was in deep dialogue with secular and Christian culture'.[37]

Two of Alexander's occasional hymns are particularly inviting of further study, not least because, despite owing their existence to the same Irish occasion, they stand in direct opposition to each other and highlight Alexander's remarkable flexibility of voice. In 1871 she penned a doleful composition, 'Look Down, Lord of Heaven, on Our Desolation!', to mark the disestablishment of the Church of Ireland in 1869,[38] to which she was vehemently opposed. It has not been preserved in the hymnals, but it was sung in Derry Cathedral to mark and mourn the occasion. The hymn continues, 'Fallen, fallen, fallen is now our country's crown, /

The life, work and politics of hymnist Cecil Frances Alexander

Dimly dawns the new year on a churchless nation, / Ammon and Amalek tread our borders down'.[39] Alexander here aligns herself with conservative contemporary thought.

It is ostensibly surprising, therefore, to turn to another hymn born of disestablishment, 'St Patrick's Breastplate' (1889),[40] in which Alexander conveys, in the most positive of terms, a sense of Celtic heritage and national pride. These seeming oppositions may be reconciled by the fact that the movement towards disestablishment required the Irish Anglican Church to write itself into the long history of Christianity in Ireland in order to claim lineal descent from the 'uncorrupted' (that is, the already 'reformed') so-called 'Celtic Church'. Thus, although Alexander opposed disestablishment itself, in its wake she arguably participated in the judicious and necessary process of identifying Irish Protestantism with early Christianity in Ireland with a work such as 'St Patrick's Breastplate'.[41] The politically charged cultural agenda to promote Irish antiquities by eighteenth-century ascendancy patriots has been considered to have laid the groundwork for the 'reclamation' of a 'lost' civilisation during the revival even as it did the work of writing Protestant Ireland into that heritage,[42] but 'St Patrick's Breastplate' suggests that the cultural productions that emerged out of disestablishment may well be a relatively neglected waystation in considering that journey.

'St Patrick's Breastplate' was a commissioned piece, and despite her clearly voiced conservative leanings, such was the esteem in which Fanny Alexander was held that she was the first and obvious choice. Brown offers a detailed account, worth quoting at some length, of how this beautiful hymn came into being:

> In the half century from 1839 to 1889, Irish scholars, Roman Catholic and protestant, especially Petrie, O'Donovan, Todd, Cusack, Hennessy, Ferguson, G. Stokes, Wright, and W. Stokes, sought out ancient Irish manuscripts … [and t]he Lorica, or 'Irish Hymn,' as it was called then, was first available to the English-speaking public in a translation by George Petrie … In 1855, [Trinity College Dublin librarian James H.] Todd published Trinity's *Liber Hymnorum, or Book of Hymns of the Ancient Irish Church*, containing the 'Lorica Patricii' (*Luireach Phádruig*) or 'Breastplate of St Patrick' … Soon after disestablishment … there was a desire to expand *The Irish Church Hymnal*. The hymnal revision committee was eager to include hymns from ancient Irish sources to emphasize an identity rooted in

Ireland's past. 'The Breastplate of St Patrick' was high on its list of possibilities. Of the many translations of the hymn then available, however, not one was suitable for singing … Thanks to the skillful pen and well-tuned ear of a woman who exemplified in her own life and work the best of her two traditions, Anglican and Celtic, our worship has been enriched by the words of Ireland's patron saint, who called upon his Lord for protection in life's journey.[43]

Alexander completed the task at the age of seventy-one after a single week's work.[44] One might compare Alexander here to her near peer Lady Gregory, another woman whose best work was produced in what would have conventionally been considered her dotage. Indeed, Lovell suggests that Alexander's talent transmuted what had been a crisis into artistic gold: 'Disestablishment was to provide a considerable stimulus to the development of hymnody in the Church of Ireland. In particular we may be grateful that it was to supply a further outlet for Cecil Frances Alexander's genius.'[45] Alexander attended scrupulously throughout to history, voice and adaptation, bringing professional rigour, consummate artistry and national pride to her project, which can perhaps be considered an early example of revival writing.[46] The result is a spellbinding poem, masterful in its use of incantatory repetition and potent imagery, and irrefutable evidence that Alexander can step outside her own traditions and perspectives in the service of her art. For example, Christ's invincible 'power' is emphasised with energy and conviction in these visually evocative lines, a call to faith to all Irish Christians:

> I bind this day to me for ever,
> By pow'r of faith, Christ's incarnation;
> His baptism in Jordan river;
> His death on Cross for my salvation;
> His bursting from the spiced tomb;
> His riding up the heavenly way;
> His coming at the day of doom;
> I bind unto myself to-day.
>
> I bind unto myself the power
> Of the great love of Cherubim;

Alexander also vividly foregrounds the physical beauty and power of nature in her homage to the glory of God:

The life, work and politics of hymnist Cecil Frances Alexander

I bind unto myself to-day
The virtues of the star-lit heaven,
The glorious sun's life-giving ray,
The whiteness of the moon at even,
The flashing of the lightning free,
The whirling wind's tempestuous shocks,
The stable earth, the deep salt sea
Around the old eternal rocks.

Christ's supreme role, however, is that of saviour, comforter and protector. He is the Christian's armour, their spiritual breastplate, always and everywhere:

Christ be with me, Christ within me,
Christ behind me, Christ before me,
Christ beside me, Christ to win me,
Christ to comfort and restore me,
Christ beneath me, Christ above me,
Christ in quiet, Christ in danger,
Christ in hearts of all that love me,
Christ in mouth of friend and stranger.[47]

This project, executed in the spirit of national unity, paradoxically brought out the best in Alexander, despite her opposition to disestablishment. Moreover, in importing into English the rhythm and starkly direct descriptions of nature from the Irish of centuries past for a contemporary audience, 'St Patrick's Breastplate' functions as a John the Baptist to Gregory's later role as the revival's Messiah.[48] Despite her achievement, a recent chapter on 'St Patrick's Breastplate' does not mention her version, only those of the previously discussed male writers and scholars.[49]

An obvious interest in storytelling and ballad metres appears early in Alexander's writing. She liked to narrate, and focus on a specific occasion. 'Once in Royal David's City' tells the Christmas story, for example, and 'There Is a Green Hill Far Away' explains why Jesus had to die in a way that is accessible to children. These and many other of Alexander's hymns are written in a ballad-like format, and employ metres and rhyme schemes typically associated with ballads. She gravitates to tetrameter,[50] both iambic and trochaic, and frequently uses an abcb rhyme scheme. Therefore, the leap to the production of a secular ballad like 'The Legend of Stumpie's Brae' (discussed below) is not a huge one. The hymn 'There Is a Green Hill Far Away' also begs consideration of what Brown terms Alexander's ballad-like 'sensitivity to place'.[51] According to local lore quoted by the current rector of St Augustine's church in Derry,[52] the opening lines referring to Calvary outside Jerusalem, 'There is a green hill far away / outside a city wall', were actually inspired by the hill overlooking the Bogside outside of Derry. Alexander is herself buried just outside the city walls. Examples of regional and local writing abound throughout Alexander's *oeuvre*: one of the better-known of these is 'The Grave by St Columba's Cross', written in memory of a beloved rector in Raphoe diocese, County Donegal, in 1858:

> Bear him gently, bear him fondly, by the bay-indented shore,
> 'Neath the purple-shadowed Errigle, from far and lone Gweedore.

Loving attention is also paid to landmarks like 'the roar of the Atlantic, rushing madly on the Horn', 'Muckish, like a giant huge', and 'the winter woods of Ards'.[53]

Lastly, a pair of ballads that, considered together, serve to demonstrate that Alexander is an artist whose allegiances are not always easy to locate. 'The Siege of Derry' is one of her best-known historical ballads; it is vivid, evocative of its time and place, and rooted in staunch unionism. It is an example of narrative versification at its best; Alexander here favours a strong rousing trochaic octameter, with an abcb rhyme scheme throughout:

> 'Twas the Lord who gave the word when His people
>   drew the sword
> For the freedom of the present, for the future that
>   awaits.
> Oh Child! Thou must remember that bleak day in
>   December,
> When the 'Prentice-boys of Derry rose up and shut
>   The Gates.[54]

Schirmer places this ballad in context: it 'retells the story of the holding of Derry City against James II's forces in 1689, as important a symbol for unionist ideology as the 1798 rebellion was for nationalism. Alexander's poem is set on the day that the Unionists broke the siege, and is structured

The life, work and politics of hymnist Cecil Frances Alexander   23

around a dialogue between a widower and his daughter inside the city walls'.[55] Note the lovingly detailed recreation of the actual moment in lines like these: 'Where the river joins the brine, canst thou see the ships in line? / And the plenty of our craving just beyond the cruel boom?'[56] While this ballad obviously cannot be claimed as an early example of revival writing, it does showcase Alexander's skill as a balladeer, her sense of place, her attention to history, and the presence of ordinary local people who bear witness to this historical event.

As is often the case with Alexander, however, more ambiguous politics are detectable if one looks elsewhere. 'The Legend of Stumpie's Brae' (*c.*1839), a 'fearsome' and 'grisly comic' verse in the murder ballad tradition that she composed in faux Ulster-Scots dialect, was inspired by an eighteenth-century Donegal folk legend about a poor elderly farming couple who kill and then mutilate a travelling pedlar in order to steal his belongings.[57] The travelling man's height requires that the couple chop off his legs at the knee in order to conceal his corpse in his own backpack. After his burial on their farm, the clomp of the pedlar's stumps is heard by the couple until their dying day. Interestingly, Alexander departed from the source legend by concluding her ballad with the couple fleeing the ghost by emigrating to the American colonies, but 'the very first sound' they hear on the deck of their ship is 'the tappin' o' them bare knees'. The chilling third-last verse develops the horror:

> Out in the woods of wild America
> Their weary feet they set;
> But Stumpie was there first they say,
> and haunted them to their dying day.
> And he follows their children yet.[58]

The use of what Alexander's own footnote to the ballad refers to as 'the peculiar semi-Scottish dialect spoken in the north of Ireland'[59] is a return to the Burns-inspired deployment of local dialect of the eighteenth-century Ulster weaver poets,[60] and also looks forward to the use of that dialect in self-consciously Ulster regional literature of the twentieth century such as Sam Hanna Bell's celebrated *December Bride* (1951). Although the ballad may be a celebration of rural Protestant culture linguistically, any such sense is undercut thematically. The ballad suggests Ulster-Scots culpability in violence in Ireland and perhaps even in colonial America in evoking such weighty matters as the history of strife between settler and native and yeoman and unsettled, the manner in which emigration was a conduit for those fleeing unsettled conditions in Ulster, the cyclical nature of history in Ireland, which was an unfinished history that often travelled with the Irish to the New World, and, most suggestively, in light of the marriage she made and the pan-Protestant politics of 'The Siege of Derry', tensions between Protestant denominations in Ireland. Certainly, a County Donegal website that attempts to read the ballad for clues to the exact locale and people involved in the real murder case upon which the local ghost story and Alexander's ghost ballad were based pinpoints the historical case as involving a 'Planter' couple.[61] Interesting too is that the ballad was composed on the eve of the Famine that would profoundly alter emigration patterns in Ireland and bring issues of the economic insecurity hinted at in the action to crisis point. Altogether, 'The Ballad of Stumpie's Brae' is at once, as Patricia Craig notes, both Alexander's 'most robust composition' and a literary 'oddity' that could bear much more analysis than there is room for in this essay.[62]

Cecil Frances Alexander died in 1895, just as the Irish literary revival began to peak, and the degree to which a highly suggestive work such as 'The Ballad of Stumpie's Brae' barely registers in the Irish canon speaks volumes in terms of all the work still to be done to insert this writer more fully into her Irish literary and historical contexts.[63] Alexander remains uncelebrated in her city of birth and was officially commemorated with a blue plaque in her adopted city only a century after her death. This neglect is ironic when one considers that millions of Christians in various churches and nations continue to sing and to know her better-known hymns by heart, even if they are not, in many instances, particularly curious about her name or story. It may not be an exaggeration to state that Alexander may be the Irish writer whose actual words are most intimately familiar throughout the world today. Many millions may know the names of James Joyce and even that of his creation Leopold Bloom, but it is arguably the other resident of Eccles Street whose words they could quote by heart should they be prompted to do so. The poignant fact remains, of course, that the name of the author who penned certain famous hymns is much less known today, even as her compositions are as popular as ever.

CHAPTER TWO

Shovelling out Ireland's permanent deadweight during the Great Famine: the Cork workhouse paupers sent to New Brunswick in 1850[1]

Gerard Moran

While an estimated eight million people emigrated from Ireland between 1815 and 1914, it is now accepted that it was not a homogenous experience for those who left. Until recently the sheer scale of the exodus meant that historians, demographers, sociologists and others concentrated on overall patterns and trends without any in-depth analysis of regional features or specific groups who did not conform to the overall norm.[2] While the last thirty years has witnessed a major upsurge in the study of Irish emigration and the diaspora, and according to J.J. Lee the amount of research since 1990 has been staggering, many areas still remain unexplored and unassessed within the overall emigration context.[3] The majority of Irish emigrants in the nineteenth century left by having their passage paid by friends and relations who had already settled in North America or the other destinations where the Irish settled. However, there was a constituency who did not have the resources or contacts to start a new life in a foreign country, but had their passage paid by the government, the colonial authorities, landlords, philanthropists or the poor law. Up to 300,000 left the country through these schemes and, while there has been a renewed interest in this exodus in recent times, we are only scraping the surface as to these forgotten emigrants.[4] While the

25

Peter Robinson scheme to Peterborough, Ontario, from the Blackwater district of north Munster between 1823 and 1825, the landlord schemes to Canada and the United States during the Great Famine, and the assisted endeavours of James Hack Tuke, Vere Foster and Rev. James Nugent in the 1850s and 1880s have been documented, the role of the poor law in the emigration process has been largely ignored or forgotten, except for the Female Orphan Scheme to Australia between 1848 and 1850.[5] This is surprising, considering that between 1849 and 1891 the poor law assisted 67,376 people with their emigration by providing the full passage fare to those who were inmates in the workhouses or subsidising the travel of those who wanted to join family members who had already settled in North America or Australia.[6] The period 1848–55 saw the bulk of these emigrants leave, with the main group, nearly 15,000, being sent to Canada.[7] While the information is rich for those female paupers who went to Australia under the Female Orphan Scheme, which accounted for 4,114 workhouse girls, unfortunately the same cannot be said for those that were sent to Canada. However, there are instances where the information is available on individuals or groups assisted to British North America, which enlightens us as to the type of pauper sent out and the approach of individual unions in sending out their surplus population.[8] One such group was the eighty inmates sent from the Cork workhouse to St Andrews, New Brunswick, on the *Susan* in October 1850.

I

While the initial *raison d'être* for the poor law when it was established in 1838 was to provide support for Irish paupers, before long its functions were extended as a result of the failure of the potato crop in the late 1840s. From late 1846 mounting pressure on the workhouse system was evident, as in Ennis where it reached its capacity to accommodate the paupers and for the rest of the Famine years was overcrowded.[9] The first inmates were admitted to Kenmare workhouse on 25 October 1845, nearly one month after the blight was first reported. The full impact of the potato failure only occurred in the summer of 1846, and by September of that year the workhouse system was full to capacity.[10] Even workhouses in what were regarded as prosperous regions had difficulties with the numbers seeking relief. By March 1847 the workhouses in Coleraine, Magherafelt and Ballymoney were over capacity.[11] By 1847 nearly all of the workhouses were full and unable to accommodate any more paupers, and over the following six years the position was exacerbated as a result of the government's decision to wind down the public relief works, and the massive clearances carried out by landlords, when between one quarter and half a million people were evicted from their farms, with counties Clare, Galway and Mayo the worst affected.[12] The problems of destitution and the evictions were most evident in west Clare: in Kilrush union, 6,090 were evicted between July and December 1848. George Poulett Scrope, the radical English MP, estimated that between 1847 and 1849 20,000 people were evicted in the union. Most of these people were forced to seek refuge and relief in Kilrush workhouse, but shelter was not always available. By June 1849 over half of the population of the union was dependent on the poor law for survival.[13] Evictions on the Shirley estate in County Monaghan in early 1850 also left the poor and destitute flocking to Carrickmacross workhouse, forcing the local guardians to increase the inmate capacity by 500 places.[14] By June 1851 there were more than 256,000 pauper inmates in the workhouses, placing major financial burdens on the administration of the poor law as the unions struggled to collect the poor rates which funded the system and attempts were made to reduce the spiralling costs due to the increasing number of paupers that entered the workhouses. By May 1849 it was costing £640 a week to administer the poor law in Skibbereen, while even the more affluent unions were in financial difficulties, as in Enniskillen which had a debt of £5,000 by May 1847.[15]

By 1848 the poor law unions looked at various ways to reduce expenditure and restrict the numbers entering the workhouses. The Ennis guardians implemented proposals whereby the infirm and helpless inmates were encouraged to leave the house and avail of outdoor relief, while in January 1848 the Galway vice-guardians restricted admission to the workhouse to the aged and infirm, and to widows and their children under fifteen years.[16] To reduce the pauper population in Sligo workhouse, the guardians decided to remove all widows with two children and place them on outdoor relief, and this was followed by the displacement of all widows with one child.[17] Other measures taken to control expenditure included the reduction in the quality and quantity of food that the paupers received at meal time, and to lower the pay of union officials.[18] However, such measures failed and other, more radical proposals were suggested, including a recommendation by R.J.T. Orpen, a landowner with property in the Kenmare union, in his evidence before the Select Committee on the Poor Law in March 1849, that a portion of the pauper inmate population be sent to the colonies, 'because the country is not able to support them'. He stated that if 600 able-bodied paupers were assisted from the Kenmare workhouse the union would once again become economically viable and 'I do not see how it can be remedied except by emigration'.[19]

Under the 1838 legislation the poor law was permitted to provide assistance to emigrate to the colonies, and over the following ten years amendments were introduced allowing the unions greater scope in sending out their paupers. However, few unions availed of these provisions because ratepayers feared it would lead to higher taxation. Guardians were not opposed to the principle of sending those who wished to emigrate, but lacked the experience of assisting paupers to be removed to the colonies. The main unions who availed of the provisions in the 1844–6 period were from Ulster, when 244 emigrants were sent to Canada.[20] With the failure of the potato, the attitude within many unions changed as the guardians examined the available feasible options that would result in the removal of a section of the inmate pauper population. In late 1846 a number of unions saw the problems which the increasing number of inmates created for their financial position and realised that in the future they would be unable to cope with a further rise in the inmate population. Ratepayers were already paying exorbitant rates, which led to the inhabitants of Galway issuing a petition that the principle of property being made responsible for poverty should not continue.[21] Opposition to funding the emigration provisions can be seen from the evidence of the parish priest of Abbeyfeale to the Select Committee on the Poor Law in March 1849, when he said that an additional rate was unacceptable, because the poor rate was already high and ratepayers had great difficulty paying it.[22] Some form of assisted emigration which would alleviate the crisis was suggested. In November 1846, the poor law guardians of Kilrush, which had one of the highest destitute populations in the country, sent a memorial to the prime minister, Lord John Russell, also circulated to other boards of guardians, which suggested assisted emigration as a solution to Ireland's problems. It said,

> We do not hesitate to suggest that every great feature, leading to, or now exhibited by the present crisis, points to an extensive system of emigration, as the remedy not only best adapted to relieve the distress, but also to become a means of increasing our Empire, by reclaiming to the use of man, some of the large uncultivated tracts of our colonies.[23]

The Cork workhouse paupers sent to New Brunswick in 1850

In some instances, the emigration proposal was initiated by local poor law inspectors, as with Edward Senior in the north-east and R.A. Duncan in the south-west, who argued that it was a way of getting rid of the 'permanent deadweight' from the workhouses, who would otherwise remain a long-term financial burden on the poor rates at an annual cost of £5 per person. Various arguments were put forward in favour of sending the emigrants to the colonies: the paupers would have a better future than spending the rest of their lives as workhouse inmates, and as the colonies needed settlers these could be provided by the surplus workhouse population. Bolton Massey, in proposing that the Kilmallock guardians send 1,000 females to Canada in May 1850, said,

> You have them immured within your walls, a drag chain upon you, perhaps to die there; send them away; they are stalwart and able to earn a livelihood in a foreign land, which I regret they cannot do here. By their industry abroad they will acquire the position of independence and be able to remit money for some of their relatives which they may leave after them.[24]

However, the real motive was financial, a point mentioned by a number of its advocates including the poor law commissioners, who in 1848 stated, 'In this mode some of the permanent deadweight in the workhouse may be got rid of at a cost to the Electoral Division of about £5 or about one year's cost of maintenance.'[25] It was estimated that a pauper could be sent to Canada for as little as £4, a one-off payment, but as the assistant commissioner of the poor law, C.G. Otway, stated in 1849, this was a benefit 'because we are getting rid of a class likely to become a burden upon the public support …'.[26] By this stage the sending out of paupers was increasingly seen as 'an economic remedy' to overcome the problem of congestion in the workhouses.

While there was a policy which promoted emigration through the poor law, there was not a uniform attitude among the unions. Some, such as Kenmare and Strabane, promoted and appointed emigration commissioners who actively encouraged the inmates to leave. Others opposed any involvement, mainly in the congested districts along the west coast where emigration was needed most. Many guardians opposed the emigration process prior to 1848 because it would lead to increased expenditure and place an additional tax burden on ratepayers. In Carrickmacross the guardians feared that if emigration was introduced, large numbers would enter the workhouse so that they would have their passage paid to North America.[27] There is evidence that this happened in Ennis and Kilrush, where large numbers of girls sought admission into the workhouses after the unions had paid the passage fares of a large number of female inmates to North America.[28] When the emigration proposal came before Castleblaney union the guardians decided not to pursue the issue because of the great financial burden that ratepayers would face.[29] Up to 1848, while nearly all unions favoured pauper emigration, they did not wish to place an additional burden on the ratepayers, instead wanting the government to finance the schemes. However, the events of 1848 changed this.

II

The initiative for the large-scale emigration from the workhouses came not from the poor law authorities but rather from the colonial officials in Australia. In an attempt to reduce the gender imbalance in the colony, where there were eight men to every woman, the authorities decided to look to the mother country to secure the necessary female emigrants. After the initial attempts to recruit the girls from the workhouses in England and Wales failed, the authorities turned to Irish female workhouse paupers in 1848, and over the following three years 4,114 girls from 118 workhouses were sent to Australia. The poor law guardians were enthusiastic supporters because the colonial authorities paid the passage fares, and the only outlay for the Irish unions was the passage fares of the orphans to the port of embarkation at Plymouth and new clothes for the girls. Given the increasing numbers in the workhouses, and in particular the number of young females, assisted emigration was seen by the poor law unions as an opportunity to get rid of a large number of inmates who otherwise would have remained a major financial burden on the rates. From the time the application process was opened the demand from the Irish workhouses was great, with the number seeking to leave exceeding the available places. When the first phase of the scheme ended in 1848 the authorities were pressurised by the poor law unions to have it reopened so that more inmates could be sent. When the scheme ended in 1850 the unions saw the advantages of assisting large numbers of the inmate population to emigrate to the colonies, and the poor law commissioners came under pressure to make more favourable financial arrangements available so that the workhouses could be cleared of the existing female pauper inmates. The Female Orphan Scheme to Australia put structures and procedures in place that were replicated in relation to the selection of candidates, their travel arrangements and how they would be looked after in the colonies.

Throughout 1848 and 1849 there were growing demands by the poor law unions that the financial arrangements be changed so that a greater number of paupers could be assisted to the colonies. Audrey de Vere told the Select Committee on the Poor Law that the funding was inadequate, especially in those areas where there was great poverty, as the guardians were unable to collect the rates and there was little enthusiasm among the ratepayers to pay an additional tax for emigration.[30] In 1849 two new measures were introduced which made assisted emigration more attractive to the unions. They were now permitted to extend the scheme to the United States, as it was a more attractive destination than the colonies for emigrants and it was hoped that more of the inmates would travel there. William Monsell, MP for Limerick and a firm believer that emigration to the British colonies was the solution to the problem of Irish poverty and congestion, had legislation enacted which allowed the poor law unions to borrow money for emigration purposes, but a provision was inserted that intending emigrants had to be resident in the workhouses for at least one year, instead of three months. This was to ensure that the workhouses did not become depots for the poor to use up their time before being forwarded to North America.[31] These new provisions were a timely development for the unions as the workhouses were crowded with young people: by May 1849 the Skibbereen workhouse had 1,482 inmates, although it was built to accommodate 800.[32] By early 1850 there were 4,000 inmates in Ennis workhouse, while overcrowding in Galway workhouse was so great by March 1849 that the paupers were sleeping four and in some cases five to a bed, leading to a demand that the number of inmates be reduced by 425.[33]

The guardians were very concerned with the large number of female paupers who had come to rely on the workhouse for survival, and it was feared that they would become a long-term burden on the system. By the end of June 1850 there were 3,565 inmates in Gort workhouse, of whom 1,265 were women and 896 girls aged between two and twelve, while there were 999 inmates in Mountbellew, of whom 382 were women and 199 girls aged between nine and fifteen years.[34] Many found refuge in the workhouses after their fathers and husbands had left to seek work, often in North America. The authorities classified them as deserted, but this was not always true, as the intention was that the men would send for their relatives once they were settled and in a position to remit the passage fare.[35] However, the authorities were convinced they would become a permanent deadweight, and it was these inmates that they wanted to send to the colonies. Some members of the Irish administration felt that young female orphans resident in the workhouses should be assisted, and afterwards consideration would be given to sending out males. Thomas Reddington, a Catholic landowner from County Galway and a member of the Dublin Castle executive, indicated that only those chargeable to the union for a long period should be considered.[36]

Despite the progressive reforms in relation to emigration, many poor law unions maintained a cautious attitude, and had little interest even as a partial solution to the problem of workhouse overcrowding. While prepared to assist individuals who applied for special assistance, they were not prepared to avail of those provisions allowing them to borrow money towards emigration. Trevor Parkhill describes the schemes of the late 1840s as a 'too little, too late' response to the Famine crisis and the problems of the poor law system.[37] Between September 1848 and September 1849 only 871 inmates were assisted by eighteen unions, principally in Wicklow and Clare, at a cost of £16,563.[38] Some unions displayed ignorance of the provisions. In November 1848, the Galway vice-guardians were informed by Fr Peter Daly and Thomas Birmingham that provisions could be made for the ninety-three people who had been evicted in the Kinvara region to emigrate. The vice-guardians did not appear to be aware of the procedures.[39]

While Australia was the initial destination for most of the early workhouse inmates, it was not long before the guardians were sending paupers to Canada, although Wexford union decided to assist their emigrants to the Cape Colony.[40] Canada became the primary destination over the next ten years for economic reasons. The cost of sending the first group of Belfast workhouse girls from Plymouth to Australia on the *Earl Grey* in early 1848 was £14 per person for the passage alone, but the transport fare to Quebec could be obtained for £4. There was also a more positive response in Canada to the paupers. Throughout the first half of the nineteenth century the Canadian authorities welcomed Irish emigrants provided they were able to contribute to the development of the colony. While the authorities had been critical of the type of emigrant that was assisted during the Famine, those mainly sent by landlords from their Irish estates, there was a different attitude towards the single workhouse

The Cork workhouse paupers sent to New Brunswick in 1850   33

females.[41] Compared to those assisted from the Palmerston, Fitzwilliam and other estates, the girls arrived in a healthy state with new clothes. By 1850 there was a growing demand in Canada for female domestic servants and those sent between 1850 and 1854 were employed within a short time of their arrival. In 1852 the Canadian authorities stated, 'this class of emigrant is much needed in this colony, owing to the difficulty in obtaining female domestic servants throughout the country ...'.[42] The main strategist behind the schemes was the chief emigration agent in Quebec, A.C. Buchanan, who throughout the 1850s informed the poor law guardians that the colony could accommodate all of the young female paupers that were sent. Some 700 girls were assisted to Canada by the poor law unions in 1851, and the authorities reported that they had secured employment within two weeks of their arrival.[43] It appeared that Canada could accommodate all of the young female inmates from the Irish workhouses, but some unions saw it as an opportunity to send inmates who did not meet the criteria set by the Canadian authorities. The guidelines were similar to those of the Female Orphan Scheme: no girl should be over thirty-five years of age; they should be free of any mental or physical defects likely to impair their usefulness as settlers; they should be vaccinated against smallpox; their character for industry should be satisfactory; they should be able to read and write, be accustomed to washing and cooking, and have some experience in domestic service as housemaids and nurses. However, the eighty inmates forwarded by the Cork guardians to New Brunswick on the *Susan* in October 1850 did not meet these criteria.

III

Throughout 1848 and 1849, as conditions deteriorated in the countryside, the number of people seeking refuge in the workhouses increased dramatically, in particular in the larger urban centres, as the rural destitute flocked to the towns in the hope of securing relief and shelter. In January 1851 the guardians in Castlebar said the town was overrun with vagrants from other parts of the county who ended up in the workhouse, while the Carrickmacross board of guardians refused to admit large numbers of paupers who had come into the town the same month because the workhouse could not accommodate them.[44] However, it was in the larger urban centres such as Dublin, Cork, Limerick and Galway that the problem was most acute. In Limerick, the workhouse built to accommodate 1,600 paupers had 3,400 inmates by January 1849, and at its peak had 5,838 occupants.[45]

The increased pauper population in these large centres meant there was a greater interest in securing positions for the inmates in Ireland and abroad. Between 1848 and 1860, 750 inmates were assisted from Limerick workhouse: 74 under the Female Orphan Scheme to Australia, 480 under a number of group schemes to Canada, and 175 individual or family groups who required partial or full assistance.[46] The females included a group of eighty who left on the *Anna Maria* in August for Quebec, forty of whom were forwarded to employers in Kingston and the rest to Montreal, and one hundred girls who arrived on the *Theron* in June 1854 and who were sent to work in Montreal.[47] Other opportunities were also seized on when they arose: when John Ryan, in Limerick workhouse for four years, applied to the guardians for £5 to enable him to travel to the United States to rejoin his sister, who had been assisted a year earlier, one of the guardians, C. Delmarge, asked, 'Would it not be better for the boy to take a gun and fight the Russians?'[48] While female inmates were the concern in the more rural unions, in the larger urban workhouses there was also a large male population that needed to be dealt with. There was also the problem that while the inmate numbers started to decline in the rural workhouses in the early 1850s, in the larger urban centres they remained static or even increased: the South Dublin Union relieved 9,185 people in 1852, but three years later this had increased to 14,375.[49]

Like those in other large urban centres, the Cork union experienced a major increase in its inmate population in the 1847–9 period: from 3,254 in June 1847 to 6,911 in June 1849, when the workhouse capacity was 6,300.[50] However, it was more proactive in assisting its paupers to emigrate than most unions. This was largely because the experience of sending the poor to the colonies already existed among the city's institutions before the workhouse was opened in March 1840. Paupers had been sent to New South Wales from St Mary's, Shandon, in 1835, with the government and private subscribers contributing to the travel expenses of 130 girls.[51] Cork was one of the few unions to actively engage with the emigration provisions of the 1838 legislation, and in March 1841, twelve months after the workhouse opened, arrangements were made to send 191 paupers to any place that would take them. The project never took place because the guardians were prepared 'to bend the rules' and were severely reprimanded by the poor law commissioners.[52] This episode indicated that the guardians were not always prepared to comply fully with the regulations. Personal

The Cork workhouse paupers sent to New Brunswick in 1850   35

initiatives by individual guardians were also carried out so that inmates could be sent overseas. In October 1848, while the Female Orphan Scheme was taking place, one guardian, Richard Dowden, devised a plan to send female paupers to Shawneentown, Illinois, where they would take up positions as domestic servants, and a list of females willing to emigrate was compiled. The guardians were informed 'that the girls will not be shielded from want and deprivation, but will be received with credible families where they will be justly and kindly treated'.[53] It is unclear if this scheme went ahead, but it highlights the guardians' determination to avail of every opportunity to reduce the pauper workhouse numbers.

It was not only female inmates that the guardians attempted to offload during this period as there was also a large male pauper population. Attempts were made, with varying degrees of success, to try and get boys to join the navy and army. In September, the Cork guardians wanted the commander of a local ship to take a number of the pauper boys off their hands, and were unhappy when he only agreed to take twenty-seven.[54] Perhaps the most controversial initiative was their involvement in sending 400 boys to work as labourers on the construction of the Panama railway. They arrived in Central America in February 1854 in a good physical condition, although there were a couple of deaths on the journey. Unfortunately, the working and climatic conditions that they encountered in Panama were extreme and there was a high mortality rate, so that by 1861 most had died.[55]

While overcrowding and financial pressures caused the Cork guardians much concern, there were other problems which they were having to deal with, and which made emigration an attractive option. There were increasing levels of tension and insubordination among the inmates in the late 1840s, resulting in a number of riots which the authorities had difficulty containing. In November 1848 the poor law inspector, Capt. Bradling, was attacked by over 600 female inmates who hurled stones, bottles and tins at him. As the authorities lost control of the situation, the constabulary and a company of the 70th regiment had to intervene to restore order. Five of the ringleaders were brought before the courts and given prison sentences. The cause of the riot is unclear, but most of those involved had been in the workhouse for a long period.[56]

As a result of the new terms and conditions under the 1849 legislation, it was inevitable that the Cork guardians would avail of the opportunity to borrow money to send their pauper inmates to Canada, and in particular young girls. Between 1848 and 1860, 1,200 girls were assisted from the

36   *Navigating Historical Crosscurrents in the Irish Atlantic*

workhouse and, while the majority went to North America, sixty-one were sent to Australia under the Female Orphan Scheme. During the summer of 1850 arrangements were made to assist 353 of the workhouse inmates, by far the largest number from any workhouse. A total of 184 left for Quebec on the *Sofia M'Kenzie* in June, of whom 109 were young women, and while most got positions as domestic servants shortly after their arrival, there was an outbreak of ophthalmia during the voyage which resulted in twenty being hospitalised after their arrival. In September, another sixty-eight females from the Cork workhouse arrived in Quebec on the *Try Again*.

It was the final group, the eighty inmates who travelled on the *Susan*, which caused most concern for the New Brunswick officials when they arrived in St Andrews in October 1850. There were fifty males and thirty females. According to the information provided by the Cork guardians, thirty of the emigrants were aged between ten and nineteen years, with John Leary the youngest at twelve years; thirty-three were aged between ten and twenty-nine years, five were between thirty and thirty-nine years, five were between forty and forty-nine years, and three were over fifty, with Patrick Driscoll the oldest at fifty-nine years. The inmates had resided in the workhouse for between five and ten years, with Eliza Magner, aged thirty years, being the longest resident. All had been admitted to the workhouse before the Famine, indicating that many were institutionalised and unlikely to be able to cope outside the institution's environment, which led one New Brunswick official to state, 'Their former mode of life had disqualified them for hard labour.'[57] There were three widows in the group: Honora Doody, who was forty years; Honora Duggan, aged thirty-five years; and Johanna Smith, aged twenty-four. All were accompanied by dependants. There were two families, including Thomas and Johanna Leary and their six children, who ranged in age from twelve to twenty-four years and had been resident in the workhouse for seven years. While the guardians acknowledged that it was a large family, they justified it 'as a set-off to the [parents'] age and infirmity'. Fifty of the adults were classified as labourers, while there were four bakers and Patrick Driscoll who was a weaver.[58] However, the documentation forwarded by the Cork guardians did not correspond with what the New Brunswick authorities were to discover. Eight on the original list did not travel and were replaced by other inmates, including Hanah Leary who was fifty-two years and Margaret Ryan who was forty-two years. The Canadian authorities also discovered that fourteen of the paupers were over forty years, the eldest

The Cork workhouse paupers sent to New Brunswick in 1850

being Thomas Leary who was seventy-six years and Patrick Driscoll who was sixty-two and not fifty-nine years. While Ellen Leary, who was eleven years, was stated to be the daughter of Thomas and Johanna Leary, she was not related to the family and left after the group disembarked. A number of the passengers were also not suitable for resettlement in New Brunswick as they were infirm and unable to look after themselves, such as Owen Rogers and William Connell who were both blind, while Hanah Leary and Patrick Driscoll had problems with alcohol. While some of the emigrants travelled to the United States and a small group decided to return to Ireland, a group of fourteen stayed in New Brunswick and continued to be a burden on the New Brunswick ratepayers. The cost of looking after them continued to be borne by local ratepayers and was estimated at £350 for the twelve months after their arrival, or as the assistant emigration officer at St Andrews stated, 'Young people and single people … we could dispose of almost in any numbers; but the aged, infirm and diseased must become chargeable on us.'[59] Thirteen of the group were unable to care for themselves and became a charge on the authorities almost immediately, as they were aged, infirm or insane. The others were said to be worthless or the women shameless or profligate.

An examination of the list provided by the Cork guardians and the New Brunswick census records indicates that in 1851 fourteen of the paupers were still residing in the colony, thirteen living in St Andrews, and John Corkery, who was twenty-five years old, was now in St George.[60] The pattern that emerges is that the younger Cork emigrants left the colony in search of employment elsewhere. Those who were in St Andrews were the thirteen that had to be looked after by the New Brunswick authorities from the time of their arrival and these included Timothy and Mary Driscoll, both aged thirty years, William Creedon who was twenty-eight years, Cornelius Desmond who was twenty-five years and James Murphy who was seventeen years. Sixty-six of the group had moved on or returned to Ireland, indicating that not all of the paupers had become institutionalised from their time in the workhouse, but had the initiative to move to places where employment opportunities were available. Some may have left feeling it was better to move on rather than remain in the colony where they would be classified as the 'pauper emigrants'. It was inevitable that Owen Rogers would become a charge on the colony because of his disability, but there is no indication that William Connell, who was also blind, was living in New Brunswick in 1851, suggesting that he was one of those returned to Ireland. Patrick Driscoll, described by the

38   *Navigating Historical Crosscurrents in the Irish Atlantic*

colonial officials as having a serious alcohol problem, also does not appear to be living in New Brunswick in 1851.

IV

One of the aspects which is not entirely clear is why the Cork guardians sent the emigrants to New Brunswick and not to Quebec, considering that the other two groups of pauper emigrants that it assisted in 1851 were sent to the latter destination. The Quebec authorities, and A.C. Buchanan in particular, in that year had indicated that the colony would accept and look after all assisted pauper emigrants. Already a clear hostility existed in New Brunswick to Irish pauper emigrants since 1847–8.[61] In 1847 the authorities had publicly criticised emigrants sent to its jurisdiction by a British cabinet minister, Lord Palmerston, from his County Sligo estate on the *Eliza Liddell* and the *AEolas*, with no provision being made for their welfare in the colony.[62] The New Brunswick officials were also critical of the one hundred families sent out by Earl Fitzwilliam on the *Star* in May 1847 from his County Wicklow property apparently to work on the construction of the St Andrew to Quebec railway.[63] The authorities were unhappy that the Famine emigrants became a charge on local resources. Under the New Brunswick Poor Law, responsibility for the relief of newly arrived emigrants rested with local parish authorities, resulting in aid being reluctantly provided. Many taxpayers felt that the expense of maintaining poor immigrants should be shared by the whole province and not just those areas that the emigrants came to. They were annoyed because they were having to pay for emigrants who were largely transient, as it was estimated that only one-third of the emigrants settled in the colony. The sick and weak remained in the colony while the healthy and strong moved to New England and other parts of the United States. The Cork guardians must have been aware of this situation, but still decided to send the *Susan* emigrants to New Brunswick. They may have felt that while the strong and healthy were being encouraged to come to Quebec they took a chance of getting rid of a long-term 'permanent deadweight' group in the hope that the New Brunswick authorities would not repatriate them back to Ireland. In the past the New Brunswick officials had threatened to repatriate paupers, and had actually sent back destitute emigrants to Ireland.[64] The guardians' failure to provide the authorities with exact information on the paupers would support the contention that

The Cork workhouse paupers sent to New Brunswick in 1850 39

the emigrants would not be sent back. While the New Brunswick officials complained about the calibre of emigrant that was being sent to the colony, they received little consolation from the Irish poor law commissioners, who stated 'that the selection of good colonists from such an institution cannot always be secured'.[65] The descriptions and terms used by the New Brunswick officials of the emigrants were similar to what applied to those sent under the landlord schemes in 1847–8: they were prepared to accept emigrants who were industrious and hard-working, but the Cork paupers were felt to have little to offer. The assistant emigration officer at St John, Captain Jones, said of the Cork emigrants,

> I can scarcely say to you the annoyance, vexation and trouble I have had with them; the greater part are the worst emigrants that ever came here. They are helpless, idle, ignorant and dissipated, without the desire or pride to help themselves.[66]

The officials were still complaining about the Cork workhouse paupers as late as the summer of 1851. They probably remained the focus of attention because no other workhouse inmates came to the jurisdiction during this period.

There are many indications that the operation was poorly organised by the Cork guardians, a charge that could also be levelled at other unions. The Canadian authorities wanted the unions to forward 'landing money', which would be used to transfer the emigrants to those areas where there was a demand for labour. In some cases, inadequate funding or none was forwarded. When the forty-four paupers assisted by the Cootehill guardians arrived in Quebec in July 1850, the Canadian officials had not received the landing money even though the emigrants were adamant each adult was promised £1 and each child 10/-; while the group from the Waterford workhouse in July 1851 received nothing from the emigration agent although the guardians had promised them 15/- when they arrived in Montreal.[67] Another problem arose where the guardians paid the 'landing money' directly to the paupers before they left, but this was then spent on board the ship purchasing alcohol and other goods which the crews provided at inflated prices, and they thus arrived in Quebec penniless. It was not until 1852 that Buchanan reached an agreement with the poor law commissioners in Ireland whereby the unions were notified that £1 per adult and 10/- per child 'landing money' should be forwarded to the emigration agent in Quebec before the emigrants' journey commenced, and this would be distributed upon the emigrants' arrival. This was largely adhered to after 1852 by the participating poor law unions, although there were instances where this did not happen, as with the girls sent out by the South Dublin Union in 1854 who arrived drunk having spent the landing money on board the ship.[68] While the Cork guardians had forwarded £70 landing money for the *Susan* emigrants, this was inadequate to meet their needs, and in late 1851 the New Brunswick officials stated that it cost five times that amount to maintain them.

The absence of proper coordination and planning between the Cork guardians and the New Brunswick officials is also highlighted in the time of year that the *Susan* emigrants arrived in the colony. Again, this criticism was not just confined to the Cork guardians. There were problems in securing employment for emigrants, not just those from the workhouses, when they arrived in the colony late in the year; job opportunities were scarce, and the new arrivals had to depend on their own resources or public charity until the labour market opened up in late spring. Many of the emigrants who came to New Brunswick through the landlord schemes in 1847 and 1848 encountered great deprivation when they arrived in September and October. It was not an issue in 1849 when 871 workhouse paupers arrived in the British North American colonies. Alarm bells sounded in 1850 when some of the emigrants arrived late in the season, as with the *Susan* emigrants. If the Cork paupers had arrived earlier in the season, they probably would not have attracted the same negative publicity as they would have dispersed throughout the colony and further afield. While a small group would have remained a charge on the public rates, the group would not have received the same high-profile attention. Assisting workhouse paupers to British North America so late in the year continued to be an issue in 1851, when groups from Strokestown, Carlow, Croom, Kilflyn and Newcastle workhouses arrived in Quebec in September and October.[69] Some had to be assisted by the authorities. In October 1851 the poor law commissioners refused to allow the Gort guardians to send twenty-nine inmates from the workhouse to St John, New Brunswick, because it was too late in the season and the commissioner adjudged many of those selected to be 'young children for whose protection and support it is not stated what provision has been made'.[70] It was only in 1852 that the poor law unions sent their paupers early in the season after a directive from A.C. Buchanan in February and a circular addressed to the unions by the poor law commissioners that the

The Cork workhouse paupers sent to New Brunswick in 1850

emigrants should arrive in the colony before the end of June so that they could secure employment.[71]

The *Susan* affair also highlights the contrasting attitudes towards emigration among the poor law unions. While the overall pauper emigrant numbers from all of the unions for 1848 and 1849 is small, the Cork guardians adopted a more proactive approach, evident in that it assisted more emigrants than any other union in 1850. Other unions adopted a more cautious approach and wanted to see how the paupers from other unions fared in North America before committing themselves. Drogheda guardians in September 1849 deferred sending eighteen orphans to Quebec because of a newspaper report which said that workhouse girls had been barbarously treated by the ship captain on a voyage to Canada.[72] In April 1852, R.A. Duncan, the poor law inspector for the south-west, indicated that a number of unions under his charge were contemplating sending up to 1,000 single girls to Quebec providing there were significant employment opportunities and the colony would be able to absorb them.[73] He also wanted to see how the emigrants from other unions fared before committing large numbers to the colonies. This approach suggests a more compassionate position by some unions regarding the sending out of pauper inmates, which was not evident with the *Susan* passengers. The guardians were responsible for the emigrants from the time they were selected to their departure, when they were handed over to the ship captain, who was employed by the shipping agent who had the tender. In some cases, the unions sent a representative to inspect the arrangements with the shipping agent or employed a chaperone to accompany the emigrants, but once they arrived in Canada they were no longer the responsibility of the boards of guardians. While some unions made arrangements in North America for the emigrants to be looked after, others like the Cork guardians made limited contact. As early as 1849 C.G. Otway, the assistant commissioner of the poor law, told a Select Committee on the Poor Law that close cooperation between Canadian officials and the unions in Ireland when the poorer classes were sent out was essential, as a hostile response from the local population would jeopardise future schemes.[74] Otway was no doubt fully aware of the impact the landlord-assisted emigration schemes had on Canadian sentiment towards Irish emigration to the colony. The Canadian authorities, while in favour of Irish emigrants coming to their shores, stated the scheme would have to be properly coordinated, as they were opposed to 'the introduction of such hordes of beggars and vagrants as have been so unceremoniously thrust on this young and thinly-populated country'.[75]

It was inevitable that the Canadian 'open door' immigration policy towards the workhouse paupers would result in problems, as seen with the *Susan* emigrants. While the Australians encouraged female emigration to their colony, they were selective as to who was acceptable. As they funded the passage fares, they were centrally involved in choosing the candidates, and their representative, Lieutenant Henry, visited the workhouses and selected the girls from a shortlist that the guardians had compiled.[76] The Australian authorities thus ensured that the girls who arrived in the colony under the Female Orphan Scheme were young and healthy, the calibre of emigrant that was needed. The Canadians never had any input into the pauper emigrants that came to their jurisdiction; they provided no financial assistance and depended on the poor law union officials in the selection of suitable candidates. While the majority of those sent were suitable, the selection process was built on trust and inevitably some unions took advantage of the process, as with those who sailed on the *Susan*. The Cork guardians were not the only ones to breach this confidence. By the late 1850s some unions were sending widows and young children to Quebec in an attempt to clear their workhouses of long-term dependants. The Canadian authorities quickly showed their displeasure with the Gorey guardians in 1858 and 1859 when twenty widows accompanied by twenty-eight young children arrived in Quebec. While the first group were accepted and positions found for the seven widows, the Canadian authorities reacted angrily in 1859 when another thirteen widows were sent, and the officials in Quebec stated that this action 'pointed out the cruelty of this class of helpless poor [being sent] to a country in which no provision whatever existed for them'. They threatened to return to Ireland any such paupers that were assisted to the jurisdiction.[77] The following year the Canadian authorities did repatriate three paupers sent from the New Ross workhouse, 'owing to their ill health and infirmity rendering them unable to support themselves in this country, and dependent on casual public charity'.[78]

The Cork guardians were not deterred by the negative publicity and condemnations in relation to the *Susan* affair. Over the following ten years more paupers were sent to North America from Cork than from any other workhouse. Between 1852 and 1854, 800 inmates were sent to Canada, the majority young females, with 300 leaving in 1853 and 360 in

The Cork workhouse paupers sent to New Brunswick in 1850

1854.[79] The guardians regarded it as a Malthusian solution to their problem of overcrowding in the workhouse, as no attempt was ever made to discover how the emigrants fared in Canada. As Nicholas Mahony, a Cork poor law guardian, told the Select Committee on the Poor Law in 1861, no effort had been made by the union to ascertain the fate of the 1,200 girls that had been assisted from the workhouse between 1848 and 1860.[80] The evidence from most of the poor law minute books shows that there was little or no contact between the pauper emigrants and the board of guardians in any of the unions. The guardians had got rid of a long-term problem and other issues had now to be prioritised. The paupers probably also felt there was no need to keep up contact. As former workhouse inmates they wanted to make a fresh start and forget their past.

The *Susan* episode is important, as it indicates the calibre of emigrant that the poor law unions were prepared to export in an attempt to reduce the financial and discipline problems in their institutions. While the poor law unions sent nearly 15,000 paupers to Canada between 1849 and 1860, we know very little about who they were, their ages or how long they had been resident in the workhouses. It is thus impossible to chart the lives of these individuals from their time in Ireland to what became of them in Canada. These are the 'invisible emigrants' of the Great Famine. However, this in a small way is addressed by the story of the Cork paupers who were sent to New Brunswick in 1850.

CHAPTER THREE

Ireland, America and transnational radicalism

David M. Doolin

To say that the Irish diaspora in America were central to Irish nationalism might seem counterintuitive if one only perceives the nation as relating to the territorial state; that is, if one confuses nation and state.[1] Instead, when conceiving the Irish nation it is more apt to understand nation as 'a community of people with a common cultural identity and an attachment to a particular territory, whereas a state is a political organisation covering a particular territory. Because nations politicise space in their desire to become legitimate political entities in state form, however, and because the political identity of states is often manifested as nationalism, the two terms are often conflated'.[2] It is important to keep this in mind when we assess Irish nationalist sentiment among the diaspora, since the diaspora inhabit a place of legal citizenship elsewhere; in this case the United States. As such, an examination of Irish immigrants in the United States who prompted, promoted and operated physical force nationalism uncovers a distinctly representative nation beyond geographical borders. Stepping beyond 'the frame of the nation' and into the frame of the transnational, challenges '[...] bounded views on national belonging [...] opening up new perspectives for the internal differences and relational connectedness of nations'.[3] When one examines the role of those Irish in the United States who worked to achieve Irish independence from Britain through physical force, this notion of the transnational reveals a thread of revolutionary impetus that was pivotal to Irish republicans' insurrectionist efforts through time. As David Brundage explained, 'Irish nationalism in the United States was

Ireland, America and transnational radicalism

not the unmediated expression of some timeless, primordial Irish identity but rather an ongoing work of political invention and imagination, involving multiple generations of men and women.'[4] In taking that on board and giving overseas insurrectionists' efforts a framework for understanding, one can find the concept of the transnational to be apt. Richard Weiner, for instance, recently wrote, 'Transnational space is the discretionary space of enterprises and associations acting across nation-state and associational borders. Territory/place does not disappear; rather, it becomes embedded in broader and more fluid constellations – as in a plasma of flow and movement powered by heterogeneous forces.'[5] Irish efforts to free themselves from the yoke of Britain reflect this, in that the insurrectionist movement was directed by assorted forces, influenced and controlled by enterprises and associations which flowed across and through state boundaries.

In the eight decades from 1820 up to 1900, a staggering 3.9 million Irish had emigrated into the United States. That figure does not include the sons and daughters of Irish incomers born in the United States, who were very often defined by their Irishness, both externally from a hostile Anglo-Saxon and Protestant America, and internally, roundly steeped in a sense of ethnic identity. Accordingly, perhaps it is understandable that:

> [...] Irish nationalism would no longer be contained within the island of Ireland. The point was not lost on the British home secretary as early as 1855. Writing on Christmas Eve, he made this telling point: 'In former Irish rebellions the Irish were in Ireland. We could reach their forces, cut off their resources in men and money, and then to subjugate [them] was comparatively easy. Now there is an Irish nation in the United States, equally hostile, with plenty of money, absolutely beyond our reach and yet within ten days' sail of our shore' [...]. In short, the United States presented Irish nationalism with a second front; it was to be utilized to the fullest extent.[6]

With that in mind, this chapter aims to outline some of the long history of Irish transnational intrigue which manifested among the groups involved in advanced, or physical force, nationalism primarily across the Atlantic Ocean. The work undertaken by Irish immigrants in America for Irish freedom seems largely prototypical in its innovativeness. The following, for instance, from an 1880s printed pamphlet in the United States 'to Irish Nationalists Everywhere', underscores the sentiment that speaks to a transnationalism most evident in the trajectory of revolutionary activities, perpetrated by those we label Fenians.[7] It reads:

> In placing this pamphlet before our people as an aid to Irish national endeavour we emphatically state we shall never sanction nor permit one to break United States laws in trying to free Ireland. This is our home and we must be good and worthy citizens, and sustain and honor the laws of this glorious republic, and as in the past, so in the future, we shall be among the foremost to sustain her constitution [...]. But no laws of God or man can prevent us from contributing MONEY and KNOWLEDGE [sic] to our sore oppressed people in Ireland.[8]

It is in examples like this that we see the Irish discernible on a transnational scale, where the idea of the state as an independent political entity is not needed for political activism to manifest, or for identities to be forged.

As Adrian Mulligan stated, '[...] a transnational perspective is essential to understanding the lives of a great number of migrants, who [...] live their lives in more than one nation-state'. Indeed, in the Irish context, nation-building is about 'the telling of a story about the origins of a community, its moments of character building and hopes for the future. The nation can thus be regarded as a "transitional social reality", and an ongoing process of negotiation and articulation [...] forged by diasporas [...]'.[9] In the US, during the nineteenth century, we can espy the strongest sentiments of Irish nationalism abroad. This was evident and facilitated by efforts such as the Gaelic revival in America, where Irish-Americans promoted the Gaelic language and the GAA, but it also became part of the effort to recruit Irish immigrants and their offspring to a revolutionary cause.[10] Nationalism, as much a cultural project, is often facilitated by activists and intellectuals deploying memories of the past to build movements in the present, through publications, lectures, songs, art, memorial. Indeed, 'The "American connection" [...] was never just a matter of "guns, money, and influence". Even more important was the fact that the American Irish were often the main proprietors of collective memory.'[11] Irish-American women were central to the promotion of these transnational rhizomes and the transatlantic entanglement through their promotion and deliverance of different elements of Irish nationalism. From earliest examples, like Matilda Tone, to the late nineteenth- and early twentieth-century efforts of Mary Jane O'Donovan Rossa, Irish

Ireland, America and transnational radicalism   47

women in America were central in lecture tours, concert performances, publishing pamphlets, books and newspapers, and helping to raise money for the cause of Irish, *revolutionary* independence.[12]

Within this transnational conception, a radical, insurrectionist nationalism was resuscitated, or perhaps incubated, awaiting a time to strike for Irish independence. So, not only were the Irish migrants and their offspring in America important in the way that they laboured to maintain a sense of Irishness, however much tinged with or subsumed by Americanness that became. History shows us that what became the Republic of Ireland's great foundational, historic moment was replete with the story of Irish-American influence. The central point here is to outline some of the threads, a continuum, in the global network of Irish revolutionary leaders and actors, and their ideas and actions, across space and time. Indeed, as Timothy Meagher wrote, 'Nationalism – the commitment to restore some political autonomy to the old country – was an essential part of Irish-American life […]. From the United Irish Exiles in the 1790s and early 1800s to the Repeal movement in the early 1840s to the Fenians of the 1860s, the Land Leaguers and Home Rulers in the 1880s to the Friends of Irish Freedom and members of the American Association for the Recognition of the Irish […] and […] Clan na Gael […] Irish-Americans have invested considerable resources of time and money into freeing the old country.'[13] As a starting point, the nineteenth-century organisation known as the Fenian Brotherhood (FB) especially informed a more radicalised version and effort for an advanced national agenda. Initially founded in 1858 in New York, to act as a potentially powerful supporter, politically and financially, to the Irish Republican Brotherhood, the IRB, in Ireland, the Fenian Brotherhood in America were part of a transnational flow that became central to the work of Ireland's physical force nationalists.

The idea of creating a revolutionary wing in the United States among the ever-burgeoning diaspora there was due to the planning of former Young Irelanders – men involved in a failed 1848 rebellion in Ireland – namely James Stephens, John O'Mahony, and for a while at least Michael Doheny. These three men had escaped the British authorities after the '48 uprising and found themselves in exile in Paris, at a highly charged political time there. This particular web's thread, then, is anchored between 1840s famine Ireland, Paris' cafes and bars, and eventually the United States.[14] It was Michael Doheny who first left Paris for New York at the end of 1849. Once there he helped establish the Emmet Monument Association

(EMA),[15] through which he began raising funds for some future Irish revolution. In the meantime, James Stephens and John O'Mahony forged a mutual alliance weaving a conspiracy that envisioned an uprising that would unbridle Ireland from the British yoke. This vision involved a recognition of the fast-expanding diaspora. After several years of planning in Paris, O'Mahony left for New York to join Doheny and help organise support for a new Irish revolutionary idea. And Stephens, noted as the pivotal founder of this new Fenian machination, returned to Ireland to organise men across the country for a sustained revolution in the 'not-too-distant-future'. What is stand-out about the Fenian organisation is the centrality of the transatlantic element from the very outset. It was hoped that in the republican environment of the United States, a physical force Irish nationalism could further harness the sympathies and the will of the diaspora to help finance and arm the coming rejuvenation of the geographically contained Irish nation.

The FB flourished among the Irish in the United States, reaching a climax in the 1860s. Fenians fostered, in the arena of advanced Irish nationalism, not just a voice but resources, ideas and inspiration to rebellion. Arguably the Fenian Brotherhood of the 1860s in its transatlantic guise, therefore, was a central part of a transnational constant that continued to breathe life into ideas of rebellion and what advanced nationalism could achieve through insurrectionary activities. Not only did the FB offer a large number of disgruntled Irish immigrants an opportunity to air their grievances at British misgovernment in Ireland as the cause of their exile, but these transnational revolutionaries also managed to mobilise a collective group to do something significant in addressing those grievances.[16] With Fenianism thriving in North America, it was within an American political environment that a healthy contingent of Irish immigrants changed their views about what they could do for Ireland. The American social and political environment at this historical juncture reoriented Irish-American nationalist thought and perception, while at the same time attempting to alter American ideas, at least vis-à-vis Britain and British North America. And it is that recognition of a unique transnational space on offer in the United States which subsequently shaped a lineage of evolving schemes, concocted by advanced Irish nationalists beyond Ireland's borders.

To offer further context, then, between the years of 1858 and 1863 the Fenian Brotherhood gained a home in the United States as it slowly expanded. At the outset Irish patriots encouraged disgruntled immigrants

Ireland, America and transnational radicalism 49

to join Irish militia groups, and as more and more migrants of a similar disposition arrived in the late 1800s, a section of Irish America had a decidedly martial prerogative. This kind of activity was for some, as argued elsewhere, merely a form of recreation or socialisation.[17] But clearly, for a large contingent it signalled something else. It seems that the utilisation of the liberty afforded to republican-minded Irish 'exiles' in the United States also informed a sense of opportunity. The Irish in America, now comparatively free to express pride in their ethnicity (despite US nativism), demonstrate a transnational consideration of identity in helping to sustain ideas of revolution. Despite the millions of migrants who settled down and rejected at least the physical form of Irish nationalism, many more had a complex rendition of the immigrant experience, illustrated by the founding of organisations like the EMA, the FB, Clan na Gael, Jeremiah O'Donovan Rossa's infamous dynamiters and Clan na Gael's public front, the Friends of Irish Freedom. These groups tried to harness the Irish immigrant experience of 'displacement, victimhood, cultural hybridity, and cultural struggles'[18] that had burgeoned among Irish migrants in the US, especially in the context of post-famine migration. Thus, for a large contingent the 'Irish question' did not fade away, but instead crystallised, even enflamed, with a less constrictive hegemony over the Irish population (as compared to in Britain) in the US. At the same time, of course, there were plenty of people who found the American environment one that was not suitable to the nationalist cause. Regardless, Irish nationalists at home and abroad believed that the diaspora could and should play a key role, if any plans for rebellion at home were to gain success. Stephens wrote, 'if properly directed the Irish here [in America] would be got to do much for their country, and I will add, for themselves; without this direction they can (with few exceptions) do nothing for either'.[19] This example accentuates how many within the diaspora remained focused on Irish affairs across the Atlantic.

To expose how the American environment influenced a changing nationalist-Irish mindset, by the early 1860s bold declarations by the Fenians showed an awareness of the protection they were afforded within America to expedite their ideas. At their first convention in 1863, the Fenians declared themselves to be a fixed and permanent institution in America, pledged to make Ireland free of Britain. However, nothing was inevitable and everything contingent upon whatever else cropped up locally, nationally, internationally. Subsequently, it was the US Civil War that reoriented the trajectory for many Irish-American nationalists, exposing them to new ideas about what they might do for Ireland. Irish migrants who had signed up to fight in that war, if not already Fenian members, were soon enrolled. By the time of the second Fenian Brotherhood convention in January 1865, the FB clearly understood their position, as an entity with a highly experienced cohort of trained military men that was beyond the reach of the British government. With candour and confidence Irish radicals proclaimed, 'We are ourselves beyond the reach of British malignity, as far as regards our persons and property. It is only by sowing discord in our midst that our enemies can defeat us. Let us then, with common accord, crush the slightest symptoms of that fell bane of Ireland wherever it appears.'[20] With this in mind, it is clear that the Fenians were not operating as a geographically bound entity concerned with the fixity of borders that defined nation states. The Fenians representing advanced Irish nationalism characterised themselves from within a kind of liminal enterprise – a nation beyond boundaries – while simultaneously utilising a sense of duality, both Irish and American. In order to express their thorough contempt for British trespass in Ireland, these physical force Irish nationalists resident in America hoped to harness Irish immigrants' sense of scorn at British rule and redirect it back across state boundaries, galvanising revolutionary organisations.[21] To achieve this they encouraged Civil War veterans to join their cause, worked to maintain political and cultural mores, while advocating and actively planning for rebellion on behalf of Ireland against Britain.

While often dismissed due to its ultimate failure, the American Fenian efforts to incite a war with British North America in 1866 (at the close of the US Civil War) is a much more important event than is usually depicted. The multiple reasons for that have been argued extensively elsewhere, but one central reason was that the motivation for an invasion of Canada was a conscious tactic to pressure the United States into taking a position regarding British imperialism at large, and the Irish question therein.[22] Fenian leader John O'Mahony wrote of the invasion plans: 'Unless it drags the U.S. into war with England it can only end in defeat to those that engage in it. But it is worth trying in the hope that it may lead to war.'[23] That is, an Anglo-American war. This underscores the view among an important group within the leadership that Fenianism, as a transnational phenomenon, could forcibly shape an Irish vision for the Atlantic world. In terms of the trajectory of an organisation like the FB, following the failure of their ostentatious effort to embroil Britain and America in war, it is true that the Brotherhood began to decline.

Ireland, America and transnational radicalism   51

Nonetheless, it signalled the persistent focus, motivation and audacity of Irish nationalists who found themselves in the United States largely due to their views on revolt and the dreams of achieving an independent republic for the island of Ireland. As such, the legacy of Irish insurrectionaries remained strong, such that similar efforts to spark revolution continued. Two stand-out Irish-American immigrants working in that vein were Jeremiah O'Donovan Rossa and John Devoy. By the time Devoy and Rossa had arrived in New York in 1871, the Fenian Brotherhood had been practically torn asunder. Nevertheless, lessons were being learned, both in terms of errors made and the memories and romanticism that embellished revolutionary methods. While the FB itself began to fade, it was very quickly replaced by a new and more sophisticated organisation in the form of Clan na Gael.

When former Irish Fenians who had been exiled from Britain for seditious activities arrived in New York in 1871 (known as the Cuba Five), two of them took up where the Fenians had left off. One was John Devoy, who suggested he and likeminded Irish nationalists in America needed 'to create an Irish party in this country, whose actions in American politics will have for its sole object the interests of Ireland'.[24] This fresh cohort of Irish nationalists arriving in New York saw an opportunity to cultivate innovative schemes centred on Ireland. As Shane Kenna suggests, '[i]t was evident that the exiles were desirous of building a broad-based, national movement uniting Irish nationalists in America behind a demand for Irish independence'.[25] The complex articulation of Irish republican radicalism existing on a global plain, and the tensions that emerged from that, can be found in both the practicalities of how insurrectionist plans played out, and the obvious paradoxes of trying to articulate a nationalist identity from outside the desired geographic state. Regardless, it is the transatlantic element around the movement to gain an independent Irish state that is central. When Pádraig Pearse, nominal leader of the 1916 Easter Rising, gave an oration over the grave of Jeremiah O'Donovan Rossa and exclaimed, 'the fools, the fools, the fools! – they have left us our Fenian dead, and while Ireland holds these graves, Ireland unfree shall never be at peace', he was indicating the matrix of connections, a sort of inheritance perhaps, between a group of Irish nationalists down through time and beyond the island of Ireland. That it was Jeremiah O'Donovan Rossa's grave at his feet and Mary Jane O'Donovan Rossa at his elbow when he spoke elevates the transatlantic nexus involved therein. It is further evidence for the contention, with regard to the history of Irish nationalist radicalism, that there is a certain evolution when it comes to the development of the changing, often cantankerous, transatlantic visions of an Irish freedom movement. It is interesting, then, to trace the approaches of the transoceanic Fenians over time, in their attempts to further the cause of Irish freedom. From the FB of the 1860s, to the actions of Rossa's dynamite campaign in the 1880s, and to John Devoy and the Clan na Gael approach towards the latter decades of the nineteenth century, each generated reactions among Irish nationalists that helped modify and amend previous approaches to the Irish cause for independence. And in doing so, the tensions that emerged reflected the complexities of an Irish national identity, specifically vis-à-vis the place of the diaspora in the story of Ireland's freedom.

What is most interesting is that O'Donovan Rossa picked up where the FB left off in conceiving of radical, transatlantic methodologies. Rossa recognised the Fenian Brotherhood's embrace of their territorial position in the United States, which provided the opportunity to act when there was reluctance or an inability to do so from within Ireland. But before his arrival in 1871 was the formidable patriot and activist Mary Jane O'Donovan Rossa, who campaigned in the United States in the late 1860s, both for the release of her imprisoned husband and for a free Ireland. It was Mary Jane who gives us a literal link between the Fenians, the invasion of Canada plot and the ongoing work of transnational insurrection. William Randall Roberts, a central player in the 1866 FB invasion of Canada, supported Mary Jane O'Donovan Rossa in New York, while her husband remained in a British jail. She stayed at one of his properties, while he helped support her on speaking tours. These tours riled up Irish nationalists in America, while also paying Mary Jane a living wage as she awaited Jeremiah's release. Mary Jane, the daughter of a Young Irelander, was convent-school educated and a brilliant writer, campaigner and fundraiser on behalf of Irish republicanism. Bringing together cultural and political nationalism in her writing while based in the United States, her guile was imperative for informing the transatlantic viewpoint on revolution. On the release of Jeremiah, reflecting the patriarchy of the era she stoically allowed herself to be somewhat backgrounded as '[…] Rossa became Irish America's celebrity. He gave speeches throughout the country and became the face of Irish nationalism as the founder of the "Skirmishing Fund" and the "Dynamite School". He wrote for multiple newspapers and gave frequent speeches […] consistently supporting rebellion in Ireland'.[26] Mary Jane continued to speak on tour and to write,

Ireland, America and transnational radicalism   53

encouraging Irish insurrection, while Jeremiah took it upon himself to try and organise an active guerrilla war campaign in Britain from across an ocean.

Significantly, Rossa's viewpoint and determination was replicated by Patrick Ford's very influential *Irish World* newspaper. The printed message of physical force nationalism became grist to the mill, spreading through Irish America and across the Atlantic to Ireland. Indeed, the political debates of the day surrounding Anglo-American relations, as they had been in mid-1860s, continued to be dominated by Fenianism when Rossa's dynamite campaign garnered momentum in the late 1870s. With the apparent stagnation in Ireland of any revolutionary activity, Rossa appealed for a 'collection of funds to keep skirmishing and keep striking England, year after year, while the Revolutionary organizations are preparing for the heavier work'.[27] Thus, the infamous 'skirmishing fund' was launched in the 1870s to help finance, plan for and direct attacks across Britain – an idea supported by Ford's paper with its wide-ranging reach into Irish nationalist opinion. The origins of Rossa's skirmishing fund are said to have come from Ford's newspaper, via a subscriber's letter, raising the idea of deploying 'terror, conflagration, and irretrievable destruction' in cities on mainland Britain.[28] By the end of 1878, the skirmishing fund had raised as much as $75,000 through donations from across America. Therein one can observe the growth, maintenance and invention of a specifically revolutionary form of Irish nationalism, devised among the diaspora, sustaining the ideas of an insurgency. Rossa took up dynamite from where the FB had left their invasion campaign, to damage the British Empire wherever it was imposed. As Ann Larabee presciently explained, 'Dynamite represented a power that could be stolen, shifting the balance to the side of the oppressed. Promoting terrorist uses of dynamite, Irish-American revolutionary leader Jeremiah O'Donovan Rossa proclaimed: "I regard these discoveries in powerful explosives as the result of the working of that eternal justice that is an active agent in the government of the universe. It is a revelation of God to the oppressed nations of the earth."'[29] Rossa was the figurehead that jumped at this opportunity to advance the Irish cause, seizing a transnational confluence to weave another thread in the web of physical-force nationalist design and activity.

Not unlike the FB's earlier intrigue, a conspiracy would once more seek to strike a blow at the British Empire, originating from the US, in order to address the Irish question. Fenian men, as Patrick Ford editorialised, '[...] *will carry on an irregular and incessant warfare against the enemy, –*

while the regular military organisations are preparing for heavier and more regular war …'.[30] With international travel becoming more popular as the late nineteenth century progressed, Irish immigrants in America pledged themselves to carry out nefarious acts, including blowing up parliament in London, or prisons and castles scattered across Britain. In the time period under investigation, from the 1860s to the 1920s, global communications had developed significantly, to the extent that cable and postal messages were becoming increasingly speedier, as indeed was travel. These improvements in communication and transport helped advance transnational developments. Furthermore, in terms of technological innovation, it was the creation of dynamite by Alfred Nobel, understood as an example at the forefront of modern science and its potential for massive social change, which interceded with the resurgence of the international Fenian conspiracy in the late 1870s onwards. At the same time that Fenian intrigue was garnering momentum, the coincidental arrival of dynamite was quickly recognised and understood by certain Irish radicals as a way to further their cause, sooner rather than later. With that in mind, Rossa explained the reason for and motivation behind the acts that he undertook: '[…] speaking in all soberness, I do not know how dynamite could be put to better use than in blowing up the British Empire'.[31] Although Rossa was certainly on the fringes of an Irish nationalist standard by the time we get to the 1880s, when the land war and home rule took precedence when it came to popular support for reform in Ireland, nonetheless his trajectory was relevant in influencing the direction of the Irish independence movement.

Often accused of merely being engaged in self-aggrandisement or showmanship, perhaps Rossa's persona blurred the picture of this transnational effort. Spearheading a newly instigated drive to not only raise money for 'skirmishing' but to affect some action, Rossa's dynamite campaign got underway with an explosion at Salford barracks in 1881. In reality Rossa's dynamite campaign was reduced to abundant rumours and several alleged near misses, when 'infernal devices' were found aboard ships by customs officers, and a few failed attempts to blow up buildings. Nonetheless, it was the perspicacity of these schemes that proved more telling. The creation of the dynamite school in Brooklyn, for example, armed men with the skills to construct timed bombing devices, which could potentially be unleashed at any time. With coercion laws implemented across Ireland in reaction to both the land war and subsequently the 1882 Phoenix Park murders (of the British chief secretary

Ireland, America and transnational radicalism   55

for Ireland and his undersecretary), popularity grew for these groundbreaking ballistic methodologies among the more militant nationalists
travelling back and forth across the Atlantic. As Shane Kenna points out:

> [t]he very idea that skirmishers were training men in America in
> do-it-yourself explosive manufacturing was a significant security
> concern to the British state. The previous year Rossa had asserted
> that, 'young men have come over from England, Ireland and Scotland
> for instruction and that several of them have returned sufficiently
> instructed in the manufacture of the most powerful explosives'.
> [Indeed] a central objective of the dynamite school was to train men
> in the [...] use of explosives in America, and dispatch them to Britain
> facilitated by advancements in trans-Atlantic communications. [...]
> graduates would share the knowledge with Fenians operating in
> Britain, seeking the destruction of British life and property.[32]

Explosions detonated in Glasgow were tangible examples of the kind of
action that these plans could bring to fruition, when the destruction of
a gasworks there raised the stakes for the British authorities. Explosions
followed in London, outside the offices of *The Times* newspaper and more
symbolically at the parliament buildings, which garnered much publicity
and led to celebration among Irish-American nationalists, swaying the
more reticent Clan na Gael members. Action, as conceived within the
diaspora, generated interest and swung the momentum towards the
radical movement for Irish independence. Consequently, Clan na Gael
took up where Rossa's skirmishers had started, orchestrating a campaign
to disrupt British life.

   One pattern that the transnational imperative commonly replicated
with these proceedings in mind was the necessity of action: acting now
and not waiting for some future event that would magically open the way
to Irish independence. The insistence on immediate engagement echoed
the FB's Canada plan, the skirmishing fund and indeed the determination
to follow through on Easter weekend 1916, despite the well-known
confusion that occurred leading up to the rising. Considering these plans,
their importance is perhaps often understated or even elided. As Jonathan
Gannt has pointed out, 'Most studies do not go far beyond labeling certain
Irish nationalists as terrorists, ignoring the serious and sustained attention
given [...] by policy-makers ... [which] shaped American relations
with Great Britain. [...] Irish-American dynamiters demonstrated [...]

an international component that required policy makers to consider real problems to Anglo-American relations.'[33] Elsewhere, one of the most prominent transnational organisers was John Devoy. Invasions of 'foreign' nations and the establishment of dynamite schools or bombing campaigns were not quite Devoy's style, although his initiatives were daring and ingenious in their own right. For instance, his role in recruiting Irish soldiers from the British army during the 1860s planning for an IRB insurrection in Dublin, which led to his exile; the outstanding organisation of the globally orchestrated *Catalpa* prison-break;[34] or the clandestine collaboration with German officials to the United States, eliciting aid for an Irish revolution during the First World War. As Terry Golway cogently wrote, 'Any exploration of the [1916 Irish] Rising as a transatlantic enterprise, as it so clearly was, must take into account the role that New York played as a source of funds and support [...] and any account of New York's role requires an examination of the formidable and perhaps irreplaceable presence of John Devoy, the man Pearse referred to as the "greatest of the Fenians".'[35] What Devoy disdained was the damage that could be caused by indiscriminate bombings, where innocent victims might be counterproductive to the overall cause. Thus, Rossa's late nineteenth-century dynamite plans were often met with disparagement by Irish-American nationalists, and Devoy was one who fell out with the hazardous Rossa.

Nonetheless, as with the 'men of action' who pursued and persisted with insurrectionist schemes, Devoy also believed talk without action meant Ireland's call for independence atrophied and ultimately perished. His biggest frustration was the lack of secrecy. Secrecy, he argued, was imperative, and proclamations of revolutionary intent should only be made if and when the time was right to do so. Devoy's influence in Irish transnational insurrection, therefore, was much more subtle. Nonetheless, his machinations showed lessons learned, as he worked tirelessly on much more mundane things, like organising networks and meetings; organising as united a front as possible among the copious Irish factions; and marshalling public opinion in the United States. A contemporary of James Stephens, John O'Mahony, Michael Davitt and Jeremiah O'Donovan Rossa, John Devoy was a tangible link to the ideas and designs of Irish transnational revolutionaries, tied to the new, young and determined generation that emerged in the 1910s, when Ireland's fight for independence was at its most critical juncture. That latter link was manifest in his ties to people like Thomas Clarke, Joseph Mary Plunkett, Roger

Ireland, America and transnational radicalism

Casement and Pádraig Pearse, the men central to the planning of 1916. There is an argument, perhaps a convincing one, that the Irish in America must surely have been out of touch with the feelings of the people in Ireland. Thus, men like Devoy, chewing over their actual exile, were seeing the plight of Ireland through a very personal and outdated lens. Thirty or forty years on since these men were ejected from Ireland, the Irish people seemed to have chosen the path to partial independence as steered by John Redmond and constitutional nationalism. Yet this misses the point entirely. Devoy was, of course, aware of Redmond's popularity, for it was sustained by Irish America too, until events like the creation of the UVF and the call by Redmond to send Irishmen to war in 1914 swung opinion back towards physical force nationalists.

Irish revolutionaries, at home and abroad, believed there was an appetite for insurrection, and no insurrectionist expects an entire population to endorse an uprising. Revolution is a slow process, as the Easter Rising itself underscored; yet it did indeed change the majority opinion on the ground, in time, as to the merits of the effort. Regardless, John Devoy was one of the most important people, a prototypical transnational figure and the central thread that linked this Irish revolutionary web across the Atlantic ocean. Terry Golway showed that upon arrival '[...] in New York in 1871 [Devoy] had worked ceaselessly to extend the struggle for Irish freedom to the shores of the United States'. In that effort, 'Any exploration of the Rising as a transatlantic enterprise, as it so clearly was, must take into account the role New York played as a source of funds and support, and as the site of negotiations between the rebels in Dublin and the German government'.[36] Devoy became the constant link in these plans. He was the man who helped to organise the return of Jeremiah O'Donovan Rossa's body to Ireland, over which Pearse gave his most famous speech leading up to the Easter Rising of 1916. But perhaps the most obvious link was the action Devoy took in employing an assistant to help him with his newspaper, *The Gaelic American*, a man named Thomas Clarke. As historian Gerard MacAtasney suggested, when writing of Tom Clarke's time in New York, one can see the centrality of transnational figures and ideas in Irish physical force nationalism: 'Without spending eight years in New York and maintaining strong transatlantic relationships on his return to Ireland Clarke would have not sustained the respect and trust of figures such as Devoy [...]. Their financial clout, political acumen and relative freedom of expression meant that they were vital cogs in the machine that produced the [1916] Rising.'[37] Thus, the trajectory, the thread, of a transnational history comes full circle. From decade to decade from the 1850s, schemes concocted by those preceding them, a more and more discerning group of Irish nationalists, emerge, continuing with revolutionary objectives in order to secure independence on the island of Ireland. It was, then, under the auspices of John Devoy that Clan na Gael in the United States took up the mantle of being the dominant, transnational Irish association helping to maintain revolutionary intrigue. What is more, the dominant place of John Devoy and Clan na Gael in the strategy known as the New Departure and the support of the land war in Ireland re-emphasises the centrality of the transnational component that informed the long Irish revolutionary period of the late nineteenth century and into the early twentieth. As well as embracing more public forms of nationalism like the New Departure, Devoy and Clan na Gael continued to organise shipments of arms into Ireland up to 1916. The 1879 New Departure arrangement that allowed Clan na Gael to acknowledge the efforts of Parnell working for home rule and Davitt for tenant rights did not mean abandoning the strand of revolutionary insurrection. Indeed, *Irish World* editor Patrick Ford perhaps explained it best as early as 1881, in a stark warning letter addressed to the British prime minister: '[...] Mr. Gladstone. You are now, unlike the past, dealing with two Irelands. The Greater Ireland is on this side of the Atlantic. This is the base of operations. We in America furnish the sinews of war. We in America render moral aid.'[38] But of course, as with all the Irish conspiracies, and considering the geographic, social, political and cultural differences and distance that inevitably developed across the Atlantic over time, this identifiable, transnational inheritance was also wrought with division and conflict.

In his efforts to promote insurrection in order to see an Irish republic created, John Devoy was never shy of pointing out the centrality of the diaspora to his brethren in Irish nationalist circles. For example, he offered an impassioned plea to Irish nationalist politician John Dillon, highlighting Irish-America's importance when it came to the question of Irish nationalism. In answering criticisms of the role of advanced nationalism emanating from the diaspora, Devoy retorted, '[...] how can you ask the Irish in America to have confidence in the majority after the exhibition they have made of their subservience to English politicians and to Irish Bishops? [...] What would you and O'Brien have to fight with and what could you effect by fighting after you would have destroyed the fighting machine?'[39] The Irish nationalism that emerged in 1916,

Ireland, America and transnational radicalism   59

then, owes much to this inheritance central to diasporic nationalists like Devoy, and his predecessors, and to the pattern of audacious revolutionary efforts advocated by those in the United States particularly. To argue over the efficacy of those campaigns misses the point. For, as we rightly acknowledge, if the failed 1916 Rising was an important moment for Ireland, then we must acknowledge the dynamite campaign, as well as the Fenians' invasion of Canada scheme, all pivotal to the Irish nationalist trajectory that gave us Easter 1916. Irish advanced nationalism was transnational and, as such, it ebbed, it flowed, grew, shrunk, was refined, evolved, formed a pattern of audacious planning and, importantly, it did not die out, but continued in light of what had gone before.

To bring us towards a conclusion, then, back at home in Ireland some nine years prior to the Easter Rising, Thomas Clarke returned from America, where he had worked closely with John Devoy, to direct the young cohorts now populating the IRB in helping to perfect the organisation in preparation for revolution. As Desmond Ryan described, '[Tom Clarke] was the incarnation of the very spirit of Fenianism. [...] What had burned into his soul was something akin to the Miltonic hate, unconquerable will and study of revenge, and most certainly a courage never to submit or yield until the flame of insurrection and a flash of rifles rounded off the tragic glory and integrity of his life.'[40] In the end, the central point is that, just like the work of the FB in 1866, the subsequent work of Clan na Gael and of figures like Devoy and Rossa, Clarke and the rejuvenated IRB in the 1910s had taken up the baton from where earlier organisations left off. Thus, a continuation of how Irish nationalism was '[...] being forged at the very margins of the globalised Irish nation; refashioned through the articulation of difference with regard to other national, ethnic and racial groupings [...]'.[41] The list speaks for itself, starting with the 1866 invasion of Canada, the *Catalpa* rescue of 1876, the skirmishing fund and dynamite campaigns of the 1880s; the New Departure into the 1890s, and the rejuvenated IRB in the 1910s; Clan na Gael, Friends of Irish Freedom and finally the 1916 Easter Rising itself; all examples of a transnational expression of advanced Irish nationalism, honed and developed in lieu of one another along a progression in time.

All of the preceding insights are by and large pointing to something that was arguably prototypical in its articulation, that of a transnational revolutionary movement that burgeoned, guided and emboldened physical force Irish nationalism. What is more, it is the innovativeness of the entire insurrectionary period over fifty-odd years that stands out, which is explicitly the result of a transatlantic transnationalism. Transnationalism's emphasis on global networks and the flow of people, things, capital and information across borders clearly informed the development of Ireland's independence movement. As a practical expression of that, in the last months of 1915 leading up to the 1916 Rising, John Devoy organised the transfer of Clan na Gael dollars to the IRB in Dublin, to the tune of $100,000, sent in increments of five and ten thousand, in cash![42] More importantly, he helped organise for Sir Roger Casement to make initial contact/liaison with German authorities to facilitate gun-running, and then to send Casement to Germany in person, at the height of the First World War, to persuade the Germans to help Ireland's cause. In 1915 Pearse would be eulogising over the graveside of Jeremiah O'Donovan Rossa, alongside his widow Mary Jane, who had been supported by Fenian Brotherhood financier William Randolph Roberts when she first arrived in New York, her husband then in jail for being an Irish revolutionary. The transfer of O'Donovan Rossa's body from New York to Dublin was facilitated by John Devoy and the funeral plans organised and overseen by Thomas Clarke, later executed in Kilmainham for his role in the 1916 Rising. Pearse, Devoy, Casement, the O'Donovan Rossas, William Roberts, Thomas Clarke: a more remarkable web of Atlantic crosscurrents and intrigue is hard to imagine. As immigrants negotiated, adapted and acclimatised, they reflected a prototypical Irish 'transnationality – or the condition of cultural interconnectedness and mobility across space'[43] – conditions from which advanced Irish nationalist pursuits emerged in tandem with the development of a transnational Irish diaspora.

CHAPTER FOUR

When history and hope rhymed: Fanny Parnell – nationalist, feminist and patriot poet

Christine Kinealy

During her short life, Fanny Parnell achieved an international reputation as an Irish patriot – a status that only a few contemporary nationalist men obtained. Born to a life of privilege and an acknowledged beauty, Fanny turned her back on the traditional path of marriage, children, domesticity and obscurity. Instead, she lived in the public eye through her writings, lectures, and her role as the founder of the Ladies' Land League in North America. Consequently, during her lifetime, her celebrity at times overshadowed that of her brother, Charles Stewart Parnell. When Fanny died prematurely in July 1882 – aged only 34 – she was a nationalist hero on both sides of the Atlantic. Her siblings not only buried their talented sister in an unmarked grave, they also buried her memory and her reputation.[1] Although revered by both men and women in her day for her political activism, today Fanny is almost only written about by women scholars and she is usually depicted as part of a sibling team, rather than as an individual. More general histories of this period, if they do mention Fanny or her sister Anna, define them by reference to Charles, not as political activists who had their own agency, abilities and followers.[2] This chapter examines Fanny's contribution to nationalist politics, especially through her poetry, and her role in raising awareness about Ireland's 'forgotten famine' of 1879–82.

61

Frances Isabel Parnell – Fanny – was born in Avondale House in County Wicklow in 1848 (or 1854, depending on the source). She was one of eleven siblings, being situated by virtue of age between Charles (born in 1846) and Anna (born in 1852). Fanny's father's family were wealthy Anglican landowners, while her Boston-born mother, Delia, was the granddaughter of Admiral Charles Stewart, a naval hero of the war of 1812 between the United States and Britain.[3] While Fanny was born into a world of privilege that typified the Protestant ascendancy, her American mother added a different, and probably anti-British, perspective to her upbringing. Moreover, the Anglo-Irish world had recently undergone a seismic shift due to the Great Famine, which had not only removed over two million people through death or emigration but had changed the structure of landowning in Ireland. While few landlords had died during the Famine, approximately 25 per cent of land had changed hands, largely due to the Encumbered Estates Acts of 1848 and 1849.[4] The Parnell family had survived these years of turmoil but, following the death of Fanny's father, Henry, in 1859, accumulated debts meant that the Avondale home had to be rented.[5] It was not sold, however, until after Charles' death in 1891.[6] Consequently, during her teenage years, Fanny lived an itinerant lifestyle, travelling with her mother and two sisters, Anna and Theodosia, to stay with various Stewart relatives in France and America.[7] The Parnell women were in Paris during the brutal Franco-Prussian War; they joined the American Ladies' Committee and worked as nurses in the makeshift field camps.[8] Following the death of Fanny's uncle in France in 1874, she and her mother returned to the family home, 'Ironsides', in Bordentown in New Jersey.

Fanny's political involvement came early, pre-dating Charles' activism. According to Thomas Clarke Luby, founder of the *Irish People*, Fanny first published in his paper in 1864, when she was aged 15.[9] As was commonplace for women nationalists, she used a pen-name – Aleria.[10] Thus, it was Fanny who first brought Fenian ideas into the Parnell home.[11] In 1865, three of Aleria's poems ('Masada', 'The Death Bed Farewell' and 'Song') were used as evidence by Dublin Castle to convict several Fenian leaders of sedition. There is no evidence that the authorities knew the real identity of the author.[12] Fanny attended Jeremiah O'Donovan Rossa's trial every day and was moved to tears when he was convicted.[13] Like Charles, Fanny did not condone violence for political ends, but her early poems suggested her belief in the need for a heroic struggle, whatever the strength of the opponent or the sacrifice it entailed:

Masada (c.1865)[14]

Wild and haggard stood the warrior, worn with watching and with
    pain;
Many a dent was on his breast-plate, on his sword was many a stain;
Loose back o'er his mailed shoulders streamed the tangled locks of coal,
Fiercely from his black eyes flamed all the tempest in his soul.

The expectation for women of Fanny's upbringing was that they would
marry within their own class and provide heirs. To this end, in January
1866 Fanny was presented with other debutantes at the vice-regal court
in Dublin Castle.[15] Seven years later, she would be presented to Queen
Victoria at Buckingham Palace.[16] Her beauty and wit were commented
on in the society newspapers. This pathway should have led to a dazzling
marriage. That Fanny viewed the marriage market with a mixture of
cynicism and amusement was evident in her penning of 'Reflections of a
Wallflower'.[17] Her viewpoint may also have been influenced by her eldest
sister Delia's marriage, which had made her deeply unhappy, even leading
to an attempted suicide.[18] For Fanny, spinsterhood was a preferable choice,
even if it was less socially acceptable. Consequently, she chose a very
different path from that of many women of her class, never marrying, and
rejecting the social values with which she had been reared, and bravely
choosing the public over the private sphere in which to live her life.

In 1875, Charles was elected to the House of Commons. Fanny and
Anna attended frequently, observing him from the Ladies' Gallery, which
they referred to as the 'ladies' cage'.[19] Charles' presence in the British
parliament provided a further step in Fanny's political education and
consolidated her support for home rule.[20] Like many, she was radicalised
by the reappearance of famine in Ireland from 1879 to 1882, and used her
increasing celebrity to challenge the British government through poetry
and prose. Fanny also intervened in a more practical way. In September
1879, she published an appeal to Irish-Americans to raise subscriptions for
people in the west of Ireland, asking:

> Will not the Irish here, who can afford it, give something from their
> conveniences to help our countrymen in their terrible need? I know
> that I do not appeal to hard hearts or closed hands.[21]

To encourage subscriptions, she herself made several donations.[22] Fanny
did not confine her appeals to the columns of newspapers, she also spoke

publicly on the issue. This included a lecture in Delmonico's banqueting hall in New York City to a mixed audience, but one primarily composed of women. A member of the audience later recalled, 'Those who heard her will never forget the impression she made on us ... with her intense, austere face, quivering, slight figure, and thrilling voice, full of all-consuming earnestness.'[23] More practically, Fanny arranged for Famine Relief Fund boxes to be placed in post offices all over the US, and she devoted on average ten hours a day to organising collections. Fanny's actions were praised in Ireland. The Dublin newspaper *The Irishman* referred to her as a 'patriotic Irish lady' and predicted that her 'name will be received with affection'.[24] Additionally, a number of Dublin newspapers offered to act as a conduit for receiving relief raised as a result of her appeals, including Timothy Daniel Sullivan, the editor of *The Nation*, who established an agency for distributing the relief within Ireland.[25]

At the beginning of 1880, Charles arrived in New York for an extended tour of North America. One of his first actions was to establish an Irish Land League Famine Relief Fund, partly to answer criticism of his indifference to the situation. Like many, he framed the food shortages in reference to the tragedy of the Great Famine. On the day of his arrival, he gave a speech in which he stated, 'In 1845, the Queen of England was the only sovereign who gave nothing out of her private purse to the starving Irish. The Czar of Russia gave, as did the Sultan of Turkey, but Queen Victoria sent nothing.'[26] In fact, Charles' recounting of the queen's contribution was inaccurate (she had donated £2,000), but he was creating a powerful, albeit controversial, narrative of English indifference to Irish suffering.[27] Parnell's comments aroused anger across the Atlantic, notably from his political protagonist and defender of unionism, Lord Randolph Churchill. Churchill accused Parnell of 'gross falsehoods'.[28] Although the Relief Fund was Charles' initiative while he was touring North America, it was left to Fanny and Anna to relocate to New York City to run the operation.[29]

Fanny, more than Charles, realised the value of the written word and of using media to win support. On the eve of Charles' tour of America, she published a treatise entitled *The Hovels of Ireland*, its purpose being 'to create and foster sympathy with Ireland amongst Americans'.[30] Proceeds from sales were to go to the Land League Fund. *Hovels*, which was sixty-five pages long, included a three-page preface by Charles, although there is a possibility it was also written by Fanny, Charles disliking the process of putting pen to paper.[31] Fanny described her motivation for writing as that

Fanny Parnell – nationalist, feminist and patriot poet

Americans had no real knowledge of Ireland and that what information they did have came from England.[32] She explained her rejection of the values of the Protestant ascendancy:

> Brought up among Anglo-Irish Tories, as I had been, and my mind filled with the bluest Tory principles, nothing less than the constant spectacle of tyranny and cold-blooded heartlessness on one side, and of suffering and degradation on the other, to which it was impossible to blind myself, which would not be thrust aside for all my circumstances of education, would have sufficed to arouse me gradually to a true view of how the case stood between landlord and tenant, between rich and poor, between Protestant and Catholic in Ireland.[33]

Although *Hovels* provided a sympathetic view of the Irish peasantry, at times Fanny chastised her countrymen who resided in 'hovels' for their own inertia: 'in Ireland there is a national hebetude, a deadly stupor, pervading the whole country, which makes of every man a desponding Rip van Winkle'.[34] Nonetheless, she challenged the stereotype of the Irish poor as hopeless and lazy.[35] She also rejected the Malthusian notion of over-population, arguing that Ireland had never been overpopulated but was, in fact, underpopulated, although no less vulnerable than it had been before 1847.[36] Rather, Fanny identified two wrongs that existed in Ireland: 'first, the wrong English rule as it exists in Ireland; secondly, the wrong of landlord rule as it exists in Ireland'.[37] It was an unequivocal attack on the class into which she had been born. It was also a rare venture by a woman into the public sphere occupied by men. *Hovels* was published in the United States, but the pamphlet and its author were also read and praised in Ireland.[38] The Dublin *Nation* – a champion of Fanny's work – opined, 'We prognosticate that this little book will meet with a large circulation, and that its publication will net a good sum for the Land League fund, for which excellent reason it first saw the light.'[39] The author herself was praised: 'Noble sentiments nobly expressed by a lady thoroughly worthy of the splendid traditions of her noble kith and kin.'[40]

While *Hovels* was well received by the nationalist community, it was for her poetry that Fanny was most celebrated. Her poems generally appeared first in the American press but were quickly reprinted in Ireland. Her output was prolific, with approximately forty poems published in less than three years.[41] Fanny used this medium to good effect, cajoling and castigating her countrymen in turn. Her poem 'Coercion – Hold the Rent' provided a poetic dimension to the policies of the Land League, leading Davitt to describe it as a 'rousing chorus' which he quoted in full in his own history of the league.[42] The poem was put to music by M.G. Giannetti and copies of the sheet music were sold in Ireland.[43] Fanny's best-known poem of that period was 'Hold the Harvest', itself based on a Land League slogan urging the tenant farmers not to allow their crops to be used to pay rent while they were starving. It was reminiscent of a poem written by another young radical woman nationalist during the Great Hunger, namely 'The Famine Year', written by Speranza and published in *The Nation* in 1847.[44] Fanny's poem was first published in the Boston *Pilot* on 21 August 1880.[45]

Hold the Harvest (1880)
Now are you men or cattle then, you tillers of the soil?
Would you be free, or evermore in rich men's service toil?
The shadow of the dial hangs dark that points the fatal hour
Now hold your own! Or, branded slaves, forever cringe and cower! ...

Oh by the God who made us all, the master and the serf
Rise up and swear to hold this day your own green Irish turf!
Rise up! And plant your feet as men where now you crawl as slaves
And make your harvest fields your camps, or make of them your
    graves! –

But God is on the peasant's side, the God that loves the poor,
His angels stand with flaming swords on every mount and moor,
They guard the poor man's flocks and herds, they guard his ripening
    grain,
The robber sinks beneath their curse beside his ill-got gain.

Within two weeks of its American release, 'Hold the Harvest' appeared in Ireland.[46] Copies were distributed at Land League meetings and it was frequently read out, including at a meeting of 5,000 in Leeds in England.[47] For Michael Davitt, an admirer of Fanny's writings, the poem represented 'The *Marseillaise* of the Irish peasant', an allusion to the anthem of the French revolutionaries in the 1790s.[48] More than anyone else, Fanny had become the poet and muse of the Land League movement.

While the instant popularity of the poem delighted supporters of the Land League, their opponents rallied against it.[49] As the following press

Fanny Parnell – nationalist, feminist and patriot poet 67

report demonstrated, poetry and poets were increasingly regarded as part of the propaganda war being fought over Ireland, and Fanny was clearly in the vanguard of the attack:

> Violent and reckless orators are not wholly responsible for inciting the Irish people to acts of indiscretion. There is a band of poets springing up, whose inflammatory verse is doing almost as much harm as the utterance of platform agitators. Prominent among the number, we are told by a correspondent, is Miss Fanny Parnell, from whose pen several poetical effusions have recently emanated, and whose latest effort is an address to the Irish farmers, framed on the text of 'Hold the Harvest' …
>
> Miss Parnell, indeed, seems to revel in strong terms, and she scatters her maledictory substantives about in a manner that would be amusing were it not for the fact that such verse, trashy though it be, exercises a powerful influence upon the excitable Irish temperament.[50]

The London-based *Morning Post* lamented the impact the Parnells were having on Irish-Americans, singling out 'Hold the Harvest' for special condemnation:

> What effect is produced upon the Irish-American mind by this course of training and long years of secret organisation may readily be understood from the highly inflammatory poem of Mr. Parnell's sister, which is now being sung throughout the neighbouring island. The lady in question resides with her mother in the United States, and has really nothing whatever to do with Ireland and its troubles; her rhapsodical cry to arms is therefore all the more indicative of the feeling of her brother's admirers and supporters in America … This is the sort of political appeal now being constantly made in newspapers and songs to excitable Irishmen in both hemispheres; and such harangues are likely to produce more terrible fruits among American-born Irishmen than among Irishmen at home … What Miss Parnell sings Mr. Parnell speaks.[51]

'Hold the Harvest' was quoted by Attorney General Hugh Law when he prosecuted Charles Stewart Parnell and other members of the Irish National Land League for conspiracy at the end of 1880.[52] Davitt took especial pride in the attorney general reciting the poem to the jury, 'in the finest elocutionary manner', with the result being, 'every pulse in court beat faster and eyes glistened and hearts throbbed'.[53] For a second time in her short life, Fanny's writings were judged to be treasonable. In the same year that 'Hold the Harvest' was published, a collection of Land League ballads was published in New York, under the title *Land League Songs*, which included many of Fanny's poems, consolidating her position as a leading voice in the movement.[54]

As Fanny's poetry continued to both delight and disturb people in Britain and Ireland, she was developing a plan to establish a Ladies' Land League in North America.[55] Her justification was that the funds of the league were inadequate, and the male leadership were about to be arrested. Michael Davitt later admitted that the idea of women forming their own association was not universally popular: 'this suggestion was laughed at by all except Mr. Egan and myself, and vehemently opposed by Messrs. Parnell, Dillon and Brennan, who feared we would invite public ridicule in appearing to put women forward in places of danger'.[56] Davitt was adamant, however, that when the men were imprisoned, 'No better allies than women could be found'.[57] Fanny and Davitt proved to be correct, with the formation of the Ladies' Land League being reported widely within Ireland and one provincial paper predicting that, 'The three L's will occupy as prominent a position in the present agitations as did the three Fs'.[58] Suggestions were made for a similar organisation to be formed in Ireland. Shortly afterwards, in January 1881, it was announced that a Ladies' Land League was to be established in Ireland. Anna had been persuaded by Davitt to be its president. By May, there were 321 branches in the country.[59]

In addition to writing, and regardless of her history of heart problems, in 1881 Fanny also undertook an arduous lecture tour of North America, attracting large audiences. Despite her claim that the primary work of the women would be focused on 'philanthropy and humanity', her political message was evident. In the Albert Hall in Montreal, her message mirrored what she had written in *Hovels*: 'The English Government was not by any means the worst enemy the Irish people had.' She explained, 'It was the feudal government in Ireland that had created so deplorable a state of affairs in that country, and brought into existence – the greedy landlord, the land-grabber, and that meanest of all spies, the police-constable spy.' Regarding the latter, she suggested – to 'great applause' – that, 'If the women had boycotted them, very few of them would have

Fanny Parnell – nationalist, feminist and patriot poet   69

remained in the force'.[60] Many of the lectures were reprinted in full in the Irish press.[61]

The assassination of two British officials in the Phoenix Park in Dublin in May 1882 caused outrage in Britain and promoted a backlash against Charles Parnell and his supporters. Fanny tackled the issue head-on, writing a letter that was published in newspapers as far away as Australia. In it, she insisted that 'no Irish hand was concerned in the murder of the two innocent men'. She added, 'We Irish are not assassins, and it is time that we should not allow any would-be Nihilist, on paper, to take away the fair reputation of our motherland.'[62] Her intervention in this controversial matter again demonstrated her fearlessness in defence of her people and refusal to take accusations meekly. For a number of observers, however, Fanny's outspokenness was dangerous, not because of its calls for Irish freedom, but for its challenge to the traditional role of mothers and daughters. In particular, she divided opinion amongst the Catholic clergy who supported the Land League. Bishop Thomas Grace of St Paul, Minnesota, denounced the Ladies' Leagues as being 'in opposition to all their womanly instincts', while Bishop Richard Gilmour in Cleveland excommunicated several women for their participation.[63] When Fanny was in Boston, where she lectured in ten different locations, Rev. Thomas Scully of Cambridge was quoted in the *Boston Globe* saying that, while he supported the Land League, he would never favour any woman …

> … who got up on a political platform. The further women are kept from the politicians, the more virtue they would have. He had no Ladies' Land League in his parish because he was not a petty-coat priest. But the women can help Ireland by being good wives and good mothers, and by having all the children they can, and bringing them up well.[64]

Regardless of some criticisms, Fanny's popularity and value to the movement on both sides of the Atlantic can be gauged by the fact that Land League lockets, which contained Fanny's likeness, and were 'finished in the best style', were being sold in Ireland, costing from one to five shillings.[65] Her popularity with the rank and file of the movement was evident, with cheers being called for her at many meetings of male leaguers in Ireland.[66] Overall, Fanny's activities gave the Parnell women a public profile that at times rivalled that of Charles. In March 1881, the *Celtic Monthly* included a long article that praised the three Parnell women – the two sisters and their mother.[67] Charles may have been the uncrowned king of Ireland, but his popularity and success owed much to the public support of the women in his life, who made him greater than he otherwise would have been.

On 20 July 1882, Fanny met with John Dillon and Willie Redmond, leading nationalists, at her home in Bordentown. A few hours later, she was dead, possibly of a heart attack. She was aged 34. Fanny's premature and unexpected death was mourned on both sides of the Atlantic. Her funeral took place in New Jersey on 24 July. In advance of it, John Heath, a sculptor from Philadelphia, obtained a plaster cast of Fanny's face.[68] The longer-term plan was to take her remains back to Ireland, as many nationalists on both sides of the Atlantic wanted her body to be returned to her birthplace. To this end, her body was embalmed 'to ensure its arrival in Ireland … in a perfect state of preservation … where the final internment will take place'.[69] Although a removal to Ireland was Delia's preference, she wanted to 'await the action of her son'.[70] The travel arrangements were brought to an abrupt end when Charles sent a telegram saying,

> My brother, sisters and I desire my sister's remains should rest in America, the country where she was best known, where she had friends, and where she lived and worked so many years.[71]

Fanny was buried in the family vault in Boston, with no headstone to mark the location, her life, or her passing.[72] At the time of her death, Charles was negotiating with the British government and had already decided to disband both the men's and the Ladies' Land Leagues. In April 1882, he signed the Kilmainham Treaty with Prime Minister William Gladstone, which led to his release from prison on 2 May. A short time after Fanny's death, in August 1882, Charles dissolved the Ladies' Land League. Anna never forgave, or spoke to, her brother again.[73] It is probable that Fanny would have been similarly outraged.

At the time of her death, Fanny was memorialised on both sides of the Atlantic. Her long-time friend and fellow activist and writer John Boyle O'Reilly paid tribute in the Boston *Pilot*, writing, 'there was something almost mystical in her nature and her life. Like the sacred Pythoness, unlike her own slight physical self, she drew her songs quivering with force and passion'.[74] In a poetic tribute, he described Fanny as a weaver of words, who would return to life when her country was free.[75] A poem by a P. Hanley ended by describing her as 'our chieftainess Fanny Parnell'.[76]

Fanny Parnell – nationalist, feminist and patriot poet

Her loss to nationalist politics was summed up by a resolution of the Carndonagh Ladies' Land League in County Donegal:

[We] beg to tender to Charles Stewart Parnell, M.P., Miss Anna Parnell, and the other members of their afflicted family, our deepest and heartfelt sympathy in their present trying bereavement; with the millions of our race all over the world, on whose lips her name was a household word, and in whose heart the fame of her young life's exertions will last forever. We deplore her loss.[77]

While Fanny's contribution to Irish nationalist discourse was brief, it was significant. Her position as an authority on the Land League was recognised shortly before her death when she appeared in a 1,000-word history of Ireland – Fanny being the only female to be so included.[78] The book was reprinted as far away as Australia.[79] Her influence and impact were acknowledged by Michael Davitt, who worked alongside her and benefited from her activities. In his 1904 history *The Fall of Feudalism*, he acknowledged her role in founding the Ladies' Land League and described her as 'a rebel to her heart's core', praising her 'songs of liberty'. He, like so many other nationalists, likened Fanny to Speranza of Young Ireland.[80] For Davitt, her words inspired Irish nationalists, while her poetry 'electrified the crowded audience'. He singled out 'Hold the Harvest', which, 'with its fine appeal to the God of the poor, gave expression to Ireland's awakened hope to wrench the soil in one supreme struggle from the hands of the heirs to confiscation'.[81] Davitt also acknowledged that Fanny's contributions lay beyond poetry:

Miss Parnell was a practical as well as a poetic reformer, and one of her proposals, a little varied in its plan and purpose, had probably more to do with the defeat of Mr. Forster's coercion policy than all of the other plans put into action against it by the leaders at home.[82]

Just as fulsome in his praise was Francis Sheehy-Skeffington, nationalist, pacifist and innocent casualty of the 1916 Rising. In writing about Davitt, he singled out Fanny's contribution to the Land League:

Fanny Parnell was the noblest and purest minded patriot of the Parnell family, and had not her fiery soul 'fretted the pygmy body to decay', and brought her to an untimely death, her genius might have won for her a place beside the Maid of Orleans among the liberating heroines of history.[83]

72   *Navigating Historical Crosscurrents in the Irish Atlantic*

Fanny's poetry continued to be cited by Irish nationalists. Four lines from her early poem 'Masada' were included by the veteran Fenian John O'Leary in his 1896 history *Recollections of Fenians and Fenianism*.[84] He also devoted part of a chapter to her, opining that, 'These verses, like all that I have seen from this lady's hand, are, I think, rather rhetoric than poetry, though very vigorous and sonorous rhetoric indeed, giving great promise for a girl, as the writer then was'.[85] Fanny's writings appeared in *A Memorial Birthday Poem to the Poet Thomas Moore: Dedicated to the National League of America, and its kindred Irish associations, with other poems*, which was first published in Philadelphia in 1889.[86] Fanny's poetry also featured intermittently in anthologies and nationalist writings, but 'After Life' rather than 'Hold the Harvest' seemed to be the choice of her fellow poets. This poem appeared in a 1900 collection of Irish poetry written in the English language. The Introduction read:

> FANNY PARNELL
> SISTER of the late C.S. Parnell, M.P. She was born in County Wicklow in 1854, and wrote poems for *The Irish People* (1864–5) before she reached her teens. She was afterwards closely connected with her brother's political work, and died in America in 1882. She was a fervent speaker and organiser, and had much poetical ability.[87]

Fanny also featured in a series entitled *Irish Literature*, edited by Justin McCarthy, in 1904. McCarthy selected 'Post Mortem' (an alternative name for 'After Death'), 'Hold the Harvest' and 'Erin My Queen' for inclusion.[88] 'Post Mortem' was reprinted in the *Sligo Nationalist* newspaper in 1913.[89] 'After Death' was also selected by Padraic Colum, one of the leaders of the Irish literary revival in his 1922 anthology.[90] This poem was also included in Lennox Robinson's *Golden Treasury of Irish Verse*, published in 1925.[91] It was 'Hold the Harvest', however, that showcased Fanny at her most political, eloquent and polemical. It provided a vivid commentary on the causes and consequences of the famine of 1879 to 1882, showing that the intermittent food shortages were artificial and the poor should not allow themselves to be passive victims.

While Fanny was remembered by her contemporaries and by the generation of nationalists who followed, it was mostly for her poetry, rather than for her more polemical writing or as the visionary behind the founding of the Ladies' Land Leagues. Following the founding of the Free State, she disappeared from public view for some decades, possibly because of the political nature of her writings. In 1970, Irish poet Brendan

Fanny Parnell – nationalist, feminist and patriot poet 73

Kennelly included 'After Death' in a book of Irish verse that was described as 'An anthology that focused on the more obscure and generally unknown Irish poets'. In the editor's brief description, Kennelly said, 'Fanny Parnell (1854–1882). Sister of Charles Stewart Parnell. Wrote for *The Nation*. Very active in politics'.[92] In April 2001, Fanny belatedly received a headstone and recognition from the government of the Irish republic. The Irish ambassador to the US, Seán Ó hUiginn, unveiled a memorial headstone of Wicklow granite, taken from the former Parnell home at Avondale to the Mount Auburn grave. Emphasising the point that the ambassador was representing a woman president of Ireland, Mary McAleese, he referred to 'the sexism which prevented the sisters being taken seriously as political partners and strategists by the establishment of nationalist Ireland'.[93] It was a belated recognition that while the two Ladies' Leagues may not have been overtly feminist, they clearly and publicly asserted the right of women to have a political opinion and a political voice.

On a number of levels, Fanny Parnell was remarkable and defies easy classification. She can be viewed as part of an Irish tradition of patriot poets, thus linking the Young Ireland movement of the 1840s with the insurgents in 1916. She also belongs to a long continuum of women who championed Irish independence, defended the Irish poor, and, during their lifetime, were more radical and recognised than many of their male contemporaries. In this way, she bears comparison with Speranza and Maud Gonne. After Fanny's death, like so many other groundbreaking women, she was marginalised, forgotten or pilloried by later generations, a process that has been referred to as being 'eire-brushed out of history'.[94] The recovery of the lives of these women and their histories has been a slow process, but it adds a complexity and depth to our understanding of Ireland's history. The nationalism of Fanny and her siblings also throws light on the role of the Protestant ascendancy in defending the right of Ireland to govern herself. Importantly, Fanny's story, and that of the thousands of women who joined the Ladies' Land Leagues, allows a more gendered understanding of Irish nationalism and the emergence of the women's movement. Moreover, their activities showed the strength of transatlantic ties in providing a cross-fertilisation of ideas and support for independence in the first generation of post-famine survivors and immigrants. Finally, the recovery of the lost contributions of Fanny and multiple other women activists brings a richness and dynamism to our understanding of how modern Ireland came into being and of the women who helped to build it.

CHAPTER FIVE

'I cannot banish the thought of home': young Irish women's responses to urban-industrial America

Kerby A. Miller

During the late nineteenth and early twentieth centuries, a slight majority of Irish emigrants to the United States were females, predominantly single women in their late teens and early twenties.[1] In America they usually laboured as domestic servants in middle-class households or less frequently in needle- or factory-work, before most of them left the paid labour force to marry and raise families of their own.

In recent decades most historians of female emigrants from post-Famine Ireland, especially of those who became house servants, have emphasised their willingness, even eagerness, to 'escape' from rural Irish patriarchy as well as their independence, ambition and apparent success in achieving economic and/or marital goals in urban-industrial America.[2] In turn, those interpretations at least implicitly accord with several intellectually and politically dominant paradigms: first, neoliberalism, which measures personal and group worth in terms of successful adaptation to local and increasingly global capitalist markets; second, American exceptionalism, which defines US capitalism in terms of unique 'opportunity', political 'freedom' and even personal 'liberation'; third, feminism, which (when inflected by neoliberalism) stresses female agency, individual and collective, in defining and achieving marketplace success; and finally, the

Young Irish women's responses to urban–industrial America 75

primacy of racial, or in this case ethnoreligious, identity in shaping the socio-cultural frameworks in which such success is understood, pursued and celebrated. Of course, these paradigms are not always consistent, but they concur in de-emphasising or even rejecting class and class conflict as principal determinants of historical change. Likewise they challenge traditional views of Irish emigration as involuntary, unwilling 'exile', mandated by forces ultimately political, as well as the accompanying and once-common belief that the Irish in America were 'the most homesick of all immigrants'.[3] To be sure, some scholars acknowledge that Irish emigrant *males* often conformed to those older interpretations, but they contend that Irish females' rejection of Irish male repression and embrace of American capitalism either led them to defer or refuse matrimony, or ensured that, if they did become wives and mothers, they played the most important roles in acculturating and 'uplifting' Irish-American working-class families into the ranks of the *bourgeoisie* – often despite their menfolk's deficiencies and protests.[4]

Scholars' recent interpretations of Irish emigrant women are valuable and important.[5] Yet at least several of their ideological premises are problematic, as I shall contend at the end of this essay. More to the point here, however, is that much primary evidence exists to question a purely instrumental interpretation of Irish women's responses to the emigration experience. For instance, many of the transatlantic letters which Irish female emigrants wrote to their families and friends were as redolent of homesickness and alienation as those often penned by Irish emigrant males. Studies by Margaret Lynch-Brennan and Maureen Murphy have discovered a number of such documents.[6] This essay focuses on several additional letters, written by two female emigrants who left County Kilkenny for the United States in the 1880s, an analysis of which may further refine our view of Irish women's attitudes to emigration and to urban-industrial America.

The earliest and shortest of their surviving letters was written by Cathy Greene, who in the decade's early years emigrated from a 'strong farm' of about 130 acres in Ballylarkin and Ballybush townlands in Killaloe parish and Shillelogher barony, nestled in the King's River valley between the town of Callan and the Tipperary border – one of the richest farming areas in all Ireland.[7] On 1 August 1884, Greene, probably a needle-worker in her early twenties,[8] penned this anguished missive from Brooklyn, New York to her widowed mother, Mrs Catherine Greene, in Ballylarkin.[9]

Brooklyn N.Y. 1st Aug. 1884

My dear Mamma

What on earth is the matter with you all, that none of ye would think of writing to me. The fact is I am heart sick fretting. I cannot sleep the night and if I chance to sleep I wake up with the most frightful dreams to think its now going, and gone into the third month since you wrote to me I feel as if I'm dead to the world. I'm left the place I was employed They failed in business I was out of place all summer and don't know how long. This is a world of troubles. I would battle with the world and would never feel dissatisfied if I would hear often from you. And know candidly how things are going on but what to think of how ye are now forgetting me I dont know but one thing I know if I dont hear from ye prior to the arrival of this letter at Ballylarkin I will be almost dead. I dream of ye every night a few nights ago, I saw a toom[10] stone, white with black letters in memory of some person who died in 1884 the first letter of the name was 'M.' and what followed I could not realize last night I saw Johnny and the 'Mare also a lot of clay turned up.[11] I feel so nervise I faint often into a swone[12] like often now. I know its from anxiety about ye, and what is best for ye to do. I sometimes think you would come here and that health would fail and like almost all the Irish drop off one by one. There is no place like home if one could at all live there but if not dont hesitate about coming here I trust ye are well and that my frightful dreams wont be realized.

   Cathy

with love to one & all for God sake write soon
your lonely daughter Cathy

Unfortunately, little more can be discovered about the author of this letter, although, if she moved from Brooklyn to Manhattan after her employer's bankruptcy, she may have been the 'Catherine Greene, dressmaker, 381 Second Avenue' listed in *Trow's 1884–85 New York City Directory*.[13] We do know, however, that at least one of her deepest fears was not realised. Despite the great difficulties that even strong farmers suffered to pay rents in the early 1880s, when Irish farm prices collapsed and evictions soared, her mother did not go to America. According to the 1901 Irish Census, Mrs Catherine Greene, age sixty-five, still headed the Ballylarkin household alongside her also-widowed, thirty-year-old

Young Irish women's responses to urban-industrial America

5.1 (*top left*) Mary Ann Rowe. (Credit: Miller papers, James Hardiman Library, National University of Ireland, Galway)

5.2 (*top right*) Mary Ann Rowe Sutton, 1897. (Credit: Miller papers, James Hardiman Library, National University of Ireland, Galway)

5.3 (*bottom right*) James Rowe Sutton, 6 months, 1898. (Credit: Miller papers, James Hardiman Library, National University of Ireland, Galway)

daughter Honoria Tyrrell and the latter's two children.[14] Yet the Greenes were not typical: between 1841 and 1851, in the decade of Ireland's Great Famine, the population of Killaloe parish had fallen nearly 40 per cent, from 1,424 to 871, and between 1851 and 1891 it declined by another 43 per cent, to only 455.[15] As for Cathy Greene, if she escaped the high mortality (especially from tuberculosis) characteristic of the Irish in American cities, which she noted in her letter,[16] then it is probable that her remittances to Ireland were critical in enabling her mother to stay in Ballylarkin and her younger sister Honoria to marry and inherit the home for which Cathy was so 'heart sick fretting'.

Much more is known about our other emigrant letter-writer. Mary Ann Rowe was born in the spring of 1864 and baptised on 8 May in the Catholic chapel of Dunnamaggan parish in the barony of Kells, less than ten miles south-east of Cathy Greene's farm. In 1888, aged twenty-four, Mary Ann Rowe emigrated – sailing on the *Pavonia* from Queenstown, County Cork, to Boston, Massachusetts, where she arrived on 11 June. She soon settled in the town of Dedham, just outside Boston. There she worked as a house servant – the occupation recorded for her in the *Pavonia*'s passenger list – until early 1897, when she married in Dedham's Catholic church.[17]

Native white Americans generally regarded domestic service as degrading, fit only for women from the poorest groups in society such as African-Americans. However, historians of Irish female emigrants contend that the latter viewed service overseas as a desirable opportunity for economic security and capital accumulation. Certainly, many Irish-American house servants came from families far removed from destitution. For example, Mary Ann Rowe's parents were also strong farmers, who probably were almost as 'comfortable' in Dunnamaggan as were Cathy Greene's in Ballylarkin. In 1888 when Mary Ann emigrated, James Rowe and his wife Catherine Kennedy Rowe[18] held over seventy acres in Dunnamaggan's Monachunna townland beside the River Glory in mid-Kilkenny.[19]

Thus it was not poverty that impelled Mary Ann Rowe's emigration. Rather, for her as for Cathy Greene and thousands of other farmers' daughters, emigration resulted from the lack of both economic and marital opportunities for women in the post-Famine Irish countryside. In that respect, young women in wealthy counties like Kilkenny were little or no more advantaged than their sisters in Ireland's poor western districts. Indeed, many centuries earlier, Norman settlers had transplanted to

Young Irish women's responses to urban-industrial America

Kilkenny and other rich south-eastern counties the restrictive inheritance and marriage practices that accompanied their introduction of the manorial system and commercial farming. Much later, Ireland's Great Famine of 1845–52, coupled with the ongoing collapse of cottage industries and the shift from tillage to pasture farming, confirmed Kilkenny farmers' reliance on impartible inheritance and the dowry system to transmit land and capital between generations. As a result, the non-inheriting sons and non-dowered daughters of solvent farmers, as well as the children of poor smallholders, cottiers and landless labourers, were obliged to migrate to Irish cities or towns, or to leave Ireland altogether.[20]

The Great Famine's immediate impact on the Rowes' Dunnamaggan parish was apparently less severe than on the Greenes' parish of Killaloe. Between 1841 and 1851 Dunnamaggan's population fell by only 20 per cent, from 1,213 to 973. However, between 1851 and 1881 the number of inhabitants fell by nearly half, to 527, and in the distressed 1880s, when Mary Ann Rowe emigrated, it declined another 23 per cent, to a mere 409. The population of Monachunna also fell sharply: in 1841 the townland had contained three households and twenty-six inhabitants, but by 1881 only the Rowe family, with six members, remained.[21]

Prior to the 1880s, most emigrants from Dunnamaggan were probably members of the labouring classes, for, as grazing cattle replaced the tillage farming which traditionally had been the mainstay of mid-Kilkenny's rural economy, employment for hired farm workers steadily decreased. Between 1841 and 1881 the number of agricultural labourers in County Kilkenny fell 86 per cent, from over 40,000 to fewer than 6,000, whereas the number of farmers declined much less sharply, from about 12,000 to nearly 9,000, while the number of cattle in the county increased by two-thirds. Although less dramatically, the ratio of small to large farmers also changed, as substantial farmers with fifty acres or more, like the Rowes and Greenes, improved their position at the expense of their poorer neighbours. Thus between 1851 and 1911, the share of Kilkenny farms (i.e. holdings of more than one acre) that exceeded fifty acres in size increased from 17 to 25 per cent.[22] Likewise, marriage opportunities declined, although at first not greatly and perhaps primarily among the labourers and poorest farmers; for example, between 1851 and 1881 the proportion of Kilkenny women aged between thirty-five and forty-four who had never married rose only from 17 to 23 per cent, and the proportion of those aged twenty-five to thirty-four who were unmarried actually shrank slightly.[23]

Thus in mid-Kilkenny the agricultural crisis of the 1880s did not cause an unusual surge of departures as it did in the poor western counties, but rather it confirmed many of the existing causes of post-Famine emigration. Indeed, in Dunnamaggan parish the rate of population decline in the 1880s was actually slightly less (minus 20 per cent) than it had been in the relatively prosperous 1870s (minus 23 per cent). Among Kilkenny's farmers, however, the falling prices, crop failures and threats of eviction during the 1880s only accelerated the long-term trends towards pasture farming, impartible inheritance and restricted marriage. Thus, between 1881 and 1911 the proportion of women in the county aged between twenty-five and thirty-four and who were unmarried increased from 44 to 59 per cent, while the proportion of those aged thirty-five to forty-four who were single rose from 24 to 33 per cent.[24]

It is very likely therefore that Mary Ann Rowe, like thousands of other farmers' daughters without dowries, significantly improved her marital as well as her economic prospects through emigration. Nevertheless, her departure may have been less than entirely voluntary. Unfortunately, James and Catherine Rowe had no surviving male heir to inherit the farm and whose marriage might have brought to the family a dowry of sufficient size to enable *both* their daughters, Mary Ann and Alice, to marry into farm families of comparable status. Instead, only one daughter could inherit and marry; in effect, the farm itself would be her dowry to attract a husband with land or capital. Somehow the decision was made that Mary Ann should emigrate to clear the way for her sister, who would gain the farm and the Irish marriage which such an inheritance would virtually guarantee, in return for taking care of her parents in their old age.[25] Accordingly, on 22 February 1892, just five months before her father's death, Alice Rowe, aged twenty-eight or twenty-nine, married a man six years younger, David Walsh, who assumed control of the farm that James Rowe had purchased the previous year from his landlord's estate.[26] Thus the Rowe family strategy succeeded but at Mary Ann's expense. On 29 October 1888, slightly more than four months after she left Dunnamaggan, Mary Ann Rowe wrote her sole surviving letter from the United States. Perhaps significantly, she wrote it to a friend and neighbour, James Wallace,[27] with whom she might be more candid than when addressing her parents. In any case, her missive evinced little satisfaction with her situation but instead expressed profound homesickness.

Young Irish women's responses to urban-industrial America

Dedham Mass.

Octr 29th 88

My ever dear and loving friend after a long Silence I take the pleasure of writing to you hoping and wishing this note will meet ye all in good health as the departure of this note leaves me also. Dear friend I suppose ye though[t] I had forgotten ye altogether since I delayed so long with out writing to ye but My Dear Friend, it is not through any lack of friendship that I stayed so long without writing to ye I do feel so bad when I go to write to home I dont be in the better of it for a long time it renews all thoughts of home in my mind that I scarcely know what to do Oh James if I thought I would be so lonely after ye all it would be the last thing that I would ever think of doing I would never leave poor Dunnamaggin If I only thought I would be so home Sick I Cannot banish the thought of home out of my mind no matter where I go it is equal to me nothing Could Cheer, and Strange to say I am growing worse every day there is not a night but I do be dreaming about ye or Some one from home Dear James I dreamed last night that little John[28] was dying I fancyed I was looking at him and had the pleasure of kissing him before he died I hope and trust nothing is the matter with any of them Oh when I think of poor little Ellen & Jimmie how they used to Come out in the fields to where we used to be working and poor little MaryAnne how she used to Call John fancied John Oh when I look back to our former days how often we Spent an afternoon on Sunday Chatting over Some thing funny how nice we used to put in the Sunday together with the little ones around us.

My Dear James I am living with a very nice family here in Dedham they are very nice people but they are not Catholics. They are much niecer[29] than Catholics Their name is Collins it is an Irish name I dont [k]no[w] but they are Irish[30] they dont like to Say they are Irish I am within 2 or 3 minutes walk from the Church[31] there is a Splendid Church here in Dedham and 3 priests I Can go to Mass every Sunday an[d] to Confession when ever I want to go My Dear James I have Seen a great deal of rain Since I Came the weather is beginning to get Cold now I am Sure It is often I will think of poor old Ireland when it is Cold weather here I often Wondered to see how they do be prepaired for every Kind of weather they would not go out side of the door without rubber boots I would not be allowed to go out to put out the clothes without even when the dew was on the grass without rubber boots on me My Mrs is so very carefull of me – My Dear friend Dedham is a very niece place & it is a Country looking place when you look around there is nothing but trees theres any amount of different fruit apples are as plenty as they are at home I saw an orange tree in the green house it is nice to see them growing It was a young tree it was placed in a box and they were 5 Oranges growing on it it was a low little tree There is a great time here in Boston there is an Election of President for Boston[32] there is Scarcely a night they dont be marching they bands and the Irish it do often remind me of the night Mc Namarra was liberated[33] it is splendid to see how they march My Dear James if I stood writing for a week I would forget some thing I must Draw to a close for the present by sending ye all my best love give my love to Father Mother and not for getting poor Statia[34] I remain your affect. friend M A Rowe

To Mr James Wallace Ballintee until Death

At first glance, Mary Ann Rowe's acute homesickness may seem surprising. To be sure, US labour historians have argued that house servants, including emigrant Irish women, commonly endured class-based exploitation and suffered profound alienation and loneliness in the homes of unsympathetic *bourgeois* Yankee employers.[35] As noted at the beginning of this essay, however, scholars of both American women's and Irish-American history usually have painted a much more positive picture of Irish emigrant women's experience in domestic service. Moreover, by her own account Mary Ann Rowe appears to have enjoyed kind and even motherly treatment from her mistress in the Collins household. To be sure, historian Margaret Lynch-Brennan suggests that the extreme youth of many Irish emigrant women, often in their early teens, may explain the longing for home which she discovered in many of their letters. However, neither Rowe nor (probably) Cathy Greene was under twenty-one, the average age of Irish female emigrants, when they left Ireland,[36] and it is also possible that Irish emigrants such as Rowe, who was twenty-four when she left Dunnamaggan, might experience greater homesickness in direct proportion to the number of years they had spent in their family homes prior to departure.

Of course, both Rowe and Greene could expect to labour in America for five to ten years as domestic servants, before they could accumulate

Young Irish women's responses to urban-industrial America

sufficient savings to marry working-class Irishmen – while also fulfilling 'duties' to send remittances to parents in Ireland. Thus for older emigrant women, the window of opportunity for matrimony was continually shrinking. This meant that Mary Ann Rowe faced marriage prospects that were more uncertain than Cathy Greene's: first, because Rowe was nearly in her mid-twenties when she emigrated, and, second, because the gender ratios of Irish-American communities in Rowe's New England were so disproportionately female.[37] Yet, Rowe's letter does not suggest that she experienced social or religious isolation from her fellow countrymen and -women. After mid-century, Dedham and the other farm- and mill-villages in Norfolk County were transformed into Boston's outer suburbs by the extension of commuter trains and street-railways from the metropolis.[38] With suburbanisation came an influx of migrants, primarily Irish, to work in construction and to labour in the homes of middle-class commuters, at least a few of whom were also of Irish descent, as Rowe's comment on the Collins family suggests. Thus, between 1880 and 1890 the numbers of Irish emigrants in Norfolk County increased from 12,202 to 14,217, and by the latter date the county contained 24,400 Catholics, the great majority surely of Irish birth or background. Similarly, in 1890 perhaps a tenth of Dedham's 7,123 inhabitants were Irish-born,[39] and certainly a higher proportion were Catholics who worshipped at newly constructed St Mary's, the 'Splendid Church' described by Rowe: 'a magnificent stone structure', later eulogised by Boston's archdiocesan historians as 'one of the finest churches erected during that period'.[40] Rowe's letter also reflects the beginnings of Irish political ascendancy in the Boston area, as only three years earlier in 1885 Irish-born Hugh O'Brien had become the city's first Catholic mayor. To be sure, Irish emigrants only comprised 12 per cent, Catholics only 20.5 per cent, of Norfolk County's inhabitants, whereas in neighbouring Suffolk County including Boston their shares were 15 per cent and 40 per cent, respectively. However, if Norfolk County's Irish communities were smaller, they were also less congested and healthier: in 1890 census-takers recorded merely 5.29 persons per dwelling in Norfolk County (4.96 in Dedham), compared with over thirteen persons per dwelling in Boston's working-class Irish wards.[41]

It is arguable then that Mary Ann Rowe's homesickness, and also Cathy Greene's, was attributable not only to their situations in the United States but also, and perhaps even more, to the cultural influence and psychological appeal of the unusually close-knit societies they had left behind in County Kilkenny. Most Irish historians and anthropologists have associated intimate family ties and tenacious cultural traditions with the materially impoverished, Irish-speaking districts of western Ireland. However, recent studies suggest that, precisely because of their relative prosperity and stability since the middle ages, Hiberno-Norman areas such as mid- and south Kilkenny were perhaps much more resistant to at least some of the disruptive social and cultural effects of later Protestant conquests and modern capitalist 'development'. In this region, for example, centuries-old farm villages – often the remnants of medieval manors – persist even today, whereas by contrast patterns of farm dispersal have dominated most of the Irish landscape since the 1700s.[42] Likewise, the district was rich with early Christian and medieval relics and ruins, including a round tower, high crosses, and the famous priory of Kells.[43] The area was remarkable as well for cultural continuity: both Mary Ann Rowe's and Cathy Greene's letters show the influence of an Irish language which, before the Famine, Greene's ancestor and namesake Cáit Graídhin of Ballylarkin could both read and write.[44] In 1851 over a fifth of the inhabitants in the Rowe family's Kells barony were Irish-speakers, and as late as 1891 between 10 and 15 per cent still spoke Irish.[45] Other examples of cultural persistence could also be cited, and it is revealing that both Cathy Greene and Mary Ann Rowe conveyed their anxieties in the forms of dreams and omens – premonitions of the deaths of loved ones at home – which were common tropes in Irish rural folklore.[46]

However, the argument is not that in the 1880s the younger-generation Rowes were still Irish-speaking or 'traditional-peasant' in outlook (neither would be likely, given the family's strong-farmer status), but rather that their society's relative affluence, stability and cultural density might engender acute homesickness among emigrants whose memories, unlike those of destitute peasants from the west, would equate Irish home-life with material comfort and contentment rather than with deprivation, 'backwardness' and shame. Likewise, issues of social class, as well as regional and cultural factors, should be considered. Society in Kilkenny and other eastern counties was highly stratified and segregated, much more so than in the west of Ireland. In mid-Kilkenny there were enormous social and psychological distances between the members of strong-farm families, like the Rowes and Greenes, and their poor 'inferiors' among the landless urban and rural working classes.[47] Thus it is very possible that, at least in counties with sharply differentiated societies such as Kilkenny, the daughters and sons of the labouring poor had more pragmatic attitudes towards emigration, and less romantic or nostalgic memories of the

Young Irish women's responses to urban-industrial America 85

society left behind, than did those whose parents were substantial farmers or shop-owners.

* * *

Unfortunately, Cathy Greene's fate in America is not known. However, Mary Ann Rowe's longing for the intimate society she left behind, whatever its causes, may have helped bring her life in the United States to a sad and early end. Nine years after her immigration, when she was nearly thirty-three and approaching the outer limits of marriageability and childbearing, Rowe made a fateful and perhaps even desperate decision, seizing what she may have believed was her last chance for a home and family of her own. On 28 February 1897 she wed the Irish-born Patrick J. Sutton of Providence, Rhode Island, at Dedham's St Mary's church.[48] Interestingly, two photographs of Mary Ann Rowe survive, one taken before her marriage, the other one afterwards (see Figs 5.1 and 5.2). Both photographs reveal the light brown hair and pale blue eyes she may have inherited from her Norman ancestors. However, in the former picture Rowe appears confident and smiling whereas in the later portrait her features seem tense and fearful.[49] Indeed, according to family tradition (but for reasons unexplained, suppressed or now forgotten), Patrick J. Sutton proved to be 'not ... a very good husband', in the diplomatic phrase employed by the donor of this letter. And on 11 January 1898, Mary Ann died in Dedham shortly after the birth of her only child, James Rowe Sutton (see Fig. 5.3).[50] At this point her husband disappeared from both family memory and public records, but, according to Mary Ann's Irish descendants, her son was fostered out and raised by the Rowes' Tully relations in Massachusetts. As for Mary Ann Rowe Sutton, Irish family tradition also has it that she was buried 'in the New England hills', whose beauty she had admired – but whose winter cold she had dreaded – in her 1888 letter.[51]

* * *

In conclusion, the evidence of Cathy Greene's and Mary Ann Rowe's letters and lives suggests that some scholars may have overdrawn the agency, adaptability and contentment of many young Irish emigrant women, perhaps especially those who became domestic servants in late nineteenth-century America. This suggestion does not deprecate or diminish those women's efforts, intelligence, character or achievements, but hopefully promotes a more realistic understanding of their motives and experiences within their socioeconomic and cultural contexts and constraints. As historian Rita Rhodes has argued, despite the slow growth of a 'limited individualism' among young females in post-Famine Ireland, it was usually their parents' economic strategies and calculated decisions, not their own choices, that determined whether, when, how and where their daughters emigrated – burdened with injunctions to send back money, taken out of their meagre earnings, to support the households from which in effect they had been expelled.[52]

Finally, with regard to the economic and ideological paradigms in which most current interpretations are embedded, it strikes this writer as rather shallow to evaluate the lives of Irish (and other) emigrants, female or male, primarily according to whether they 'adapted successfully' to what native reformers and radicals, as well as many Irish emigrants in their letters home, criticised as the hyper-competitive, brutally exploitative and crisis-ridden conditions of late nineteenth- and early twentieth-century American capitalism. Until recently, perhaps, most historians' liberal interpretations, nurtured in the halcyon postwar decades, may have seemed justified by optimistic illusions about the alleged benignity and inevitability of 'modernisation' and its supposed compatibility with democracy and social justice. But surely now, in this new Gilded Age, it can be acknowledged that those hopes proved false and that instead the conditions of that earlier era have culminated quite logically and disastrously in today's ruthless plutocracy, gross inequality, unchecked global plunder and rapidly advancing environmental catastrophe.

More to the point, this author suggests that the homesickness and alienation experienced at least temporarily by Rowe, Greene and many other Irish emigrants reflected not simple 'failures to adapt' but rather their vague but critical recognition of American society's glaring inadequacies in light of the values and memories, expectations and dreams brought from home and not yet jettisoned as 'inappropriate', 'unrealistic' or dysfunctional in the American marketplace. To be sure, the 'spirit of capitalism' had already distorted Irish society and family relationships, forcing or persuading young women and men to emigrate. Yet, many pre-capitalist social ideals and cultural traditions still endured even in class-ridden Kilkenny. Thus Horace Plunkett, an Irish 'reforming landlord' who knew the worlds of both peasants and capitalists, observed that Irish countrymen and -women had a broader and deeper concept of 'home' than

Young Irish women's responses to urban-industrial America

the one that prevailed among the American and English *bourgeoisie*: a concept that transcended their parents' dwellings and instead embraced an entire 'social order' – the human and physical landscapes with which they had such intimate, organic relationships: 'these are the things', Plunkett wrote, 'to which [an Irish man or woman] clings ... and remembers in exile'.[53] Unfortunately, one of the functions of the Irish-American religious and political institutions, which Rowe so innocently praised in her letter, was to ensure that the emigrants' memories and initial, critical insights would be sanitised or suppressed, so that a *bourgeois*-controlled Irish America would eventually blend seamlessly, even enthusiastically, into what became an *imperium malum* even more ruthless and predatory than the one that had imposed capitalism by conquest and famine on Ireland itself.[54]

CHAPTER SIX

The Balfour war mission to America in 1917 and the Irish problem

Francis M. Carroll

The United States entered the First World War on 6 April 1917, the last great power to be caught up in this vast conflict. The Allies immediately sent missions to Washington to integrate American manpower, weaponry, industrial resources and finances into enormous efforts to defeat Germany and the Central Powers. For the British there was an additional problem of anti-British sentiment in the United States. With almost 20 per cent of the American population of Irish descent, a serious question for the British to confront was whether the unresolved Irish political situation would obstruct wholehearted American support for Britain in the war effort. Arthur J. Balfour, the British foreign secretary, and former prime minister and former Irish chief secretary as well as nephew of Lord Salisbury, led the British mission to Washington in late April 1917, the first sitting member of a British cabinet to visit the United States.[1] Would this distinguished icon of the Conservative establishment be able to reassure the American government and the Irish-American community that Irish aspirations could be satisfied, at the very least as a measure to keep Allied solidarity in the war effort?

Certainly, as United States relations with Germany deteriorated in the first months of 1917, British observers worried about the effect that Irish matters had on American attitudes towards Britain. The British ambassador to the United States was Sir Cecil Spring-Rice, a career diplomat with very good connections in many social circles in America. Spring-Rice himself was from a west of Ireland Anglo-Irish family and

88

The Balfour war mission to America in 1917 and the Irish problem   89

was sympathetic to some form of home rule. Indeed, his cousin, Mary Spring-Rice, had served as crew on Erskine Childers' boat *Asgard*, when they ran guns for the Irish Volunteers in July 1914. Spring-Rice in early 1917 tended to see German money as the source of extreme Irish nationalism in both Ireland and among Irish-Americans. 'In the forefront of German agitation against the Allies', he reported to Balfour on 11 January, will be efforts 'directed against Ireland and our policy there'. He thought Americans generally supported 'good feeling and mutual understanding' with the Allies, but he warned, 'It is very strongly felt that the Irish question is a very serious drawback and that it is a common nuisance of the English speaking world.'[2] Of course, within a matter of weeks Germany resumed unrestricted submarine warfare in European waters and on 3 February the United States broke diplomatic relations, although did not go to war. In these circumstances Irish matters took on increasing importance. Spring-Rice concluded that most Irish-Americans would remain loyal to the United States, but he noted, 'The Irish question here is the great obstacle to a good understanding with the United States and it would be a great advantage to ourselves and Canada to be rid of it.'[3] He also proposed that some form of Irish government be implemented with constitutional guarantees for religious and civil liberties such as those included in the American constitution. Two weeks later Sir William Wiseman, the special British intelligence liaison, with President Wilson's advisor, Colonel Edward M. House, wrote a memorandum for the meeting of the Imperial War Conference in London, using many of the same words as Spring-Rice, but with some of House's caution. 'The Irish question is one of the greatest obstacles to a good understanding between Britain and America. The Unionist argument was unknown and the nationalist extremists have dominated American opinion.' Wiseman went on to say, 'There are, however, many reasonable and intelligent Americans of Irish extraction who feel very strongly on this subject, and might be persuaded to lend their assistance with all honesty to the settlement of this question at the end of the war.' Wiseman dismissed figures such as John Devoy and Jeremiah O'Leary, but concluded, 'the movement is given its greatest strength by the fact that reasonable honest citizens of the type of John Quinn feel so strongly about it'. House penned on his copy that 'the President had read it and thought it a just statement'.[4] The question of how to deal with Irish-American problems came to a head for the British when Wilson finally went to Congress to ask for war. Congress complied and on 6 April 1917 war was declared.

Once the United States was in the war, the British, French and Italians sent missions to confer with Wilson's government. The foreign secretary, A.J. Balfour, headed the British delegation and the official objectives were to work out arrangements for troops, supplies and finances. However, in the circumstances Irish matters could not be avoided. Wilson sent a strong signal directly to Lloyd George less than a week after the declaration of war. On 10 April the president asked Secretary of State Robert Lansing to send a dispatch to Ambassador Walter Hines Page in London to raise the matter with the prime minister. Page was instructed to:

Take an early opportunity in conversation with the Prime Minister to convey to him in the most confidential manner the information that the only circumstance which seems now to stand in the way of an absolutely cordial cooperation with Great Britain by practically all Americans who are not influenced by ties of blood directly associating them with Germany is the failure so far to find a satisfactory method of self-government for Ireland.

Wilson, echoing the earlier warnings of Spring-Rice and Wiseman, went on to say that the concern about Ireland expressed in Congress and in the press showed that more of the population were concerned than just the Irish-Americans. He concluded with a comment that suggested British failures regarding Ireland were also a world problem, asking Page to 'frankly' point out that,

if a way could be found now to grant Ireland what she has so often been promised, it would be felt that the real programme of government by the consent of the governed had been adopted everywhere in the anti-Prussian world.[5]

It was a very bold statement for the head of one government to send to the head of another government, asserting that the moral position of the Allies was compromised by British inaction in Ireland. Page was able to raise the matter with Lloyd George in social circumstances at the ambassador's residence. Lloyd George responded very agreeably; in Page's words,

He instantly understood and showed that he already knew the facts that I presented and was glad that the President had instructed me to bring the subject up. He had the American situation in mind

The Balfour war mission to America in 1917 and the Irish problem　　91

during the whole discussion of home rule and he was doing his best. Then he asked me to request the President to give his views to Mr. Balfour as soon as possible after his arrival.[6]

This, in turn, was an equally remarkable request, but it was in keeping with the decision to send Balfour to the United States. Indeed, on 10 April, the very day Wilson drafted his letter for Page, the British war cabinet gave instructions to Balfour, urging that he 'undertook to make special enquiry, and to telegraph to the War Cabinet, as to the importance of the Irish question in connection with our relations with the United States of America'.[7] These instructions were reinforced by Spring-Rice, who cabled several days later, 'There can be no doubt that the President will speak of the Irish question', noting that Irish matters were a political issue in the United States and were a constant source of criticism against Britain's claims on behalf of the rights of small nations.[8] So in addition to arranging the practical working relations between the two warring partners, Balfour was instructed to take the measure of what the Americans would accept as a solution to the Irish problem. Could he and would he?

Balfour and his entourage sailed secretly from Greenock, Scotland, on 13 April on the White Star liner *Olympic*, landed in Halifax on the 20th and travelled by special train to Washington. Secretary of State Robert Lansing escorted Balfour and Spring-Rice to the White House on the morning of Monday 23 April to introduce him to the president and to open discussions about the issues confronting the two countries, now partners in the Great War. This was followed by a dinner at the White House in honour of the British mission and a reception. Later Wilson confided in Colonel House that these talks had not gone to his satisfaction. He suggested a private dinner at the White House on 30 April with Balfour, House and his family, to be followed by more penetrating talks for two and a half hours about war issues.[9] These were the first of at least four private conversations between Balfour and Wilson in Washington. In his brief memoirs written years later, Balfour said 'no subject connected with the war was excluded'. But was Ireland discussed? Balfour cabled the Foreign Office on 1 May, a day later, that 'Neither President nor any Member of the Government has said a word to me about Ireland', although many private citizens had raised the matter with him.[10] On the other hand, after talking with Spring-Rice at the embassy, Shane Leslie confided in his diary the next day, 'Learnt that Balfour was confronted with Irish Q[uestion] on first visit to Wilson.'[11] The documents do not provide clear evidence as to

6.1 Robert Lansing, secretary of state (1915–20), greeting A.J. Balfour, Washington, DC, 1917. (Credit: Library of Congress, Prints & Photographs Division, photograph by Harris & Ewing [repr. number LC-DIG-hec-08329])

whether Wilson did or did not discuss the Irish question with Balfour, as Lloyd George had suggested that he should. When President Wilson's secretary came to him with an appeal from a political supporter to make a statement on behalf of the Irish, Wilson replied on 5 May not to mention this, but 'I have been doing a number of things about this which I hope may bear fruit'.[12]

In fact, Wilson's secretary of state would confront Balfour with the Irish problem that very day. On Saturday 5 May Secretary of State Lansing arranged a quiet meeting with Balfour at Gunston Hall, the eighteenth-century mansion just a few miles south of Washington along the Potomac river, out of sight of journalists and politicians. Lansing recalled that they spent over three hours talking about problems arising out of the war, focusing specifically on the current military situation and relations between the Allied powers. However, Lansing also raised the question of American relations with Britain, which had never been as cordial as those with France. Part of the reason for this, he explained, was the legacy of the American War of Independence, but anti-British feeling was also kept alive by the failure of Britain to implement some form of self-government in Ireland. Lansing told Balfour,

> The failure of his government to respond to the intense longing of the Irish for the freedom of Ireland from British rule by conceding to them a measure of independence made thousands of Irish-Americans bitter enemies of Great Britain, pointing out to him that this was a situation with which our government found it difficult to cope.

This was a remarkably frank commentary on the obstacles to close Anglo-American relations as the two countries prepared to embark on joint military efforts, the result in large part of British domestic political inaction in implementing some form of home rule. Lansing's assertions described very much the American political situation that Ambassador Spring-Rice had regularly conveyed to his government. Lansing went still further:

> I urged him to do something to remove this hostility of persons of Irish blood and of their American sympathizers and he promised to lay the matter before his government when he returned to England.[13]

This was an incredible charge for the American secretary of state to make directly to the British foreign minister, even if delivered in informal circumstances. Would it prompt Balfour to move his government to action? Lansing mused, looking out across the gardens of Gunston Hall

94   *Navigating Historical Crosscurrents in the Irish Atlantic*

to the Potomac and the shores of Maryland opposite, on the irony of holding this discussion at the eighteenth-century home of George Mason, the author of the Bill of Rights, the first ten amendments to the United States Constitution, guaranteeing religious freedom and civil liberties, the very issues so much an anxious concern for the opponents of Irish self-government.

Surprisingly, in view of Balfour's regular dispatches to the Foreign Office and private cables to Lloyd George, he seems never to have mentioned his Saturday afternoon meeting with the secretary of state. Earlier that day, 5 May, Balfour had sent a detailed account of a meeting with a deputation of Irish-Americans (to be discussed below), but not with this elaborately arranged meeting with Secretary Lansing at Gunston Hall.[14] In fact, only in his final report on the work of the war mission did he make an oblique and negative mention. 'The President never referred to it [the Irish problem] at all; the Secretary of State never referred to it officially.'[15] In the world of diplomatic practice there are certainly levels of nuance in which official and unofficial communication have recognised standing. A meeting of two ministers in the foreign office of one of them would constitute official communication. The meeting with John Quinn's group would certainly have been well down on even the unofficial scale, but it merited an immediate report by Balfour and an elaborate account of the talks. Why then was there not even a mention of Balfour's unofficial meeting and discussion with the secretary of state? Perhaps the concerns expressed by Lansing were simply more than Balfour was prepared to admit to his government.[16] In circles close to the White House there was confidence that pressure had been put on Balfour and the British government. Shane Leslie, with contacts with Wilson's secretary Joseph Tumulty, confided to Redmond almost two weeks later that 'the President has not been indifferent to the Irish Questions I can assure you privately', and he confidently asserted, 'I think we may take it that we shall owe Home Rule to him.'[17]

Many private citizens had exactly the same worries as Lansing about the effect to be had on the American public and specifically the Irish-American community by the ongoing failure of the British government to extend some form of self-government to Ireland. On one level there was a growing awareness that Lloyd George was about to announce new plans for Ireland. John Quinn, a successful New York financial lawyer and art collector, organised the sending of a cable signed by twenty-seven leading Irish-Americans to John Redmond on 22 April deploring the possibility of a partitioned Ireland and asserting that minority rights could be perfectly protected in Ireland as they were in the United States.[18] At the same time, Lord Northcliffe had solicited statements from prominent Americans, about the importance of an Irish settlement, to be published in *The Times* and also the *New York World* on 26 and 27 April, in the midst of Balfour's visit. Distinguished contributors were former presidents Theodore Roosevelt and William Howard Taft, 1904 presidential candidate Judge Alton B. Parker, James Cardinal Gibbons of Baltimore, New York mayor John Purroy Mitchell, Harvard University president Charles W. Eliot, and Columbia University president Nicholas Murray Butler, among others. At the core of their statements were powerful arguments in favour of some measure of Irish self-government as a means of securing political stability for the British Empire and closer relations with the United States.[19] And on 28 April some 140 congressmen sent a cable drafted by Congressman James A. Gallivan of Massachusetts to Lloyd George, urging him to implement home rule as soon as possible.[20] In addition to the importance of giving Ireland the form of self-government that it had earned through the parliamentary process, there was behind these statements and appeals the desire to improve Anglo-American relations through this process.

It was in this context that Sir Horace Plunkett talked with Balfour on 24 April. Plunkett, a younger son of Lord Dunsany, had ranched in Wyoming, served in parliament and pioneered the co-operative agricultural movement in Ireland. Although his hour-long meeting with Balfour dealt primarily with Britain's need for food from the United States, they also talked about the Irish situation.

> I explained the enormous importance of getting the Irish Question settled as a means of enlisting American sympathy with England. He agreed. It was arranged that he would see a small (3 or 4) number of Irishmen if I decided that it was well for him to do so.[21]

The following day Plunkett talked by phone with both John Quinn and Colonel House, and he wrote to Balfour saying he would be in touch with several of those who had written pieces for *The Times*. He promised to tell Balfour who among them would be 'likely to be helpful for you to see privately, two or three responsible Irishmen and allow them to state for your information views which they would like you to place before the Cabinet'.[22] Since Plunkett was about to leave the United States to return to Ireland, he turned over to John Quinn the organising of a deputation to talk with Balfour. Quinn had been mentioned by Sir William Wiseman and Colonel House as a reliable and moderate Irish-American. Plunkett assured Balfour's private secretary that Quinn was 'quite reasonable as Spring-Rice will tell you' and that 'nothing but good could come of a quiet talk with these men', who Quinn would bring.[23] Quinn put together a deputation of remarkable Irish-Americans to meet Balfour: Judge Morgan J. O'Brien, the former presiding judge of the appellate division of the New York Supreme Court and former vice-president of the New York State constitutional convention; Colonel Robert Temple Emmet, a West Point graduate, holder of the Medal of Honor, and a descendant of the Irish martyr/patriot Robert Emmet; Lawrence Godkin, a prominent New York lawyer and son of Edwin Lawrence Godkin, editor of the *New York Evening Post*; John F. Fitzgerald, the mayor of Boston for six years and congressman for six years; and of course himself. O'Brien and Fitzgerald were Catholic, Emmet and Godkin Protestant, and Quinn described himself as 'neutral'. Arrangements were made to meet with Balfour in Washington at the headquarters of the British Commission on Friday afternoon, 4 May, where his private secretary Sir Eric Drummond and his parliamentary secretary Sir Ian Malcolm accompanied him.[24]

The deputation was introduced to Balfour, who was courteous and receptive, and a relaxed conversation lasted for two hours. The group emphasised the importance of extending some form of self-government to all of Ireland, that the exclusion of parts of Ulster would be seen as a betrayal of the integrity of the island. Fitzgerald emphasised how the failure to implement home rule had drawn Irish-Americans and German-Americans together, which threatened the unity of the United States in the current war crisis. To illustrate the point, he told of how just four days earlier an Irish-American crowd at Faneuil Hall in Boston had cheered at the statement that German submarines had sunk 400,000 tons of Allied shipping. Quinn asserted that as a result of the United States entering the war and the Irish-German situation, 'the Irish question had now in a sense become an American question'. He also argued that the exclusion of parts of Ulster from any settlement, together with the appointment of Sir Edward Carson to the cabinet, 'would generally be felt here that Ulster and Carson had won'. Quinn said that Americans were puzzled that the British allowed 'disaffection' in Ireland and 'general disaffection here over three or four counties in the north of Ireland', and he suggested a united Ireland was not too great a sacrifice to make in the war. Quinn also acknowledged the collapse of support for John Redmond and the

The Balfour war mission to America in 1917 and the Irish problem　　97

Irish Parliamentary Party and noted that Britain was going to have to work with the moderate elements of the Sinn Féin movement. In this vein he urged the release from prison of Eoin MacNeill. Quinn concluded his case by claiming that a settlement of self-government for a united Ireland would be enthusiastically welcomed by President Wilson, former presidents Roosevelt and Taft, the American Catholic hierarchy, and reasonable Americans across the country.[25]

Balfour himself responded by taking a very modest position, protesting that he was unable to speak on Irish matters. 'I have no authority whatever to speak upon it', which was a surprisingly restrictive understanding of his cabinet instructions and Lloyd George's comments to Ambassador Page. And he claimed to be out of touch since he left London with the initiatives that Lloyd George had taken that would lead to the Irish Convention. He said he appreciated how the matter of Irish self-government had become a problem in American public affairs, as indeed it had in British politics, and had jeopardised the war effort. However, he argued that over the past several generations major reforms had broadened the electorate, ended religious restrictions, provided the means for small farmers to purchase land from large landowners and created a Catholic university, which would have been unconstitutional in the United States. In a political sense, Balfour argued, 'Irishmen … are as free as any American citizen or wherever free institutions on the British model have been extended.' By contrast, and *apropos* the so-called Irish–German alliance in the United States, Balfour described the current discriminatory treatment of Poles in Germany. As for Ulster, Balfour did not think there was any basis for worry about religious discrimination or economic exploitation, nor did he feel that some form of constitutional safeguards would change any sentiments. The fact was, however, that a large majority of the population in parts of Ulster identified themselves as an integral part of the United Kingdom and simply did not want to leave. As for forcing Ulster into a united Irish government, 'I think it would be felt that our condition really would be made worse by an attempt to settle the Irish question in that way.'[26]

Quinn records that his group came away from their two-hour meeting impressed by Balfour's courtesy and evident interest in their remarks. In Quinn's words, Balfour 'was in complete sympathy with the objects of the visitors'.[27] Several weeks later Quinn wrote to a friend confidentially that Balfour 'cabled [to the British government] our judgment that any attempted settlement "that divided Ireland would be worse than useless"'.[28]

98   *Navigating Historical Crosscurrents in the Irish Atlantic*

A less sanguine view of Balfour's assurances was conveyed by one of his secretaries to a friend, noting that 'Even the Irish deputation to whom he said nothing in particular, were enormously pleased at his receiving them, so Quinn told the Ambassador.'[29]

Balfour cabled a report about the meeting to Lloyd George the next morning. He summarised the general arguments of the deputation that the failure to implement home rule for a united Ireland made difficult, if not impossible, important cooperation between Britain and the United States during the war. Balfour himself attempted to explain to them the complexities of the Irish situation, and he noted that he had no powers or authority to deal with the problem. However, he did warn the prime minister that the Irish question 'is apparently the only difficulty we have to face here and its settlement would no doubt greatly facilitate vigorous and lasting cooperation of the United States Government in the war'. He added that the group generally supported Sir Horace Plunkett's plan for a solution to the home rule impasse, which would include the unionist counties of Ulster in a united Ireland but with the power to opt out after a period of five years. However, Balfour concluded with a 'Most Secret' message that,

> Shane Leslie has stated confidentially that though [the] deputation had to reject any scheme involving partition, if such a scheme was all that could be agreed to[,] a considerable portion of Irish moderate opinion here would rally to it.[30]

Leslie was from a prominent Anglo-Irish family which was largely unionist, although he himself had converted to Catholicism at Cambridge and become a supporter of Redmond. The cousin of Winston Churchill and brother-in-law of Congressman W. Bourke Cockran, Leslie was very well connected in Britain and the United States and was in mid-1917 working closely with Spring-Rice and Quinn. Balfour's singling out Leslie's opinion, not a member of Quinn's deputation nor an American, in this context is puzzling and effectively undercut his accurate summary of what the Irish-Americans had said. As a realist and a supporter of Redmond, this statement is surprising. In his own report of the meeting to Redmond he gives no indication of any consent to partition.

> I have just returned from Washington where the moderate Irish have used every possible and honorable means to save the British

Mission from the error of supposing that Irish opinion can be over-ridden in this country … But even at this late hour the moderate Irish can check and guide it into channels parallel to the aims of the Allies. But we must have the means, the excuse, the rallying cry and the lever to do so – these are all included in Home Rule, and your political vindication.

Leslie briefly summarised the discussion at the meeting and gave no indication of having anything other than the understanding of home rule for the whole of Ireland. He spoke of the moment in the war crisis as an opportunity: 'There is a general desire to do under American auspices what might have been brought about in Ireland had the Govt. kept its word with you.' And he saw the sending to the United States of A.J. Balfour, who was still remembered in Ireland as 'Bloody Balfour' for his heavy-handed dealing with protesters while chief secretary, in a peculiar light.

> The Irish as a whole refuse to take a neutral view of Mr. Balfour. Either, they say, he has been sent in contempt of them or to make a dramatic reconciliation between the Irish and English peoples as the climax of his mission. In their present temper it would be extremely dangerous to disappoint even our moderate friends in their hope.[31]

This was a role that Balfour specifically declined, agreeing only to convey to his government the views that were expressed to him.

Balfour's mission was unquestioningly a success in building good wartime Anglo-American relations. Balfour himself seems to have made a personal connection with Wilson, whom he described as 'not merely friendly, but open, frank, easy, and exceedingly pleasant'.[32] Balfour was given the honour of addressing the House of Representatives on 5 May and the Senate on 8 May, after which he shook hands with the members. President Wilson attended the latter occasion and joined the reception, congratulating Balfour on his remarks. 'Your man has disarmed us,' one Congressman told the *Times* correspondent, 'he is some salesman.' In an ironic twist, Balfour was the first foreigner to address Congress since Charles Stewart Parnell in 1880.[33] Later he travelled to New York, where he was warmly greeted by Mayor John Purroy Mitchell, the grandson of the 1848 rebel John Mitchell, and feted at a banquet whose guests included former presidents Theodore Roosevelt and William Howard

Taft, governor Charles S. Whitman, former ambassador Joseph Choate, and other notables. Balfour was also the guest of honour at a dinner given by Congressman Medill McCormick, the brother of the Chicago newspaper baron. At this gathering he met a second group of Irish-Americans. His parliamentary secretary later commented that, 'Even the Irish Nationalists, after their interviews with him ... professed themselves sorry that they were unable to persuade a gentleman whom, otherwise, they were delighted to have met.'[34] After almost two months in North America, Balfour sailed for home on the *Olympic* on 9 June.

When he returned home to Britain he submitted a comprehensive report on 23 June on what had been achieved by his mission in the United States. In this report he devoted considerable attention to Irish matters. He said Irish issues were an important element in American public life because of the large number of citizens with Irish connections, and that the frustrations of this community were exploited by the 'boss' politicians. For this element, 'if the existing Irish Question were solved, a new one would have forthwith to be invented'. Much of the rest of the American community resented this Irish intrusion into American public life and were 'deeply concerned that no solution has yet been found for this ancient problem'. Balfour concluded that Americans generally 'regard' a solution to the problem of Irish self-government as 'the one obstacle which stands in the way of close friendship between their country and ours'. As for his meetings with Irish-American groups, he reported that 'I saw two deputations, composed of men of character and position, who advocated Home Rule in an undivided Ireland', and he generously added that 'their observations were most moderate, both in tone and substance'. All things considered, he conveyed accurately the substance of their arguments for the need for self-government for a united Ireland.

Balfour's comments on high-level talks about Ireland are more ambiguous: 'The President never referred to it [Ireland] at all; the Secretary of State never referred to it officially.'[35] Balfour seems not to have even acknowledged his private meeting with Lansing at Gunston Hall, never mind Lansing's specific remarks. In that respect, he deliberately misled the war cabinet. Clearly Lansing and Wilson, the moderate Irish-American deputations, and much of the American public hoped for the implementation of some form of Irish home rule that would end the 'Irish question' in American politics and facilitate British–American cooperation during the war. Balfour did honestly articulate public opinion, while not conveying his discussions with either Wilson or Lansing – essentially the urgings of the American government.

Balfour himself moved steadily closer to supporting some form of home rule, but he also held fast to the exclusion of those counties in Ulster which were determined to remain in the United Kingdom unchanged. As Professor Shannon has explained, 'Balfour proved more willing than other Unionist leaders to accept the destruction of the Union, provided, of course, that the six counties were to remain free from Dublin rule.'[36] She correctly concluded in her account of Balfour's assessment of the Irish problem in America that he 'underestimated … the growing American sympathy for Sinn Féin as well as the strength of American opposition to partition'. In her analysis of Balfour's meeting with Quinn's deputation she suggests that Balfour singled out Shane Leslie's remark that the moderate Irish-American community would accept partition in Ireland if home rule were actually put into operation because this proposition was 'congenial to his own views'.[37] Unquestionably a shrewd assessment. It is also ironic that Sir Horace Plunkett, who had done so much to put Balfour in touch with moderate Irish-American spokespersons, worried in his diary that Balfour would take away the wrong impression of opinion in the United States. 'I fear the [British] commission will be completely misled about the real feeling of the American people by Washington Society's excitement over Balfour', which certainly seemed to be the case.[38] None of Balfour's reports carried a tone of urgent crisis sufficient to force the government to impose the kind of Irish settlement even the moderate Irish-Americans favoured. But perhaps events were moving too quickly. On 16 May Lloyd George proposed to the leaders of the several Irish parties either immediate implementation of home rule with the exclusion of the six counties of Ulster or a convention where all the various Irish parties could work out their own constitutional form of self-government. News of the Irish Convention, chaired by Plunkett, was received with great relief and enthusiasm in the United States as the solution to the Irish problem. However, by the time the work of the convention came to an indecisive conclusion eight months later, America was fully integrated into the war and both Britain and America were focused on new crises.

PART 2

Crosscurrents: identities and incarnations

CHAPTER SEVEN

'Ireland's family re-union': the 1932 Eucharistic Congress

Mary E. Daly

During the 1920s the Irish Free State made serious efforts to establish a presence on the international stage: by promoting an active and independent membership of the League of Nations, establishing an Irish diplomatic service and issuing Irish passports. It was also determined to strengthen links with emigrants and those of Irish descent. In 1926 W.T. Cosgrave, president of the Executive Council of the Irish Free State, broadcast his first St Patrick's Day message to the USA.[1] The Tailteann Games, which were staged in 1924, 1928 and 1932, offered a combination of competitive sports and cultural events; competitors had to be of Irish birth or descent.[2]

Although the Eucharistic Congress in Dublin in 1932 was part of a regular sequence of international meetings that attracted participation from Catholics worldwide, the 1932 Congress assumed a specifically Irish dimension – regarded as an opportunity to showcase Ireland's significant presence in worldwide Catholicism. This essay examines the Eucharistic Congress from the perspective of the Irish diaspora, with particular emphasis on the contrasting attitudes of the Catholic communities in Britain and the United States. Although the Irish diaspora in the United States and Britain included both Catholics and Protestants, in the United States the Catholic Church and Catholic institutions, especially Catholic schools, played a major role in sustaining an Irish identity. Kevin Kenny described the Catholic Church as 'arguably the single most important institution in the lives of Irish immigrants in the nineteenth-century United States'.[3] By contrast, in Britain, the association between

Catholicism and Irishness was much more problematic, despite the large number of Irish-born religious ministering in Britain, and there is evidence of that contrast in British reportage and involvement in the 1932 Eucharistic Congress. A secondary theme of this essay concerns timing. The Congress was held at the height of the 1930s depression, which undoubtedly reduced the number of Irish-Americans who could attend, and reducing the capacity of the Congress to strengthen and re-establish links between an independent Ireland and Irish-America. It also took place shortly after Éamon de Valera's Fianna Fáil party took office, with a determination to remove the vestigial traces of British authority in Ireland, and this fraught political climate coloured British Catholic attitudes towards the Congress.

The title of this essay comes from a sermon given by the archbishop of Liverpool, Dr Richard Downey, in St Mary's Cathedral Kilkenny on St Patrick's Day 1932, where he linked the fifteen hundredth anniversary of St Patrick's coming to Ireland with the forthcoming Eucharistic Congress. Dr Downey, born in Kilkenny, educated by the Christian Brothers in Enniscorthy,[4] and subsequently in Liverpool, became bishop of Liverpool in 1928 at the age of forty-seven, the youngest bishop in the English hierarchy. John Belchem, historian of the Irish in Liverpool, describes him as 'the doyen of the Kerry gang of priests in the Liverpool archdiocese'.[5]

Dr Downey described the Eucharistic Congress as:

> Ireland's family re-union ... no secular celebration of her national emancipation nor a commemoration of her independent status in the commonwealth of nations great as these achievements are; no, her sons and daughters are gathering from the ends of the earth to rally around the Eucharistic Throne and give corporate expression to their loyalty and homage towards the Saviour in the Sacrament of His love. Other people have national bonds of kinship but the Irish are not only united in ties of blood, but are welded together still closer in the quickening of the spirit, in the prompting of the Faith delivered to their forebears by Patrick fifteen hundred years ago.[6]

The Eucharistic Congress was, first and foremost, a spiritual event. It was dedicated to Christ the King, a theme promoted by the papacy in the 1920s in opposition to fascism and secular nationalism. It was an international religious celebration, a gathering of Catholics from throughout the world. The Congress is often seen as a triumphant

'Ireland's family re-union': the 1932 Eucharistic Congress   107

celebration of the Irish Free State. David Holmes claims that 'the Irish nation, not just the Irish religion, was redeemed by the Eucharistic Congress'.[7] Several contemporary articles on the Congress suggest that Ireland's history of defeat, disaster and mass emigration was divinely engineered in order to spread Catholicism throughout the world; on that basis the 1932 Congress, held in a newly independent Ireland, could be seen as a celebration of that mission, and the culmination of Ireland's divine destiny.

The editorial in the English Jesuit periodical *The Month* in January 1932, titled 'Ireland's Year', stated that,

> The Celtic *diaspora* which resulted from her national misfortunes, carried knowledge of the Faith and the Eucharistic worship over large portions of the globe, where, to this day, the terms 'Catholic' and 'Irish' are considered practically synonymous. And thus the Congress will be attended by many who have a filial affection for St. Patrick and who look upon Ireland as the mother-land of their Faith.[8]

The advance programme anticipated a large attendance by Irish emigrants and their descendants:

> In 1932, the sea-divided Gael will return again to the land of their origin, and with them will come the descendants of those Irish saints and soldiers, scholars and pioneers. They will foregather to honour in common with the nations of the Earth that King for Whose sake their nation was broken and dispersed to the four winds of Heaven.[9]

The pontifical letter carried by the papal legate to the Congress, Cardinal Lauri, opened by referring to 'the Irish people, whose ancestors carried forth the religion of their fathers, and widely diffused it in very many parts of Europe, in North America, in South Africa, and in the distant lands of Australia and New Zealand'. He referred to the almost 800 churches worldwide dedicated to St Patrick, and claimed 'that it can truly be said of the Irish people, "their sound hath gone forth into all the earth"'.[10]

In his opening address welcoming cardinals, clergy and laity from all over the world, Dr Byrne, archbishop of Dublin, observed that, 'Many of them are exiles come back to the land which bore them, and now, with a mother's love, welcomes them home again'.[11] Cardinal Lauri referred to 'this immense throng of sons and daughters of this Ireland, comprising so many members of the Sacred College of Cardinals, Archbishops, Bishops and other prominent personages, come from all parts of the world'. He saluted 'pioneers of the Catholic Faith, brought by you to many lands, and not only brought by you but preserved by you and kept flourished by you in many parts of the world'.[12] Dr Downey's sermon, quoted above, provides some additional glosses on the theme:

> It would indeed seem as though in the designs of Providence the Irish Church had a special mission, that she was cast to play a leading part in preserving upon the face of the earth the Faith once delivered to the saints and to the Catholic culture that went with it.

He referred to the 'island of saints and scholars' that brought Christianity and learning back to Europe before moving rapidly to more recent times. At the Vatican Council[13] – 'Saint Patrick had more mitred sons present than the patron saint of any other country. Truly the world is spiritually the richer for Ireland's material misfortunes.' He expanded at some length on the

> Irish of the Dispersion – forced to leave her shores … If you seek their monument, look around. The world over, they have raised up cathedrals and churches, built monasteries and convents, and laboured as priest and laymen for the salvation of souls …
>
> To visit the New World … is to see the grandchildren of those who left the shores of Ireland in sorrow and distress now shaping the destinies of continents and moulding history to a more humane pattern than that which drove their ancestors into exile. In America and in the Colonies the Irish are no longer merely hewers of wood and drawers of water. They are conspicuous among empire-builders, governors of states, captains of industry and international financiers.[14]

The reference to 'international financiers' was probably inappropriate, given that in 1932 the United States and much of the developed world was in the depths of the international depression, and the depression forms an important backdrop to the participation of Irish-American Catholics in the Eucharistic Congress. If the Congress had taken place in 1928 or the summer of 1929, there would have been a much larger attendance from

'Ireland's family re-union': the 1932 Eucharistic Congress

the US. In his 1931 St Patrick's Day address to the United States, W.T. Cosgrave claimed that the Irish Free State, as a predominantly agrarian economy, was much less affected by the depression than other countries.[15] He urged Irish-Americans to visit Ireland for the Eucharistic Congress. This prompted many letters from the US, where several correspondents wrote about the impact of the depression on their lives.[16]

On 5 January 1929 the Boston *Pilot*, the newspaper of the largest Catholic archdiocese in the United States, publicised the forthcoming celebrations in Dublin marking the centenary of Catholic Emancipation and linking these with the 1932 Eucharistic Congress. The same edition of the *Pilot* carried advertisements for trips to Ireland by Cunard, Hapag Lloyd, White Star and Thomas Cook lines; such advertisements featured in practically every edition of *The Pilot*. The Ancient Order of Hibernians (AOH) was planning a special excursion from New York to Ireland coinciding with the Catholic Emancipation celebrations;[17] one advertisement was headed 'Going Home to Ireland', the itinerary of which included a visit to the Patrician site, Croagh Patrick. *The Pilot* gave extensive coverage to the Catholic Emancipation ceremonies in advance and after the event, and their accounts contained detailed descriptions of places of historic significance to Irish Catholicism: the Lough Derg pilgrimage, celebratory masses at the ruins of Muckross and Mellifont abbeys, planned restoration works at the Rock of Cashel, the annual pilgrimage to Cruagh Patrick (as they styled it) and the anniversary of the Knock Marian apparition. *The Pilot* did not give background information about Croagh Patrick, Lough Derg, Cashel, St Brigid or St Ita; it assumed that these sites and names constituted an essential part of the religious tradition of its readers. In other words, the dominant cultural repertoire of this Boston Catholic newspaper was Irish.

By contrast, while Daniel O'Connell's contribution was extolled at a major Catholic Emancipation centenary rally in the London Coliseum in February 1929,[18] Catholic Emancipation was celebrated as an achievement for English Catholicism and England's Catholic heritage. A joint pastoral issued by the hierarchies of England and Wales marking the occasion stated that the Catholic Church was

> the legitimate heirs of those who professed and maintained the united and unbroken Faith of the Catholic Church in this our land ... The Emancipated Church is the same Church as the British Church; as the Saxon Church; as the Norman Church; as the Church

which having made England became in a new and clearer sense the *Ecclesia Anglicana*, the Catholic Church in England and the Church of the English. The pastoral went on to recall the English Martyrs and 'the dark days of persecution'.[19]

It made no mention of the Irish Catholic community in England and its contribution to 'the Emancipated Church', not even a reference to the fact that Catholic Emancipation was secured by the Irishman Daniel O'Connell. Even a cursory look through *The Tablet* or the English Jesuit periodical *The Month* shows that Irish saints and places of pilgrimage do not feature in the articles, which is perhaps not surprising, given that England has its own saints and pilgrimages, which they are keen to celebrate. Nevertheless the contrast with the Boston *Pilot* is obvious.

AMERICAN CATHOLICISM AND THE EUCHARISTIC CONGRESS

On 16 May 1931, under the headline 'Sea of Welcoming Lights', the Boston *Pilot* explained that 'lighted candles displayed in windows … will symbolise the Light of Faith and welcome pilgrims'. Thousands of Irish people across the world 'have taken with them the Light of Faith … many of those same will be returning' for the Eucharistic Congress, and a decision had been taken to encourage people to display a lighted candle in their window as a welcoming gesture.[20] By the summer of 1931 ships were being chartered to bring pilgrimages to the Congress, by groups such as the Maryknoll Missionaries, and US dioceses and archdioceses were announcing which prelate would accompany their pilgrimage. An editorial in the *Pilot*, on 1 August 1931, titled 'The Pilgrimage to Ireland', claimed that enquiries about places on liners were coming from throughout New England. It went on to describe the statue of Christ the King by Andrew O'Connor, which would be erected in Dún Laoghaire at the start of the ceremonial route to the city.[21] Most US pilgrims stayed on boats moored in Scotsman's Bay close to Dún Laoghaire harbour. The papal legate would arrive in Dún Laoghaire and travel from there to the city.

The Boston archdiocese chartered the Cunard liner *Lancastria* for a pilgrimage to be led by Cardinal William Henry O'Connell. Subsequent issues carried reports of heavy bookings and great enthusiasm, but the relentless repetition suggests a desperate effort to drum up business. In September 1931, an official letter from Cardinal O'Connell about 'next year in Dublin' was read at all masses. Over Christmas/New Year 1931/2 the *Pilot* reported that emigrants' remittances to Ireland had fallen considerably, emigration from Ireland had ceased, and a number of other articles confirmed the impact of the depression. Nevertheless in January it announced that the archdiocese was substituting a larger pilgrimage ship – the *Samaria*. Yet at the same time as the paper carried announcements that all places on the *Samaria* had been filled, Thomas Cook was offering reduced prices, 'due to present shipping conditions'. On 30 April Cunard cut rates by 20 per cent and announced a deferred payments plan, though it would appear that the *Samaria* was genuinely full. Meanwhile Filene's, Boston's main department store, was advertising new luggage for 'your trip to Dublin'; the *Pilot* reminded pilgrims who were not US citizens that they must carry a permit permitting them to re-enter the United States.

On Tuesday 14 June 1932 Cardinal O'Connell and 800 pilgrims were seen off by an estimated 5,000 spectators. The cardinal was escorted to the ship by Boston city and state police. Mayor Curley and city officials were at the waterfront to greet him and they went on board to bid the passengers farewell. Each pilgrim was given a small US flag, which they waved as the ship sailed, decorated with US, Irish and papal flags.[22] The US Jesuit weekly *America* claimed that 20,000 Americans travelled to the Congress in sixty pilgrimage groups, 'despite the economic blight which made many cancel their plans'.[23] Some 600 pilgrims travelled from Galveston, Texas, to Cobh. *America* claimed that the US attendance included three cardinals, ten bishops and 500 priests and nuns; later issues described the 'constantly overcrowded "Yankee" section at Phoenix Park, [which] brought her [Ireland] eloquent assurance that her faith was alive, and growing upon the living Christ, in that "new" world she had done so much to win for Him'. Some of the descriptive language in *America* was more suited to a performance by Bing Crosby or Barry Fitzgerald than a religious gathering:

> There never has been a day in Ireland that will equal the days from the twenty-second to the twenty-sixth of June. And never has there been such a flock of visitors to 'the little bit of heaven that dropped from out of the sky' as there will be to this paradise prepared on earth for the coming of the King of Heaven.[24]

Ireland's contribution to US Catholicism was a recurring theme during the course of the Congress. There were a series of national sessions, focusing on Catholicism in various countries, and as part of the US session, Rev. Peter Guilday, probably the leading US historian of Catholicism,[25] gave a paper on Ireland's contribution to the progress of Catholicism in the US, which included the history of the AOH, and the contribution by leading Irishmen – name-checking Charles Carroll of Carrolltown, the only Catholic to sign the Declaration of Independence, James Hoban, the architect of the White House, and many others. Replying to the paper, Dr Joseph Schrembs, bishop of Cleveland, opened with a cry of 'God Save Ireland' and in similar expansive mode said that 'to-day Good Friday was past, Easter Sunday had come, and the triumph and glory of the Ascension had spread over Ireland. Almost the first thing done by free Ireland was to hail Christ her King in the great Eucharistic Congress' (applause).[26]

The celebrant at the High Mass on Sunday 26 June, the final day of the Congress, which was attended by an estimated 1 million people, was Dr Michael Curley, archbishop of Baltimore, who was born in Athlone, as was the famous tenor John McCormack, who sang *Panis Angelicus*. After the closing ceremony Cardinal O'Connell made a live broadcast to Boston, where he proudly stated that the 1,500 pilgrims from Boston constituted the largest single group. His address was lyrical and nostalgic:

> Here the faithful came from all over the world … here in Ireland, where our forefathers lived and suffered for the Faith, they have made a renewal … The one prayer prominent in the minds and hearts of the pilgrims is that God's blessing may rest upon this country and that this solemn act of adoration will bring new life and health to those who are burdened with the government of the nations, so that they may see the real true condition of things as they exist in the world today.

As he concluded, the cardinal mentioned that he was heading off to visit 'the beautiful shrines of Ireland'.[27] The *Pilot's* editorial in the issue, published immediately after the Congress and titled 'Ireland the Conqueror', was a full-blown testimony to the suffering of the Irish people in the past – an outstanding example of what Liam Kennedy has termed the MOPE[28] theme, that the Irish were the most opposed people ever, coupled with a wish for a brighter future:

> Here is a people the first of all those wronged, as history proves for centuries, struggling under difficulties enough to drive another

nation to despair. They were robbed of their lands. Attempts were made to crush them, to extirpate them. Yet from the start to the finish, at the Congress there was a cheerfulness and contentment of soul and a spiritual happiness which was absolutely unmistakeable.

No one can read Ireland's history and remain at the end untouched by the magnificent faith and fortitude which lighten the dark distressed pages. Ireland, the oldest nation in Europe, has at a great price saved the integrity of her soul. Over her have swarmed the Danes, the Normans, and the Englishmen. Dreadful famine years have decimated her population. During centuries of unremitting persecution her budding industries were destroyed, her schools were closed, and religious consolation denied to her dying.

Historians, who from their studies are familiar with the ruinous effects wrought on national character by centuries of repression, marvel at the cheerful, even hopeful disposition of the Gael. He has conquered his victors and has won from his enemy the supreme tribute of imitation ... more Irish than the Irish themselves ...

It will be the ardent prayer of all who tasted this beautiful Irish hospitality and of Ireland's friends all over the world, that the dark clouds which now hover over the late scene of the 31st Eucharistic Congress may be speedily dispelled ... now serious questions press for solution. That this gallant sorely tried Catholic nation may enjoy the peace it has so richly merited.[29]

BRITISH CATHOLICISM AND THE EUCHARISTIC CONGRESS

The coverage of the Eucharistic Congress in the British Catholic media was predictably more restrained and more limited. There were few updates on advance preparation, and some of these were of a rather snide variety; for example, reassuring readers that Dublin would be capable of coping with the Congress; fears of chaos were unfounded. As part of this reassurance *The Tablet* suggested that estimates of the numbers who were expected to attend had been grossly inflated, so there would be ample accommodation.[30] *The Tablet* carried advertisements for the Congress – the liner Britannia would travel from Liverpool with the archbishop of Liverpool on board. As in the case of the American groups arriving on chartered liners, pilgrims would live on board and have most of their meals on board, together with morning mass, though the Britannia would moor in Dublin at Sir John Rogerson's Quay, not in Dún Laoghaire. The advertisements, like those in the United States, repeatedly offered the 'last remaining spaces', again suggesting that bookings were slow. The Catholic Association offered a luxury package; other advertisements encouraged readers to order programmes or Congress badges from Veritas, the Catholic Truth Society bookshop in Dublin's Lower Abbey Street. Veritas was also selling a limited number of tickets at 5/- each for the official Congress garden party at Blackrock College. Readers were warned that once these were gone no other tickets would be available. Other advertisements offered accommodation in private homes and the issue of 18 June, the last before the Congress opened, carried advertisements for day trips to the event from major English cities by rail to Holyhead and boat to Dún Laoghaire. The English Catholic publishers Burns, Oates & Washbourne opened a shop in Dublin's D'Olier Street shortly before the Congress.

The Eucharistic Congress was the main theme in the Lenten pastoral issued by Dr Bourne, the archbishop of Westminster. The English hierarchy had postponed its triennial national congress until 1933 to avoid a clash with Dublin. The pastoral suggested that,

> The Congress … ought, with God's blessing, to surpass all the Congresses which have gone before. It will meet in the midst of a Catholic nation, known the world over for its unswerving attachment to the Faith which fifteen hundred years ago was brought to it by St Patrick and for its devotion to the Holy Mass. No year, therefore, could be more fittingly chosen than this year, 1932, for the first international Eucharistic Congress on Irish soil. It will have the full support and assistance of the National Government. Nowhere, it would seem, could such a Congress meet under more favourable circumstances. As we have already said, it is our earnest desire that we, who are united to our Irish brethren so intimately by our Catholic Faith, and so closely by bonds of friendship, and in many cases by ties of friendship and blood, should share as largely and as fully as possible in the coming Congress.[31]

America, the US Jesuit weekly, estimated that 20,000 pilgrims came from England and Scotland, which was similar to the number who travelled from the USA. The *Irish Independent* Eucharistic Congress souvenir listed twenty archbishops, bishops and coadjutor bishops from England and Wales, plus four lord abbots, four Scottish bishops and two

'Ireland's family re-union': the 1932 Eucharistic Congress   115

abbots.[32] The English delegation was led by Cardinal Bourne, who was paying only his second visit to Ireland, despite the fact that his mother was born in Dublin.[33] The cardinal was often regarded as anti-Irish. His entry in the Oxford Dictionary of National Biography suggests that he supported Irish self-government, but wanted Ireland to retain its links to the crown, and the empire,[34] which would have meant that he was out of sympathy with Éamon de Valera's government. In contrast to Irish-American prelates, Cardinal Bourne did not proclaim his Irish heritage.

An editorial in *The Tablet* examined the by-now familiar theme of the Eucharistic Congress and Ireland's Catholic diaspora:

> Members of the Congress have already set out … Some of these are Catholics of Irish blood who have never before pressed their feet upon the ancestral soil. Others are Irishmen or Irishwomen who were exiled from Erin in early youth by some stern necessity and have never since revisited the homeland. From intimate letters which have been shown to us, we know that many such visitors to 'the' Congress have been saving their money for years to pay for this journey. Missionaries have postponed their infrequent leave for a whole year, or even two … and have cheerfully gone on labouring in unhealthy fields from which they have sorely needed a respite. It is pleasing to think that just as the Christmas dinner reunites widely scattered families, so the Eucharistic Feast is winning back Americans and South Africans, Australians and New Zealanders to one common hearth, in company with non-Hibernian fellow-believers from every clime.[35]

There is one glaring absence from this list of countries, Britain, and this is not an isolated omission. Dr Downey's sermon in Kilkenny, cited earlier, also conspicuously failed to mention Britain in his litany of the Irish diaspora. *The Tablet* stated that thousands from England, Scotland and Wales would attend the Eucharistic Congress, but there is no suggestion that many pilgrims might have an ethnic relationship with Ireland and its people. The national sessions at the Congress again show the contrast between British and American Catholicism. The English session consisted of papers on theological subjects by Ronald Knox and Fr Cyril Martindale, SJ; the Scottish session had a paper on the causes of the downfall of the Catholic Church in Scotland, but there was no indication of any effort to highlight the role of Irish Catholics in the British church, whereas national sessions from the Argentine and Canada included tributes to the work of Irish missionaries in their countries.

Part of the explanation lies in the ethnic background of the respective hierarchies. By 1900, 62 per cent of US bishops were Irish, half of these were Irish-born, half of Irish descent. Irish Catholicism spanned the Atlantic.[36] The archbishop of Baltimore, the premier US archdiocese, was Athlone-born Michael Curley; both parents of New York Cardinal Patrick Joseph Hayes had emigrated from Kerry, and there are many such examples. With the possible exception of Dr Downey, who toured Ireland extensively in 1932, receiving the freedom of Limerick and an address of welcome from Enniscorthy Urban Council, and preaching in several other locations, presumably as part of a fundraising effort for Liverpool's Catholic cathedral, few members of the English hierarchy proclaimed their Irish antecedents, if they had any. Cardinal Bourne is a noteworthy example.

Despite the rhetoric describing the USA as an ethnic melting pot, hyphenated identities were widespread and they were encouraged in both religion and politics. In the larger cities the US Catholic Church supported ethnically distinct parishes, with priests and saints to match.[37] By contrast in England the emphasis was on assimilation and promoting English Catholicism and its historic traditions. Thomas Greene remarked that 'English Catholics were inclined to be critical of Irish matters in any event: they had viewed the Irish issue from their own nationalistic perspective for over a century.'[38] Given the history of the English Reformation and the fact that English Catholicism had been associated with treason in the past, Catholic schools in England placed a strong emphasis on affirming Englishness and loyalty to king and country: 'Catholic school children were taught that their church was more English than that of the Anglicans, which was merely the creation of bad King Henry VIII.'[39] Catholics remained an insecure minority in the 1930s, and *The Tablet* expressed fears that the Dublin Congress would provoke anti-Catholic rhetoric.

The political context was important. *The Tablet* was highly critical of de Valera's government – elected in the spring of 1932 – and their efforts to remove the last vestiges of British authority in Ireland: snubbing the governor-general (the king's official representative) during the Congress and more generally; taking steps to remove the oath of allegiance to the crown, ceasing to pay land annuities to Britain. In an editorial titled 'The Few Flies in the Abundant Ointment', which appeared in the issue of 25

'Ireland's family re-union': the 1932 Eucharistic Congress

June (on the eve of the Congress closing), *The Tablet* noted that, 'Fiercely jealous of Ireland's magnificent Act of Faith, the unflagging enemies of our holy religion in England and Scotland are peering through their strongest glasses in order to magnify every little gnat into a dragon'. The treatment of the governor-general was a 'big and poisonous' fly in the ointment, which caused 'deep grief to English Catholics'.[40] On the front page of the same issue they expressed concern that what they described as 'this arbitrary and untimely attempt to treat the King's headship of Ireland as already abolished is to be exploited to the utmost by the various Protestant Societies at a Demonstration in Kingsway Hall'.[41] And indeed the United Protestant Council convened a mass demonstration in London, reflecting concerns throughout the empire and among the loyalist Irish people in the Free State and Northern Ireland at de Valera's attempts 'to repudiate the covenant made between Britain and the Irish Free State'. The public notices for this meeting claimed that the Eucharistic Congress in Dublin was being used 'to deepen and extend the false belief that St. Patrick ... was an emissary of the Pope'.[42] *America*, the US Jesuit weekly, was also critical of the treatment of the governor-general, and it carried articles by A.E. Malone on the oath of allegiance and the land annuities which were highly critical of de Valera's actions. But the overall treatment was much warmer. In February 1932 (admittedly before de Valera's government had moved to repudiate links with Britain), *America* sent congratulations and best wishes to de Valera 'on his assumption of the Presidency' (of the Executive Council), noting that their newspaper 'in times past has been closely joined with him in his endeavours'.[43]

De Valera's actions posed no threat to US Catholicism, regardless of how they were viewed by the State Department or the White House, and the economic depression, which coincided with a tightening of US immigration quotas, had resulted in a collapse in Irish emigration to the US. Emigration to Britain, however, continued without restriction, and there was growing hostility in Britain to Irish men and women who were taking jobs from English people, and allegedly claiming welfare, on a fraudulent basis.[44] Belchem writes of 'a sustained campaign to stigmatise migrants from the Free State ... Ready scapegoats for Liverpool's economic decline, new arrivals were condemned as both job-taking "scabs" and welfare scroungers'. Bishop David – the Anglican bishop of Liverpool – was a leading member of this campaign, goaded by local Evangelicals.[45] There was a strong argument therefore against the English Catholic Church highlighting its Irish connections.

Domestic politics divided English Catholicism from nationalist Ireland. For many decades the English Catholic Church had supported the Conservative party because they protected denominational education, whereas the Liberals and Labour parties were very much opposed. Cardinal Bourne, archbishop of Westminster, was hostile to the post-1906 Liberal government because of its policy on education, and he was not unique among the English hierarchy in his views.[46] English Catholic journals tended to regard the Irish Free State as not sufficiently Catholic. According to Thomas Greene, 'The distinction noted between aspiration and reality was especially significant'.[47] The editorial in *The Month* in January 1932, titled 'Ireland's Year' – the tenth year of statehood, the fifteen-hundredth anniversary of the coming of St Patrick, the year of the Eucharistic Congress – claimed that 'the one interest is to see how a nation ninety-three percent Catholic has succeeded in embodying in its Government and its political conduct the principles of Christian civil, social and industrial life as taught by the Catholic Church'. It asked,

> whether the country is resolutely determined to recover its full Catholic heritage, whether those who, through education, station or office, are the leaders of the people know in what directions they should lead, and are making reasonable progress. Never before in the world's history has there been a people so united in their Catholic belief.

The verdict of *The Month* was that the Irish Free State should 'try harder' to achieve a truly Catholic state and society.

> Much remained to be done before the Saorstát can claim to represent, as it ought, the political mind of a Catholic people – much in the way of suppressing excessive gambling, of purifying stage and cinema, of banning the propaganda of birth-prevents, of thoroughly Catholicizing its University education, and, in the economic sphere, of developing Irish industries and agriculture ... The conclusion is that it will be an uphill struggle to create a truly Catholic state.[48]

The Month returned to this theme in its August issue, after the triumph of the Congress, asking, 'Does that mean that in Ireland there may ultimately emerge a wholly Catholic government, one whose policy will always be in harmony with the moral law and whose legislation will never, even indirectly, make the practice of the Faith more difficult?'[49]

'Ireland's family re-union': the 1932 Eucharistic Congress   119

British coverage of the Eucharistic Congress, even in Catholic periodicals, was predominantly political. G.K. Chesterton opened his series of articles on the Congress by noting that 'Dublin is full of flags; and London is full of stories about flags'. He went on to play down reports that the Union Jack had been pulled down, emphasising that the dominant flag was the papal flag, the Congress was not a political occasion.[50] Irish politics and US–Irish relations were of little interest to US Catholics who attended the Eucharistic Congress: they could indulge in nostalgia, visits to relatives, and see Ireland through a less critical lens.

CHAPTER EIGHT

Differing with the American cousins: the Irish Catholics of Canada fight the Great War, 1914–18

Mark G. McGowan

If anything, Father C.J. McLaughlin was courageous. In July 1916, as the British army's offensive on the Somme had faltered, claiming thousands of allied dead, and just two months after British General John Maxwell ordered the execution of Irish republican leaders, this Canadian priest prepared to address the plenary meeting of the Ancient Order of Hibernians in Boston. It was anticipated by the Canadians present that the largely Irish Catholic American delegates would be unsympathetic to McLaughlin's message:

> Patriotism ever burns in the heart of the Hibernian. I would remind you Mr. President and brothers that this organization is composed of members owing allegiance to different flags and, sir, may I inform you that the fires of patriotism burn not the less bright within the bosoms of the Canadian Hibernians for the British flag than it does within the breast of the American citizens for the Star Spangled Banner … Hibernian that I am I am also a British subject. Britain's flag is our Talisman. The Roman citizen of old gloried in the title of Roman citizenship. Let me, sir, assure you today that the Canadian delegates here assembled glory in the proud title of Canadian-British citizenship, and, sirs, I would indeed be unworthy of the race and the land from which I came if I were to sit here this morning and offer

120

no protest to some of the remarks that I have heard made here ... If
the Dublin people followed John E. Redmond and his Nationalists
we would not today be mourning the loss of life in that unfortunate
affair ... Let me answer it here by telling you that the hearts of the
Canadian Irish beat true and that Canadians of all classes, Irish
included, are prepared to stand by Britain in this crisis to the last
man and the last dollar.[1]

The New Brunswick Catholic paper the *New Freeman*, of which
McLaughlin had been a former editor, reported that his speech was
received warmly by 'hundreds' of delegates and that some of the resolutions
on foreign affairs against which he protested were subsequently modified.[2]
His speech was reprinted across Canada upon his return and during his
subsequent speaking tour. Unafraid to test this message at home, the
Canadian branches of the AOH applauded him, and in Moncton, New
Brunswick, he was greeted with repeated cheering.[3] McLaughlin's speech
underscored profound differences between Irish Catholics in Canada and
America, both in the manner in which the Irish should engage in the
Great War and in the current Irish crisis.

Among the majority of Canada's Irish Catholics during the war period,
there was no contradiction in supporting the British war effort, while
advocating constitutionally inspired home rule for Ireland. It was clear
in the writings and speeches of prominent Catholic leaders that Ireland
should enjoy the autonomy within the British Empire that was enjoyed by
Canada, Australia or New Zealand. The Canadian Catholic press strongly
supported constitutional nationalists in Ireland like John Redmond,
and some Canadian politicians had even advised him on how home
rule might look for Ireland, particularly in light of a hostile Protestant
minority in Ulster.[4] While many American-Irish Catholics, particularly
within the AOH, had abandoned constitutional nationalism by 1914 and
become overtly anti-British and pro-German until the American entry
into the war in 1917,[5] Canadian-Irish Catholics adopted British imperialist
rhetoric, raised thousands of dollars for the war effort, and enlisted in the
Canadian Expeditionary Force (CEF) by the tens of thousands. The war
experience bitterly divided the Ancient Order of Hibernians itself, with
the Canadian branches threatening succession from the ardently Irish
republican and German-sympathising parent body in the United States.
The war and the Easter Rising helped to underscore the diversity of
Irish Catholic identity, experience and opinion in North America;[6] while

religion and ethnicity may have united Irish Catholics on both sides of the border, it was clear that differing cultural contexts, politics and history separated these 'cousins' from one another.

Unlike the experience in the United States, where the president and Congress would decide the nation's entry into the war, Canada, as a member of the British Empire, was automatically a belligerent when Britain declared war on the Central Powers in August 1914. Irish Catholics in Canada embraced the war effort, particularly in light of the passage of the third Home Rule Bill in 1912, and Redmond's enthusiastic support of the imperial effort as a sign of Irish loyalty. Constitutional Irish nationalism had deep roots in the Canadian provinces, where Catholic leaders, both clerical and lay, had historically regarded Canada as a constitutional example of what Ireland might become. While there were pockets of physical force republican nationalists in Canada, they were small in number, less vocal, and generally without much of a following since the failed Fenian raids on Canada of the mid-1860s. Over time, the Irish Catholic communities in Canada had come to adopt a greater sense of British imperial citizenship, in their school curriculum, benevolent societies, and in political partisanship.[7] As early as the second Boer War, 1899–1902, Irish Catholic Canadian politicians, such as federal justice minister Charles Fitzpatrick, openly supported the British military action in South Africa. As he told the Canadian House of Commons:

> I say that the time had come, not only because of what was going on in South Africa … but because of mutterings on the continent for British subjects the world over to prove once and for all that the British Empire is no mere geographical expression for a number of sundered and disunited provinces – the time had come when it was necessary for the whelps of the lion to rally to the defence of the old land. The time had come when every man must be made to understand whether on the European continent or in South Africa, that blow for blow whensoever the blow might come, must be struck back by the British, and would be struck as freely from Australasia and Canada as from the heart of the Empire itself.[8]

A similar chorus of support came from William Wilfred Sullivan, chief justice of Prince Edward Island,[9] Senator Lawrence Geoffrey Power of Nova Scotia,[10] and even Cornelius O'Brien,[11] the archbishop of Halifax, who himself was a member of the Imperial Federation League. Irish

Catholic men, particularly from Nova Scotia and Ontario, were notable in their enlistment, constituting about 7 per cent of the Canadian voluntary forces destined for South Africa.[12] So strong was the Irish Catholic imperial feeling in Canada at the outset of the Great War, in 1914, that some Catholic newspapers cited Catholic participation and voluntary enlistment during the Boer War as a clear precedent for the current struggle against Germany and Austro-Hungary.[13] In Winnipeg, Manitoba, the *Northwest Review* commented that Canadians were 'loyal to the Motherland. The spirit that animated their forefathers a century ago when invasion [by Americans] threatened this infant nation, the spirit which impelled her sons to brave the dangers of the African veldt – that spirit, the surest defence against aggression, animates them still'.[14]

Given the hierarchical power structure of the Roman Catholic Church, it is not surprising to discover that Irish Catholic Canadian support for the British war effort may have been influenced by the rhetorical examples set by Canada's bishops. All of Canada's English-speaking bishops and most French-Canadian bishops were vocally enthusiastic in their support of the British war effort. While the speeches of many bishops might be cited as evidence for this support, Archbishop Neil McNeil of Toronto, who was of mixed Irish and Scottish ethnicity, was one of the most respected prelates in Canada and one of its most eloquent. His words would have been heartily supported by his episcopal colleagues:

> There are duties to our fellow-men in general and to our country in particular which events press upon us, and to which I call your attention. The first duty is prayer to God for peace … You do not need to be reminded of the duty of patriotism. You are as ready as any to defend your country and share in the burdens of Empire. But those of us who are remote from the scene of conflict, and cannot leave Canada, may be tempted to think that our part is simply that of interested spectators. It is not. We can all help, and therefore should all help, by taking care to stop all unnecessary expenses in our homes and in our daily lives. It is no time for luxuries or festivities when millions of men are in mortal combat, and the poor everywhere are likely to need all we can spare.[15]

McNeil's colleagues in sixteen Celtic-led dioceses, out of a total of thirty-eight dioceses across Canada,[16] echoed his remarks, speaking in variations on his themes of prayer, service and loyalty.[17] One colleague,

Archbishop Michael Spratt of Kingston, Ontario, even offered a theology of recruitment, likening the sacrifice of the Catholic soldier to the *Imitatio Christi*.[18] Given the overwhelming support of the war effort by their bishops, Catholic priests across the country publicly endorsed the imperial war effort from their pulpits, at public meetings, on recruiting platforms, and by leadership in the many fundraising initiatives during the war.[19] There was no way that an Irish Catholic layperson in Canada could have mistaken the position of the institutional church on the British war initiative.

If an Irish Catholic still had any doubt about where good Catholic loyalties lay in Canada, he/she might only have to look at the six English-language Catholic newspapers across the country – all of which unequivocally supported Britain and its allies. In Antigonish, Nova Scotia, Michael Donovan, editor of the *Casket*, wrote, 'It is our deliberate conviction that the smashing up of the British Empire would be a tremendous blow to the welfare of mankind.'[20] In a 'no-holds-barred' approach, he challenged Ulster unionists for their reliance on Germany during the civil strife after the passage of the third Home Rule Bill, as an overt rebellion against the crown. Catholics would do no such thing. Moreover, disavowing any position that the current conflict was not Canada's war, the *Casket* boldly proclaimed that 'Canada's future is, at the moment, being fought for on the banks of French rivers, and Canada's safety was fought for, to some extent, last week, off the coast of Chile'. Quite simply, the empire's war was Canada's war.

To the west, in Toronto, Ontario, the editor of the *Catholic Register*, Monsignor Alfred E. Burke, a noted imperialist and Conservative party supporter, told his 13,000 subscribers[21] in no uncertain terms where their loyalty as Catholics ought to lie:

> It will be for us beyond peradventure that we as Canadians are Britishers to the core and that Britain's troubles are our troubles, Britain's shield our safety. We must sacrifice something for this protection. Where would we be today but for the Empire's Navy and the Empire's men? Our part is to give generously what is our honest toll, whether it be for the army and the navy ... what we need is to finish the work effectually – so effectually that Pax Britannica may rejoice the world for another half century. The God of Armies is great and wonderful in his dispensations.[22]

The Irish Catholics of Canada fight the Great War, 1914–18

While not as wedded to imperial rhetoric as Burke, the editors of the *Canadian Freeman* (Kingston, Ontario), the *Catholic Record* (London, Ontario), the *New Freeman* (St John, New Brunswick) and the *Northwest Review* (Winnipeg, Manitoba) echoed the necessity of Canada's Catholics to rally to the imperial cause.[23] These members of the fourth estate were joined by the patriotic pro-British speechmaking of Canada's notable Irish Catholic politicians, including Charles J. Doherty, member of parliament for St Anne's riding in Montreal, and the minister for justice in Sir Robert Borden's Conservative government in the federal parliament at Ottawa. Never a wallflower, former Liberal privy councillor and chief justice of Canada Sir Charles Fitzpatrick also invoked the glory of the empire in his speeches.[24] Irish Catholic war fever crossed the Canadian partisan divide.

With Irish Catholic leadership, both clerical and lay, so strongly and loudly in support of the imperial war effort, it should not be surprising that Irish Catholics, both Canadian and Irish-born, enlisted in large numbers during the voluntary phases of recruitment. Sir Robert Borden's Conservative government initially pledged one infantry division to Britain, although the recruitment effort would expand monumentally over the next three years.[25] Much of the first Canadian contingent consisted of expatriate British and Irish men enlisting in the hopes of filling the imperial ranks quickly and ending the war by year's end.[26] Unrequited hope of a quick victory and the stagnation brought about by trench warfare on the western front prompted Canada to initiate two further phases of voluntary enlistment from 1914 to 1917.[27] With Catholic leaders preaching this as a war for Christian values and civilisation, the liberation of Catholic Belgium, and the principle that small nations should be free, Irish Catholic Canadians were prominent across the country for their voluntary attestation to fight in King George V's army overseas. The military records are uneven and incomplete in providing a religious breakdown of the recruits to the CEF. Father John J. O'Gorman, a prominent Ottawa-born priest, offered some of the most complete statistics on Catholic enlistment. O'Gorman, who had been serving as a frontline chaplain, was wounded and returned to recuperate in Ottawa, where he filled his time with gathering valuable information to defend Catholics from zealous Anglo-Protestants who were suspicious of Catholic loyalty.[28] He presented to the Department of Militia and Defence a detailed report of Catholic recruitment indicating that, when the French-Canadian Catholics were removed from the count, there remained 36,512 Catholics of Irish and Scottish descent. This group of English-speaking Catholics, argued O'Gorman, was second only to the Anglicans in terms of their proportion of the general population.[29] If O'Gorman's calculations are to be trusted – and the numbers have been substantiated in other Militia and Defence records – it is clear that Irish Catholics in Canada recruited strongly during the voluntary phases of enlistment.[30]

Further study of the Militia and Defence records and soldiers' and nurses' personnel files offers a portrait of Irish Catholic volunteers. Most Irish Catholic recruits were Canadian-born, most appeared to be the product of upwardly mobile families with respect to occupation, and many had seen previous service in local militia units and regiments. The story of Irish Catholic recruitment, in fact, appears to mirror the general patterns of voluntary recruitment across the country regardless of religious denomination. Irish Catholic men were prominent at the local voluntary enlistment depots in 1915 and 1916, but, like other Canadian-born recruits, they appeared to be less represented in the initial wave of voluntary enlistment in 1914, which tended to be dominated by the British-, Welsh- and Scottish-born immigrants who were eager to return home and take up the king's good cause. When asked to sign registration cards during the period of national registration in 1916, Irish Catholics followed the encouragement and direction of their priests and bishops in participating in the programme, and consequently were often among the first to be conscripted in 1918 under the terms of the Military Service Act. Similarly, after 1917, the conscripts of Irish Catholic descent appeared to be little different from conscripts of other faiths and ethnicities; many were engaged in agriculture or lumbering or were single men in blue-collar occupations. Any suggestion that Irish Catholic recruits balked at national service because of the 'Irish question' after the Easter Rising of 1916 does not bear up to empirical scrutiny. In fact, the evidence supports the claims of Catholic bishops that English-speaking Catholics were second to none in the performance of their duty. Although there may have been dissent over some political and religious issues among Irish Catholics, these individuals did not represent the majority within the new generations of Irish Catholic Canadians.[31]

As was the case for other Canadians, a range of motivations compelled Irish Catholics to enlist in the Canadian Expeditionary Force. Many, inspired by patriotism and strongly held imperial loyalties, responded to the calls made in the press and by the leading politicians of the day.

The Irish Catholics of Canada fight the Great War, 1914–18

Others were members of militia units, which in the second phase of recruitment (in 1914 and 1915) became the primary source of men to form battalions for the second and third overseas contingents. Families also provided a nursery for soldiers: brothers frequently enlisted together – or in succession as younger siblings came of age. Given the unemployment levels in 1913 and 1914 in many of Canada's major cities, many Irish Catholics facing underemployment or unemployment were attracted by the $1.10 daily pay for private soldiers and the early prognostications of victory by Christmas. No doubt, many young men were also attracted by the romance and adventure associated with donning khaki and travelling to parts of the world they might otherwise never see. There were many reasons why a man might elect to serve or to stay behind, but most left no lasting record of how they came to their decision. It is left to historians to piece together inferences and hypotheses as to why so many chose to enlist. When they did sign up, Irish men often joined friends and family in local battalions, or in special battalions which had ties to local militia units. The latter was typical in Halifax, Nova Scotia, where young Irish Catholics joined the 25th and 40th battalions, which had ties to local militia units long supported by the Charitable Irish Society.[32]

The recruitment of Irish Catholics in Canada was not restricted to Irish speciality regiments and battalions, of which there were several. In Toronto, the 208th Canadian Irish, and in Montreal the 199th Irish Rangers, were the best-known ethnic Irish battalions established during the war in Canada. The 199th was raised in Quebec and eastern Ontario[33] and was primarily filled with Canadian-born Irish Catholics under the watchful eye of chaplain-designate William Hingston, SJ.[34] In Toronto, although it had a more pronounced Protestant flavour (its chaplain was Methodist) than its Montreal counterpart,[35] the 208th was reported to have attracted 'one hundred fair Irish colleens', primarily Catholic women, to act as recruiting sergeants on St Patrick's Day, 1916.[36] Catholics constituted only about 15 per cent of the battalion's strength, and of the ninety-nine Catholics in the unit, about eighty-four, or 12.8 per cent, were of Irish birth or descent.[37] Known as the 'fairy godmother of the battalion', Catholic philanthropist Teresa Korman Small donated $5,000 of the $7,000 raised for the 208th's recruitment drive.[38] The 208th battalion appeared as the great irony of the alleged 'Belfast of Canada': a largely Protestant and Irish battalion underwritten with the money and hard work of Irish Catholic women. The handful of other Irish speciality battalions were hardly Irish at all. The Edmonton 'Irish Guards' or 218th battalion, for example, contained only thirty-seven Irish-born Catholics, accounting for only 5.8 per cent of its total strength, whereas Russian-born members of the unit accounted for 159 men, or a whopping 25.1 per cent.[39] Based on birth alone, the 218th ought to have been renamed the 'Slavic Guards'. The empirical evidence suggests that Irish Catholic men were more likely to join neighbourhood or provincially based battalions than hold out for membership in Irish-named units, with all of the associated Celtic iconography. There was no Canadian equivalent of New York's 'Fighting 69th'.[40]

As Irish Catholic Canadians rallied around the Union Jack, it is not surprising that, in the fora where Irish-Americans and Canadians directly met, there might be some disagreement. The large group of Irish physical force nationalists in the United States would certainly be unnerved by the ease with which Canadian-Irish Catholics set forth their imperial arguments. The Ancient Order of Hibernians, which was arguably the largest fraternal association of Irish Catholics in North America, was a case in point. In Winnipeg, Manitoba, the local Ancient Order of Hibernians chastised American-Irish nationalists of the parent branches for being out of touch: 'The Ireland of today is far removed from the oppressed isle of our forefathers.' In a backhanded swipe against Irish-Americans who did not fully appreciate how far Ireland had come under the Irish Parliamentary Party (IPP) leader John Redmond, the *Northwest Review* commented, 'It is to be feared that the Irish Parliamentary Party is to be judged by a standard which is not recognized across the water.'[41] For at least this branch of the AOH, constitutional Irish nationalism was strong, and there appeared to be no contradiction whatever in supporting the war effort while also supporting Redmondite principles of an Ireland with dominion-like status in the empire.

Such thoughts appeared not to be unique to the Ancient Order of Hibernians in Winnipeg. The Great War exposed growing division between radical nationalist members in the United States and members in Canada who, while holding on to their sentimental attachment to Ireland, were loyal to crown and empire. As early as 1915, AOH branches from across Canada had threatened to secede from the American AOH because of the latter's pro-German and anti-British stances. In fact, the Canadian AOH demanded that the official organ of the order, the *American Hibernian*, be seized at the border as seditious literature. John H. Barry, an AOH executive from Fredericton, New Brunswick, where the order was particularly strong, was adamant that 'the order in

The Irish Catholics of Canada fight the Great War, 1914–18

Canada is worth saving though not at the tremendous cost of treason to our country'.[42] The crisis passed, but the Easter Rising in Dublin only increased the tension between the Canadian and American branches of the AOH. It was within this context that the prominent AOH chaplain Father C.J. McLaughlin made his impassioned plea to the delegates at the AOH general convention in Boston in July 1916. Irish Catholics on either side of the border approached the war and the Irish question differently and McLaughlin demanded that the Americans respect their Canadian cousins.

The Irish question would not go away, however, and differences between Canadian and American approaches would still break along constitutional nationalist and physical force nationalist lines, although there would be representatives from both camps on either side of the border. In the aftermath of the rising in 1916, most Irish Catholic Canadian leaders and the press condemned the rebels' action as foolish and cowardly, particularly while Britain and its allies were in a desperate fight with Germany. The *Catholic Register* and its new editor James Wall described the rising as 'an unspeakable outrage and colossal folly' perpetrated by a 'small and unrepresentative element'.[43] The *Register*'s provincial rival, the London *Catholic Record*, was equally strident, although like many Canadians they would mistakenly blame the Sinn Féin movement rather than the Irish Republican Brotherhood. 'The Sinn Féiners are not Irish nationalists, but the bitterest opponent of the Irish national movements. Often John Redmond and his followers protest against the puerile pleadings and insane ebullitions of this handful of mischief makers.'[44] The *New Freeman* branded the Sinn Féin rebels as 'anarchists', while the *Casket* described the rising as an act of 'folly' and 'stupidity'.[45] One poignant comment came from an Irish-Canadian soldier at the front, who learned of the rising while it was still taking place. From his encampment in France, Canadian artillery officer William O'Brien wrote in his diary that he had '[h]eard about disgraceful Sinn Féin riot in Dublin on the 24th'.[46] For at least one Irish-Canadian who recorded his thoughts at the front, the rising made little sense – the real war to be fought was in Flanders and on the Somme.

With the summary court martial and execution of IRB leaders by General Maxwell's British forces, Irish Catholic Canadians were horrified. While it did not diminish Irish Catholic Canadian support for a constitutional solution to the Irish question, it did raise considerable concern about the wisdom of British policy in the wake of the rising and the credibility of the British government itself. Most Irish Catholic leaders in Canada remained convinced that John Redmond's constitutional means of achieving home rule was still the best policy and that he was the politician worth supporting. There was a sense of frustration, however, that the misguided leaders were summarily executed, particularly given the knowledge that, in 1913 and 1914, unionist leader Sir Edward Carson and his Ulster Volunteers were prepared to engage the crown with German-supplied arms and were left untouched by authorities. According to the *New Freeman*, in St John, 'there would not be an armed man today in Ireland, excepting soldiers and the constabulary, but for Carson's rebellious policy'.[47] The inconsistency of British policy was clearly problematic for Irish Catholic editors, who now walked a fine line between promoting the war effort so that small nations might be free, and 'by association' supporting an empire that was willing to take such harsh measures against a small, predominantly Catholic nation that was the land of their ancestors. Angered by the executions, the *Northwest Review* reminded readers that the German militarism that spells 'the destruction of the natural rights of nations' must be defeated everywhere and that 'we ought not to forget what we are fighting for'.[48]

No clear consensus was reached by any of Canada's Irish Catholic editors. The *Casket* in Nova Scotia blamed Germany for fuelling the insurrection.[49] In Toronto, the conservative *Catholic Register* blamed Ulster unionists for the undercurrent of division in Ireland. It also reprinted the opinion of the Dublin *Irish Catholic*, which condemned the IRB leaders for treason.[50] The more moderate *Catholic Record* offered a nuanced understanding of the motives of the rebels as sincere, while judging their actions as 'folly'. The paper regretted the executions, but it still labelled rebel leader Patrick Pearse's actions as criminal because he and his followers failed 'to present a united front under the guidance of [Ireland's] elected leader, John Redmond, who is supported by almost the entire hierarchy of the land'.[51] The *New Freeman* agreed, as did the *Northwest Review*.[52] Perhaps the most strident voice was that of the *Canadian Freeman*, in Kingston, which was now owned and operated by the priests of the archdiocese of Kingston. While it soundly condemned the rising, it unequivocally denounced the executions as 'worse than a crime … a blunder that seems calculated to revive old hatreds and old misgivings. By her [Britannia] stupid policy of repression she has glorified a riot into a revolution. If her intention was to make martyrs out of a handful of fanatical dreamers she has succeeded admirably'.[53] For the editors of the *Canadian Freeman*, the constitutional approach as opposed to the recourse

The Irish Catholics of Canada fight the Great War, 1914–18   131

to violence was still preferable and they held up Canada as a model for Ireland: 'Were there not mutterings of rebellion in Canada before self-government was conceded?' the *Freeman* argued. 'Canada did not receive self-government because she was loyal; she is loyal because she enjoys self-government.'[54] Despite taking different tones in the debate, Catholic editors across Canada could agree that Britain should enact home rule in Ireland immediately.[55]

Accordingly, Canadian support for Redmond continued throughout 1916 and 1917 as he attempted to trust in the promises made to him that home rule would be honoured, at the very least following a victory in the war – whenever that might come. The survivors of the rising, such as Éamon de Valera, however, were breathing new life into Sinn Féin, which was fast becoming the principal rival of Redmond's Irish Parliamentary Party and highly critical of Redmond for being too cooperative with the British. While not abandoning their constitutional nationalist position, several Canadian Catholic newspapers and the AOH continued to make resolutions demanding that the new government of Lloyd George enact home rule for all of Ireland immediately, in order to secure Irish loyalty to the war effort. According to the *Canadian Freeman*, the reasons for urgency on home rule were clear from a Canadian perspective. Irish-Canadians are loyal, remarked the editor, because 'they enjoy the priceless boon of liberty [and] … they believe that Canadian liberty is worth defending'.[56] Coinciding with St Patrick's Day 1917, prominent Irish Catholic Canadians joined with rank-and-file Catholics to demand that the Borden government apply pressure on Lloyd George to effect home rule in Ireland immediately. From across Canada, petitions and words of support came from the AOH, the Irish Catholic Benevolent Association, Archbishop Spratt of Kingston, Bishop Fallon of London, Member of Parliament Charles Murphy, J.J. Leddy, the Catholic Conservative scion of Saskatoon, and former mayor of Montreal Patrick Keane, among many others. The plea was for constitutional change and to honour the principles for which Canada was fighting in Europe.[57] None of the leading subscribers to these resolutions would be considered cool to the war effort; in fact, support came from Charles J. Doherty, Borden's minister for justice and a prominent Irish Catholic MP for Montreal.[58] Privately, Doherty thought the rising and the stalling on home rule might have hurt Irish Catholic recruitment in Canada.[59] For the editor at the *Canadian Freeman*, such demonstrations 'dispelled forever the suspicion that [Irish Canadians] were apathetic about the Home Rule issue'.[60]

Once again in the minds of leading Irish Catholic Canadians the participation of Canadians in the war effort and the calls for home rule in Ireland were inextricably linked. While some Irish-Canadians had thought that Irish-Canadians should stop fighting the Germans until Ireland was given her autonomy, this was not the position put forward by Father J.J. O'Gorman, the wounded chaplain and indefatigable priest from the archdiocese of Ottawa. As was his habit, O'Gorman put his ideas to paper and developed a position whereby Irish Catholic Canadians could continue the fight against Germany, while professing their loyalty to the British Empire, and while continuing to demand home rule in Ireland. With his customary eloquence, O'Gorman developed the idea of 'double duty'. He was still convalescing from wounds in Ottawa when he decided to approach a secular paper, the *Ottawa Citizen*, as a means of assuring a wider dissemination of his ideas to Catholics and Protestants. His interview was reprinted across the country so that a national audience could now understand the 'true' Irish Catholic position on imperial policy:

> To answer the question [no recruiting unless there is home rule in Ireland] we should consider the double duty of the Irish Canadian – the duty he owes to Ireland, and the duty he owes to Canada. For there certainly exists this double duty. There are some who claim that we of Irish descent are Canadians pure and simple; that Ireland was indeed the land of our ancestors, but it is not our land, and that consequently we have nothing whatever to do with it. This claim we Irish Canadians cannot admit. Ireland has bequeathed to us, in addition to the Catholic faith of St Patrick, an intellectual, moral, emotional and artistic inheritance which is of the highest spiritual value. It is our right as it is our duty to know Ireland's history, her great saints, her mighty men and women, to impregnate ourselves with the ideals which they realized, that we their descendants may be imbued with their high spirituality … Canada is indeed our native land, but Ireland is our fatherland, all the dearer and nearer and we will be second to none in 1917.[61]

O'Gorman identified that the loyalty of his people was bifocal, and it was an identity based on a debt to one nation and a present obligation to their Canadian home.

O'Gorman used the interview to take aim at those who argued against further recruiting, knowing full well that revived war industries in Canada and casualty rates in Europe were already causing voluntary enlistment

The Irish Catholics of Canada fight the Great War, 1914–18   133

in Canada to falter. He eschewed the anti-conscription movement in Australia and the anti-English lobby in the United States. While he admitted that there was anger in the Irish-Canadian community after the executions in Dublin, he claimed that the reasoning in any 'anti-recruiting' movement was flawed because '[i]t directly aids the enemy and weakens our allies'.[62] Arguing that such a policy was one of 'sulk[ing]', he advocated a 'policy of self-sacrifice', reminding Irish Catholics of their double duty:

> [T]he duty we owe to Ireland coincides with the duty we owe to Canada … The interests of Canada, as a nation, as a part of the British Empire, and as a member of the world's family of nations, demanded that we enter this war against the Turco-Teutons, and that having entered it, we should prosecute it till we finish it or it finishes us. The few voices that are raised here and there, asking that we should halt till Ireland gets Home Rule, have rightly been disregarded by the vast majority of Irish Canadians. We do not intend to do wrong that good may come … No matter how unjust be the policy of England towards Ireland, we shall not change. For our patriotism is the result, not of the changing conduct of individuals or institutions, but of principles as unchanging as our Catholic faith.[63]

He did not mince words about the failure of the British government to handle the rising and its aftermath effectively, but he did not see this as sufficient to divert Irish-Canadian attention away from winning the war. For O'Gorman, Canada had to be a voice at the table as an advocate for small nations, and he recognised in Prime Minister Borden an equal partner with the British, as a strong voice for Canadian interests. His position won praise, even from the intensely Irish nationalist staff at the *Canadian Freeman*; for this paper's priest-editors, the war was about Christianity prevailing over *Kultur*, a struggle that could not be lost.[64]

In 1917 and 1918 Canadians faced a crisis over the implementation of conscription, which seriously divided the country along religious and linguistic lines. Most French-Canadian Catholics opposed its implementation, claiming that the Borden government had made promises that no man would be forced, against his will, to take up arms. The French-Canadian hierarchy, prominently Archbishop Louis Nazaire Bégin of Quebec City and Archbishop Paul Bruchési of Montreal, felt personally betrayed by Borden, who they had publicly supported in nearly all of his initiatives for the war effort.[65] In some ways French Canadians could not depend on their Irish co-religionists for support. Irish Catholics themselves were divided on the question, with sizable factions of politicians and editors on either side of the conscription issue.[66] The Celtic Catholic hierarchy, while generally not directly engaged in politics, supported conscription as a means to win the war.[67] The division among lay leaders, however, became more palpable when, in 1917, Prime Minister Borden formed a union government out of his Conservative caucus and pro-conscription members of the Liberal Party. Robert J. Manion, a demobilised military doctor (and a former Liberal), and C.J. Doherty, the minister for justice, were prominent Irish Catholics on the union side, while Charles Murphy and war veteran Charles Power were outspoken opponents of conscription on the dissenting Liberal side of the House of Commons. During the election of December 1917, one of the most bitter in Canadian history, the Unionists won a decisive majority, but secured only three seats in the primarily French-speaking province of Quebec.[68] A critical feature of the lead-up to the election was the support given to the Union Party by Bishop Michael Francis Fallon of London, one of the most prominent and outspoken Irish Catholic prelates in Canada, and who was despised by many French Canadians for his less than fair treatment of Francophone Catholics in his own diocese. In a public letter, just days before the election, Fallon wrote, 'In the approaching election, the issue which dwarfs all others is Canada's effective continued participation in the war. This is the issue that compels us to disregard all others, however important they might be at another time.'[69] This was an application of 'double duty': win the war and all else should fall into place.

In November 1918, the Allies won the war, but Canada was a divided nation. Irish Catholics had gained some respectability in the eyes of Protestant clerics and politicians for their loyalty, but had become estranged from their French-Canadian co-religionists. Although the Great War was over, Irish Catholic Canadians continued to be greatly concerned for the events unfolding in Ireland. In Canada, bishops, Irish Catholic clergy, and most of the Catholic weeklies clung to their support of the dreams proffered by Redmond's successors, confident that the remnants of his IPP could bring to Ireland the autonomy within the empire that Catholics in Canada enjoyed.[70] With the massive Sinn Féin electoral victory in late 1918, and the deployment of the brutal paramilitary 'Black and Tans' to keep the peace in Ireland, Irish Catholic Canadians became louder in their demands that Ireland enjoy the constitutional rights that Canadians already possessed.[71] It is on this point that the editors at the

Catholic Record were most eloquent: 'Canada has a form of Home Rule which secures for her the utmost liberty of action in arranging her own affairs, developing her resources and framing her laws. Her people are happy ... The reason is because our ancestors fought for and obtained their rights, just as the people of Ireland are doing now.'[72]

Once again, the Great War played a key role in Irish Catholic thinking: if Irish Catholics fought the empire's war so that small nations might be free, it only stood to reason that this principle must be applied in Ireland. According to the *Canadian Freeman*, which had been among the most sympathetic supporters of Sinn Féin's approach to home rule after 1920,[73] there was a clear link between the Great War and Irish autonomy: 'Irish people are rightly struggling to be free; Irish people must rightly choose their course according to the principles fought for by the allies; Canadian soldiers fought for this principle of self-determination; the British army of occupation [of Ireland] is a direct threat to "Liberty and Democracy". Irish towns are being sacked, homes burned, citizens murdered ... Canadians will not deny others the freedoms that they enjoy.'[74]

In the minds of many Canadian-Irish Catholics, there was no contradiction between taking pride in their participation in the Great War as an imperial player and demanding that the empire be a place where the principles for which the war was fought be honoured. It was logical that constitutional Irish self-determination be supported.[75] As a matter of justice, sentiment towards the birthplace of their ancestors, and outrage at the atrocities committed by the Black and Tans, a large number of Irish Catholic Canadians, from coast to coast – including newspaper editors, clergy and the Ancient Order of Hibernians – sent subscriptions to the Irish Relief Fund to assist the cause of home rule.[76] By 1920, there was also widespread Irish Catholic Canadian support for the Self-Determination League for Ireland, which pressed for home rule by holding 'monster' meetings in several Canadian cities, including Vancouver, Winnipeg, Halifax, Montreal and Ottawa. Notable at the Toronto meeting on 5 July were local Irish Catholics who had been prominent in their support for the war effort: these included Thomas O'Hagan, a poet, and AOH leader C.J. Foy, who had supported Borden's Unionists in 1917.[77] Public meetings were not without controversy. In Winnipeg, Archbishop Alfred A. Sinnott prohibited the use of a church hall for a self-determination rally, preferring that politics be kept out of the church. *Northwest Review* editor Patrick Henry retreated from his support of the use of the church hall, carefully stating that the archbishop's disapproval did not signal a lack of sympathy for the cause but merely reflected caution, since his 'diocese includes so many races and languages [and he] must be neutral and fair to all'.[78] In Montreal, the city's Irish Catholic 'double minority', who tended to wear their Irishness more vociferously than most other Irish Catholic communities in Canada, were viewed as natural allies of Henri Bourassa's French-Canadian nationalists.[79] The AOH was most vocal in its support for Sinn Féin, although some Irish Catholics in Quebec, including Charles Fitzpatrick, disapproved of such demonstrations, which appeared to be anti-England.[80] A small minority of Irish Catholics, the most notable of whom was journalist Katherine Hughes, favoured a 32-county republic for Ireland.[81] They were an exception to the prevailing constitutional nationalist spirit among Canada's Catholic Irish, who embraced the Anglo-Irish Treaty and supported Michael Collins and the Free State thereafter.[82]

Canadian-Irish Catholics blazed a different pathway from their American cousins during the Great War and the Irish home rule crisis. As British subjects they did not have the flexibility of the American Irish in espousing republican ideas, nor revolutionary-style physical force solutions to Ireland's problems. In Canada, generations of Irish Catholics had assented to living under the Union Jack, or at least the Canadian Ensign, which also bore the Jack in its top left corner. As Catholics they had negotiated a place for themselves amidst the English Protestant majority in the country and within a church that was dominated by Francophones. They came to understand that in Canada itself, an autonomous portion of the British Empire, there existed a space in which they could be loyal citizens of the empire while being free to practise their faith openly and carve out new and independent lives for themselves. It was sometimes a delicate balancing act, and it was by no means perfect given periodic sectarian disturbances, but it offered an alternative model for Ireland. For the Irish Catholics in Canada, constitutional nationalism for Ireland implied their 'motherland' enjoying the same rights, privileges and opportunities in an independent Ireland, but within the context of a larger British Empire. As the American Irish Catholic communities became increasingly radicalised in their support of an Irish republic, their Canadian cousins would labour to keep Ireland in what would become the British Commonwealth. As Father C.J. McLaughlin might add, the 'fires of patriotism' for Ireland burned intensely in each community on either side of the border – but differently.

CHAPTER NINE

The *Gaelic American*, 1921–8: reporting on the Anglo-Irish Treaty and the Irish Free State

Michael Doorley

The *Gaelic American* newspaper was founded in New York in 1903 and covered news from Ireland and the United States for its mainly Irish-American readers. From the beginning, its news coverage reflected a radical Irish nationalist lens. Its first editor, John Devoy, was also the leader of the Clan na Gael, a secret Irish-American nationalist organisation based in New York which sought to establish an Irish republic by revolutionary means. However, the newspaper also defended what it perceived to be the interests of the Irish 'race' in the United States, as expressed in its full title *The Gaelic American: A journal devoted to the cause of Irish independence, Irish literature and the interests of the Irish race*.

This article will examine how the *Gaelic American* reported on a dramatic period in Irish history, from the signing of the Anglo-Irish Treaty in 1921 which established the new Irish Free State, to the death of John Devoy in 1928. It will show how the bitter legacy of the dispute which wracked the Irish-American nationalist movement in 1920 influenced its coverage of subsequent Irish events. It also explores how, increasingly, American isolationist preoccupations dominated *Gaelic American* headlines as the Irish question faded from the headlines in the United States. These isolationist concerns and a deeply ingrained anti-British impulse influenced the newspaper's coverage of developments in the Irish Free State and American domestic and foreign affairs.[1]

The Irish struggle to secure national liberation from Britain was a key motivation in the establishment of the *Gaelic American* in 1903. There were significant differences of opinion within the Irish-American community as to how best this could be achieved. For much of the second half of the nineteenth century and until 1914, constitutional nationalists, in the form of the Irish Parliamentary Party (IPP), captured the allegiance of a majority of Irish opinion on both sides of the Atlantic. The IPP advocated peaceful parliamentary means to achieve a limited form of independence known as home rule.[2] However, a minority of Irish nationalists who formed the Irish Republican Brotherhood (IRB) in Ireland advocated a more revolutionary approach aimed at securing an Irish republic completely detached from the British Empire. The *Gaelic American* and the Clan na Gael supported this latter approach to the Irish question, which had been advocated by a long line of revolutionary nationalists going back to the 1798 rising. In a 1910 edition, the *Gaelic American* proudly proclaimed 'our allegiance to the principle and policy of the United Irishmen, of John Mitchell and the Fenians …'.[3]

At the time of the *Gaelic American*'s foundation, it had already become customary for Irish nationalist leaders of all persuasions to tour the cities of the United States looking for financial and political support. According to the American census of 1900, almost 5 million Americans were either Irish-born or had at least one Irish parent.[4] Not all of the Irish-American community in the United States took an interest in Irish political affairs but significant numbers did so, especially during times of political or social tension in Ireland, as during the Irish land war of the 1880s and Ireland's War of Independence in 1919–21.[5] In the first two decades of the twentieth century, John Redmond's IPP had its own American support organisation in the form of the United Irish League of America (UILA). The IPP also enjoyed the support of the largest Irish-American newspaper, the *Irish World*.

Meanwhile, at the other end of the Irish-American nationalist spectrum, the New York-based Clan na Gael, led by *Gaelic American* editor John Devoy, was closely aligned with the Irish revolutionary organisation the Irish Republican Brotherhood. Since his arrival in New York in 1871 after a spell in a British prison, Devoy had pursued the Irish revolutionary cause with a relentless determination.[6] By the beginning of the twentieth century, the Clan had survived several splits and its secrets had been betrayed by British informers, yet it continued to be a key source of funding and support for revolutionary activities in Ireland.[7]

Reporting on the Anglo-Irish Treaty and the Irish Free State

Given the dominance of the IPP in Ireland and the UILA in America, Devoy believed that the cause of Irish republicanism in the United States could best be served by the establishment of a newspaper that would promote the nationalist ideology of the Clan. Writing in an edition in 1925, Devoy declared, 'The Clan needed a defender in the press, and a public voice to enunciate its principles.'[8] By 1913, the *Gaelic American* had established itself as one of the leading Irish-American newspapers and had also doubled its circulation base from approximately 15,000 copies in 1907 to 30,000 in 1914.[9]

In founding and promoting the *Gaelic American*, Devoy secured the assistance of an Irish-American lawyer and fellow Clan member Daniel Cohalan (1865–1946).[10] Cohalan is listed as the principal director of the 'Gaelic American Publishing Company' on the company's share certificates.[11] Daniel Cohalan typified the second-generation Irish-American nationalist. Though fully immersed in American political and social life, he was nevertheless willing to devote his time and energy to the Irish cause. Cohalan was the son of Famine emigrants from Cork and joined the Clan as a young man. By 1902, he had become chairman of the Clan in New York. Devoy valued Cohalan's close connections to the Catholic Church, the New York corporate world and most of all to the Democratic Party organisation in New York, Tammany Hall.[12] Indeed, the *New York Times* viewed Cohalan as the 'brains' of Tammany boss Charles Murphy. Cohalan's close association with Murphy led to his appointment to New York State Supreme Court justice in 1911.[13] Following this appointment, Cohalan resigned from the board of the *Gaelic American* and ended his formal role with the Clan. However, according to Patrick McCartan, an 'envoy' to the United States from the Irish nationalist movement Sinn Féin, Cohalan worked closely with Devoy in determining the paper's 'editorial attitude'.[14]

As noted in the introduction, the *Gaelic American* viewed events in Ireland through a strongly nationalist lens. Devoy had wanted to call the newspaper *The Nation*, the title of an earlier Irish-American newspaper that had failed for financial reasons. However, Cohalan insisted that the paper should be called the *Gaelic American*.[15] This title indicated sympathy with the aims of the Celtic revival then taking place in Ireland. The newspaper promoted the activities of organisations associated with this revival such as the American branch of the Gaelic League (1893), which, as in Ireland, sought to revive the Irish language. Likewise, the sporting activities of the Gaelic Athletic Association (GAA), which had been founded in 1884 to revive the ancient Celtic sports of hurling and Gaelic football, received extensive coverage. In the 1920s, as in previous decades, Irish emigrants in the United States looked to the *Gaelic American* for information on how their county teams were performing back home. A typical article from the newspaper's May 1928 edition reported on a closely fought Gaelic football National League final between Kerry and Kildare at Croke Park stadium in Dublin. The paper reported that Kildare 'were within an ace of at least levelling up just before the last whistle'.[16]

The *Gaelic American* also offered both Irish immigrants in the United States and second-generation Irish-Americans an opportunity to maintain their ethnic heritage. Irish cultural events, dancing and music were frequently advertised. By way of illustration, the *Gaelic American*, in February 1923, advertised 'a splendid entertainment including songs, recitations, music and the presentation of an Irish play' all before an evening of Irish dancing at the Brian Boru Club Ball on New York's East Side.[17]

Although the Celtic revival was a cultural rather than a political movement, it became associated with resistance to what many Irish nationalists viewed as the anglicisation of Irish society. Many of the members of these cultural organisations, both in Ireland and the United States, had strong nationalist sympathies. While the old Fenian John Devoy was often sceptical of the contribution of Irish cultural nationalism to the Irish revolutionary cause, this was not true of younger Clan members. Daniel Cohalan, who was fluent in the Irish language because of his west Cork parentage, also served as head of the Gaelic League's finance committee in New York and corresponded frequently with Gaelic League president in Ireland Douglas Hyde.[18] Moreover, Irish resistance to anglicisation in Ireland was easily translatable to Irish-American resistance to Anglo-Saxon assimilationist pressures in the United States. Indeed, Cohalan saw how the *Gaelic American* could be used to resist these pressures and de-anglicise American culture. In a letter to all Clan members in 1903 urging them to purchase stock in the Gaelic American Company, Cohalan justified his call on the following lines:

> We want to reach out to young men and women of the Irish Race who are fast falling away from Irish ideals. We want to reach the children of Irish-American families so that they may be taught that they belong to a race that was great in war – in literature, in art, and in music before the barbarous Anglo-Saxons emerged from the primeval forests.[19]

Reporting on the Anglo-Irish Treaty and the Irish Free State

Cohalan's ethnic defensiveness, in the face of what he saw as the White Anglo-Saxon Protestant (WASP) domination of American society, was not unusual at this time. Historian Alison Kibler, in her work *Censoring Racial Ridicule: Irish, Jewish and African American struggles over race and representation, 1890–1930* (2015), has explored how the Irish Catholic ethnic group in the United States at this time was portrayed as drunken and violent.[20] In an earlier article entitled 'The Stage Irishwoman' (2005), Kibler described how vaudeville theatre productions typically portrayed Irish women as inept and 'manly' domestic servants who could not be controlled by their more civilised Anglo-Saxon mistresses.[21] From its foundation in 1903, the *Gaelic American*, like its main Irish-American newspaper rival the *Irish World*, attacked such negative portrayals of the Irish in its editorials and features and reported favourably on Clan protests against such productions.

The defence of the Irish race in the United States was a constant theme in the *Gaelic American* and it saw the Gaelic League as an important tool in this battle. In a speech to the Harlem Gaelic Society in 1904, and reported in the *Gaelic American*, Cohalan argued that the goals of the league should focus on banishing 'such monstrosities as the stage Irishman' and correcting the 'falsifying of American history'.[22] However, by the 1920s, the *Gaelic American* had shifted its attacks from vaudeville theatre productions to several early silent films which it felt caricatured the Irish race in 'vulgar and vile' ways. In an October 1927 edition, the paper called for the banning of *The Callahans and the Murphys*, a movie produced by the Metro-Goldwyn-Mayer corporation. This campaign, which had the support of Irish and Catholic organisations across the United States, eventually led the producers to withdraw the film.[23]

As part of its efforts to correct the 'falsifying of history', the *Gaelic American* frequently highlighted the Irish role in the American colonial settlement and Irish service in the revolutionary war against Britain. Cork-born historian Michael J. O'Brien, who served as an official historian for the American Irish Historical Society (AIHS), contributed many articles on this theme in the 1920s. An article appearing in June 1923 highlighted the service of Irishmen Patrick, Timothy and William Murphy to the American Revolution under the headline 'Brave Soldiers of the Virginia Continental Line'.[24]

The *Gaelic American* also linked the defence of the Irish race to the defence of the United States itself. The paper continually argued that pro-British elites in America, in league with the British government abroad and British-sponsored agencies in the United States such as the Carnegie Institute, were trying to ensnare the United States into an alliance with the British Empire. In a July 1924 article, the paper bitterly condemned the nomination of John W. Davis as the Democratic candidate in the upcoming presidential election, arguing that Davis served as a trustee of the Carnegie Endowment for International Peace and 'is the white-haired boy of the un-American Ku Klux Klan'.[25]

This battle against the prospect of an Anglo-American alliance became a constant feature of the *Gaelic American*'s coverage of international affairs in the 1920s, but it is important to note that this isolationist impulse can be traced right back to the early years of the newspaper. In 1911 and 1912 the *Gaelic American* had vehemently opposed a proposed Anglo-American Arbitration Treaty which was then being debated in the American Senate. This proposed treaty provided for the peaceful resolution of any remaining territorial disputes between the United States and Britain. The *Gaelic American* argued that such a treaty would undermine the treaty-making powers of the Senate and pave the way for an Anglo-American alliance that would only play into the hands of the WASP elite. In strident tones, the *Gaelic American* declared, 'The propaganda carried on in favor of the Treaty is essentially pro-English and offensive to citizens of other races, who now constitute a majority of the population of the United States.'[26]

It would be impossible to estimate how influential this press campaign was, since the *Gaelic American* worked with other Irish-American societies and newspapers in this campaign. Nevertheless, senators and congressmen representing Irish-American districts came under sustained pressure. In the end, the Senate modified the treaty to such an extent that President Howard Taft refused to sign the measure into law.[27] The *Gaelic American* came to believe that it had single-handedly defeated the measure and in the 1920s, the paper recalled this 'victory' against Britain. An article in March 1924 entitled 'Deep Significance of Defeat of the Anglo-American Alliance' argued that this earlier British attempt to entrap the United States should serve as a warning for the future.[28]

The *Gaelic American* opposition to American involvement in the First World War can also be seen in this isolationist context, though this goal also had a strong Irish nationalist motivation. Before the outbreak of the war in Europe in 1914, the *Gaelic American* had mocked Redmond's 'bogus' home rule proposals as a betrayal of the Irish nationalist cause, claiming that even Irish customs and excise would still be 'controlled and managed by Great Britain'.[29] In this campaign against the IPP, the

Reporting on the Anglo-Irish Treaty and the Irish Free State 143

Gaelic American was a minority voice within Irish America, especially as a home rule parliament seemed about to be established in 1914 despite the opposition of the Ulster unionists and the Conservative opposition party in Britain. Yet events dictated otherwise. After Britain's entry into the war in August 1914, the Liberal government postponed the implementation of the measure for the duration of the conflict.

Despite this setback, which he believed to be only temporary, John Redmond encouraged nationalist Irishmen to enlist in the British army in the belief that home rule would be granted after the war. This decision undermined his standing with Irish-America. Even the *Irish World*, the *Gaelic American*'s main newspaper rival, which had supported Redmond in the past, now withdrew its support. Redmond's support organisation, the United Irish League of America, also went into decline.[30]

The *Gaelic American* welcomed these developments and the new militancy within Irish-American nationalism. This provided the ideological space for Devoy and Cohalan to found the new Friends of Irish Freedom (FOIF) organisation at the First Irish Race Convention in New York in March 1916. Emerging just six weeks before the Easter Rising, the organisation was in place to exploit Irish-American outrage at the British executions of the rebel leaders following the rebellion. The *Gaelic American* provided extensive coverage of these FOIF protests. A front-page headline in May 1916 reported that a crowd of 20,000 people had assembled outside New York's Carnegie Hall to denounce 'England's ruthless murder in cold blood of prisoners of war'.[31]

The *Gaelic American* did everything possible to promote the expansion of the FOIF in the year after the rising. However, once the United States itself had entered the First World War in April 1917, the paper felt compelled to support the nation. Irish-American nationalists had always taken pride in the heroic Irish role in the American armed forces and the *Gaelic American* now celebrated the heroism of Irish-American soldiers at the front. More strategically, with an eye to the postwar peace settlement, it linked Ireland's demand for independence to President Woodrow Wilson's claim that the war was being fought for 'democracy and civilization'.[32]

Following the conclusion of the war in November 1918, the *Gaelic American* took a more strident position in favour of Irish independence. It also campaigned vociferously against Wilson's proposed League of Nations, which it felt would only bolster the British Empire. In a March 1919 edition, the *Gaelic American* recorded a speech by Cohalan where he argued, 'How clever the Englishman who devised the term, but oh, how much more strongly an appeal a "League of Nations" makes to mankind in general than a League for the preservation of the British Empire.'[33]

In June of 1919, Éamon de Valera, the leader of the Irish nationalist movement Sinn Féin, arrived in the United States. Sinn Féin was now the leading nationalist party in Ireland having secured an overwhelming victory over the IPP in the British 1918 elections. Unlike the IPP's pursuit of home rule, Sinn Féin called for the establishment of an Irish republic in keeping with the objectives of the failed rising of 1916. At this time, Sinn Féin's military wing, the Irish Republican Army (IRA), became engaged in a bloody conflict with the British army in Ireland itself. Given these shared objectives, one might have expected a close working relationship between de Valera and the *Gaelic American*. Certainly, this was the case initially and the paper welcomed de Valera as the president of Ireland. The paper also lauded his American birth and boasted how he had made his way undetected to the United States after a daring escape from a British prison.[34]

Yet, not long after de Valera's arrival, conflicts began to emerge between de Valera and his supporters on the one side and Cohalan and Devoy on the other. Broadly, these various disputes related to whether Irish or American objectives should come first and who should have overall control over the Irish movement in the United States. Some leading members of the Clan such as Tyrone-born Joe McGarrity believed that Irish objectives should take precedence.[35] Other Irish nationalists such as Cork-born Diarmuid Lynch, who had fought in the 1916 rising and had become national secretary of the FOIF in 1918, argued that Irish-Americans could do more for Ireland in the United States as Americans rather than being seen as the servants of a foreign leader.[36] This latter allegation had frequently been levelled at the Irish by members of the WASP elite.

Some of these differences of opinion related to fundraising, such as the management of a so-called Victory Fund which had been inaugurated at the Third Irish Race Convention in Philadelphia in March 1919. While some of these monies were used to finance de Valera's mission to the United States and the Sinn Féin mission to the Paris Peace Conference, another portion of this fund was used in the FOIF campaign against the League of Nations. De Valera objected to the use of these funds in this way and was also sympathetic to the idea of a 'real League' which would protect the rights of small nations in a predatory world of great

Reporting on the Anglo-Irish Treaty and the Irish Free State

powers.[37] Yet, both Devoy and Cohalan, as reflected in the pages of the *Gaelic American*, remained adamant in their opposition to the league, believing that it would strengthen the British Empire and pave the way for an Anglo-American alliance.

The *Gaelic American* became directly involved in these escalating tensions within the Irish-American nationalist movement. This can be illustrated by its critical reaction to de Valera's so-called 'Cuba interview'. In February 1920, de Valera, in an interview with a reporter from a British newspaper, the *Westminster Gazette*, cited the Platt Amendment, which governed relations between Cuba and the United States, as offering a possible solution to Britain's security problems in the event of an independent Ireland. One of the Platt Amendment's provisions stipulated that Cuba could not make a treaty with any other foreign power which might endanger American security. De Valera indicated that he would have no objection if an independent Ireland adopted a similar measure to reassure Britain.[38]

De Valera's interview was seen as a step too far by the *Gaelic American* given Cuba's subordinate relationship to the United States at that time. In a series of critical articles on de Valera, the *Gaelic American* argued, 'You cannot cite the Platt Amendment without bringing in the whole text of it, which gives the United States rights in Cuba which it would be suicidal to give England in Ireland.'[39] In a famous exchange of letters between de Valera and Cohalan, de Valera accused the *Gaelic American* of seeking to undermine his mission to America. In response, Cohalan, in critical tones, pointed out that he had no control over the contents of the *Gaelic American*. He also defended Devoy's right 'to comment upon, or discuss your public utterances, or those of any man who speaks for a cause or a people …'. More fundamentally, Cohalan questioned de Valera's authority to dictate policy to Americans and Irish-Americans: 'Do you think for a moment that American public opinion will permit any citizen of another country to interfere, as you suggest, in American affairs?'[40]

This conflict, which had been stoked by the *Gaelic American*, soured relations between Cohalan and de Valera. It meant that Irish nationalists and Irish-American nationalists were unable to coordinate their approach to winning American diplomatic support for Irish independence during the 1920 American presidential election year. The increasingly fraught relationship between Cohalan and de Valera became evident once again at the Republican national convention in Chicago in June 1920. Cohalan, and a delegation representing Irish-American church and political leaders, sought to persuade the Republican Party resolutions committee to include a policy plank supporting Irish self-determination. If inserted, an incoming Republican administration would, in theory at least, have committed itself to secure Irish self-determination. However, de Valera, who arrived unexpectedly at the convention, demanded a resolution in favour of an Irish republic. In the end, the perplexed committee accepted Cohalan's resolution but voted against de Valera's proposal. In response, de Valera publicly disavowed Cohalan's proposal and, as a result, the committee decided to wash their hands of any reference to the Irish question in the Republican Party policy platform.[41] Not surprisingly, each side blamed the other for the debacle.

In this dispute, the *Gaelic American* loyally supported Cohalan. At an FOIF National Council meeting after the Chicago convention, Cohalan issued a report severely critical of de Valera. The *Gaelic American* welcomed the report, under the headline 'Cohalan Sustained by National Council'.[42] Despite attempts at reconciliation, relations between Cohalan and de Valera continued to deteriorate and by November 1920 matters had come to such a head that Harry Boland, a close associate of de Valera, formally severed the links between the IRB and the Clan in a press release in October 1920.[43] In turn, before his return to Ireland, de Valera founded his own support organisation in the United States known as the American Association for the Recognition of the Irish Republic (AARIR). De Valera's rejection of Devoy and Cohalan impacted severely on the regular membership of the FOIF, which fell from 100,749 in November 1920 to just 20,000 in mid-1921.[44] Even before Boland's press release, the *Gaelic American* bitterly resented the hostility directed towards them by Sinn Féin leaders in the United States. The paper claimed that, 'No better work for Ireland was ever done in living memory and yet those who did it are treated as enemies of Ireland.'[45]

As the Irish War of Independence intensified in 1920, the *Gaelic American* staunchly supported the actions of the IRA in its attacks on British forces. It also reported extensively on atrocities committed by British forces in Ireland. The paper's front-page headlines of August 1920 reported, 'The British Hun is Loose in Munster. Murder, house-burning, raids on the houses of the people, rioting and indiscriminate shooting by soldiers and constabulary are everyday occurrences in the south of Ireland'.[46] Meanwhile, the paper continued to defend its actions during the recent dispute. In successive editorials, the paper blamed de Valera for destroying the unity of the Irish-American organisation, which had done

Reporting on the Anglo-Irish Treaty and the Irish Free State

so much for Ireland. The newspaper also condemned the AARIR as the new 'wreckers organization'.[47]

In July 1921, the Sinn Féin leadership signed a truce with the British government to allow peace negotiations to begin. While this was welcomed by the *Gaelic American*, the paper argued that the Irish side in the coming negotiations would be weaker because of de Valera's actions in the United States: 'Whether he fully realized what he was doing or not, his action here created a situation that weakens the Republic and is favorable to compromise on Home Rule lines. His personal responsibility for the split, which hurts Irish influence in America, is beyond all doubt.'[48]

After several months of negotiations in London, the British government published draft proposals in December 1921 which provided for dominion status for Ireland. These terms were similar to what had already been granted to Australia and Canada. The treaty that followed also confirmed the partition of Ireland, which separated the six north-eastern counties, with a majority unionist population, from the new mainly Catholic Irish state. These six counties had already been given their own home rule parliament under the Government of Ireland Act of 1920.[49]

In Ireland, the terms of the treaty provoked a split within the Sinn Féin movement between those who believed that it was the best deal possible given the military situation and those who felt that it represented a betrayal of the men who died for the republic proclaimed in 1916.[50] Michael Collins, who had masterminded the IRA campaign against British forces during the War of Independence, led the pro-treaty faction within Sinn Féin while Éamon de Valera lent his support to the anti-treaty side. Much of the opposition centred around the oath of allegiance to the British king which new members of the Irish Dáil (parliament) had to take. Interestingly, the issue of the partition of Ireland did not loom large in the treaty debates. Most members of the Dáil at this point believed that a boundary commission, which the treaty provided for, would transfer so much territory to the Free State that Northern Ireland would prove unviable as an economic and political entity.[51]

The *Gaelic American* was initially critical of the deal, but following acceptance by a majority in the Dáil in January 1922 it reluctantly supported the measure. The pro-treaty majority now formed the 'Provisional Government of the Irish Free State', which again received the support of the newspaper. Indeed, in a letter to Michael Collins in February 1922, Devoy wrote, 'Although they remain Republicans, our best men, under existing conditions, favor giving the Free State a chance to do what it can for Ireland.'[52] The fact that de Valera led the anti-treaty faction within Sinn Féin may also have persuaded the *Gaelic American* to support the treaty. In April and May of 1922, the paper bitterly attacked de Valera for his opposition to the measure, arguing that he was encouraging civil war in Ireland.[53] Yet the *Gaelic American*'s support for the treaty was not motivated solely by opposition to de Valera. The Irish-dominated American Catholic Church and most Irish-American political leaders also supported the measure, though a minority within the Irish community opposed it. In a major boon for the anti-treaty side, the *Irish World* came out against it, describing it as a 'Treaty of Surrender' and the Free State as 'The Freak State'.[54] When in the June 1922 general election the pro-treaty side gained an overall majority of seats in the Dáil, the *Gaelic American* gloated at de Valera's defeat but warned that 'routed in elections he seeks by Mexican methods to overcome the decision of the people by force'.[55]

As Francis M. Carroll points out in his comprehensive study *America and the Making of an Independent Ireland* (2021), most Irish-Americans, irrespective of their position on the treaty, were appalled by the outbreak of civil war between the pro- and anti-treaty wings of the IRA.[56] Many chose to take a neutral stance. However, the *Gaelic American* was unflinching in its support for the Irish Free State. In reporting the Civil War, the paper exaggerated de Valera's ability to control events once the fighting had started. In a vengeful editorial, Devoy thundered, 'He is a monster who must be punished for his crimes. Eliminate him and the trouble will soon end. He is not fighting for the Republic but for his own personal advancement.'[57] In a further editorial in February 1923, the paper declared, 'De Valera is doing no fighting, but he is getting other men to fight and to devastate Ireland and destroy her economic resources for the purpose of restoring his leadership.'[58]

The *Gaelic American* supported the draconian punishments meted out to captured anti-treaty prisoners by the Free State authorities. After the killing of Seán Hales, a pro-treaty member of the Irish Dáil, the government executed in reprisal four captured anti-treaty prisoners. The executed men included Liam Mellows, who had once worked as a journalist with Devoy on the *Gaelic American*. Under a headline 'Executions to Protect Nation's Life', the *Gaelic American* explained that such actions were 'vital to the existence of the nation' in response to 'a definite plan to decapitate the nation by extermination of the Government and Parliament'.[59]

Reporting on the Anglo-Irish Treaty and the Irish Free State 149

The *Gaelic American* welcomed the victory of the pro-treaty side in the Civil War and praised the efforts of the new Irish Free State in restoring order. On the other hand, it did not hold back from criticising what it perceived as the 'reactionary' tendencies of the new Irish government led by president of the Executive Council William T. Cosgrave. In April 1923, the paper described the Free State's application to join what it described as a pro-imperialist League of Nations as a 'bad blunder'. The paper argued that Irish membership would only strengthen the hand of American 'Anglomaniacs' who were themselves plotting to bring the United States into the league.[60] In the event, Ireland did join the league, and in a letter to Cohalan, President Cosgrave patiently explained 'that while many imperfections might exist, the league was really the only available machinery which small nations had'.[61] There is no evidence to suggest that such pleas had any impact whatsoever on the editorial stance of the *Gaelic American*, though its relations with the new Irish state still remained broadly cordial.

In reporting on economic developments in the Irish Free State, the *Gaelic American* frequently called on the Irish government to break the dependence on Britain and forge new economic ties with the United States.[62] In their reports to Dublin, Irish government officials in the United States noted such criticism. In April 1927, Timothy Smiddy, the Free State's minister plenipotentiary in Washington, noted with some exasperation that, 'On two occasions recently I took the opportunity, when I met Judge Cohalan, of introducing the subject of the attack on our Ministers by the Gaelic American. I failed to change his views though I endeavoured to make him realize that the *Gaelic American* had not all the facts …'. In his report, Smiddy lamented that because of high American import tariffs, there was 'little prospect of any substantial increase in our exports to the USA'.[63]

This dispute, reminiscent of the conflict between de Valera and Cohalan over the *Gaelic American*'s coverage of the 'Platt Amendment proposal', once again highlights how the paper's focus on an American agenda could lead to tensions with Irish political leaders. In this case, Cosgrave diplomatically avoided any public conflict with Devoy or Cohalan. At least in public, relations still remained cordial, and the *Gaelic American* ruled out support for de Valera's new opposition party, Fianna Fáil, founded in 1926. The paper also welcomed the official visit of President Cosgrave to the United States in 1928 and Cohalan played a key role in the reception committee which met the Irish president in New York.[64]

After the end of the Irish Civil War in 1923, Irish-American interest in Ireland declined and the *Gaelic American* now shifted most of its attention to American matters. In January 1925, the paper altered its overall masthead to better reflect these priorities. Under the traditional title '*The Gaelic American*', the rest of the newspaper's title now read *Devoted to the Cause of Irish Freedom and the Preservation of American Independence*. In 1925–6, this mission to preserve American independence can be seen in the newspaper's campaign to prevent American participation in an International World Court. Article 14 of the Covenant of the League of Nations had envisaged the setting up of a Permanent Court of International Justice to provide advice on the settlement of international disputes and the court had begun its work in 1921.[65]

Throughout the second half of 1925 and into 1926, when pressure on the United States to join the court intensified, the *Gaelic American* continuously ran front-page headlines condemning the court. In June 1925, a typical headline, citing a speech by Cohalan, warned, 'New York Jurist says Foreign Tribunal is a Snare to Entangle America'.[66] In a familiar refrain, the paper condemned the efforts by Britain and the other Great Powers that made up the League of Nations to secure American participation in the court. Given the American isolationist mood of the 1920s, the United States never recognised the court, but the *Gaelic American*'s preoccupation with this issue illustrates once again how American concerns now dominated the coverage of the newspaper, often to the exclusion of Irish issues.

On 6 October 1928, the *Gaelic American* reported on the death of its famous editor John Devoy at the age of eighty-six. In bold headlines the paper proclaimed, 'Irish Race Mourns John Devoy: Ireland claims body of Fenian chief'. The main feature article then explained how Devoy's body would be transported to Ireland for burial in Dublin's patriots' plot in Glasnevin Cemetery. The entire edition of 6 October was devoted to presenting the story of John Devoy in heroic terms.[67] Words of praise from James Reidy, the new leader of the Clan na Gael, highlighted Devoy's role in the revolutionary struggle to liberate Ireland. The newspaper also included a message from President Cosgrave, who voiced the 'sympathy of the Irish people' on the death of John Devoy. Despite its previous criticism of the Irish Free State, the *Gaelic American* still valued the Irish government's positive affirmation of its dead editor.[68]

Finally, the *Gaelic American* also included a message of sympathy from Senator James Reed of Missouri. Reed, a close ally of Cohalan in the

Reporting on the Anglo-Irish Treaty and the Irish Free State   151

battle against American participation in the League of Nations and the World Court, lauded Devoy's defence of the Irish race in America. Again, this had always been a key objective of the *Gaelic American* and would now become even more pronounced after Devoy's death.[69]

Throughout the 1930s, the *Gaelic American* focused much of its attention on combating what it perceived as British attempts to end American isolationism. As the international situation deteriorated and the prospect of another war in Europe increased, the paper expressed fears that the United States would once again be drawn into a new global conflict on the side of Britain.[70] In an edition following the outbreak of war between Britain and Germany in September 1939, the paper cited isolationist Senator William Borah's warning against American participation in 'Europe's ever-recurring wars'. However, after the Japanese attack on Pearl Harbor in December 1941, the paper once again reversed its stance on neutrality as it had done in April 1917. The *Gaelic American*'s headline of 13 December 1941 declared, 'War with Japan! Irish here will fight to last man for honor and glory of United States'.[71]

A study of the *Gaelic American* newspaper in the period 1921–8 highlights how a radical Irish-American nationalist newspaper had other agendas besides the cause of Irish independence. As we have seen, these agendas, such as the defence of the Irish race in the United States and the 'preservation of American independence' from entangling alliances, were visible at the very establishment of the newspaper in 1903. A study of the *Gaelic American* in the 1920s illustrates how this American agenda became even more pronounced once Ireland's struggle for independence had faded from the headlines.

CHAPTER TEN

Duelling mythologies of James Michael Curley

Suzann Buckley

Surely you are not going to vote for 'that crook and jailbird', said Catherine Shannon and her siblings to their Auntie May in 1949. Her reaction was swift and defiant. We were in her kitchen, and she picked up a big cast-iron frying pan from the top of the old iron stove, held it aloft and said, 'If you say another word against that good man, I'll dash this within your liver.' Needless to say, we shut up, returned to the suburbs and never uttered another bad word against 'his honor'.[1]

In this recollection, Catherine is referring to James Michael Curley, a dominant and colourful presence in Massachusetts politics, especially in Boston, for most of the first half of the twentieth century. During that time Curley was elected once to Boston City Council (1909), four times to Congress (1910, 1912, 1942, 1944), four times as mayor of Boston (1914, 1921, 1929, 1945) and once as governor (1934). He ran unsuccessfully several times: six for mayor (1917, 1937, 1941, 1949, 1951, 1955), twice for governor (1924, 1938) and once for senator (1936).[2] For Auntie May, Curley was a good man who used his political position to help his Irish-American constituents deal with adverse conditions by such actions as finding them jobs, building free medical facilities and providing parks and playground spaces. But young Catherine, who lacked her aunt's long perspective and need for assistance, was merely stating the obvious. Curley had recently served six months in federal prison for mail fraud.

After Curley's defeat in the 1949 election for mayor, the disagreement between Catherine and her aunt might have become academic. Curley, aged seventy-five, could have gone quietly into retirement, written his memoirs and followed a defeated politician's usual course of gradually

152

Duelling mythologies of James Michael Curley   153

disappearing from public memory. The contrasting black and white views of Curley might have receded to a forgotten or hazy past. But Curley remained in the public arena. He ran unsuccessfully for mayor in 1951 and 1955, declared his candidacy for senator and then governor in 1954, and ran successfully for delegate-at-large to the 1956 Democratic convention. He also continued on the Democratic National Committee. During those years he was denounced as a crook when he sought a pension from the state in 1952 or praised as a good man in 1956 when he publicly portrayed himself as the protagonist in Edwin O'Connor's novel *The Last Hurrah*. Even his death in 1958 did not end the conflicting views of Curley. Journalists, politicians and academics in the Boston area continue to put forward the contrasting interpretations, albeit for the most part more nuanced impressions than the binary one proffered by Auntie May and young Catherine. What explains this continuing interest in Curley and disagreement about his reputation? For some it is a desire to understand how he maintained support despite his nefarious reputation, and they conclude that 'he was the idol of a cult, arbiter of a social clique and spokesman for a state of mind' of ethnic resentment.[3] Within that context he is a freebooter or a rascal king, a rouge. For others, Curley is a way to link their political actions or experiences with a long-standing local leader they admire for both his social justice views and his role in the struggles of the Irish immigrants in Boston. Yet for others again, Curley serves as good copy. There are innumerable anecdotes about Curley and using one to depict him as either a good man or crook can still attract readers, especially those with only superficial knowledge of the history of Boston or politics. Examining Curley's reputation during his life and in subsequent decades can illustrate the role Curley played in shaping his contested reputation and how later generations have modified and used the reputation, thereby keeping the debate alive.

Curley was born in 1874 in one of the parts of Boston settled by Irish immigrants. Like so many of his contemporaries in the city, Curley was a child of poor Irish immigrants from Galway. His father died when Curley was a lad of twelve, which forced him to leave school after grade 8 in order to help support the family. Despite these challenging circumstances, he focused on educating himself and finding opportunity in politics, one of few areas open to Irish immigrants in Boston. He was ambitious, or, as the author of the main biography of Curley sweepingly generalises, Curley's 'ambition never fell before the corrosive self-deprecation so habitual among the American Irish'.[4]

Curley worked hard in the local political and parish organisations and in the Ancient Order of Hibernians, thereby developing a number of skills and connections that would shape his future as well as provide him with first-hand observations of the negative consequences of the economic privation in his ward. In 1897 and 1898 he ran unsuccessfully for Common Council, the lower chamber of the city's then bicameral form of government. These unsuccessful campaigns taught him the importance of ward politics, and he teamed up with the ward bosses to get elected to the council in 1899. He soon became a ward boss himself by forming his own club, named Tammany, modelled on the New York Tammany organisation. He was elected to the council in 1900 and then ran successfully for the state House of Representatives in 1902.

In 1903 and 1904 two events occurred that would set the stage for Curley to turn the situation to his political advantage, use the event and his communication skills to gin up his constituents' resentment against those who opposed him, shock both Republicans and Democrats, and delight those who appreciated that Curley could triumph against all odds. The events would also provide ammunition against Curley for the rest of his life. In 1903 Curley and three compatriots were each found guilty of defrauding the US government by taking a civil service exam for another person. Judge Francis Cabot Lowell imposed a lenient sentence of two months at the very minimum-security Charles Street Jail. Curley and one of the other defendants, Thomas Curley (no relation to James), unsuccessfully appealed and went to jail for two months in November 1904.

While awaiting the decision on his appeal, Curley continued his campaign for a seat on the Board of Aldermen, then the upper house of Boston's legislature. He won the election, and the next year, while serving his jail sentence, he handily won re-election. Undaunted by the scandal of being in jail, he established himself as 'a good man' in the eyes of many of his unemployed constituents by widely publicising that he had taken the exam solely to help a friend who needed a job. He was thirty years old, and his success made it clear to many that the old political establishment and norms faced a serious challenger. But within seven months of his release he would get the label 'crook' added to his jailbird reputation by being one of several aldermen accused of taking a bribe. A grand jury refused to indict any of them, and Curley would demonstrate his developing oratorical talents and the results of his rigorous self-education, by quoting Othello on the theft of a good name. Yet, for many, Curley was

Duelling mythologies of James Michael Curley

now a jailbird and a crook, and this reputation would negatively affect his behaviour and forever overshadow his career and thwart his ambitions.

Prior to Curley's rise in Boston politics, Irish-American politicians had served as mayor. Both Hugh O'Brien (mayor from 1884 to 1888), the first Irish Catholic mayor of Boston, and Patrick Collins (mayor from 1902 to 1905) ran business-like administrations, kept peace among the fractious Irish ward bosses and stressed repeatedly that 'there are no Irish voters among us'; we are all Americans and Americans we will remain.[5] O'Brien, Collins and others assimilating into the Yankee culture had sought to ensure the Irish would be a tolerated minority in Boston and that the Democratic Party in Boston would be integrated into the Democratic political party at state and national levels in order that its Boston leaders could enjoy a power beyond city limits.

In *The Boston Irish: A political history*, Thomas O'Connor draws upon the work of historian John William Ward to argue that, in Boston, Collins and others abided by what Ward calls 'rational politics', a coherent system of bureaucratic politics designed to work in the public interest and one that seeks out a leader that resists selfish interests, pressure groups and single-issue constituencies in order to better serve a common good. In 1906, with the sudden death of Mayor Collins, a different political approach began to gain public ascendency. Ward labels this approach 'ethnic politics', a political culture that celebrates the personal and individual rather than the general and the universal, that emphasises family and friendship and sees the role of government as providing help and opportunity. In Boston, this type of politics had to be couched in the rhetoric of ethnic and religious chauvinism lest it be seen as socialism, a concept anathema to William Henry Cardinal O'Connell, a very powerful force in Massachusetts politics from 1911 until his death in 1944.[6]

Curley was poised to take advantage of the unhappiness of his economically distressed Irish constituents and the ascendancy of 'ethnic politics'. He did this in several ways that served him well as elected member of the newly created Boston City Council, as two-term member of Congress and in his early terms as mayor. As congressman (1910–14) he tended to the needs of his constituents, got on well with both the Democratic Party leadership of Champ Clark and with Republican President Taft, and endeared himself to many immigrants, including his Irish constituents, in 1912 by taking a leading role in defeating the restrictive immigration bill strongly supported by Senator Henry Cabot Lodge, Sr, from Massachusetts. As member of the city council (1909–10) and as mayor of Boston (1914–18, 1922–6, 1930–4), first and foremost he provided jobs and invested heavily in such public works as parks, Boston City Hospital, schools, libraries and roads. Many of the projects directly benefited his constituents by providing employment or health care or educational and recreational space. They also assisted him financially, as those on his preferred list of contractors paid to play. When the press ran negative stories, especially ones condemning Curley as corrupt, he would attack the reporters and claim that attacks on him as a crook were but a thinly veiled vilification of his Irish Catholic constituents. And when his opponents railed against 'the jailbird' he would trot out his campaign slogan, 'I did it for a friend'. In the process Curley became 'a master in all the ways that politics can entertain, beguile and divert'.[7] Among other strategies he staged enormous, raucous, entertaining rallies filled with both divisive attacks on the Brahmin overlords and inspiring oratory about the many contributions of the Irish to America.[8]

Praise for his oratorical talents were perhaps the only point of agreement for fans and critics of Curley. His fans credited him with being the best orator since Daniel Webster and even his critics admitted that he had 'a gift of gab almost unrivaled in America'.[9] He spent years taking speaking lessons and reading the classics to develop a distinctive style of oratory, and his speaking style was so compelling that one election opponent found himself applauding enthusiastically until advised by his wife to sit on his hands.

Curley, a great fan of theatre, also applied symbolic uses of appearance in many venues. Soon after being elected mayor, he built an elegant house on the Jamaicaway, far from the Ward 17 of his youth. But his residence was not viewed by his supporters as a rejection of them, because he promoted it as a credit to the Irish success against those who would prevent their rise in status. He underscored this point by having the shamrock design carved into the house's large shutters and opportunistically called his constituents' attention to that tribute by publicising a fabricated complaint about the shutters from one of his Yankee neighbours. The bogus complaint fanned ethnic resentment and silenced critics who had the temerity to claim that Curley must be crooked to be able to afford the house. The house served as a powerful statement that the Irish had arrived. And arrive they did, because Curley took care to make sure to welcome them whenever they arrived with their petitions for help.

Curley also did not hesitate to use dramatic stunts to enhance his reputation as a 'good man', as attested by the favourable media coverage

Duelling mythologies of James Michael Curley

he engendered from the Democratic national convention in 1932. In the delegate fight prior to the convention, the Massachusetts party leaders supported the Irish Catholic Al Smith, but Curley supported Roosevelt. The leaders prevailed, and political obituaries for Curley were being written. Undeterred, Curley went to the convention and got himself selected as chairman of the delegation from Puerto Rico. With great fanfare Jaime Miguel Curleo, the delegate from Puerto Rico, cast the delegates' six votes for Roosevelt. The once hostile press then portrayed him as the little guy who had bucked the establishment and come home a winner. Such favourable coverage helped him to assuage the anger and disappointment of his constituents who had wanted him to support Smith. In addition, he confirmed his 'good man' reputation by assuring his constituents that he still fought for them. In a movie and stump speech about 'the forgotten man', as he campaigned nationally for Roosevelt, Curley spoke about the need for jobs, especially to counter the effects of the Depression. Franklin Delano Roosevelt, he declaimed, was the one hope for 'the forgotten man and the return once more of opportunity for all men'.[10]

Curley also skilfully built a public image as a 'good man' by focusing on being seen as a friend of the people, mayor of the poor, and a welcomer of other ethnic groups. He presented himself as a man with a heart, a message that he would refine into a repeated refrain: it is as 'friend and defender of the poor, the alien and the persecuted that I hope to be remembered – as the Mayor of the Poor'.[11] He broadcast this message widely and coupled it with publicising his support for working women. One of the oft-repeated stories about Curley was how he changed working conditions for the scrubwomen in City Hall (many of whom were Irish-American). On his first day in power, he ordered that long-handled mops replace the scrub brushes because 'the only time a woman should be on her knees is when she is praying to Almighty God for better days'.[12] As a champion of the working woman, especially the Irish-Americans, he seemed to have no equal in their eyes. Helen McDonough, whom Curley had hired as a maid and cook shortly after her arrival from Knock in 1938, 'saw only the good in him. She never saw anything that Curley did that was anything but upright to her.'[13] He was also connected with women on a personal level by calling attention to the death of his first wife and several children in his campaigns. His first wife, Mary, died of cancer in 1930, and by 1934 only four of his nine children were alive. His female constituents, many of whom had experienced the death of a spouse or children, grieved for, and with, Curley.

But even Curley's skills could not continue his electoral success indefinitely and keep his negative reputation at bay, especially once he left City Hall for the governor's office. In 1934 his Republican opponent Gaspar Griswold Bacon campaigned against him with two main points: Bacon would bring clean government and business-like government to the state house, and he would keep the name of Massachusetts untainted.[14]

Curley won, but he was soon besieged by setbacks in getting federal funds, scandals, a hostile Republican legislature, angry Democrats, President Roosevelt's disdain for him as a crook, and an inability to change his own self-destructive behaviours. After one year in office Curley announced that he would run for Senate, instead of seeking a second term as governor. Despite his aspiration for a Senate seat, he did little to change his conduct, curb his lavish personal spending or deliver on his promise of work and wages. Instead, he generally fulfilled Bacon's fears of Curleyism and besmirching of Massachusetts. National publications denounced Curley as the Huey Long of the Bay State, and many in Massachusetts concurred. Curley tried to deflect the damage from these criticisms in his Senate campaign booklet *This Man Curley, 13 Years a Faithful Public Servant Endorsed by 2,617,142 voters.*[15] It included a detailed breakdown of the fiscal problems in the state that his administration had inherited and the dire national economic situation, as well as several of his radio speeches about what he had achieved in progressive legislation despite objections from many in the Republican-controlled legislature. The legislation included improvements in working conditions, mortgage relief and additional social services as well as funding for some aspects of work and wages. As ever, Curley presented himself as 'the friend of the common man' and warned voters against believing his opponents' claim that he was no longer their champion. Would 'this man of action, of achievement, whose humanitarian accomplishments were the prideful memories of a whole public career', act differently in the governor's office?[16] Many believed him, and were grateful that he had made state government accessible and understandable. But not enough of them would vote for him for Senate in 1936, and he lost to Henry Cabot Lodge, Jr.

He lost again in 1937 for mayor, to his protégé Maurice Tobin, and the next year for governor against Leverett Saltonstall, and again in 1941 for mayor against Maurice Tobin. By this time, he had remarried, lost most of his savings in a failed investment in a mine in Nevada, and had been ordered to pay the city of Boston $42,735 for his share of the profit from the $85,000 the city had paid to settle a damage claim of $20,000.

Duelling mythologies of James Michael Curley   159

It appeared that 'Boston, recognizing the wreckage of a great career by Curley's own hand, [had] had enough' of the jailbird and the crook.[17]

But Curley was not one to fade away. He decided that his best chance for a victory was to run for Congress. In keeping with the times, he offered a new aspect to his 'good' reputation – a Catholic fighting godless communists. In 1942 he won a congressional seat in a new heavily Irish-American and Italian-American district by framing the election as Curley or communism. He won, and was re-elected two years later, gaining support from some for his progressive voting record. Despite this success, he readily responded to Joseph P. Kennedy's offer to pay off his debts in agreement to run for mayor in 1945 instead of for re-election to Congress in 1946. He thus opened the seat for a run by John F. Kennedy, who won election for Congress, while Curley won for mayor.[18]

In his mayoral campaign, although he was seventy-one years old, diabetic and under indictment for mail fraud, he had campaigned vigorously by making explicit another aspect of his reputation with the slogan 'Curley gets things done!' He had won nineteen of the twenty-two wards with the biggest margin any mayoral candidate had ever received, and he had won 58 per cent of the vote from those between the ages of twenty-one and twenty-nine. One can speculate that some of their aunts had told them that Curley was more of a good man than a crook, and that he would deliver jobs and social services. They would have been right to some extent.

Although Curley would be in Danbury federal prison from the end of June to the end of November 1947, when President Truman commuted his sentence, he had provided jobs and social services. By 1948 the number of city employees on Boston's payroll was 45 per cent higher than the average for the eight largest cities in the country. One in fourteen residents lived in public housing, a greater ratio than in any other major US city. Per capita expenditures for welfare, health and hospitals were the nation's highest, as were expenditures for police and fire departments, handy employment bureaus for Curley. In 1949 it appeared that Curley would be re-elected to another term as mayor as he campaigned on his record of what he had built for the public during his long tenure as an office-holder – bathhouses, branch libraries, schools, clinics, parks, playgrounds – and his often-stated belief that government was not created to save money and to cut debt, but to take care of people. His main opponent, John B. Hynes, who had served as acting mayor during Curley's incarceration, argued that the city could not afford city bosses anymore and that it was possible to have better government – one that preserved and protected the interests of the homeowner, the rent payer and the businessman. The election brought a record turnout, with Curley getting almost 10,000 more votes than he had ever received, but Hynes won by 12,000 votes, boosted by support from the more affluent supporters in the outer city wards.

A few months after the election defeat, Curley would suffer the tragedy of having two of his adult children die within hours of one another from cerebral haemorrhages. Two months later, President Truman would pardon him for both of his convictions (1904, 1947). Curley would run again for mayor in 1951, but once again be defeated by Hynes. Shortly thereafter he tried to put into practice his belief that government was meant to take care of people by convincing Thomas 'Tip' O'Neill, speaker of the Massachusetts House of Representatives, to push through a bill that would enable Curley to have a $12,000 annual pension. This time, a leader of the taxpayers' association who had been fighting Curleyism since the 1930s worked with the local press to produce such a hue and cry that Curley renounced the pension.[19]

At the age of eighty, he ran for mayor again in 1955, but could not muster enough votes to make the run-off, and Hynes was re-elected. Curley continued in politics as a member of the Democratic National Committee and as a speaker for other candidates, but he was a somewhat diminished figure, physically and politically. His career had in fact ended with his defeat in 1949. A biography of him published that year concluded that his time had passed. He was 'the last of the political buccaneers, ungovernable, unmanageable, irrepressible, incorrigible …'.[20] In effect, Curley was both a good man and a crook, with the latter public image increasingly prevailing.

That image shifted significantly in 1956 to an emphasis on Curley primarily as a good man with the publication of Edwin O'Connor's *The Last Hurrah*.[21] The plot focuses on an unsuccessful mayoral election by veteran politician Frank Skeffington, aged seventy-two, as he runs for yet another term. The protagonist, Skeffington, is a flawed but humane man with many achievements to his credit. His major failure: corruption as a result of government by favour and graft, and his disinclination to address the issue. O'Connor depicts Skeffington as beholden to many interests and thus unable or unwilling to reduce what foes and even some friends saw as corruption in government. This behaviour is treated sympathetically and placed within the context of the time and place of a chieftain responsible for the well-being of tribal members. His tribal constituents are depicted

Duelling mythologies of James Michael Curley 161

as needing government by favour, especially those with few opportunities and beset by economic challenges, and Skeffington's perpetuation of such a system is treated as more virtue than vice. When Skeffington loses to the young, telegenic, laughable, empty suit Kevin McCluskey, the narrator explains that the election was 'a last hurrah' for the kind of old-style politics that Skeffington had mastered.[22]

O'Connor had presented an affectionate portrait of a man and his constituents who had endured so much, and this affectionate image was reinforced by Curley's co-option of the story. After threatening lawsuits and winning compensation, Curley decided that the Skeffington characterisation could work to his advantage. He championed the book as his unofficial biography, and he took a line from the book as the title for his hastily compiled memoir *I'd Do It Again* (1957). Furthermore, in an article in *Life* he pointed out some things that O'Connor had failed to include about his efforts to use government to help those who needed it. The novel was a huge success for many reasons, but one stands out: for Irish-Americans the timing was perfect. Those who had long seen good in Curley could feel vindicated, and those once embarrassed or annoyed by Curley could now accept him as the Skeffington character. More importantly, they could laugh at a past that no longer bound nor defined them. Skeffington and Curley were the past.[23]

By 1958, the year of his death, Curley's reputation as a good man had trumped critics who had railed against him for decades. Media coverage of his wake and funeral overshadowed the other big news story for Irish Catholic Bostonians – the rumour that Archbishop Cushing would receive the Red Hat.[24] As an indication that Curley had won the hearts of so many, the city came to a halt for two days as 100,000 paid their respects at his wake in the State House. The question remained, of course, if his reputation as a good man would hold in subsequent decades.

Many of those in attendance at the wake were Irish-American men who would have considerable political influence in ensuing years. One was Tip O'Neill, who had been elected to Congress in 1952 from Kennedy's seat and who would become speaker of the House of Representatives in 1977. Although increasingly opposed to Curley's behaviour of helping himself as well as others, he would join others from the Massachusetts congressional delegation in entering glowing testimonies to Curley as a good man in the *Congressional Record* – a man who helped so many in need.[25] O'Neill himself had practised helping but came to realise that it risked placing him in a negative ethnic light. As he defensively recounted in 1980:

I've done a million favors. And in that million favors, I helped the poor, the needy and the indigent and the underprivileged and I had to twist the law a little bit sometimes to be able to do it ... Thirty-five years ago it was a legitimate thing to do. But when you go over that history in light of today you ask, 'What the hell kind of scoundrel was he? A typical Irish politician?'[26]

Tip was not alone in the idea of helping constituents or projecting an image of the good man in government helping constituents. Two of the Boston nesting dolls of Irish-American politicians, Albert 'Dapper' O'Neil and Raymond Flynn, modelled themselves in varying degrees after their narrow interpretation of Curley. Dapper O'Neil was born in 1920 in Roxbury, then an Irish-American enclave.[27] He was the youngest of four children in a single-parent household, headed by his mother. He idolised Curley and started campaigning for him in the 1930s. After serving in the army during the Second World War, he graduated with a degree in oratory and ultimately landed a job with the state housing board. From 1948 to 1961 O'Neil failed in his first five attempts at elective office, despite Curley's endorsement of him in these races prior to 1958. He ran unsuccessfully for mayor (1967) and for sheriff (1970s). In 1971 he made it to the city council by appointment to a vacant seat and eventually, running as an at-large councillor, he was re-elected again and again until 1999.

Throughout his career O'Neil outraged many with his homophobic and racial slurs and his opposition to busing to desegregate some of Boston's schools. But according to Raymond Flynn, mayor of Boston from 1984 to 1993, O'Neil endeared himself to many voters through attentiveness to constituents and mastery of that old-fashioned politicking. According to Flynn:

[O'Neil] would go to four or five wakes a night. When he'd come back from the wakes, I'd see him the next morning with little pieces of paper in his pocket. We'd go to breakfast at Amrheins [a local South Boston restaurant which displayed a picture of O'Neil sitting beside a statue of Curley] and he'd pull out a little note with a name and phone number on it ... He would often walk into my mayoral office without an appointment looking for a turkey or a ham for a poor family who had been burned out by a fire or to help some

Duelling mythologies of James Michael Curley 163

veteran friend of his who got laid off from work. I would do what he asked me to, that's what politics is supposed to be about, helping people. He learned it from Curley, and I learned it from them.[28]

Raymond Flynn, born in 1939, shared Curley's idea about politics as a way of helping people. An Irish Catholic from South Boston, Flynn was the son of a dock worker hospitalised for years with tuberculosis and a mother who worked nights cleaning offices. He began his elected political career as a Democratic member of the Massachusetts House of Representatives from 1971 to '79, representing the South Boston neighbourhood during the turbulent busing crisis of the early 1970s. He later served on the city council from 1978 to 1984, before successfully running for mayor of Boston in 1983 and being re-elected in 1987 and 1991. During his time in office Flynn presented himself as 'the people mayor', and he advocated for social programmes and immigrants, especially Irish.[29]

Both O'Neil and Flynn used their positions to commemorate Curley. By keeping his image active, they not only honoured him, but cast themselves in his image of mayor of the poor. In 1975 the city council supported the use of money from a fund established in 1892 to beautify the city to erect ultimately not one, but two statues to Curley. The first has Curley seated on a bench, welcoming passers-by to sit with him. When one city councillor found the statue disrespectful because Curley 'never sat on a bench in his life', a second, more traditional life-size statue of Curley standing was commissioned. At the unveiling in 1980, Mayor Kevin White suggested that the two statutes symbolised the duality of Curley – the one the man of genuine concern and compassion for the people he served; the other the man of authority. Curley, dead for twenty-two years, was cast in bronze as a good man.[30]

Flynn continued promoting the image of Curley as mayor of the poor as soon as he was sworn in as mayor in 1984 by requesting that Curley's former desk be installed in his office. It was not to be. In the ensuing brouhaha, rumours circulated that it had been stolen by the previous mayor. When it was located some fifteen years later in 1999, Mayor Thomas Menino put it on display in City Hall. Menino, like Curley, saw himself as an ethnic minority and believed that government should welcome immigrants and help those in need of assistance. In fact, in the 1980s Menino, then city councillor, and Mayor Flynn both strongly encouraged the campaign named 'Shutter the Thought' to have the city buy the former Curley house on the Jamaicaway in order to keep it from being razed. They hoped that the house could be used as a museum of immigration history, in addition to serving as a memorial to Curley.[31]

One might argue that, years after his death, with two statues, his desk back at City Hall and his former house saved from developers, Curley's status as a 'good man' was set in stone. Not so fast. In the 1980s President Reagan and congressional Republicans, champions of small government, dismantled social programmes, propagated urban legends about welfare abuses and attacked Democrats as nothing but out-of-control tax-and-spend profligates. Perhaps this provided a timely environment to re-visit the image of the 'good man' Curley. In 1991, the public broadcasting series *American Experience* debuted a version of Curley as less than a good man in 'The Scandalous Mayor', while a year later saw the publication of *The Rascal King*, which emphasised Curley's crooked dealings and defined his goodness in personal terms: 'A faithful husband, a caring father, a practicing Catholic: by any measure he had been a "good man". But from first to last, crimes and scandals had marked his life in politics.' In academic studies, in 2005 two Harvard economists published *The Curley Effect: The economics of shaping the electorate*, which presented a model of redistribution politics to argue that Curley engaged in wasteful redistribution to his poor Irish constituents and used incendiary rhetoric to encourage richer citizens to emigrate from Boston, thereby shaping the electorate in his favour. The authors concluded that this type of politics was detrimental to all in Boston, as it was when used in other US cities (such as Detroit) and in other countries (such as Zimbabwe).[32]

More recent portrayals of Curley are more sympathetic. In 1997 The Mighty Mighty Bosstones (a ska band from South Boston) recorded 'The Rascal King' as an homage to Curley, and in 2009 William Bulger, also from South Boston, published a short biography of Curley. Bulger, who began his career in the Massachusetts legislature in 1960 and served as president of the State Senate from 1978 to 1996, may be projecting when he argues that Curley was of greater virtue than his foes. Curley, he maintains, was a man who rendered enormous public service in the face of great opposition and personal tragedy – a man of courage with a rich sense of humour and a gift for entertaining bombast. To keep his memory alive is to honour the past.

To some extent Martin Walsh, the recent mayor of Boston, seems to agree. Walsh, son of parents who had emigrated separately from villages in Connemara in the 1950s and settled in working-class Irish areas of

Duelling mythologies of James Michael Curley

Boston, was first elected mayor in 2014. One of his first acts was to install the Curley desk in his office. When reporters questioned this action, he argued that the desk had historic significance and that he identified with the positive part of Curley's legacy of public service as the mayor of the poor.[33]

Over sixty years after his death, Curley's reputation remains contested, but with the exception of the economists' article the consensus seems to be that he was both a good man and a crook, and Boston politicians find it useful to emphasise the former. Perhaps Auntie May and Catherine could now find common ground, and scholars might at long last examine Curley within the context of such duelling notions as the role of government, immigration, and disruption within political parties.[34]

CHAPTER ELEVEN

John McGahern and the historian of modern Ireland

Diarmaid Ferriter

I

John McGahern's name is regularly invoked in contemporary Ireland and not just because of his literary brilliance. People seem drawn to the idea that his persona and the subject matter of his writing underline very specific aspects of Irish identity in the twentieth century and provide an elegy for an Ireland that no longer exists in the twenty-first century. His experiences are also cited due to his central place in the history of Irish censorship. Two examples of his name being invoked in May 2012 particularly caught my attention. His fellow author John Banville, in relation to Irish attitudes to Europe, remembered, 'Years ago a reviewer, writing about one of my books, suggested that in my work I was endeavouring to "open a window on Europe". I was rash enough to mention this to my friend the late John McGahern, to which, with one of his most feral grins, John retorted, "Oh, yes – and I'm trying to slam it shut!"'[1]

A few days later, writer and playwright Michael Harding also recalled him, for a different reason:

> The first time I saw McGahern was in Maynooth where he was delivering a lecture. He never took off his overcoat and looked like a farmer on the stage as he bowed very grandly towards the illustrious clerics who sat on chairs behind him. A professor introduced him, speaking with impeccable diction and clarity, but when McGahern approached the microphone he spoke in a rustic whisper that

166

John McGahern and the historian of modern Ireland   167

suggested he might be terrified of waking the dead if he spoke too loud. Of course no one listened to the introduction but you could hear a pin dropping when McGahern started speaking. The first time we actually met he referred to that night in Maynooth. He said he was brought up to the professor's apartment afterwards for drinks and noticed, as he was using the toilet, that the taps on the bathtub were gold. 'They looked lovely,' he said, without smiling.[2]

These memories (and I should acknowledge that McGahern's widow Madeleine has strongly disputed Banville's anecdote, maintaining the Europhile John would never have said such a thing) reveal a certain devilment, a sardonic humour, a man capable of making concise and cutting observations and seemingly a man not remotely interested in the world outside of his native habitat. But they also reveal more than that. If I am to tell my first-year history students in UCD about the controversy over the banning of *The Dark* in 1965 and McGahern being fired from his teaching job, they will wonder why on earth he would have agreed to give a lecture at Maynooth and bow to 'illustrious clerics'. I might respond that this was his version of giving those clerics two fingers, or I might cite his essay 'The Church and Its Spire', which included the observation that he had nothing but 'gratitude for the spiritual remnants' of his upbringing.[3] I could explain to them that despite the censorship, McGahern was not anti-Catholic and, though an atheist, he wanted a Catholic funeral. In doing so, I would seek to underline for them the importance of nuance and context and maybe even inconsistency when discussing McGahern and the use of his work and his life story by historians.

I am also conscious that McGahern was dubious about the idea that his work represented a social history. He was someone who maintained, through Kate, the wife in *That They May Face the Rising Sun*, that 'the past and the present are all the same in the mind. They are just pictures.' He also suggested, 'the best of life is life lived quietly, where nothing happens but our calm journey through the day, where change is imperceptible and the precious life is everything'.[4]

The irony, of course, is that the author who made such assertions has, in my experience, provided the historian of Ireland with considerable riches. He maintained there must be 'emotional truth and accuracy', not uncontrolled 'self-expression', which is 'the opposite of creativity',[5] and it is that emotional truth and accuracy that speaks to me as a historian interested in the social, cultural and political history of twentieth-century Ireland. In 1993, when the renowned historian of Ulster A.T.Q. Stewart was interviewed about the difficulty of clinging to the idea of objectivity, he maintained, 'If you look at history it is about humanity and it is about emotions and some historians write as if it were not. Their view has become terribly narrow.'[6] McGahern made it clear in his *Love of the World* collection that he admired an art that would bring to light the lives and voices of people who have never thought about being witnessed or recorded, like the unselfconscious working rural Irish men in the Leitrim photographs of Leland Duncan. 'The moment and the day were everything. The past was a cutaway bog or an exhausted coal seam on the mountain. The future belonged with God. Too much talk they saw as unlucky and essentially idle. They left no records. Their presences are now scattered on the mountain air they once breathed.'[7] He too was a rescuer; such presences are scattered throughout his books, their experiences recorded in an exercise of great value to the historian.

I opened *Amongst Women* in 1990 when I was seventeen years old. Immediately, I was hooked, and began to seek out and devour his other books. I had read *The Pornographer*, as it was on my parents' bookshelves when I was a younger teenager, and I was intrigued, but I was not yet the budding historian. When *Memoir* came out I could not put it down. This for me was not just about the power of his writing; I suspect it was also because of my by now well-established passion for history. I felt I was reading both fiction and history and when I later came across a quote from John Banville about the impact of McGahern's work – 'we have not so much been reading as living'[8] – I could identify with it as one that underlined the value of McGahern's work, not just to a generation that lived through the era he wrote about, but also to the social historian.

After I became a professional historian in the early 1990s, I was occasionally asked which books had influenced me most in my study of Irish history and I cited two: Joe Lee's *Ireland 1912–85: Politics and society* and McGahern's *Amongst Women*. Here was what I said in one response: 'McGahern did mesmerising work on such a small canvas; he was such an accurate and graceful wordsmith, the material doesn't date and the dark forces in Irish family life are expertly delineated.' In relation to Lee's book I responded, 'Provocative, polemical and formidably researched, it challenges at all levels and contains sophisticated, deeply textured political analysis. It neglects social history, but his omissions provided a stimulus to other historians to fill in the gaps and build on his foundations.'[9]

John McGahern and the historian of modern Ireland   169

Both of the books, it seemed to me, complemented the other. They were published within a year of each other and, for me, came at a stage of my life when I was taking the study of history very seriously. When completing my own history of the twentieth century, *The Transformation of Ireland 1900–2000*, I came to a welcome but paradoxically dreaded point: the ending. I do not particularly like epilogues or neat or contrived conclusions, but, after some deliberation, it occurred to me that the best person to finish with was McGahern. After nearly 800 pages of text, the question that Moran asked in *Amongst Women* – 'What was it all for?' – seemed an ideal way to finish, and the final paragraph of my own book was as follows:

> Moran felt he and his comrades had fought for independence at the best time of their lives, only for native misrule to render it somewhat meaningless: 'Some of our own Johnnies in the top jobs instead of a few Englishmen. More than half of my own family work in England. What was it all for? The whole thing was a cod.' When Moran died it was perhaps appropriate that the tricolour that draped his coffin was so faded. For Moran, so alienated from public life, the republican dream had long since vanished, though his involvement in the local themes of family, survival, money and the repression of women was always apparent, making him an appropriate symbol of twentieth-century Ireland. But apart from his insight about character and what propels people, McGahern was also able to write beautifully about nature and rural Ireland, gentle small and independent communities and local concerns, employing rich dialogue and an acute sense of place. These positive aspects of Irish identity were, if not dying by the close of the twentieth century, at least being left further behind by a pragmatic, dismissive and ideologically indifferent Ireland. McGahern's work remains both an indictment of the failures of Irish independence and a celebration of Ireland's distinctiveness. It is difficult for the historian to disagree with his assessment.[10]

II

One of the tasks I set myself in writing *The Transformation of Ireland* was to uncover and showcase new sources and to use literature to enhance the historical narrative. I found McGahern's work very useful in this regard, but the use of such literary sources raised a wider question about the legitimacy and reliability of source material, which surfaced again when McGahern's memoir was published in 2005. How valid and trustworthy a source are memoirs of Irish childhood? Archivist and critic Catriona Crowe suggested, when the publication of memoirs of Irish childhood was at its height over twenty years ago, 'These memoirs run like a parallel stream of information alongside the official documentary record and complement it with their personal immediacy and vibrancy … it is the fact that we are hearing a story from the inside of Irish life that gives these books their value as human testimony. The official record can tell us what happened, but rarely what it felt like.'[11]

Her conclusions are an apt summation of the importance of a genre of writing – and I would interpret the word 'memoir' in its widest form, including some fiction – which has done much to expose what might be referred to as the 'underbelly' of Irish state and society at a crucial time in the development of modern Ireland. Much of the testimony is bleak, and at times harrowing, and there is a strong temptation to conclude after immersion in these texts that the greatest blot on twentieth-century Irish society's copybook was its treatment of children. Their value lies not only in the articulation of personal childhood experience, but the light they shed on other key themes of modern Irish history: the family as an institution, parenting, religion, education, health and welfare, institutionalisation, violence, physical and sexual abuse, class, and the significance of the environment in which a child is reared. What is certain is that the work of McGahern sheds light on all of these areas. He wrote with what Patrick Maume, in a perceptive entry on McGahern in the *Dictionary of Irish Biography* in 2011, has described as 'unobtrusively clear-eyed recognition of the victims of past cruelties and conformities and the sometimes brutal foibles of local characters'.[12]

One of the roles memoirs have fulfilled is to highlight the gulf between the rhetoric of aspiration, which coloured so many of the expressions of Ireland's supposed advantages as an unsullied rural idyll with the bedrock of the institution of the family, and the reality of a society, and indeed many families, that hopelessly failed to give credence to such rhetoric. If historians want to deal seriously with the social and cultural history of twentieth-century Ireland, they need the kind of perspective McGahern offers, not least, as has been pointed out by Patrick Crotty, because 'no characters in [McGahern's] fiction are as powerless as children'.[13] The experience and influence of mothers and fathers are other, complementary

John McGahern and the historian of modern Ireland 171

themes he excavates. We learn that motherhood in abject circumstances inevitably took its toll, and when McGahern refers to the fact that the father in his fiction 'had an intense pity for himself and would fly into a passion of reproaches if he got any provocation', he is underlining a condition that was common to many, a reminder of the need to place it alongside other memoirs, to look for patterns and commonalities.[14]

In dwelling on the duties of the woman and in his depiction of motherhood, he also addressed a common subject. In *Memoir*, his love of his mother and the heartbreak of her death are minutely recorded ('a terrible new life was beginning, a life without her, this evening and tomorrow and the next day and the next').[15] It is difficult to dislodge the image of the oppressed mother in memoirs of Irish childhood, a reminder that McGahern's work needs to be placed alongside other memoirs for a sense of what they collectively portray about suffering mothers. The mother in Paul Smith's *The Countrywomen* (published in 1962), Molly Baines, seeking survival in 1920s slum Dublin, is burdened with a violent and abusive husband and has to continually negotiate the pendulum of his moods and the tangibility of his anger and terror. Much later, Peter Sheridan in his memoir of life in Dublin's Sheriff Street also observed his mother 'at all times being careful. Being less than who she was. I watched her do all this because it wasn't safe for her to do anything else.'[16]

Those children who lost their mothers when still very young were not encouraged to reflect on their loss, deal with their grief or communicate the reality of parental absence. Seán Dunne, in his memoir of growing up in Waterford in the 1960s, recalled that after his mother died at the age of thirty-three, when he was four years old, he latched on to whatever scraps he could: 'To hear someone talk of my mother could give me thoughts for days. Yet my mother's family seemed a family of ghosts, of lives spent with suffering and drawn into death when young.'[17] Edith Devlin, reared in a stern Protestant home in the grounds of Swift's Hospital in Dublin city, was never allowed to deal with the loss of her mother, who succumbed to cancer. She wrote that 'after her death, no one spoke of her again. The word mammy was never again heard in our house.' Her father, who lived until he was eighty-five, would not mention his wife's name, and she recorded bitterly that 'unwittingly he had dammed up my natural feelings and by impoverishing my early memories had weakened me for the very future he was preparing me for'.[18] She replaced her mother with books, as did McGahern, and again it can be seen that by placing McGahern's memoirs alongside others, certain patterns emerge which do much to illuminate different aspects of the experience of family life and how loss was dealt with or ignored. Notwithstanding, as pointed out by Jamie Dockery, the way McGahern eulogises his mother can also be seen as problematic; Dockery legitimately wonders whether she really was as 'loving and tender as the father is brutal and harsh'.[19]

III

Looming large in all the issues McGahern addresses is the exercise, but also the loss, of power. In the words of Patrick Crotty, 'Power in McGahern is almost always elsewhere, or in other hands; even the patriarchs who reign tyrannically at home – Reegan, Moran, Mahoney – do so partly out of a bitter sense of their marginalization in the larger social sphere.'[20] It is clear from McGahern's fiction, non-fiction and interviews that he was particularly interested in the extent of the power that rested with the Catholic Church, but the overall assessment of religion we get from McGahern is nuanced and qualified. There is no doubt he took serious swipes at the suffocating abuse of power by the church, as seen in the description he provided of some priests who 'looked and acted as if they came from a line of swaggering, confident men who dominated field and market and whose only culture was cunning, money and brute force. Though they could be violently generous and sentimental at times, in their hearts they despised their own people.'[21] It's a description that can be legitimately cited when attempting to place in context the revelations we have become accustomed to in recent decades about the abuse of power by the church and the reliance on a network of institutions that incarcerated those deemed to be transgressive, revealed, for example, in the Ryan Commission report of 2009 that documented systematic abuse in Ireland's industrial schools.[22]

McGahern was also preoccupied with the obsession with sexual morality, the consequences of which have also been underlined by recent reports, including the McAleese Report of 2013 that examined the Magdalen laundries and the report of the Commission on Mother and Baby Homes published in 2021.[23] He also suggested, however, that 'many who entered the church at the time were victims themselves'. Many who supposedly had vocations for priestly work clearly did not, and were the very last people who should have been put in charge of children. Forced celibacy, the young age of entry to religious training and single-sex

John McGahern and the historian of modern Ireland   173

environments compounded the problems and poisoned the atmosphere these men, women and children lived and operated in. Many of the perpetrators of abuse were victims of snobbery – the internal church pecking order that deemed certain clerics to be more suited to working in industrial schools or certain nuns to working in Magdalen laundries or mother and baby homes. There is no doubt that the frustrations they experienced had devastating consequences for the children and for themselves. They were products of a uniquely Irish mixture of large families, thwarted ambitions, rigorous segregation of the sexes and lack of economic opportunity, as were the children or 'fallen women' some took out their frustration on, often in the harshest of ways.[24]

But there was more to the power and pervasiveness of Catholicism than this; in McGahern's words, 'people drew solace from its authoritarian certainties' and they were pragmatic: 'most ordinary people went about their sensible pagan lives as they had done for centuries'. Jamsie and Ruttledge in *That They May Face the Rising Sun* talk of going to mass 'to see all the other hypocrites', a description that also appears in his essay 'The Church and Its Spire'. McGahern also described his memories of the Redemptorist missionaries who came every few years to his parish like a band of strolling players and thundered hell and damnation for an entire week. There were stalls selling rosaries and medals and scapulars, and prayer books and stations set up along the church wall for what McGahern described as 'the macabre carnival'. As he saw it, they were simply brought in to purify through terror, but in his experience 'they were never taken seriously, though who can vouch for the effect they might have had on the sensitive or disturbed. They were evaluated as performers and appreciated like horror novels. "He'd raise the hair on your head," I heard often remarked with deep satisfaction. Poorer performances were described as "watery". Some of the local priests were a match for these roaring boys, and while they were feared and accepted, I don't think they were liked by the people, though they'd have a small court of pious flunkies.'[25]

McGahern was also prescient in seeing the danger of exchanging one form of intolerance for another. Shortly before he died he wrote,

> When a long abuse of power is corrected, it is generally replaced by an opposite violence. In the new dispensations, all that was good in what went before is tarred indiscriminately with the bad. That is to some extent what is happening in Ireland. The most dramatic change in my lifetime has been the collapse of the church's absolute power.

This has brought freedom and sanity in certain areas of human behaviour after a long suppression – as well as a new intolerance.

Closely linked to this was his oft-quoted observation that 'people do not live in decades or histories ... it is easy to fall into the trap of looking back in judgement in the light of our own day rather than the more difficult realisation of the natural process of living which was the same then as it is now'.[26]

The power that the church had was plainly evident in the 1950s, by which time it had become, according to one historical analysis, a mighty yet 'lazy monopoly'.[27] But McGahern challenged some of the images of hidebound Catholic conservatism, in much the same way that Brian Fallon did in his book *Age of Innocence* when he disputed the notion of Ireland in the 1950s as a cultural wasteland.[28] McGahern offers us different layers to Ireland in the 1950s than, say, Anthony Cronin did in *The Bell* in 1954 ('Here, if ever was, is a climate for the death wish').[29] McGahern's sense of the decade invited a more textured, stratified reading of that society:

> There were many good second hand bookshops in which one could root about for hours ... it was easy to get a desk in the national library ... there were inexpensive seats at the back of the Gate Theatre; Chekhov or Tennessee Williams could be enjoyed at the Gas Company Theatre in Dún Laoghaire and the city was full of cinemas ... what developed was a freemasonry of the intellect with a vigorous underground life of its own that paid scant regard to church or state ... the people I knew in the Dublin of the time acted as if they had complete freedom to read and think whatever they wanted.[30]

IV

McGahern has a central place in the history of censorship in Ireland because of the content of his literature that was deemed to be objectionable, resulting in the banning of *The Dark* in 1965 and his subsequent sacking from his teaching job. These events have been characterised as 'the last major *cause célèbre* of the censorship regime and cited as exemplifying how censorship promoted a falsely idealised vision of Irish life and suppressed discussion of social problems'.[31] Again, it is important for the historian

John McGahern and the historian of modern Ireland   175

to put this into a broader context. McGahern was a victim of a wider power play that was based on the fear that the censorship battle was being lost. Despite his personal views, for example, Thomas Coyne, the secretary of the Department of Justice, was consistent in informing archbishop of Dublin John Charles McQuaid in the early 1960s that the state on its own could not provide 'a wholly satisfactory solution' to preventing the circulation of objectionable literature, while Dermot O'Flynn of the Knights of Columbanus had continued to decry the amount of 'no action' decisions by the Censorship Board.[32]

Questions were also raised in the early 1960s about the legal situation regarding the publication of banned books in serial form in newspapers; this issue, for example, arose in relation to Edna O'Brien's *The Country Girls*, which an article in the *Sunday Press* in October 1963 had maintained 'will keep the city girls happy during the winter months'. In 1965 it was due to appear in the magazine *Creation* and the Censorship Board decided in November of that year 'that they had no function in the matter'. The attorney general offered the opinion that its publication in serial form would not amount to an offence because it had been banned as a book and not a 'periodical publication', although the minister for justice warned the magazine's publisher it had to be careful and selective in the extracts it published as such extracts 'might, of themselves, constitute a ground for prohibiting a periodical publication in which they appear'.[33]

The emergence of fault lines and uncertainty was relevant to McGahern's case; there was clearly a desire to reassert traditional controls. The episode also revealed a continuity of deference and fear of offending the powerful, reflected in the stance adopted by the Irish National Teachers' Organisation (INTO), which refused to defend and protect McGahern. D.J. Kelleher, the general secretary of the INTO, met McGahern, having first braced himself with whiskey, and McGahern's account of this provides us with a wonderful image: "'If it was just the auld book, maybe – maybe – we might have been able to do something for you, but with marrying this foreign woman you have turned yourself into a hopeless case entirely," he said, "and what anyway entered your head to go and marry this foreign woman when there are hundreds of thousands of Irish girls going around with their tongues out for a husband," he added memorably, especially since not many of them had been pointed in my direction.'[34] McGahern decided not to contest the banning of *The Dark*, maintaining a public silence and discouraging protests on his behalf by other writers, including Samuel Beckett. 'I was secretly ashamed.

Not because of the book, but because this was our country and we were making bloody fools of ourselves.' To join the protest, he felt at the time, 'would do the whole sorry business too much honour'.[35] But the hurt was immense, just as it had been for Seán O'Faoláin and others thirty years previously.[36]

Nonetheless, the banning of the book was also something of a turning point; it is no coincidence that shortly afterwards the appetite to liberalise the censorship law gathered momentum. Certainly, the McGahern episode meant there was more ridiculing of the perceived heavy-handedness of the approach to censorship; in 1966 English novelist and essayist Brigid Brophy, who had controversial views on sex and feminism, wrote in *Don't Never Forget*: 'A year or two ago I stood, an invisible woman (and author of banned books) in one of the finest bookshops in Dublin and copied down the notice pinned to one of the bookcases: "There are over 8,000 books banned in Ireland. If, by chance, we have one on display, please inform us, and it will be destroyed."'[37] Writing in the *Guardian* newspaper in 1965, Peter Lennon considered the 'cowardice and indifference' of Irish politicians when it came to obstacles towards the emergence of a more mature attitude towards censorship.[38]

It became clear over the next few years that some politicians were not content to leave the old systems and the old personnel unchanged with regard to the policing of morality. As minister for justice, Brian Lenihan began planning a change in the censorship laws because definitions of what constituted obscene had changed so dramatically and other writers and campaigners against the misuse of censorship turned up the heat publicly in the aftermath of *The Dark* affair.

A memorandum on censorship appeared in Archbishop McQuaid's office in 1967 and referred to 'a number of reds, some parlour pinks and a few Catholics who wished to be considered as belonging among the "intelligentsia"' and who were manufacturing letters 'in the Palace Bar and the Pearl Bar' to the *Irish Times* on the subject of censorship reform. Lenihan's predecessor Charles Haughey, ever keen to placate McQuaid, had made a number of old-style pronouncements about the contemporary world being 'inundated with a great tide of pornographic publications and indecent films ... the argument for some form of censorship is, in my opinion, unanswerable, though there may be some scope for honest disagreement on the form it should take'.[39] But in liberalising the law on censorship, Lenihan decided on a different approach and justified his decision in a number of memorandums. He was also clear about

John McGahern and the historian of modern Ireland 177

what would not change: 'The question of whether a book advocates the unnatural prevention of conception etc. is one of fact and the problem of changing standards does not arise in the case of the banning of books in this category.'[40] Between 1946 and 1965 the total number of books banned was nearly 8,000; 314 decisions had been repealed and 220 were successful. Lenihan elaborated on his own reasoning for introducing the bill that allowed books to be re-examined by the Censorship Board after the passage of twelve years:

> Critics of the Board and of the system of censorship generally often point out that many books stand banned which are recognised the world over as being of considerable literary merit (some of them by Irish authors) and defenders of the present system are embarrassed by the undoubted truth of these assertions. The fact is that, until an entirely new board was appointed in 1957, the members were, in general, extremely narrow in their outlook and were especially prone to ban books by Irish authors. Many of their worst decisions were upset by the Appeal Board but there are still a number of books banned for all time under the law as it stands whose presence on the register can only reflect discredit on the whole system of censorship. Apart from the particular problem associated with the membership of the Board, it is a fact, in the minister's opinion, that standards of propriety do change and have changed greatly since 1946 in this country and he considers that, for that reason alone, the finality of a ban on a book on the ground that it is 'indecent or obscene' is indefensible in principle.[41]

A note sent to Lenihan by a civil servant revealed that in some respects the wheel had turned full circle on this issue, in that it was the writers rather than the bishops who were now being looked to for guidance and approval with regard to the censorship question: 'Seán O'Faoláin in today's papers recognises that the social conventions of 20 years ago and more which gave rise to the standards of prohibition of that time have changed radically. That is your justification.'[42] Ultimately, that was the main justification Lenihan used, and O'Faoláin can be legitimately seen as one of the midwives of the new birth in 1967. But so too, indirectly, was McGahern.

V

McGahern's work has also been cited in the context of the multitude of revelations about the extent of child sexual abuse in twentieth-century Ireland. In an article in *Studies* in 2010, Peter Guy wrote about reading McGahern in light of the Murphy Report, published in November 2009 (officially titled the Report of the Commission of Investigation, Catholic Archdiocese of Dublin, and chaired by Justice Yvonne Murphy).[43] The report had its origins in the 2002 broadcast by RTÉ television of a documentary produced by the acclaimed Irish journalist Mary Raftery, *Cardinal Secrets*, which investigated the handling of child sex abuse allegations in the Dublin Catholic archdiocese. Following the broadcast, the government pledged to establish a full independent judicial inquiry into the archdiocese's handling of abuse allegations, which led to the setting up in 2006 of an investigation into the handling of those allegations by church and state authorities from 1975 until 2004. It found that four successive archbishops of the Dublin Catholic archdiocese handled allegations of child sexual abuse badly, with 'denial, arrogance and cover-up', and did not report their knowledge of abuse to the Irish police over a period of three decades. The structures and rules of the Catholic Church facilitated the cover-up of abuse. Many auxiliary bishops of Dublin were also aware of complaints of child sex abuse, yet assignments of priests to parishes were often made without any reference to child sex abuse issues. The report detailed cases involving forty-six priests, and more than 320 children, most of them boys. Senior members of the Irish police force regarded the actions of priests as being outside their remit, and some of them reported complaints to the archdiocese instead of investigating them. The Murphy Report's use of the phrase 'avoidance of public scandal' underlines the determination to hide and deny rather than confront.[44]

Why is McGahern relevant in this regard? Because as early as 1965 in *The Dark* McGahern's suggestion of a clerical disposition towards abuse is apparent in Chapter 12. He also wrote about abuse in domestic settings; children, he wrote in *The Dark*, 'knew their place; they were merely pawns', or as is said in one of his collected stories as a child's belly is being rubbed by his father: "'That's what's good for you, Stevie. Isn't that what you like, Stevie?'" The sexual excitement derived from administering punishment in his story 'The Recruiting Officer' is also apparent.[45] Commenting after McGahern's death in 2006, novelist Joseph O'Connor wrote, 'His work spoke to readers about their own lives; its silences were also ours.'[46]

John McGahern and the historian of modern Ireland 179

Undoubtedly this was true of sexual abuse; McGahern wrote in *Memoir* that his father 'never interfered with me in an obviously sexual way, but he frequently massaged my belly and thighs' while he masturbated. More generally, the preoccupation remained with what was seen and heard publicly as opposed to what went on behind closed doors. In this sense, the controversy over *The Dark* is understandable. The response of the *Irish Independent* to its publication in 1965 was a contention that 'the novel is unreal … unreal especially in its picture of provincial Ireland today'.[47]

Fintan O'Toole suggested just after McGahern died that he had accurately described

> the human interiors of Ireland … The starkest example of this is the issue of child sex abuse. When it hit the headlines in the 1990s, it was spoken of as a stunning and awful revelation, a secret that hardly anyone knew. Yet it is there in black and white in *The Dark*, thirty years before. The description is eerily like something that would be spoken aloud in Ireland decades later in *States of Fear* [Mary Raftery's television exposure of abuse in the industrial school system that led to the commission to inquire into child abuse in residential institutions] or the Ferns Inquiry [of 2005, which investigated child sex abuse in the diocese of Ferns in Wexford]. 'His hand closed on your arm. You wanted to curse or wrench yourself free but you had to lie stiff as a board, stare straight ahead at the wall, afraid before anything of meeting the eyes you knew were searching your face.' Such awful privacies were unspoken and, in the case of *The Dark*, unspeakable. Officialdom had no place for them, and though most Irish people knew about them, they did not want to really know them. But McGahern's calm persistence, his unrelenting integrity, drove them into our collective heads. The very conservativeness of the surface, the avoidance of shrillness or stridency, made the act of insinuation all the more explosive.[48]

Notwithstanding, I think O'Toole has exaggerated the extent to which McGahern 'overturned a nation's self-image' or 'altered our sense of reality'. Perhaps he was too introverted for that; like his characters, he kept a certain silence around himself. O'Toole's point that McGahern's avoidance of stridency 'made the act of insinuation' regarding sexual abuse all the more explosive is valid, but decades after he wrote about that, children were still being abused; after all, we've heard an awful lot in recent times about a catalogue of horrific abuse well after the era of *The Dark*'s publication.

McGahern also addressed other taboos in relation to sexuality, the history of which has often amounted to a history of what went wrong. Perhaps the aspect of this that made McGahern most angry was continued sexual activity that would put the life of the mother at risk as conception could worsen existing illness, in his mother's case the cancer that killed her. Some of the most disturbing passages in McGahern's memoir relate to the continuing risk that pregnancy posed to the recurrence of his mother's cancer, but his parents continued to have full sexual relations. His mother's letters to his father frequently referred to whether or not her 'visitor' (period) had arrived; in the spring of 1943, 'In her letters to my father she states matter of factly that her 'visitor' has not arrived, but by Easter she is certain she is pregnant.' McGahern's father wrote to his mother's oncologist at the Mater Hospital in Dublin and received a contradictory reply from him, with an unexpressed acknowledgement of the difficulties of lack of access to contraception, couched in archaic and ambiguous language:

> I can assure you, though I have advised against what has happened, I can readily appreciate the position and I see no reason why either of you should be worried ... It is a fact that if the possibilities of recurrence are present, that rapid progress [of the cancer] may be brought about by the present condition of 'affairs'. In November of that year, she gave birth to her seventh child and resisted her husband's desire for the child to be called Jude 'after the patron saint of lost causes because of her cancer'.

But it was indeed a lost cause. McGahern wrote about the situation early the following year: 'Amazingly, they were still risking sexual intercourse in the light of all that had gone before – fasting, novenas, Dr Corcoran's warnings. In a letter written that February, my mother reassures my father that he has no cause to worry further since "her visitor" had just arrived.'[49] She died that year, and McGahern's father refused to have any contact with her in the last months of her life, as if she was contaminated and had betrayed him. This is a reminder of the factual reality of what had appeared in fictional form in *The Leavetaking*, where the couple are told that if the woman conceived again it would be dangerous after her mastectomy:

John McGahern and the historian of modern Ireland   181

'Is it alright?' He drew her to him.
'It's a dangerous time.'
'I'll be careful.' Starved for sexuality, he could not hold back.
She turned to him. It was her duty.[50]

I wonder are there any three more dangerous words in the history of Irish
sexuality than 'I'll be careful'?

                                    VI

In relation to the era of the Irish revolution from 1912–23, about which
there is much contemporaneous discussion due to the current decade of
centenaries and commemorations, the question of the meaning and legacy
of that period is debated in some of McGahern's work, most obviously
in *Amongst Women*. Moran comments acidly in one exchange that the
revolution had produced a country, "'if you'd believe them".[51] He clearly
did not accept church and state pieties and pretensions in that regard.
Significantly, Moran refused to apply for a military service pension based
on his time in the IRA during the revolutionary era. His old comrade-in-
arms Jimmy McQuaid says to him, "It makes no sense your not taking the
IRA pension. You earned it. You could still have it in the morning.'" His
response is, "I'd throw it in their teeth." Moran clenched and unclenched
his hands as he spoke … "Many of them who had pensions and medals
and jobs later couldn't tell one end of a gun from the other. Many of the
men who had actually fought got nothing. An early grave or the emigrant
ship. Sometimes I get sick when I see what I fought for.'"[52]

The ongoing release of approximately 300,000 military service pensions
files, part of the Military Service Pensions Collection documenting
the War of Independence and Civil War activities of men and women
active in the republican movement from 1913 to '23, and the largest piece
remaining of the archival jigsaw relating to the revolutionary era, indicates
that Moran's decision not to apply for a pension was 'unusual for his
time'.[53] The Pension Board's decisions were a reminder of the longevity of
battles over the legacy of the War of Independence and Civil War in the
state that was created at the revolution's end. The archive, with its wealth
of information on military service, engagements, tactics and strategy,
will provide historians of the War of Independence and Civil War with
abundant material to deepen an understanding of the nature and logistics

of the wars, but also the battles over status, survival and profit in their aftermath.[54]

There are approximately 121,000 files for those who applied under 1934 legislation, but up to July 1957 only 10,832 awards were made. Even allowing for dubious or even dishonest claims, such a gulf between the numbers of applications and awards meant it was inevitable that there was a very large constituency of people who would have been, at the very least, disappointed at the decisions of the assessors. The archive of the military service pension files is littered with letters expressing disappointment and containing desperate pleas against what must have seemed like a cold, harsh bureaucracy. Financial penury was certainly a factor in prompting applications, but intertwined with that were issues of pride and status and the difficulty of verifying the historical record, particularly thirty years after the events. For those seeking to survive or eke out a bare subsistence in the 1930s and '40s, every penny generated by War of Independence service was precious.[55]

For Moran, however, the pension issue was not about money but a means for him to contrast past and present; his critique of post-revolutionary Ireland is no-holds-barred. He spits out the reality, as he sees it, of the failed promise of the southern Irish state and laments a time when things were more ordered and courage more prized: as he rants at Quirke in the barracks, "'I wore the Sam Browne too, the one time it was dangerous to wear it in this balls of a country.'" He detests the crowd of 'small-minded gangsters' running the country, and has no illusions about his part in the history of the Republic: "'Don't let anybody fool you. We were a bunch of killers'"; or even more robustly: "'The war was the best part of our lives. Things were never so simple and clear again. I think we never rightly got the hang of it afterwards. It was better if it had never happened.'"[56]

What of McGahern's personal attitude to that period and the politics and conflicts of his own era? He did not hoist the flag of nationalism; it was foolish, he thought, as 'one is given the place one is born into, but first and last one is a human being. And the humanity is much more interesting than the locality or nation'.[57] But he was undoubtedly interested in the revolutionary period, counting Ernie O'Malley's *On Another Man's Wound* (1936) as a classic. McGahern was livid at the accusation at the Booker Prize ceremony by an English critic who suggested *Amongst Women* glorified the IRA: '*Amongst Women* glorifies nothing but life itself and fairly humble life. All its violence is internalised within a family, is not public or political; but is not, therefore, a lesser evil. If the novel suggests anything, it is how difficult it is for people, especially women who until very recently had no real power at all in our society, to try to create some space to live and love in the shadow of violence; how they manage to do that in the novel becomes their uncertain triumph.'[58]

McGahern made it clear in *Memoir* he did not like the idea of sacrificing the individual for a political or religious cause. He did engage with some contemporary concerns and was critical of the Provisional IRA during the Troubles. In *That They May Face the Rising Sun*, an IRA man – who is also the local auctioneer – is at work in the local town. Every year there is a procession to commemorate an ambush by the Black and Tans of young rebels. McGahern's gentle alter ego, Joe Ruttledge, speaks out savagely against violence towards the end of the book. In *Love of the World*'s essays, IRA fighters haunt the landscape; and the essays, like the novels and stories, refer back to past conflicts, killings and vendettas, but also the betrayals, failures and exiles of the state that came into being in 1922–3.[59] In McGahern's view, the spirit of the Proclamation of 1916 'was subverted in the Free State … rights and freedoms were whittled away from the nation as a whole in favour of the dominant religion … Church and State became inseparable, with unhealthy consequences for both'. The essays spell out forcefully 'the political opinions that provoked, and darkly underlay, his deliberately non-political fictions'.[60] He spoke acidly in private conversation of the hypocrisies and corruptions of local and national politicians, expressing great admiration for political journalist Dick Walsh.[61]

The trenchant declaration made by McGahern in reaction to the accusation of glorifying historic violence was an interesting moment, as it contains an accurate summary of one of the difficulties of the social historian – getting to the essence and the practice of 'life itself and fairly humble life'. Leszek Kołakowski, the Polish philosopher and critic of historical determinism, offered one plausible, and frequently cited, reason to study history: 'We learn history not in order to know how to behave or how to succeed, but to know who we are.'[62] It is for that reason the writing of McGahern is important and revealing for the historian of modern Ireland.

CHAPTER TWELVE

Wild Atlantic Ways

Gearóid Ó Tuathaigh

In 2014 Bord Fáilte (the dedicated tourist agency of the Irish government) launched a new marketing initiative branded 'The Wild Atlantic Way'. This describes a tourism trail covering the nine western counties of the Atlantic seaboard, from Donegal to Cork (a 2,500 km route), with a brand represented by public signage featuring a white 'wave' icon on blue background. This is but the latest iteration of representations of the 'west' of Ireland as a distinctive territory, place or habitat, in terms of both physical and broadly cultural characteristics. Among earlier initiatives in state policy that focused on the specific condition and needs of 'the west' was the package of measures introduced by the Balfours in the 1890s, the origins and effects of which formed part of Catherine Shannon's scholarly discussion of Arthur Balfour and constructive unionism.[1]

The ascription of 'wild' as the qualifying adjective for the 'west' became a commonplace of English commentaries on Ireland virtually from the outset of the early modern era of conquest and colonisation, even if the territorial extent of the west remained fluid and imprecise.[2] Nor was there a fixed or singular meaning connoted by the adjective 'wild': over the centuries it was applied to the rugged and sublime physical landscape of the Atlantic rim, to aspects of the economic retardation and 'primitive' methods of husbandry and general agricultural practice, to the 'condition of the people' (housing, dress, diet, poverty), and to religious beliefs and practices and other cultural habits and customs. It was also used to signify a propensity for violence among the native people and a general indifference to the law established by the conqueror. Thus, it was embedded in folklore that the fate of the Catholic leadership defeated and dispossessed by Cromwell was to be banished from their eastern

Wild Atlantic Ways

lands 'to hell or to Connacht' (though few of these leaders actually moved west). A century later (in 1761–2) Baron Willes, on his circuit of the Connacht assizes, remarked of Iar-Chonnacht (West Connacht) that it was 'inhabited by the antient Irish and has never yet been made amenable to the laws'.[3] No doubt, the language difference accentuated further a sense of 'otherness': the western rural districts were still overwhelmingly Irish-speaking up to the early nineteenth century.

However, reporting on the more coastal districts of the west remained very much a rarity, even as the number of travellers' accounts of Ireland increased from the mid-eighteenth century. Accessibility to the coastal settlements – by road and by sea – remained variable and challenging. The presence of an 'improving' (though not necessarily popular) landlord in a remote district frequently attracted a visit from celebrity visitors anxious to observe and report on signs of improvement, economic and moral, among the population. George Hill at Gweedore, W.H. Carter in Belmullet, the Blakes at Renvyle were examples of such energetic landlords. The few intrepid landlords who determined on establishing new urban settlements at the periphery – for example, John D'Arcy at Clifden from the 1820s – were dependent for success on the construction of a good road. Thus, travellers could, increasingly from the later 1820s, access north Connemara along the Galway to Clifden road: but south Connemara, along the northern shore of Galway Bay, remained largely *terra incognita* well into the nineteenth century.[4]

The Act of Union of 1801 and Ireland's incorporation into the United Kingdom ushered in a powerful wave of surveys and enquiries, to discover, describe and 'anatomise' the condition of Ireland and its people. The systematic surveying of the western districts was a prominent feature of this wider culture of enquiry that marked the early decades of the union era – to enable the (new) rulers of the state to become informed about the condition of Ireland: Wakefield's (1812) and Shaw Mason's (1816–19) statistical surveys, the county statistical surveys under the auspices of the Royal Dublin Society, the bogs survey, the ambitious Ordnance Survey project, and later Griffith's Valuation. Security considerations, taxation options and, in time, development initiatives would all benefit, or so it was intended, from this opening up of Ireland – the landscape, people and total resources of the island.[5]

As the population of Ireland increased – from *c*.5 million in 1801 to *c*.8.3 million by 1845 – the base of the social pyramid widened dangerously: by the 1840s perhaps a third of the population was dependent, almost exclusively, on the potato for their subsistence diet. The pressure of population generated predictable social tensions: poor seasons for crops triggered emergencies that called for special relief measures from the state and voluntary agencies. The state assumed, incrementally, a more active role in the lives of the people – in elementary education, policing and poor relief.

Pressure on resources was especially acute on the poorer lands of the west, even as state institutions (police barracks, post offices, coastguard stations) and the enhancement of communications gradually reached into hitherto isolated districts on the western periphery. The pre-Famine decades were punctuated by local crises in the food supply to the proliferating poor, in response to which the emergency relief measures adopted by state and voluntary bodies showed increasing signs of strain. Likewise, though the infrastructure of the Catholic Church (the church of the overwhelming majority) expanded, it found it difficult to minister effectively or to provide vital social support to its ever-increasing congregations of the poor. A number of Protestant evangelical societies established missions among the poorer communities, notably in Irish-speaking districts of the west; establishing schools, providing vital resources, including food, but also exciting resentment and opposition from Catholic leaders. The competing pressures of, on the one hand, traditional religious loyalty to one's 'tribe' and, on the other, the desperation to access the means of subsistence, added further to communal tension in a number of western districts.[6]

Fundamentally, the surge in population in the poorer western periphery during the years *c.*1780 to 1820 was related to a surge in British demand for all agricultural produce during the French wars and a sharp intensification of rundale farming, chiefly among the coastal communities of Connacht and Donegal, and it turned on the growing dominance of the potato in the diet of the poor. A sustained period of plentiful herring shoals gave part-time fishermen an income boost, and other contributions to the household income of families struggling on minute holdings of variable land came from harvesting kelp and from an assortment of occupations in cloth manufacturing. If ready access to fuel (turf) is added, the total resource base of the community was capable of sustaining the growing population, albeit at a low standard of living. The clear signs of increased economic activity in the peripheral areas encouraged the establishment of such new urban centres as Clifden, Belmullet and Binghamstown from the 1820s.[7]

Wild Atlantic Ways

The downturn of the agricultural economy that followed the end of the Napoleonic wars, a sharp fall-off in the herring shoals and the geographical contraction of linen manufacture to the mechanising north-east heralded a progressive deterioration in the economic condition and living standards of the western poor. Failure or partial failure of the potato crop precipitated subsistence crises in parts of the country – particularly severe in the west – in 1816–17, 1822 and 1831. The government responded with emergency relief measures, notably public works, with supplementary assistance from charitable bodies. The sheer numbers and vulnerability of the Irish poor increasingly attracted commentary by economists, social reformers and, ultimately, by the government, which in 1833 established a royal commission to enquire into the condition of the poor in Ireland.[8] The commission's recommendations, when it reported in 1836, were largely ignored. The institutional system actually adopted by the government for dealing with Irish poverty (the workhouse system) was inadequate and ill-suited to the scale of the problem and was quickly overwhelmed when the major calamity of the potato famine struck during the years 1845–51.

The calamity of the great potato famine of 1845–51 was a subsistence crisis of unprecedented scale and severity, with mortality rates and general misery and suffering especially heavy in the counties of the western seaboard. The relief efforts of both the state and voluntary agencies struggled – and ultimately failed – to get to grips with the sheer enormity of the human calamity. A particular obstacle to effective relief in the west was the underdeveloped state of the communication and distribution network. This is not to deny that in the early years of the nineteenth century the gradual reach of a retail market had already begun to integrate even the more remote corners of the Atlantic rim into a commercial trading economy. Thus, for example, Patrick Knight, writing in the 1830s (and advocating the construction of a railway link to a port on the Atlantic coast for transatlantic sailings), offered the following comment on Erris in west Mayo:

> There is nothing peculiar in the customs, manners or dispositions of the natives of Erris … Hospitable, good-natured, generous … and industrious when given opportunity … Twenty-three years ago when I first visited Erris, there were some peculiarities in costume, particularly among the females, which the constant intercourse produced by the roads with the interior of the country, and the introduction of cheap English goods into shops at their own homes, has now nearly obliterated.[9]

It is important not to exaggerate the speed or thoroughness of the maturation of a genuinely competitive retail, monetised economy along the western periphery. Monopolist local traders, controlling terms of credit, were a feature of numerous smaller, less accessible communities up to the close of the nineteenth century. But during the second half of the century – and notably in its final third – the combined effect of improved communications, retail and wholesale expansion, and an expanding post office network, relentlessly, if unevenly, moved the western districts into a more open relationship not only with the rest of the United Kingdom but with the wider anglophone world.

The reporting of suffering, starvation and disease during the Famine calamity – by a variety of observers, charitable bodies and local leaders – provides harrowing evidence of the consequences of chronic poverty and vulnerability to disease in the western districts. Despite exceptional efforts by various relief agencies and individuals, mortality was severe in these districts during the Famine. Of particular value was the evidence – and the relief efforts – provided by the Quakers, who established a special relief committee shortly after the arrival of the blight. The fact-finding visits to the stricken areas of the west and north-west, from late 1846, of such concerned Quakers as William Forster and his son William Edward, Jonathan Pim, Richard D. Webb and, most notably, James Hack Tuke not only publicised the scale of the suffering and excited public sympathy and financial support, but also informed their own practical schemes of relief, including the establishment of a model farm as an exemplar of good practice – the kind of long-term developmental action that would be resumed more systematically in the 1890s.[10]

While the generation following the Famine saw significant transfer of land ownership in the western counties – notably through the Encumbered Estates Court – many of the new owners, understandably intent on generating a commercial return on their investment, frequently sought to stock the land with sheep or cattle rather than tolerate the intensive cultivation that might support, however precariously, the large numbers of poor cottiers and labourers who formed the 'congested' underclass of rural society. The potential for commercial farming rested, of course, in the quality of the land: but shifting the balance from tillage to livestock would have major implications for the demand for labour.[11]

In the western districts of Connacht and Donegal, seasonal migration remained an important aspect of family income until late in the nineteenth century. It may be claimed that the seasonal earnings not only kept many

Wild Atlantic Ways   189

subsistence families solvent, where the yield of the smallholding would not be sufficient to meet rent and basic family living costs, but additionally probably staved off the day when more drastic choices had to be made. Permanent emigration was one such choice. Emigration rates from the poorest western counties did not run ahead of the national average until the last two decades of the century. And, while there were earlier schemes of assisted emigration, it was only for a brief interlude during the 1880s that limited assisted emigration was employed in efforts to alleviate the problem of congestion on poor land in Connemara and west Mayo.[12] By this time, however, 'voluntary' emigration from the western counties was above the national average.

A recurring concern of many travellers' accounts of Ireland from the late eighteenth through to the third quarter of the nineteenth centuries was with providing English readers (including those presumed to have influence on government policy) with an understanding of Ireland's distinctive problems and of the reasons for its sharp deviation from the British 'norm'. Many of these accounts of the state of Ireland by travellers, whether sombrely investigative or breezily touristic in tone, were as much prescriptive as descriptive. Certainly, for readers of these accounts, the 'west' meant, more than anything else, poverty and deep-seated problems of backwardness. But for some commentators, in the shadow of the Famine and in its immediate aftermath, it also meant potential for development, as yet unexploited. Yet, even the most upbeat promoters of investment and its potential returns had to acknowledge the daunting realities of the most congested districts. Thus, in 1849 the noted agriculturalist James Caird, while eloquent on the potential for economic development in north Connemara and the 'interior' hinterland of the lakes, conceded that there was no such prospect on the stony croppings along the coast road west of Galway.[13]

The gallery of visitors who spent time observing living conditions in the west was not exclusively comprised of social and economic reformers, philanthropists and religious evangelists, nor were the accounts of individual travellers always exclusively concerned with economic difficulties and their remedy. The wild scenic beauty of the west attracted favourable comment from visitors, even if their numbers were limited. The engineer George Preston White, visiting Connemara in 1849, was 'astonished' at how few visitors had discovered its beauty, and hoped his remarks might direct 'attention to a district hitherto unnoticed ... I might almost say unknown'.[14] Issues of access and shortcomings in the tourist infrastructure were, no doubt, factors inhibiting growth. Yet, even the arrival, in Galway in 1851 and Westport in 1866, of the railway did not presage anything close to the spectacular growth in tourist numbers experienced by the Scottish Highlands from early in the nineteenth century. The great entrepreneur of mass tourism, Thomas Cook, claimed to have taken 40,000 tourists through the Highlands between 1846 and 1861.[15] The Irish west experienced nothing like this. Economic backwardness, cultural recidivism and an instinct for turbulence remained firmly fixed as components of the image of the Irish 'west' with which the outside world was most familiar.

While the wild scenic beauty and the potential for development attracted commentators in the post-Famine decades, there was a further – darker – sense in which the west was described as 'wild'. This was the sense of its being not quite amenable to the rule of law, that its inclination to remedy and resolution of disputes and grievances – notably in relation to land issues – was more immediate, direct and frequently violent. This view was already deeply embedded in commentaries at the time of the union, and despite the extension of the network of police barracks, local courts and magistrates throughout the hitherto poorly accessible enclaves of the western districts from the 1830s, the reputation of these western areas as being somehow outside the law and civility endured.

The official view is well captured in the comment of the lord lieutenant, Earl Spencer, following a five-day tour of the west of Ireland in September 1882. Spencer's tour had included a visit to the remote Maamtrasna district – the scene of a horrific and widely reported multiple murder of the Joyce family the previous month. Spencer reported to his colleague Lord Granville in the following terms:

> My trip was delightful ... I was very heartily received everywhere where no one could get at the people. In Westport they were apathetic and no doubt had been ordered to be so. I rode three days about 25 or 36 miles a day over a wild moor country. We visited the scene of the Joyce massacre. I could not have believed that 6 human beings could have lived in such a hole. It was deeply interesting. I fancy the people round have neither education or religion ...[16]

The railway may have made Galway or Westport more accessible from Dublin, but journeying further west to the Atlantic coastal districts or to more remote valley or mountain settlements remained a challenge.

Wild Atlantic Ways

Even as the general prospects improved in the post-Famine decades, a poor season for potatoes or for the commercial grain crop brought the threat of acute distress to the struggling occupiers of poor land in the western districts. It was such an acute crisis in the late 1870s and early 1880s – several successive poor seasons coinciding with a general fall in agricultural prices – that led to the founding of the Irish Land League and the outbreak of the land war. Initially triggered in Mayo by the crisis of the western smallholders, the Land League quickly subsumed the struggling westerners into a nationwide movement of tenant farmers, demanding rent reductions, compensation for improvements, and fixity of tenure based on 'fair' rents.

The land war was a turbulent struggle in which an array of legal tactics combined with direct action (including violence, intimidation and the boycotting of uncooperative landlords and their agents) were deployed by the Land League, to which the government responded with strong doses of emergency (i.e. coercive) legislation, accompanied by incremental concession of the main demands of the tenants. Ultimately, successive governments decided to provide capital funds to enable tenants to buy out their farms and to incentivise the landlords to sell. But it took thirty years to arrive at this 'solution' to the Irish land question.[17]

Presiding over this protracted struggle to find the formula that would secure peace and stability in the Irish countryside was the burning issue of Irish 'home rule', the political demand – supported by four-fifths of the Irish MPs elected at successive general elections from 1885 to 1910 – for devolved self-government for Ireland. Whatever the calculations of short-term political advantage prompting the Conservative party's adoption of a firm unionist position in 1886, its resolute anti-home rule stance hardened in the years that followed, inevitably provoking bitter denunciation by Irish nationalists. However, as the Conservatives assumed office in 1886 (with the support of former Liberals who had refused to support Gladstone's home rule proposals), they had to rule Ireland in the face of strong nationalist opposition.

This was the challenge facing Arthur Balfour when he became chief secretary for Ireland in 1887. A new phase of land agitation had resumed and the law was being challenged. He first took a strong line in confronting the land agitators and vindicating the law – earning him the title 'bloody Balfour' in nationalist denunciations.[18] But Balfour was also determined to introduce constructive measures to deal with 'genuine' Irish grievances. The programme of constructive unionism, initiated by him, was later continued by his brother, Gerald (chief secretary 1895–1900), and George Wyndham (chief secretary 1900–5). This suite of constructive initiatives in the twenty-five years before the Great War included improved housing for labourers, a series of progressively more ambitious land purchase schemes, light railways (reaching out to outposts on the Atlantic rim), representative local government from 1898, a Department of Agriculture and Technical Instruction (1899) and, in 1891, the establishment of the Congested Districts Board (CDB).[19]

We need not dwell at length here on the well-rehearsed debate on whether Balfour's constructive unionist initiatives had as much to do with the political management of different elements of support for continued Conservative government at Westminster as with producing a coherent reform programme for Ireland, calculated to take the wind out of the home rule sails ('killing home rule with kindness', as described by Gerald Balfour in 1895), but his identification of the particular challenge posed by backwardness in the western districts came relatively early in his term of office. Writing to his uncle (and the prime minister) Lord Salisbury, 31 October 1889, he explicitly spoke of the western congested districts: '… I think we ought to deal with them: and though the question is beset with almost insuperable difficulties, I think my method of solving it worth consideration …'.[20]

Balfour's tour of the congested districts of Connemara, Mayo and Donegal from 25 October to 8 November 1890 provided him with direct, observed evidence of conditions in these districts, while also sending a clear signal to people of the government's interest in doing something constructive about the west's special problems. Despite being a hate figure for nationalist politicians, Balfour was well received by community leaders throughout his tour. In addition to contemporary newspaper reports of his fact-finding journey, Balfour's itinerary was captured in a remarkable photographic album, later presented to him in recognition of his support for the Galway–Clifden railway. The photos were taken, a few years after the original Balfour journey, by the distinguished Belfast-based photographer Robert J. Welch.[21]

In retrospect, the establishment of the CDB in 1891 may be seen as a radical departure. Established as a board independent of Dublin Castle, initially for a period of twenty years but with the possibility of extension, with its own modest budget, the board membership included persons with expertise and with a track record of service in the relief of distress. Its early function was to improve all aspects of agriculture, forestry, livestock

Wild Atlantic Ways

breeding, poultry and pigs, household improvements and husbandry, weaving, spinning and craft work (with a focus on female participation), fishing (boats, nets, gear, salting and storage facilities), harbours, piers and slipways. Its schemes had immediate impact. After 1899, its work and resources were increasingly redirected towards land acquisition and the consolidation of scattered strips into modest, but viable, farm units. This concentration on land reform (which saw many of its earlier schemes diverted to other state agencies) was accentuated by an act of 1909 which more than doubled both the land mass (including towns) and the population now covered by a reconstructed board.[22]

Ciara Breathnach's verdict, that 'Historians have judged the Congested Districts Board very harshly because it has been viewed as part of the legacy of Constructive Unionism, which failed to "kill home rule"', requires some qualification.[23] Certainly, constructive unionism's boast of 'good government' ultimately failed to trump the nationalist demand for self-government. More pertinent to a verdict of failure, several economic historians have questioned the overall impact of the CDB's work, citing its excessive timidity in dealing with obstructive vested interests (notably credit and retail monopolists), the limited success of its land policies and its rather conventional ('husbandry to hearth') attitudes to the role of women in rural society.[24] But the radical character of the CDB lies in the very concept that it embodied: the need for an independent board dedicated to western economic and social regeneration.[25]

Of course, the CDB didn't 'solve' all the problems of the communities in which it operated. Even during the 1890s serious distress in several western districts prompted traditional relief action from dedicated societies established to respond to the emergency. And agrarian agitation by smallholders against extensive 'ranchers' punctuated the final years of the union.[26] What is incontestable, however, is that the CDB, notwithstanding its limited resources, undertook a wide-ranging programme of activities and schemes to raise living standards in the congested districts and that its efforts were appreciated. The popular memory of the CDB and its numerous schemes of improvement was generally positive.[27]

However, in the decades in which the CDB and constructive unionism sought to effect improvements and to raise living standards in the congested districts, the sense of what the 'west' meant underwent a radical change from an altogether different source. For the leaders of the Irish literary revival and the champions of the Gaelic revival, the 'west', far from being a problem territory needing nursing into the modern world, was elevated as the source of national cultural redemption and renaissance.[28] For the cohort of enthusiasts in the Gaelic League movement, dedicated from the early 1890s to the revival of the Irish language as the dominant vernacular in the country, it is not difficult to see why the 'west', in which were situated the surviving Irish-speaking communities (the Gaeltacht), would assume a unique, not to say sacral, significance. For the predominantly urban and middle-class language-learners of the Gaelic League, the immersion in the Gaeltacht experience was transformative, providing a setting not only for acquiring a grasp of the ancestral language but, in effect, for many, acquiring a new sense of 'belonging' in their own country. The 'west', in the context of the language revival, was the hallowed, uncontaminated ground of the old Gaelic civilisation and the hope of the cultural future that beckoned.

But it was not only the survival of the Gaeltacht communities, largely dispersed along the Atlantic seaboard from Donegal to Kerry, that invested the 'west' with a privileged meaning, as the habitat of the ancient, immemorial, authentic Irish culture. The fascination with the 'communal' – the virtuous community with a close sense of reciprocal obligation and shared welfare – runs through the fictional writings of Canon Sheehan and would colour early anthropological studies of the rural west. The idealisation of an essentially heroic simplicity and integrity constituted the core of the 'hard primitivism' that characterised the society of the Aran and other off-shore islands, and of other western communities, for successive cultural evangelists seeking an escape from – an alternative social milieu to – the increasingly urbanised, individualistic values of advancing consumer capitalism.[29]

This investing of the 'west' with cultural meaning proved enduring and was central to the representation of Ireland as a distinctive tourist brand throughout the decades following the founding of the Irish Free State (IFS). As Catherine Nash has observed, 'Though presented primarily in terms of its physical features, the West's image holds cultural meaning which has been significant in terms of Irish identity and involves issues of how the country has been presented to others and to the state itself.'[30] Tourism strategies revolve around product differentiation. Ireland's attractiveness must, therefore, be seen to reside in its distinctiveness. For cultural nationalists of the Irish revival period (c.1880–1914), as for many tourist promoters in later decades, 'the West came to stand for Ireland in general, to be representative of true Irishness ... a way of access into the Irish past through its language, folklore, antiquities and way of life ...'.[31]

Wild Atlantic Ways 195

The visual representation of landscapes and peasant dwellings characteristic of the west (Paul Henry), or of the rituals, customs, pastimes and physical traits of its people, on land and sea (Jack B. Yeats, Charles Lamb), further reinforced this sense of identity.[32] Nor was celebration of the cultural distinctiveness of the west necessarily incompatible with frank acknowledgment of the social problems of the inhabitants. It was on a commission from the *Manchester Guardian* that J.M. Synge and Jack B. Yeats undertook a month-long tour of congested districts in Connemara and Mayo in June 1905, reporting on the distress in these districts. Yeats provided sketches and drawings to accompany Synge's prose accounts, published serially under the title 'The Congested Districts'.[33]

EPILOGUE

When in 1928 Arthur Balfour described the fledgling Irish Free State as 'the Ireland that we made', his claim did not want for evidence.[34] Key structures and institutions of governance – parliament, representative democracy, the judiciary, the basic shape of the civil service, the system of local government, the centralised apparatus of policing and law enforcement – were all clearly the legacy of the systems of governance that had evolved in the union era. Moreover, the legacy of the land acts of the closing decades of the union (and for which Balfour himself and the governments in which he held office had a considerable measure of responsibility) was a highly dispersed rural society of peasant-proprietors, overwhelmingly stable, conservative and generally resistant to any further convulsions in the countryside. Land hunger had not been assuaged, but land redistribution to smallholders would prove hugely challenging and controversial for successive governments of the new Irish state. However, with regard to the specific measures devised for western regeneration in the twilight years of the union, Balfour's verdict demands qualification.

The CDB was abolished in 1923 – with some of its functions and schemes redistributed among departments of the new Irish Free State. In the half-century after the establishment of the IFS in 1922, all of the counties in the original territory served by the CDB experienced continued population loss at every decennial census.[35] And throughout these decades the continuing population loss, together with the economic retardation and social anaemia that both prompted and followed it, inspired a succession of voluntary groups and community leaders to attempt to mobilise resources (including political interests) in a series of campaigns dedicated to 'saving the West'.[36]

The network of light railways, which had been constructed in the 1890s to reach to the most remote (scenically beautiful but economically retarded) reaches of the Atlantic rim, was not long maintained (still less developed) by the native government. By 1935 the Connemara line was closed, the Achill line in 1937. In the decades that followed, the old track-lines became overgrown and derelict – the silent arches and causeways ghostly relics of earlier ambitions. More than a century after their construction (and more than eighty years after their abandonment) the remnants of these railways to the Atlantic edge have in recent years been recognised (and some have begun to be refurbished) as potential greenways, for walkers and trekkers attracted by environmentally sustainable 'active tourism' in the western districts. Once again, remnants of Balfour's legacy are pressed into service, as the wild Atlantic way beckons.[37]

CHAPTER THIRTEEN

John Hume and the evolution of power-sharing in Northern Ireland

Seán Farren

John Hume, one of the key political leaders in Northern Ireland from the late 1960s until the early 2000s, was an ardent supporter of the case for a mandatory partnership or coalition government for the region. This article discusses the evolution of Hume's thinking over the period 1963–75 with respect to how Northern Ireland should be governed. Hume, then a young schoolteacher in his native city of Derry, entered into public discussion on the issue of how Northern Ireland should be governed in 1964 with a two-part article for the *Irish Times*. Hume argued for a strong opposition to hold the unionist government of Northern Ireland to account. In so arguing he accepted the constitutional status quo whereby the majority party in the Northern Ireland parliament, invariably the pro-British Ulster Unionist Party (UUP), provided the government, with the other parties, mainly representing the nationalist community, assuming the role of opposition. According to Hume, a key weakness in Northern Ireland's parliamentary system was the failure of the main nationalist party to provide the kind of strong opposition he believed was needed.

When first elected to the parliament in 1969, Hume set himself the goal of developing that kind of opposition. To achieve his goal, he joined with other like-minded members on the opposition benches. However, events inside and outside parliament gradually forced Hume to rethink that approach and to move to the conviction that what was needed was

197

a partnership/power-sharing government consisting of representatives from both Northern Ireland's main communities, nationalists as well as unionists. The British and Irish governments also became convinced of this proposition, and for a time in 1974 it seemed as if partnership government would be the answer to building a society in which both communities would work together to the mutual benefit of both, rather than remain in constant conflict. A partnership government of the kind envisaged by Hume was agreed and took office in January that year. But with its collapse only five months later in the face of opposition from extreme unionists and the IRA's campaign of violence, the case for partnership government suffered a severe setback. Furthermore, with the failure of the Northern Ireland Convention in 1975–6 to agree a form of government, the partnership model was put on ice, not to be seriously considered again until the inter-party negotiations leading to the Good Friday/Belfast Agreement in 1998. Then, the partnership approach would be given wide endorsement in 1998 in the referendum on the agreement that same year. Despite several suspensions of the institutions agreed in 1998, the power-sharing/partnership model remains the only basis upon which a regional government can be sustained in Northern Ireland. All the major parties now accept that proposition, even if they do not all agree on the conditions for its implementation.

While John Hume is closely associated with the concept of a power-sharing/partnership government for Northern Ireland – consociationalism to use its technical name – this was not a concept to which he was wedded from the outset of his political career. Indeed, with regard to power-sharing/partnership government in Northern Ireland, when he wrote what many regard as his seminal political article for the *Irish Times*, 18 May 1964, on political relationships within Northern Ireland, he certainly was not. Instead, he clearly accepted that, because unionist MPs always won a majority of the seats in the Northern Ireland parliament, representatives of the unionist community would continue indefinitely to form the government. That meant that representatives of the nationalist community, because they were in the minority, would remain in opposition indefinitely. Nevertheless, Hume did advocate change in the manner politicians behaved towards each other across the political divide, especially in the approach of representatives from his own nationalist community. For those representatives, he argued it was time to abandon what he regarded as their sullen, anti-partitionist approach and, instead, to adopt a more positive approach in which they would, where possible and desirable, cooperate

John Hume and the evolution of power-sharing in Northern Ireland   199

with unionist representatives for the greater good of all in Northern Ireland. His strong advice to nationalist politicians was, therefore, to set aside their emotional flag-waving, their simplistic anti-partitionist, anti-British stance, and what he regarded as the futile abstentionist politics that had them sometimes in and sometimes out of parliament.

In advancing this argument, Hume would have been conscious of the fruitless campaign of the pan-nationalist all-Ireland Anti-Partition League which had petered out in the early 1950s, and of the disastrous IRA (Irish Republican Army) terrorist campaign of the late 1950s which had won little support within the nationalist community and had caused several deaths as well as the destruction of property. Such campaigns, he argued, neither advanced their declared cause of Irish unity, nor addressed the social and economic problems of the nationalist community. Indeed, he excoriated nationalist politicians as a whole for their failure to provide positive leadership:

> They have – quite rightly – been loud in their demands for rights, but they have remained silent and inactive about their duties. In forty years of opposition, they have not produced one constructive contribution, either on the social or economic plane, to the development of Northern Ireland, which is after all a substantial part of the united Ireland for which they strive.[1]

PEOPLE BEFORE TERRITORY

In those remarks Hume expressed what was to become one of his most constant political messages, i.e. a concern for people's well-being above territory. In other words, people mattered, and it was their daily needs and their relationships with their neighbours that should be the primary concern of politicians. Unusual for someone from a nationalist background at the time, he argued the need to develop respect for the unionist tradition and for the need to build bridges between the communities. Doing so, he believed, would gradually convince those opposed to Irish unity that it was a worthwhile and desirable enterprise. In other words, consent based on conviction was an essential ingredient, if a united Ireland was to be achieved.

Given that Hume was writing at a time when inter-communal tensions were lowering, and when, due to the benign effects of the Second Vatican

Council, inter-church relationships were improving worldwide, not least in Northern Ireland, his message resonated more positively than it might have some years previously. So, when some prominent unionist politicians, notably Terence O'Neill, Northern Ireland's prime minister since 1963, were, rather tentatively, expressing a greater willingness to positively recognise the place of nationalists, Hume obviously felt the need to acknowledge the moves and the possibilities they offered for improved community relations. O'Neill, for example, spoke of his commitment to improving the circumstances of all in Northern Ireland:

> ... Today we have to persuade the people of Northern Ireland that we have forward-looking policies which will improve social conditions ... I want all sections of the community to feel committed to the task. It is important to convince more and more people that the Government is working for the good of all in Northern Ireland – not just those who vote Unionist.[2]

Hume seemed to be reciprocating when he wrote that nationalists should:

> ... recognise that the Protestant tradition is as strong and as legitimate as our own. Such recognition is our first step towards better relations. We must be prepared to accept this, and to realise the fact that if a man wishes Northern Ireland to remain part of the United Kingdom it does not necessarily make him a bigot or a discriminator.[3]

PRECURSORS

Hume's views were not completely novel within the nationalist community. Some years earlier G.B. Newe, a prominent Catholic who was secretary of the Northern Ireland Council for Social Service, and a founder member of a cross-community ecumenical group called PACE (Protestant and Catholic Encounter), had expressed similar views at a social studies conference in 1958 and, later, at a conference of Catholic organisations in Belfast in 1963.[4] Newe had called on Catholics to play a greater role in civic society than had hitherto been the case and suggested that the Nationalist Party become the official opposition in the Northern Ireland parliament, views not dissimilar to those expressed by Hume

John Hume and the evolution of power-sharing in Northern Ireland   201

some years later. He argued that the impression Catholics had created among their Protestant and unionist neighbours was that they were not interested in the general welfare of the whole community and were only interested in their own sectional requirements. In the late 1950s Newe's arguments received little by way of a positive response, especially not from nationalist politicians or the press. The nationalist daily, the *Irish News*, was highly critical of the argument that nationalists were, even to some extent, responsible for their own non-participation in civic life. Instead, the *Irish News* put the onus on unionists to let 'kindness, generosity and freedom from bigotry prevail on all sides and not one side alone'.[5] Nevertheless, Newe's views obviously would find a supportive echo from within the nationalist community, some years later, in John Hume's words.

COMMUNITY ACTIVIST

Despite his focus on politics in the *Irish Times* article, throughout most of the 1960s Hume did not directly engage in political activity. Instead, he demonstrated his commitment to addressing local concerns by immersing himself particularly in developing the credit union movement in his home city of Derry, and more widely throughout Ireland, becoming president of the movement in Ireland in 1964. He was also prominently involved in the 'university for Derry' campaign, the Derry Housing Action Committee, and eventually in the civil rights movement through the Derry Citizens' Action Committee. From each he gained very practical experience that prepared him for the commitment to politics that was to be all-consuming during the rest of his public life. So, when he did eventually enter the political arena in 1969, Hume stressed that he envisaged a future in which people of both communities, notwithstanding their political and religious differences, cooperated to create 'a society in Northern Ireland in which Catholic, Protestant and Dissenter can work together to build a new community and base political action on political attitudes rather than use religion as a political weapon'.[6]

This was clearly a very different political message to the traditional nationalist messages which condemned partition, regarded it as an unjustifiable denial of Ireland's 'right' to unity, and, ignoring the long history of sectarian division in Northern Ireland itself, heaped blame for partition exclusively on the British, while eschewing opportunities to cooperate with their unionist neighbours in building a peaceful, prosperous society. For Hume, working together was also the only worthwhile basis upon which the goal of Irish unity could be achieved. He believed that genuine cooperation would develop mutual trust and promote mutual respect for each other's traditions.

POLITICAL ARENA

Hume could not, however, avoid addressing the corrosive effects on community relations of the darker side to life in Northern Ireland. He was well aware that to maintain its political control over Northern Ireland the Ulster Unionist Party frequently disregarded its obligations to equity and justice when it perceived that control to be threatened, however minimally. Employment opportunities were often denied to Catholics in the public sector because they were seen as likely to use such positions to subvert the state, something Hume himself had experienced when he had applied, unsuccessfully, for a position with the local education board in Derry. Blatant discrimination had also produced electoral boundaries intended to ensure that the city's Protestant and unionist minority retained control of the corporation, including the provision of social housing, vital in reinforcing that situation. To these injustices were added the decisions to close some of the city's rail links and to locate Northern Ireland's second university in the predominantly unionist town of Coleraine, and not in Derry which already had a third-level institution, Magee College, that could have been developed into a full university. Action to address these issues propelled Hume towards the political arena and eventually to a reconsideration of his views on the nature of Northern Ireland's government.

With his background of considerable involvement in community work, Hume was urged on several occasions to enter the political arena by prominent nationalist figures in Derry anxious to see a new political leadership emerge there. He eventually agreed to enter the electoral fray when in January 1969 Prime Minister O'Neill called a snap general election to test support for his policies. Hume was nominated to contest the seat held since 1953 by the leader of the Nationalist Party, Eddie McAteer. His manifesto showed that Hume still firmly accepted the traditional government and opposition parliamentary conventions as he committed himself to:

John Hume and the evolution of power-sharing in Northern Ireland   203

... work for the formation of a new political movement based on social democratic principles, with an open membership and an elected executive to allow the people full involvement in the process of decision-making ... The movement must provide what has seriously been lacking at Stormont, namely a strong and energetic opposition to conservatism, and pursue radical social and economic policies.[7]

Hume won the seat but was soon to witness a violent outburst of street politics in his own city that would force him to that reconsideration of how Northern Ireland should be governed. In August 1969, five months after he was elected to the Northern Ireland parliament, the city's Bogside area experienced several days of intense rioting following altercations at the annual demonstration by the Apprentice Boys – an exclusively Protestant organisation – in the city. The police besieged the area in an attempt to quell the riots but met strong resistance from residents armed with petrol bombs and other missiles. When eventually the rioting ceased and order of a kind was restored, British soldiers were on the streets and a new era in Northern Ireland's politics was dawning. As a result, Hume became convinced that constitutional change aimed at involving both communities in decision-making, and political initiatives to eliminate injustice and promote reconciliation and cooperation between the communities, offered the only viable and worthwhile way forward.

CHALLENGING UNIONIST DOMINANCE

If persuading nationalist leaders of the value and, indeed, of the necessity to move from their long-entrenched attitudes and practices was one challenge, persuading unionists was a more formidable one. For unionists, majoritarianism in politics – i.e. the winner takes all – was a fundamental principle. In Northern Ireland, where the region's external boundaries had been established so as to guarantee a unionist majority, that majority had governed at central and at local level on that same principle. The principle was, after all, one which was recognised and accepted in many countries throughout the democratic world. Not surprising then – since majoritarian politics meant the unionist community was always in power and the nationalist community always in opposition – that persuading unionists that the principle ill-suited circumstances in Northern Ireland would not be easy.

For Hume, deciding what form cooperation would take in the political sphere was not something to which he had a ready answer. During his first year or so as a public representative he remained determined to work as effectively as possible within the parameters of traditional parliamentary practices. He made no explicit mention of seeking a role in government for representatives of the nationalist community. However, as Hume's involvement in public affairs intensified, a noticeable change of language became apparent. While not yet fully advocating power-sharing, he began hinting at that possibility. In a submission to the Crowther Commission that was examining devolution possibilities within the UK at the time, Hume described what he believed was a critical fault line in Northern Ireland's politics:

> Normal politics have been impossible and anyone holding the perfectly legitimate view that Ireland should be one political entity has been branded and treated as a disloyal citizen. Where one has a permanent minority with no share in power or in decision-making, then one has a permanent situation of instability, which is likely to produce periodic outbreaks of unrest as people strive by extra-parliamentary means to find what has been impossible by parliamentary channels – a say in moulding the nature of the society in which they live.[8]

In this submission, he was beginning to build the case for a greater say in political decision-making for the 'permanent minority' than was possible in the 'winner takes all' parliamentary practice followed in Northern Ireland. Against the backdrop of growing unrest, inter-communal violence and consequent political instability, there was an increasing emphasis in his remarks on nationalists being excluded from decision-making and, by implication, on the need to address this absence if political stability and inter-communal harmony were to be achieved. Obviously, full cross-community power-sharing would provide the greatest say, but, as yet, he was not in a strong enough political position to advance that proposition, and may not yet have fully accepted the proposition himself. At the time Hume was only one independent voice in the Northern parliament. He still had a party to found, and that became his immediate priority.

Interestingly, in the same submission Hume also argued for regular referenda to test public opinion on the constitutional position of Northern Ireland. He did so in the belief that this would prevent the issue infecting

John Hume and the evolution of power-sharing in Northern Ireland   205

day-to-day politics. It was a proposal that, along with power-sharing, would be formally endorsed in the Good Friday Agreement thirty years later.

A NEW PARTY IS BORN

At the launch of the Social Democratic and Labour Party (SDLP) in August 1970, there was no mention of power-sharing in its basic manifesto. Subject to the principle of consent, the new party accepted the existing constitutional arrangements and emphasised that it would provide strong opposition from a left-of-centre position, and that it would organise and contest elections in every constituency. However, events on the ground and in parliament would soon change the new party's approach. In June 1971, against a background of intensifying paramilitary violence, an opportunity for significant reform seemed to present itself when the Ulster Unionist Party leader Brian Faulkner indicated that he was willing to explore ways in which nationalist representatives might be able to play a greater role in parliamentary decision-making. Faulkner's proposals focused on strengthening the role of parliamentary committees, two of which he suggested could be chaired by members of the opposition. While such a practice is not unusual in parliamentary democracies, from a unionist perspective it appeared to be a significant move towards involving the opposition in decision-making, even if it did not amount to the root and branch reform that Hume and his colleagues had by then begun calling for. For them, the demand was now the replacement of Northern Ireland's constitution, the 1920 Government of Ireland Act, with legislation that would allow nationalists a right to be directly involved in decision-making at the highest – in other words, cabinet – level. They now argued that 'it is time the whole constitutional framework of Northern Ireland was re-examined so that the sections of the community who had not been given a voice in the past could be given an opportunity to express themselves'.[9]

So, while Hume indicated that the SDLP would consider Faulkner's proposals, the party made clear it would only engage in meaningful negotiations if other proposals could be included on the agenda. In the event, following the killing in Derry of two young men by the British army, the SDLP withdrew from parliament when the government refused its request for a public inquiry into the circumstances surrounding the killings. The party's withdrawal was made irreversible when, a few weeks later, the British and Northern Irish governments introduced internment without trial to try to end the growing number of IRA killings and bombings. Hundreds of men were detained and placed in makeshift prison camps, many of whom were subjected to what was later judged by the European Court for Human Rights to have been 'inhuman and degrading treatment' in the course of their interrogation. Northern Ireland teetered on the brink of outright civil war, and the SDLP set about making arrangements to establish an alternative assembly for nationalist representatives. At the same time, at its first annual conference, the party made explicit its demand for fundamental reforms to the manner in which Northern Ireland was governed. Among these reforms were a right for the minority to participate in government and for the establishment of North–South inter-governmental institutions to address all-Ireland concerns. Power-sharing and an Irish dimension had become Hume's and the SDLP's twin constitutional demands. These demands were to be reinforced by a totally unforeseen and extremely tragic occurrence.

A SHARED IRELAND

The formal suspension of devolved government followed the killing of thirteen unarmed civilians at an anti-internment rally in Derry in January 1972 on what became known thereafter as Bloody Sunday. The killings added a considerable urgency to resolving the grave political crisis that was gripping Northern Ireland. Direct responsibility for the region now came under the control of the British government, with immediate responsibility in the hands of Secretary of State William Whitelaw. This meant that, with the proviso of no change in Northern Ireland's position within the UK without the consent of a majority, the slate had been wiped clean as far as any future forms of devolved government were concerned.

The SDLP now engaged in the task of formulating precise proposals for that prospect. These were contained in the party's first policy document, *Towards a New Ireland*.[10] While several hands had a part in drawing up the proposals, John Hume's fingerprints are clearly evident. The document rehearsed his analysis that the Northern state, as then constituted, was inherently unstable, and that only a united Ireland achieved by consent could provide lasting stability. In the meantime, the region should become the joint responsibility of the British and Irish governments and both communities should be jointly involved in its day-to-day governance. In

John Hume and the evolution of power-sharing in Northern Ireland   207

preparation for unity, the SDLP document also proposed that a senate, representative of North and South, be established to administer matters of mutual concern to both parts of the island.

This document was avowedly united Ireland in its content and much more radical than what had been expected from a party that had been preaching partnership and the principle of consent. Hume later admitted that *Towards a New Ireland* was more an opening bid than a position to which the party was firmly wedded, and that despite criticism for being orientated towards a united Ireland, its principles were those of partnership/power-sharing and respect for the will of a majority on the issue of constitutional change. But he added that reforms along lines not dissimilar to those in the SDLP proposals would have to be introduced if the parliamentary process were to regain its primacy in addressing the crisis facing Northern Ireland.

A NEW NORTH

That reform along the lines of the SDLP's partnership proposals would be introduced soon became apparent when in October 1972 Secretary of State Whitelaw published a British government discussion paper, *The Future of Northern Ireland*.[11] The paper indicated that for the return of devolved government 'there are strong arguments that the objective should be achieved by giving minority interests a share in executive power'.[12] In other words, future governments would have to consist of representatives of the nationalist and unionist communities. Furthermore, in a section entitled 'Irish Dimension', the paper argued that a settlement should recognise Northern Ireland's position in Ireland as a whole. Hume and the SDLP's twin demands for government in Northern Ireland and for North–South relations had now received British endorsement. Consequently, they became central to the inter-party negotiations in October 1973 which followed assembly elections earlier in June.

Meantime, in an attempt to allay unionist fears and to try to convince their community that the SDLP believed a partnership, cross-community government was the best means of achieving a better Northern Ireland for all, the party placed an advertisement in the *Irish News* and *Newsletter*, the main voices of the nationalist and unionist communities, respectively. This outreach was unprecedented. Entitled *A Policy for Partnership*, the advertisement argued the value of cross-community dialogue and partnership government in order 'to end forever the sectarian conflict that has caused so much bitterness and suffering throughout our long history'.[13] To answer unionist concerns about nationalists in government, the SDLP stressed its acceptance of the principle of consent for constitutional change, i.e. such change could only come about with the consent of a majority of the electorate in Northern Ireland.

The inter-party negotiations involved the UUP, led by Brian Faulkner, the SDLP, led by party leader Gerry Fitt and his deputy John Hume, and the Alliance Party, led by Oliver Napier and Bob Cooper. They took place against a background of continuing IRA and loyalist paramilitary violence. If Faulkner faced opposition from extreme voices within the unionist community led by the fiery Protestant cleric Ian Paisley, the SDLP also faced opposition from sections of the nationalist community. Like the IRA, this opposition rejected the prospect of any form of devolved government and demanded nothing less than an immediate British declaration that it would withdraw from Northern Ireland within a given time frame.

MINISTERIAL OFFICE

Standing firm against such pressure, the SDLP emerged from the negotiations with three key government departments under its control: Department of Commerce to be held by John Hume, Department of Local Government by Austin Currie, and the Department of Health and Social Services to be held by Paddy Devlin. In addition, the deputy prime minister was to be Gerry Fitt, while two further junior departments were to be held by SDLP politicians. They would all share executive authority with ministers from the UUP and from the Alliance Party. A few weeks later agreement involving the British and Irish governments on establishing a Council of Ireland sealed a set of agreements that were broadly in line with SDLP policies. So, when the new power-sharing executive took office on 1 January 1974, Hume optimistically greeted the new arrangements saying, 'Partnership has replaced conflict as the basis of our political and constitutional thinking. New institutions of government have been set up based on the whole concept of partnership ... It is for us now to use those institutions and the powers they give us to improve the quality of life of our people.'[14]

John Hume and the evolution of power-sharing in Northern Ireland   209

For a short while that optimism appeared justified, and it seemed possible that politicians from both sides of the community could work together. As Minister of Commerce Hume was an enthusiastic ambassador for the new arrangements, along with Prime Minister Brian Faulkner, he opened a new Northern Ireland Office in Brussels, faultlessly addressing a news conference in French. In the US he encouraged business leaders to invest in Northern Ireland, while at home he helped ensure government investment in the Harland & Wolff shipyard, whose workforce was predominantly and often militantly unionist. He and his SDLP colleagues were determined to demonstrate their commitment to working for all.

Despite the efforts of its members to demonstrate their capacity for genuine cross-community government, this power-sharing experiment lasted just over four and a half months. It collapsed when unionist support for it dwindled, caused by exaggerated fears that power-sharing and the Council of Ireland would lead to a united Ireland, fears exacerbated by the ongoing IRA campaign. Unionist opposition to both power-sharing and a Council of Ireland had been loud and determined ever since the publication of Whitelaw's proposals. Throughout the autumn of 1973 while the inter-party negotiations were taking place, at parliamentary and street level unionists opposed to both proposals had made clear that they would use every means to prevent either being realised. Despite what the SDLP said about respecting the principle of consent for constitutional change, and about its policies for partnership government, a large section of political unionism had rejected such assurances.

SECOND CHANCE

A year after the collapse of this first power-sharing experiment, a constitutional convention was convened to explore the possibility of some form of partnership government being restored. Once again, the SDLP provided the sole representatives from the nationalist community. On the unionist side several anti-power-sharing parties combined to form a majority, with the result that the negotiations failed to reach any agreement. It was at the opening session of the convention that Hume delivered one of his most powerful analyses of why a partnership, power-sharing administration was essential. As a pre-condition for that to be effectively achieved, he argued that it was essential that leaders in both communities re-examine their beliefs about each other, and their attitudes towards each other, so as to develop more positive attitudes that would enable them to cooperate in a spirit of true partnership:

> The SDLP challenged both traditions to break with the shackles of the past – they would urge the loyalists to break with the ascendancy and siege mentality and to recognise that their rights and traditions were best protected by their own strength. The loyalists should realise that no constitutional change was possible without their consent. To those who adhered to the Irish dimension the party urged a turning away from a 'spiritual' concept of Ireland which had been used to justify violence and death in an impossible struggle. The SDLP offered a long hard road of partnership to get rid of mutual fears and to enable people to build together a much better new Ireland and new North, through the co-operation and sweat of all our people.[15]

For many, in both communities, more than forty years from Hume's exhortation, that re-examination remains to be undertaken. Not surprising, therefore, that a sense of political instability continues to persist in Northern Ireland. So, while Hume's messages of partnership and power-sharing shaped the Good Friday Agreement, there are still those in both communities who attempt to frustrate the full and wholehearted implementation of that agreement. Critically, they fail to produce a viable alternative, most probably because there is none.

CHAPTER FOURTEEN

Boston's three Irelands: busing, class and Irish ethnic identity, 1970–2015

Matthew O'Brien

In the eyes of many Americans, not least among them its own residents, Boston is a quintessentially 'Irish' city – perhaps the most so of any in the United States. Other metropolitan areas have their Irish-American neighbourhoods, often sites of previous settlement during periods of immigration, such as Beverly on the South Side of Chicago, Woodlawn in the Bronx, or Kensington in Philadelphia. Yet few cities come close to the pervasive citywide influence that the Boston Irish enjoy, putting hardnosed Dorchester and Charlestown at the forefront rather than genteel Brookline or Cambridge. Whether it has to do with the basketball Celtics, the Kennedy political dynasty or Irish-flavoured bands like the Dropkick Murphys, the association between Boston and Irish America distinguishes it, ethnically speaking, as the greenest city in America.

Yet this identification sits uncomfortably with another identification of Boston, left over from the 1970s, as the 'Birmingham of the North'. In a city that served as the birthplace of the National Association for the Advancement of Colored People (NAACP) and counted Booker T. Washington, W.E.B. Dubois and pre-conversion Malcolm X (nee Malcolm Little) among its residents, the stock image of Irish ethnic pugnacity often conveyed, and conveys, a more ominous tone. The accompanying violence appeared in newspaper photographs of South Boston protestors throwing rocks at school buses of incoming African-

211

American kids in Dorchester Square, or the iconic and disturbing shot of 'The Soiling of Old Glory', where a young white man attacked an African-American bystander with a pole bearing the American flag. These images drew condemnations from Irish activists such as Bernadette McAliskey, and retain their shocking force today.[1] Long after the putative rehabilitation of the cities of the 'New South' (such as Atlanta or New Orleans), the ironic sobriquet of 'the Deep North' seems explainable mainly through the atavistic nature ascribed to the Boston Irish.

It is interesting, therefore, that among the many references to the Boston Irish as an ethnic bogeyman, there has been little work done by historians of Irish ethnicity on the accuracy of such an image. This is not necessarily surprising given the hagiographical work of the 1960s and 1970s, with its laudatory portrayal of fair-minded public officials and dedicated citizens. Nevertheless, the reflexive condemnation by the ensuing whiteness school was only marginally closer to the truth of the story, at least in terms of the summary indictment it made of the city, and through that, Irish America as a whole.

Nearly thirty-five years after its initial publication, J. Anthony Lukas' monumental account, *Common Ground*, remains the best resource for understanding the Irish ethnic dimension(s) of the conflict, expressed alongside its penetrating accounts of the legal principles, political dimensions, and exploration of the sociological ramifications of neighbourhood gentrification.[2] But as perhaps the most chimeric aspect of Lukas' analysis, most subsequent retellings have elided the intra-class antagonisms between the suburban 'two-toilet Irish' of the middle-class suburbs and the 'shanty Irish' of the urban enclaves. More recent critical accounts of Irish America, in particular, have dismissed the ethnic background of the chief architect of the busing programme, Judge W. Arthur Garrity, as well as its defenders, such as State Board of Education lawyer Sandra Lynch and Senator Ted Kennedy, as well as its (admittedly reluctant) chief administrator, Mayor Kevin White. On the whole, most accounts seem to accept the claims of ethnic authenticity made by the opponents of busing at face value, treating the predominantly Irish-American composition of the obstructionist Boston School Committee as a facile indication.

The fractious nature of this relationship goes even deeper than the evocative descriptions offered by Lukas, as shown in a number of letters that appeared in collections of correspondence to Judge Garrity, Mayor White and others. One Boston letter-writer offered the ethnically

Busing, class and Irish ethnic identity, 1970–2015   213

invested declaration that the judge had 'disgraced the name of Garrity' for his decision.[3] Another writer 'of Irish descent and proudly so' explained that she or he was 'distressed to see fellow "clansmen" so vehemently on the other side of this case', especially since the correspondent '[knew] the vehemence that division causes within the family, Catholic, Irish and Jesuit'.[4] Another item from a Cambridge resident 'with Irish blood' copies an item the correspondent had written to local papers, supporting Garrity with quotations from John Boyle O'Reilly about the laudatory qualities of African-Americans from the Boston *Pilot*.[5]

One full-throated letter of support for Judge Garrity, written under the pseudonym 'A White Irish American', praised Garrity's decision as 'inspired, courageous and positive'. This stood in contrast to the correspondent's condemnation of the 'South Boston mentality', declaring that its 'hostility is vented upon a broad scope of people, to include any and all obvious non-residents of their area' and condemning the leadership of 'educators and politicians in So. Boston'.[6]

The letters to Mayor White that invoked Irishness were even more strongly worded and returned fire over authenticity by invoking the working-class backgrounds of the protestors. A letter from Roxbury praised 'Boston's very well behaved and law abiding Black Community', while conversely condemning the 'stupid manner' and 'racist tactics' of 'South Boston's Irish Community'. Calling for an end of efforts to 'molly-coddle' the 'South Boston Irish' and their 'racebaiting leadership of Louise Day Hicks and other racist oriented politicians', the writer referred to the injustices inflicted on previous generations of Irish arrivals during 'Yankee vs. Irish' conflicts. Using the insider terminology of Irish-American ethnics, the letter castigated the '*cruel* and *bestial* "shenanigans" of South Boston's *non-lace curtain Irish*' [author's emphasis], noting the leadership role of older adults on children as speculating that the education of those involved 'certainly must have stopped at about the six [*sic*] grade level'. Finally, the writer concluded, 'This must certainly have been somewhat of an embarrassment to the better educated Irish People.'

These letters offer reflections of individual perspectives on Irish-American ethnicity and busing. In an attempt to pursue a wider, more collective base of evidence and more directly address the role of socioeconomic class in this relationship, the rest of this paper will examine the attitudes that have appeared in three specific publications: the *South Boston Tribune*, the *Boston Irish News*, and the *Boston Irish Reporter*, each of which offers a specific and distinct view of the busing crisis.

SOUTH BOSTON IRISHNESS IN THE 1970S

Although the first of these newspapers, the *South Boston Tribune*, lacked an overt identification with Irish ethnicity, it unmistakably reflected the pervasive and profound identification that most of the residents in Southie felt with Ireland. Founded in the early 1930s, the *Tribune* boasted a self-reported circulation of over 10,000 copies on a weekly basis that gave it an estimated audience of between 30,000 and 40,000 readers – an impressive figure that nearly equalled the entire population of South Boston. There was little question about the ethnic orientation of the *Tribune* as well, reflected in the shamrocks that often adorned advertisements, to the more developed pageantry of the special annual Saint Patrick's Day double-issue, filled with political advertisements and pictures from the iconic holiday parade.

The specific nature of this identification was not quite straightforward, however, as the link to Ireland reflected a reconstructed transatlantic connection.[7] Judging from the surnames of the residents of South Boston, as well as other details from many of the self-provided genealogies, most of the later-generation Irish-Americans in that neighbourhood had ancestral roots in the western or southern counties of Connacht or Munster, with particular concentrations from Galway, Cork, Kerry and Clare. Nevertheless, in the wake of the Troubles and the advent of the busing crisis, the South Boston Irish instead turned to the six counties of Northern Ireland to define their ethnic home, as exemplified by Northern Irish-style wall murals found in the neighbourhood.[8]

This identification also offered inspiration (at least initially) for Michael Patrick MacDonald in his powerful account of coming of age during the busing crisis, *All Souls: A family story from Southie*. As they moved their belongings into South Boston, MacDonald described his mother excitedly pointing out 'all the shamrock graffiti and IRA and Irish Power spray-painted everywhere, and said it looks just like Belfast and that we were in the best place in the world' – a memory that comes back especially vividly to the narrator during the busing riots.[9] Later, when trying to explain the appeal of rioting, MacDonald mentioned that the quixotic nature of the protests 'made us even more like the Irish, who were always fighting in the songs even if they had to lose and die a glorious death'.[10] In other ways, MacDonald explained the familiar demonisation of the villainous supporters of busing, who were initially tarred as communists, then 'rich English' and then 'White Anglo-Saxon Protestants'.[11]

Busing, class and Irish ethnic identity, 1970–2015   215

The *South Boston Tribune* also carried these well-worn descriptions of the busing conflict, defining 'authentic' Irishness as the exercise of neighbourhood loyalty through the expression of ethnic pugnacity. Whether it was the verbal fusillades emanating from anti-busing leader Louise Day Hicks, the fiery rhetoric of politician Jim Kelley, or the erudite indignation of sophisticated orators like state senator William Bulger, this willingness to mix it up 'for a good cause' served as the cardinal virtue of the South Boston Irish for *Tribune* readers. As one letter to the paper declared, Ted Kennedy's support for busing was not only disappointing, but disqualifying, as it stood in contrast to the virtues of his 'splendid' brothers Jack and Robert, who 'understood what it meant to fight for a principle.' The theme of fighting also emerged in a column reprinted from the *Patriot Ledger* by Rev. John McMahon of Quincy, which the editorial praised as 'an excellent analysis of the whole subject'. In it, McMahon explained that the members of the anti-busing movement were 'fighting for the restoration of their own alienated rights', couched in the context of the American Revolution, but readily identifiable in the context of Irish-American patriotism.

This mutually reinforcing complement of loyalty and fighting also offered a means to disqualify suburban Irish-Americans who were supportive or even lukewarm in their opposition to busing. In one editorial, titled 'Get Them Out!', the paper took a break from civic-minded admonitions to citizens with overdue public library books to rail against 'these suburbanites, who don't want any part of our problems, who lecture us about them in the venal metropolitan press, [and] who heave their bags of garbage onto our sidewalks in the dead of night!' Other criticisms got more personal, with a special bitterness towards Irish-American advocates of busing. In his occasional column in the *South Boston Tribune*, written under the title of 'Community', a young Ed Forry singled out Congressman Michael Harrington from Salem for his 'bias' and 'political hypocrisy' in sending his children to private schools while 'blindly suggest[ing] that court-ordered busing is right for everyone else's children'. But the chief figure of ridicule, besides 'Wendell from Wellesley' (as Southie critics called Garrity), was Teddy Kennedy, whose invited appearance at a Knights of Columbus communion breakfast in Quincy drew a hostile crowd of more than 200 protestors.

Finally, the *Tribune* seldom referred directly to Ireland, but it shared in the neighbourhood's view that the Troubles (which had entered an increasingly dark time by the mid-1970s) were central to its ethnic identification. In addition to occasional announcements about meetings of the Irish Northern Aid society (Noraid), there were pieces such as the call for readers to attend a Noraid benefit concert by Sean Roche and his Irish-American showband. Given the prominence of a front-page article, the author confidently wrote, 'I'm sure that we will all be happy that we were able to help support this struggle for freedom.' This appears with another announcement, about a performance of the purposefully named 'Irish Volunteers', in an advertisement presented on a shamrock background.

By the spring of 1976, about a year after the peak of South Boston's opposition to busing, the *Tribune* took on an increasingly exhausted tone. The paper's decline was partially hidden by its self-reported circulation estimates, and in the early 1980s its half-century run of publication came to an end. (During its waning years, the South Boston Information Center (SBIC) would attempt to print a more overtly politicised monthly publication, named *The Marshal* after the self-designated title of SBIC workers, but this only lasted for a handful of issues.)

RESPECTABILITY AND THE *BOSTON IRISH NEWS*

As the *South Boston Tribune* began its descent in the mid-1970s, it was passed by another Irish-American publication that had emerged during the waning years of the busing crisis, the *Boston Irish News*. With a monthly publication schedule that allowed for more columns and fewer short-term announcements, the *Boston Irish News* started out with an initial run of 5,000 copies. Its publisher, Don Mooney, arrived with a network of support drawn from his previous careers as a lounge singer and a sergeant in the Boston Police Department. Mooney took an unusual approach in his self-described attempt to establish 'a journal of opinion', offering the paper for free and relying entirely on advertising revenue rather than subscriptions.[12]

The *Boston Irish News* also took a different tack in courting readers, pursuing a geographically expansive middle-class audience. In an early issue Mooney announced that he envisioned a readership that spread to expand beyond city or even state boundaries, in contrast to the intensely local focus of the *South Boston Tribune*. Reaching out to 'the greater Boston Irish community', the paper's coverage would be 'by no means limited to the city limits nor to the metropolitan area', extending to southern New

Busing, class and Irish ethnic identity, 1970–2015

Hampshire, Maine, Vermont and Connecticut in a bid 'to reach as many Irish homes or places of congregation as possible'.[13]

The break with its predecessors was not complete, however, and there were signs of the archetypal Irish-American pugnacity in the first issue, such as a front-page story by Dick Sinnott that seemed to share the *Tribune*'s occasional defensiveness. With a long local reputation as a conservative commentator, Sinnott also brought established credentials as a fiery defender of neighbourhood mores, first in a public career as Boston's last official city censor and then later as a talk radio host and a columnist for several neighbourhood newspapers in the city. The article began with an appeal to ethnic boosterism, calling for the construction of a public memorial to the iconic Irish-American politician James Michael Curley. Throughout his hagiography, Sinnott offered occasional grievances and derogatory references to liberalism, bemoaning the free-spending reputation of 'Taxachusetts' and condemning 'a sick society [that] saluted persons named Jerry Rubin or Fr Groppi'.[14]

The larger context of the new enterprise showed up more effectively in an unsigned statement of purpose, presumably written by Don Mooney, titled 'The *Boston Irish News*: Two major goals'. Reaching back a bit further than Sinnott by invoking the spirit of St Brendan and 'an Irish navigator named McGuire', the article seemed to share some of Sinnott's dissatisfaction in its criticism of 'the public and sectarian press of the Hub' for its 'deficient' and 'inaccurate analysis of Irish activities'. Yet Mooney's message was more aspirational than reactionary, declaring that the new paper would focus on 'Ireland's social and cultural heritage as it is retained in varying degrees in New England', with coverage that was 'politically objective, socially aware and culturally attentive'. Reaching beyond the embattled provincialism of ethnic Boston in the mid-1970s, the *News* sought to 'rekindle a pride in [Irish] heritage by focusing on those achievements and influences which can be traced to Ireland in origin'.

Later in the first issue, the *News* provided the means by which this enlightenment would take place. A tribute to Dr Eoin McKiernan cited the renowned scholar as an exemplary apostle, praising his public addresses 'on college campuses, at Rotary and other service club meetings … about the true Ireland and the part the Irish played in the development of the US'. Another story celebrated the recent foundation of a Boston chapter of the Dublin-based Comhaltas Ceoltóirí Éireann, with its mission of promoting and preserving traditional Irish music and dance. Working from such stories of inspiration, the paper also wasted no time calling for an umbrella organisation that might link the many pre-existing Irish cultural, athletic and social groups in Boston, and informed readers about Irish-language instruction in the city as well an Irish-language mass in West Roxbury. Although the paper insisted to its readers that there were no prerequisites for beginners in these programmes, it was clear that the *News* was aiming for a middle-class audience.

This deliberate distinction appeared in the first issue's editorial tribute to the Irish immigrants of the 1950s. The paper hailed them as 'a window to the real Ireland, one not influenced by pseudo-nostalgic strains which originated in places like Tin Pan Alley'. Twenty years later, 'their discernment has spurred interest in Irish culture', and 'Saint Patrick's Day is returning to a status of honorable festivity in many areas where it is again fashionable to be Irish and sober at the same time'. The creation of a new cultural centre would further bolster this trend, since 'the many Irish enclaves which perpetuate the purer traditions of this heritage are much stronger in number than they realize themselves'.[15]

Although the *News* avoided direct discussions of the busing fight, which its opponents had lost through attrition by the late 1970s, there was a certain timeliness to its contributors' attempts to get the Boston Irish to expand their perspectives. In his column titled 'On Being Irish, in Boston and America', John Tracy McGrath cited an old admonition from his father regarding the core of Irish-American ethnicity, 'There's not much point in being Irish … unless you're smart.' As McGrath wrestled with the 'terrifying and wonderful' assimilative pressures that accompanied upward mobility, he called for his counterparts to return to certain traditional ethnic attributes, such as the Irish 'excellence and pride in the arts', 'love of learning' and 'a hunger for social justice'. McGrath followed up the standard warnings about materialism and complacency by calling for his readers to step outside their anachronistic enclaves. Offering an ethnic *examen*, the author called the Boston Irish to ask themselves whether they 'still act clannish and self-protective' or 'allow our politicians to dance away to the sound of bugle calls of other wars now long gone and won'. For McGrath, being 'smart' meant being self-aware, offering the warning that 'when Irish-Americans now recall their great heritage, they must be sure that their pride is pride and not merely prejudice'. Avoiding ethnic chauvinism and the demagoguery that constrained so many South Boston Irish, McGrath's narrative of Irish-American ascension shifted the basis of Irish-American authenticity from reflexive neighbourhood loyalties to a deeper appreciation of past ideals.

Busing, class and Irish ethnic identity, 1970–2015

The paper's coverage of Ireland reinforced this message of contrast with Southie. Although the paper occasionally carried pictures of 'Brits Out' protests and announced Noraid meetings, Mooney's opening announcement quickly disabused any readers who might be looking for IRA support: 'Before anyone jumps to premature conclusions, let it be established that the goal here is not to set up a new political party, or to rally local Irishmen for some military campaign.' In a swipe at disaffected members of the conservative right and paramilitary sympathisers, Mooney brusquely informed his audience that such long-held dreams had 'about as much a chance of success as a Nixon comeback'.[16]

For the *News*, most Irish coverage focused on Dublin rather than Belfast. The lead headline of the first issue celebrated a visit from Massachusetts governor Michael Dukakis, and later society columns constantly featured notices about Bostonians visiting their 'home counties', usually in Munster and Connacht. This focus on the Republic also pertained to political coverage, with regular attention to the decisions of the Fine Gael and Fianna Fáil governments. When Northern Ireland appeared in the paper, writers treated it as innately tragic rather than heroic, sometimes with more than a trace of middle-class American condescension. When the *News* called for Irish-American engagement, it largely eschewed calls for boycotts or potentially disruptive protests about the Troubles and instead appealed to self-designated roles as guardians and proponents of Irish culture. Even then, the paper's call for Irish-American influence stressed elements of propriety rather than summoning disruptive protestors. When the *News* called for mounting an appeal to the Irish government in order to include Boston on an upcoming national tour by the Book of Kells, the call framed any activism in a strictly respectable framework. While less-refined groups were ready to mount unruly picket lines, the paper announced that 'we advocate no demonstrations in this regard', since 'a simple petition should suffice' with well-placed letters and calls to follow up the effort.

This determined but respectable tone also pertained to domestic issues in Boston, as the *News* made its judicious case for inclusion within institutions that *Tribune* writers portrayed as innately hostile and worthy only of scorn. The regular 'Irish Rover' column, for instance, often pushed for recognition from the city's pro-Garrity newspaper of record in Boston, pointedly asking, 'Does the *Boston Globe* really have an Irish reporter?' The same was true for colleges, with relentless agitation about the lack of funding for Irish students everywhere from the state university system to Harvard University (where the columnist pressed for more public recognition of the Celtic Studies programme), and even the Massachusetts Council on Arts and Humanities. An optimistically titled article by Gaelic Club member John McGrath also proudly provided an account of the recent history of the Harvard programme, including the extension courses taught on the Irish language.[17]

Although the *Boston Globe* estimated the paper's circulation at 40,000 copies, its status as a free publication probably made for a smaller readership than would be accorded to a subscription newspaper.[18] By 1989 this figure had dropped by half, and the average length of Mooney's publication had shrunk to twelve pages, except for its annual triple-sized issue for Saint Patrick's Day. Although he remained optimistic about the Irish ethnic market in general, Mooney closed the *News* the next year in the midst of an economic recession. But if the Irish-American readership seemed to be losing momentum, the arrival of the 'New Irish' immigrants, many of them undocumented, brought a new generation of Irish-born readers, and bolstered the circulation of two New York-based weeklies, the *Irish Voice* and *Irish Echo*, with their self-reported Boston circulation of 8,000 and 7,500, respectively.[19]

THE *BOSTON IRISH REPORTER*

Within a year of the closure of Mooney's publication, another monthly paper stepped into the gap. This time the new paper, the *Boston Irish Reporter*, combined some of the neighbourhood elements of the *South Boston Tribune* with the self-criticism of the *Boston Irish News*. By the end of the following year, however, a veteran local reporter had stepped into the gap. Founded by longtime Boston journalist Ed Forry and his wife Mary Casey Forry, the *Boston Irish Reporter* pledged to 'Tell the Stories of Boston's Irish'.[20] For Ed, this was somewhat familiar territory, given his publication record in a number of neighbourhood papers, including the *Tribune*.

The *Boston Irish Reporter* cultivated this image of neighbourhood paper from the start. The paper's roots came from Forry's initial publishing venture, the *Dorchester Reporter*, which he launched in 1982 under a masthead that promised 'The News and Values around the Neighborhood' and a front-page declaration that 'the main goal of the *Reporter* is to provide information to you – about your church, your school, your neighborhood, your local merchants'. Twenty-five years later, the special

Busing, class and Irish ethnic identity, 1970–2015

anniversary issue noted the pride that Ed Forry took in the awards that recognised the *Dorchester Reporter* as a beacon of community journalism, including the designation of 'Boston's Best Neighborhood Newspaper' from a local Boston publication.[21]

The neighbourhood ethos also came through in the *Reporter*'s regular features on local figures, which frequently invoked ethnic points of reference from Dorchester and nearby South Boston, such as Catholic parishes, the Old Harbor housing projects, or the unofficial South Boston anthem, 'Southie Is My Hometown'. Nearly without fail, the paper held up honourees for their exemplary blend of humility and loyalty conveyed in the cardinal virtue of 'never forgetting where they came from'.

Yet the *Reporter* was more than just a mere throwback, and these tributes often included progressive messages about race relations. A 2012 feature on Dorchester-born MSNBC host Lawrence O'Donnell mentioned his father's willingness to reach across racial lines as a lawyer, including a willingness to take on the Boston Police Department for a wrongful death case involving an African-American victim. Acknowledging 'the prevailing racial animosities that were at an all-time high in the mid-to-late 70s in Boston', the *Reporter* cited this case as a crucial moment for O'Donnell's career as a writer, sending him on a nationwide campaign to investigate police shootings of African-American men.[22] The paper's profiles of Fr Richard 'Doc' Conway and Fr William Francis, for example, specifically praised them for their bravery during the busing crisis, as they rode alongside African-American schoolchildren on the buses that were targeted by rock-throwing locals.[23] In the case of Fr Francis, the *Reporter* explicitly noted that he 'bucked the stereotype of the intolerant Southie Irishman', and continued to call for the church to make overdue accommodations to recognise the growing presence of new ethnic and racial groups in formerly Irish parts of Dorchester.[24]

If the *Boston Irish Reporter* was another neighbourhood paper, it nevertheless involved a redefinition of the conventional (racially homogenous) understanding of a neighbourhood. This became even more apparent with the addition of Ed Forry's son Bill, who joined the staff of the *Reporter* not long after graduating from Boston College. When told about the longstanding separation between the African-American and Haitian neighbourhoods in North Dorchester and the Irish-American concentration in South Dorchester, the younger Forry replied, 'Well, some of us are working for it to be one Dorchester, and the more folks talk about divisions, the harder it will be to change.'[25]

In fact, the *Reporter*'s racially inclusive approach to Dorchester also reflected a larger demographic trend within the city, as a new wave of immigrants arrived during the late 1980s and 1990s. While the so-called 'New Irish' obviously drew the most attention, the undocumented status of many of these new arrivals evoked an ecumenical approach from the *Reporter*, which adopted the same spirit of open-ended advocacy that marked new organisations like the Irish Immigrant Center (IIC). As the number of immigrants of colour from Central America, the Caribbean and Asia grew significantly, the *Reporter* revived a diasporic understanding of Irish identity that distinguished the paper from its immediate predecessors, joining a groundswell of publications and radio programmes in the early 1990s that increased the number of foreign-language news outlets in the area to more than thirty.[26]

This trend was particularly apparent in the comparisons that the *Reporter* made between Irish immigrants and their Haitian counterparts. An early column by an Irish-born correspondent, Colm Renehan, provided an account of the poverty and desperation that he saw in Haiti during a trip that included IIC members. The experience led Renehan to reassert the role that the hardships of migration had played in forming the identity of the Boston Irish community, noting the 'great collective historic memory we all, as Irish men and women, share with this desperate oppressed people'. Writing that 'our prosperity and future security depends entirely on our refusal to allow such events to recur', Renehan insisted that it was incumbent on readers to 'recall to memory our own experience of fear and flight and demand an end to the government's complicity in, and support of, this island people's suffering'.[27] A decade later, a Haitian-born contributor, Caleb DesRosiers, completed the loop with reflections on his trip to Ireland.[28] The topic of Irish-American leadership once again appeared in the Irish ethnic press, but now it was a model cited by aspiring Haitian arrivals such as DesRosiers, who told the *Reporter*'s readers, 'Progress is slow, but we are working on it and have been impressed with the Irish-American model.'

The *Reporter* also proudly covered a production of the 'Annual Black and Green' celebrations during the 1990s, jointly sponsored by the IIC and the Monserrat Aspirers.[29] The paper's coverage of the Boston Peace Conference in 2000 also carried a theme of inclusion and Irish ethnic identification with the developing world. Although the *Reporter*'s correspondent mentioned the Irish delegates to this women's conference, she noted that the group included Irish Protestants as well as Catholics, and

Busing, class and Irish ethnic identity, 1970–2015   223

brought them into a larger context with references to the Sudanese women and those from eight other countries who gathered at the conference.[30]

At the same time, however, the *Reporter* was still sensitive to perceived slights as the voice of an urban neighborhood. For instance, the paper remained understandably critical of the decades-old decision by city planners to build an expressway that cut through Dorchester in order to link downtown Boston with the affluent suburbs to the south. Second, when *Boston Magazine* published a cover in April 1998 that labelled Henry Louis Gates as 'Harvard's Head Negro in Charge', the *Reporter*'s condemnation noted that the offending publication aimed for 'an exclusive, upscale mostly suburban audience'. Furthermore, the paper decried the magazine cover's derogatory portrayal of Henry Louis Gates as 'pointing the finger of racism at city people who live in Boston's neighborhoods'. Defending its constituency, the *Reporter* admitted, 'There are certain divisions in our society, and they include issues of class, economics, geography and race. But in our city, in our neighborhoods, let it be clear – *Boston Magazine*'s hateful cover story's words do not reflect the attitudes of the great majority of Boston's neighborhood people.'[31]

This defensiveness also extended to portrayals of Dorchester and South Boston in the media, such as television reporter Sean Flynn's book *Boston D.A.* Taking umbrage with Flynn's declaration that 'the Irish heritage [in Southie] becomes an Irish caricature, and a mean one at that', Bill Forry argued that Flynn was pushing an anachronistic view that dated back to 'right around 1975', and reflected 'the mind of somebody whose fundamental perception of Boston and its people was minted in the Gerry Ford administration'. The split between the city neighbourhoods and the more affluent suburbs also surfaced in his accusation that Flynn shared the tendency among 'too many of his colleagues [to] write with a suburban audience in mind and [is] eager to play into the sprawlers' worst fears of city squalor'. As a corrective, Forry offers the overlooked story of 'the broad integration of neighborhoods like ours, which "dared" to defy the myth of parochial Boston and have lived to tell about it'.[32]

REVISITING BUSING

No matter how momentous these demographic changes, however, they were not enough, in and of themselves, to address the legacy of the busing crisis and the lingering divisions between African-Americans

224   *Navigating Historical Crosscurrents in the Irish Atlantic*

and Irish-Americans in the urban enclaves most dramatically affected by Judge Garrity's programme. Reliance on the passage of time or a shift in generational understanding is simply insufficient, creating, at best, a gap in memory or, at worst, outright denial. Thus, it was the necessity of full engagement with the issue of Boston Irish racism that made the contribution of the *Boston Irish Reporter* all the more important, especially as it came from founder and publisher Ed Forry.

This willingness to engage with the original sin of American society came to the fore for the *Reporter* in 2004. As the city of Boston approached the thirty-year anniversary of the busing crisis, a couple of well-publicised comments by prominent critics of the city on racial issues drew intense public attention. At the same time, most commentators viewed the last three decades as a time of loss and disillusionment for the Boston public school system, with declining enrolment and still-damaged morale.

Rather than engaging in *schadenfreude* with busing proponents (as a number of other commentators did), Ed Forry bucked convention to hold up a mirror to the Irish of South Boston and Dorchester. When two prominent African-Americans made controversial remarks about Boston's racist reputation in the summer of 2004, Forry broke with the reflexive defensiveness that had characterised the standard reaction from Southie (and Dorchester) during the previous thirty years.

The first step in this process came with an admission. Although Forry mentioned the negative reputation of one of the sources, baseball player Barry Bonds, who had never actually visited the city, Forry then acknowledged the deeper cause of this criticism. The hard truth was that 'millions of black Americans' saw Boston as 'the Birmingham of the North, a reputation that was recklessly but sturdily built rock-by-rock, brick-by-brick by the morons who played target practice with yellow buses 30 years ago'. In fact, Forry moved beyond this admission with the deeper assertion that 'some of the same clowns are still out there, only now they're wearing suits and masquerading as respective citizens'. Repeating the observation of an expat friend who now lived in Atlanta, Forry declared that Boston's reputation for racism continued as a self-inflicted wound, since 'too many Bostonians like to pretend like the 1970s never happened'.[33]

Although Forry noted that 'both sides are living a lie', his call went beyond drawing a moral equivalence. Describing another African-American critic's visit to South Boston as 'a brave, and perhaps, appropriate gesture', the veteran reporter-turned-publisher contrasted this with the lack of such valour among the 'supremely self-righteous, "we-told-you-so"

Busing, class and Irish ethnic identity, 1970–2015   225

anti-busing crowd whose irresponsible leadership, on the streets and in the hearing rooms of the city, triggered the turmoil in the first place'. Laying the blame for the controversy ultimately at the feet of local politicians like Jimmy Kelly, the longstanding South Boston president of the city council who 'pooh-poohed the violence at Dorchester Heights', Forry cited Kelly's recent reaction to the comments in the *Boston Herald*, noting the effect of such words in light of the persistent image of Boston's racism.[34]

Moving on to an event at the Old State House marking the release of Judge Garrity's papers, Forry mentioned the retrospective insights offered by a former state senator, Jim Hennigan. Although he was on the record as opposing busing, Hennigan nevertheless played the part of Cassandra on the Boston School Committee in 1971 when he warned his fellow committee members about the doomed nature of anti-integrationist obstructionism. Standing up to protestors 'who cursed his name', Hennigan presciently warned of the repercussions that would come from refusing to integrate existing schools – a course of action happily taken by the subsequent leaders of the anti-busing movement Louise Day Hicks, Dapper O'Neill and John Kerrigan, whose demagoguery as members of the Boston School Committee Forry would blame for the crisis.

Forry's column concluded by calling for South Boston's leaders, and his readers in general, to confront their own role in the crisis. The passage of time, as Forry warned, was not enough. Instead, there needed to be honest disclosures about the 'cavalcade of men, and at least one woman, who were regularly picked to run our affairs over more than a decade', for their willingness to '[run the schools] into the ground, blatantly and deliberately discriminating against black children to soothe the racist fears of the voters'. On a wider scale, Forry said, 'Boston's largely white citizenry of the era has to take some responsibility' for the election of such officials. Calling for a deeper responsibility, the publisher of the *Irish Reporter* argued that this moral reckoning was both necessary and long overdue: 'Blaming some out-of-towner for our ills isn't the answer. It's time to start talking honestly about what happened. Until then, the "new Boston" will be nothing more than a cheap conventioneer's slogan.'[35]

CONCLUSION: THE BOSTON IRISH, AND RECONCILIATION

When J. Anthony Lukas published his monumental account of the Boston busing crisis, *Common Ground*, in 1985, it offered a kaleidoscopic view of race relations in that city. Nearly forty years on, however, there has been surprisingly little follow-up work, and almost nothing from ethnic historians, leaving Michael Patrick MacDonald's powerful memoir, *All Souls*, as the best historical work out there. This gap is especially striking in Irish Studies, where the question of racial violence of the 1970s has been presented as an indictment of the entire city, or even Irish America as a whole, but somehow deserving of little exploration or substantive analysis. In some ways, it is a version of the 2016 presidential election that remains unopened and unexplored nearly four decades later.

Although it is tempting to dismiss the Irish of South Boston as a whole as being motivated by atavistic racism – a kind of 'ur-deplorables' – a serious look at Southie uncovers seemingly incongruent facts. Judging from the hostile reaction to an NAACP float in the 1964 St Patrick's Day parade, the history of South Boston's racism extended much further back than the imposition of Judge Garrity's infamous busing order.[36] But so did the political progressiveness of its national political leadership – the foremost of whom, speaker of the house John McCormack, spent much of the peak years of his career pushing forward anti-lynching legislation in the 1950s and '60s.[37] Nor was this a mere outlier: Joe Moakley, one of McCormack's successors in the South Boston congressional seat, spent much of his political career fighting for human rights in Central America.

The perceived contradictions between progressive convictions and neighbourhood loyalties can never be fully reconciled until the partisans of each side come down from their rhetorical ramparts, abandoning the archetypal Irish-American resistance to self-analysis. When this happens, it will be in large part due to the moments of candour, conscience and self-examination that we have seen in the *Boston Irish Reporter*.

PART 3

Bridging Atlantic Worlds

CHAPTER FIFTEEN

'forever one and the same person'

Thomas E. Hachey

C atherine Shannon is indeed an abundantly worthy academic to be honoured with a *festschrift*, the German extraction connoting a collection of celebratory writings. Unsurprisingly, Professor Shannon was herself invited to be a contributor to earlier *festschrifts* honouring two notably distinguished women scholars, they also in the field of Irish Studies, namely Dr Margaret MacCurtain (in 1997) and Professor Maureen Murphy (in 2011). Even a quick review of Shannon's academic and other professional activities clearly confirms the merit in having a *festschrift* produced celebrating her distinctively varied and decidedly meritorious accomplishments.

Shannon first matriculated for a bachelor of arts degree, with a concentration in history, at the University of Toronto from which she graduated in 1960. She subsequently enrolled as a graduate student at University College Dublin, NUI, and graduated in 1963, with honours and a master of arts degree. Her master's thesis was entitled 'The Irish Local Government Act of 1898: The politics and administration', a subject that has remained an integral part of her multiple research interests to the present day.

Catherine began her teaching career in 1964 at a public secondary school in Holbrook, Massachusetts, but left three years later upon obtaining a full-time appointment as an instructor in the Department of History at Westfield State College. By 1971 she had advanced to the rank of assistant professor while also engaged in the early beginnings of a doctoral programme at the University of Massachusetts, Amherst. She graduated from that school in 1975 with a PhD in a programme that focused on modern Irish and British history. Her dissertation was entitled 'Arthur J. Balfour and the Irish Question, 1874–1922'.

Dr Shannon had, of course, begun her long career of academic and public presentations as early as 1963 when she delivered a paper on local Irish government reform at a meeting of the Dublin Historical Association. She gave another Dublin presentation on a kindred theme to the Irish Historical Society in 1965. Her next major presentation was not until 1977, two years following the award of her doctoral degree, and it was on a subject that would resonate throughout much of her academic career. It was at the 1977 national meeting of the American Historical Association in Dallas, Texas, that Catherine delivered a seminal presentation entitled 'The Roots and Symptoms of Ulster Separatism, 1828 to 1880'. It placed that 'Orange' legacy into a definable context that would anticipate her later analyses of the complicated origins and outlook of Ulster unionism.

In the meantime she presented a paper focusing upon a still more targeted subject, 'Arthur J. Balfour and Ireland', delivered at the 1982 Rocky Mountain Conference on British Studies. Both the number and variety of Catherine's academic presentations proliferated ever afterwards. In 1986, at a conference on Women in Contemporary Ireland held at the Catholic University of America, she crafted a paper focusing on 'Irish Women and the New Irish State, 1922–'85'. She next gave a discourse captioned as 'John Boyle O'Reilly: Prophet of progressivism' before a regional American Conference on Irish Studies event at Salve Regina College in 1988 and, subsequently, in 1992, presented a paper entitled 'The Legacy of Arthur J. Balfour to Twentieth-Century Ireland', for the Parnell Summer School in Avondale, County Wicklow. Her rapidly emerging interest in the gender aspect of the Troubles was skilfully explored with a paper entitled 'Hidden Heroines: Women in Northern Ireland', at Queen's University Belfast in 1993.

Over the next quarter century, from 1993 to 2018, Catherine continued to engage with an ever-increasing focus on gender as women's studies became a central focus of her work on Northern Ireland. That salient shift was perhaps most manifest in papers she delivered again at Queen's University Belfast in 1993 and at the University of Rhode Island in 1994 for a colloquium series on 'Race, Gender, and Class'. She doubled down still further on the topic with presentations on the 'Changing Status of Women in Ireland, 1960–1997', at the 1998 national meeting of the American Historical Association, and again with a paper entitled 'Representations of Irish Women in the Field Day Anthology of Irish Writing' presented at the International Conference of Irish Women Historians held at Queen's University Belfast in 2004.

'forever one and the same person'

But during that same aforementioned quarter century Catherine also found the time and energy to engage on two additional but entirely different fronts: the Irish in nineteenth-century America and the Northern Ireland peace process of the late 1990s. With reference to the former, she delivered papers between 2009 and 2013 on 'The Wreck of the Brig *St John* and its Commemoration, 1849–2008' for several Irish organisational groups in Boston, such as the Éire Society, the Charitable Irish Society, and the Cohasset Historical Society. Almost concurrent with those Irish-American programmes, Shannon also participated in a different series of presentations associated with Hofstra University's Irish Studies programme, which, in 2005, hosted a Presidential Conference on William Jefferson Clinton in a programme entitled 'Bringing Hope to Northern Ireland's Civil Society: Bill Clinton's Belfast visits of 1995 and 1998'. That general format was then repeated at the Clinton Institute-University College Dublin, and later at NUI Galway and Queen's University Belfast.

In 2011 Professor Shannon presented a paper at the University of Ulster entitled 'Randolph Churchill, Ulster, and the Orange Card', which was later expanded upon for a national meeting of the American Conference for Irish Studies at the University of Wisconsin, Madison, where the title of the new incarnation read 'Lord Randolph Churchill's Orange Card: Pure principle or pure opportunism?' On 5 July 2013, Catherine delivered the keynote address at the John Boyle O'Reilly Exhibit at the Highlanes Gallery in Drogheda, Ireland. She also was among the few chosen to be one of the speakers celebrating the life and work of Nobel laureate Seamus Heaney at the Boston Public Library in December 2013. And her successive presentations that connected the state of Massachusetts with the country of Ireland was again in evidence at the American Conference for Irish Studies international meeting at University College Dublin on 14 June 2014, where her paper was entitled 'Dublin Lockout of 1913: The view from Boston. A Comparison of the 1912 Lawrence Textile Strike and the Dublin Lockout General Strike of 1913'.

Catherine Shannon has had a clearly understandable interest in the brig *St John*, the fated 'famine ship' that had been expected to dock in Boston Harbor on 7 October 1849, when it suddenly was engulfed in a furious storm a short distance from its destination. Captain Marten Oliver decided to drop anchor at nearby Cohasset Harbor when he was next blown off his intended course. The vessel was then tossed furiously against the boulders along the water's edge and, amidst the fury of the waves and wind, promptly began to splinter. Despite heroic attempts by the scores of townspeople who sought to offer help, the weather precluded any success. There were well over a hundred passengers on board the brig *St John* and only sixteen survived, as did seven crew members. But no more than forty-five bodies were washed ashore and they were quickly placed into a trench-like common grave in the region's central cemetery. A Catholic priest, Rev. John T. Roddan from Quincy, officiated at the grave. Professor Shannon, who was born in Hingham, only a half dozen miles north of Cohasset, has lived, when not in Westfield, for decades in a home at that seaside community. She was a practised sailing enthusiast who often explored the shoreline of that harbour and well understood, as few could, precisely how perilous a landing would have been for a wooden vessel tossed about in hurricane-strength wind and rain. This was the '*an Gorta Mór*' experience up close, a terrible Famine-related tragedy involving people who had fled such dire conditions at home in Ireland, only to die in such horror on the shoals of Cohasset. It is a subject that Catherine speaks of with visible passion. And speak of it she has before academic and Irish society audiences, regularly referencing how, in 1915, the Ancient Order of Hibernians memorialised the tragedy of the brig *St John* with the placement of a large stone Celtic cross in the Cohasset Cemetery in memory of victims who will remain forever unnamed.

Shannon's focus on the Famine also extended to another memorable chapter in that epoch of human misery. On 12 April 2015, at the Elms College in Chicopee, Massachusetts, she gave a moving account entitled 'It is Not an Everyday Matter to See a Nation Starving: Captain Robert Forbes and the 1847 voyage of the USS *Jamestown* to Cork, Ireland'. In it she recounted how the USS *Jamestown* departed Boston on 28 March 1847 with over 800 tons of food and provisions for the starving people of Ireland during the darkest month of that year. Shannon described the means Captain Forbes employed in order to get those supplies successfully to the desperate populace, and the sense of horror he experienced upon arrival in mid-April at that beleaguered port. What Shannon so poignantly underscores is how remarkable and unprecedented was the source of the huge benefaction for the destitute Irish. The huge quantity of food and provisions had been made possible by the support given to the New England Relief Committee by people from both the Irish and Yankee communities who helped raise $150,000 in cash that represented fully half of the $300,000 that was ultimately sent from Boston to Ireland in 1847 for famine relief. The non-sectarian nature of that effort represented a truly historic occasion when both groups put aside long-held suspicion

'forever one and the same person'

and hostility towards one another in a joint effort to redress a great humanitarian crisis.

As with any true scholar, Catherine Shannon's legacy will be best preserved by the publications that emerged from the research that underpinned her oral presentations, and they are notable. Her first publication, 'Ulster Liberal Unionists and Irish Local Government Reform, 1885–1898', appeared in the premier journal *Irish Historical Studies* in March 1973 that was later reprinted in Alan O'Day (ed.), *Reactions to Irish Nationalism, 1885–1914* (London: Hambledon Press, 1987). In 1988 she published her masterful study of Balfour entitled *Arthur Balfour and Ireland, 1874–1922* (Washington, DC: Catholic University of America Press, 1988), which is very arguably the finest work of its kind and likely to remain so for some time. In 1989 Catherine also published 'Catholic Women and the Northern Ireland Troubles' as a chapter in a volume edited by Alan O'Day and Yonah Alexander entitled *Ireland's Terrorist Trauma* (London: Harvester Wheatleaf Press, 1989).

Shannon went on to publish almost another two dozen such contributions between 1989 and 2017. Among them were writings that predictably reflect her keen interest in, and insights regarding, Irish women and civil rights, John Boyle O'Reilly, the Irish Famine, and the Clinton legacy in the Northern Ireland peace process. Nor did she ignore her seminal interest in the Orange legacy of the North. In 2012 Robert McNamara published an edited volume with Irish Academic Press, Dublin, entitled *The Churchills in Ireland: Connections and controversies since the seventeenth century* in which Catherine quite fittingly had two chapters entitled 'Lord Randolph's Irish Apprenticeship and its Aftermath, 1877–'85' and 'Lord Randolph Churchill and Ireland: The road to and from the Orange card, 1885–1893'.

Catherine Shannon has also been engaged as an active reviewer for *The American Historical Review*, *Irish Literary Supplement*, *The Journal of Modern History*, *History Ireland*, *New Hibernia Review* and the *Canadian Journal of Irish Studies*. Moreover, her prominent visibility within the academic world won for her not only two highly competitive National Endowment for the Humanities summer fellowships, one at the University of Virginia (1976) and the other at Brown University (1982), but also two different year-long distinguished senior research fellowships, one at Queen's University Belfast (1990–1) and another at University College Galway (2001–2).

In the world not exclusively moored in academe, Catherine has been no less visible: she was elected a Fellow of the Royal Historical Society in 1991, became a founding patron of the *History Ireland* magazine in 1992, and received the Irish-American Heritage Award in 1998. She was also conferred with the John L. McDonough Award from the Charitable Irish Society of Boston on 17 March 2012, the only woman ever to be so honoured by that august body, which dates back to 1737. Numerous other credits could be added to this impressive iteration of things accomplished by the indefatigable Dr Shannon. Yet amidst the number of her continuing contributions and participations she perseveres with her scholarship agenda and is presently at work on another monograph focusing upon the role and status of Northern Irish women between 1965 and 1998.

Boston and Belfast have both occasioned strong ties for Catherine Shannon, but she will never be forgotten in any foreseeable future by Westfield State University where she not only launched her own distinguished career but also provided a presence that would be difficult to imagine anyone replicating. She taught courses that ranged from medieval Europe to the Victorian underworld and, apart from the surveys on modern Britain and Ireland, there were seminars on women in European history, literary perspectives on Irish history, as well as the usual surveys on the western experience. Shannon was awarded successive distinguished service awards and faculty research grants and, in 1994, she was conferred with the Westfield State 150th Anniversary Award for her contribution to both the college and community. Both had reason to celebrate Dr Shannon's contribution to their respective locales. From 1980 to 1982 Dr Shannon led a $54,000 curriculum development grant, funded by the US Department of Education, Ethnic Heritage Division, that targeted faculty, curriculum, resource development and community outreach. The programme resulted in a notably successful undertaking that included lectures, films, concerts and art exhibits. Those public events were attended by no fewer than 10,000 people.

Near the close of her academic career Shannon, who had been raised to the rank of full professor at Westfield State University in 1982, taught from 1995 to 2001 as adjunct professor of history at the University of Massachusetts. In 2002 she was designated emerita professor of history at Westfield State University, bringing to a close a most remarkable and accomplished tenure of some thirty-five years.

Anyone who has had the opportunity to both meet and come to know Catherine B. Shannon will almost certainly agree that she is both an irrepressible and unfailingly cordial force of nature. Her enthusiasm

'forever one and the same person'

for people and politics, particularly any subject touching upon things Irish and relating to gender and civil rights, or to the Irish linkage with America from the Famine years to the present, will encounter a tour de force that is clearly palpable. And Professor Shannon is forever one and the same person, no matter with whom she might be engaged in conversation. Whether it be a troubled student, a fellow academic, an elected politician or a victim of some mindless sectarian strife, she exudes a truly genuine concern for people and for the issues that may be affecting them. And that is the priceless quality that makes her such an invaluable asset for the underserved, whether they be exploited women or perplexed undergraduates. She is a sympathetic listener for them all and a formidable ally to each when opportunity avails. The contributors to this *festschrift* welcome the opportunity to honour such a remarkable colleague, one Catherine B. Shannon.

Lastly, the Center for Irish Programs at Boston College hosted a major symposium on 'John Hume: His vision and legacy for Ireland', on 28 April 2018, to which Professor Shannon contributed a substantive piece entitled 'John Hume and Boston's Irish-American Community: A case of positive diasporic intervention'. For over a quarter century Catherine Shannon has been an invaluable contact and/or resource for people in Irish-related sectors at Boston College, including the Irish Studies faculty, Burns Library specialists and Irish Institute professionals. She has been, and continues to be, an asset to the Boston College community and we are grateful for her presence among us.

CHAPTER SIXTEEN

Charting a course: framing scholarship and practical politics in the work of Catherine B. Shannon

Maureen O'Rourke Murphy

He makes his own events, not time nor chance;
Their logic his: not creature, but creator.[1]
John Boyle O'Reilly

John Boyle O'Reilly's words describe the work of Catherine B. Shannon: her scholarship and her service to the Irish and Irish-American communities. Irish nationalism has been the common thread tying together her teaching, her research and her service; its location has been Boston and its south shore along Route 3 from Scituate to Marshfield. She was the daughter of New York wool dealer David Shannon who settled in Boston with his wife Catherine Cannon Shannon. The Shannons raised their family in the south shore village of Hingham, six miles north of Scituate, where Catherine would have her summer home, a place with its own Irish associations.

Immigrants from Galway who arrived in Scituate in the nineteenth century discovered a local source of *Chondrus crispus*, the red seaweed known in Ireland as carrageen, and with this they supplemented their income as fishermen, clammers and lobstermen till the end of the twentieth century.[2] Today Scituate is a centre for recreational boating, as it was when the young Shannons were sailing in Scituate Harbor. Like her

Charting a course: framing scholarship and practical politics

brothers David and Christopher, Catherine was influenced by their eldest brother, Richard Tonra Shannon, who became a chief warrant officer in the United States Coast Guard and the sailing master of the USCG barque *Eagle*, the academy's square-rigger that visited Cork Harbour in 1976 as part of Op Sail.

Shannon's transforming experience was her work for her MA in history at University College Dublin with Dudley Edwards and Desmond Williams on the politics and administration of the Irish Local Government Act of 1898, for which she was awarded a degree with honours. Her life-long friendships with Joe Lee and Margaret MacCurtain date from her UCD years. She continued with her study of Modern Irish and British History when she returned to a teaching position at Westfield State College in Westfield, Massachusetts, and to the graduate programme in Modern Irish and British History at the University of Massachusetts-Amherst. She was awarded her PhD in 1975 for her dissertation 'Arthur J. Balfour and the Irish Question, 1874–1922', the work that was the basis of her magisterial study *Arthur J. Balfour and Ireland, 1874–1922* (1988), her clearly reasoned account of Balfour's response to the complicated matter of Ireland, a problem he solved for Conservatives with the Government of Ireland Act that institutionalised partition. Shannon's ability to carefully and clearly examine a position with which she might not be sympathetic prepared her well for the later work she would do on the Troubles in Northern Ireland.

The same year that she published her study of Balfour, Shannon began to speak and write about the Irish-born journalist, poet and political activist John Boyle O'Reilly (1844–1890), who died at his summer home in Hull, Massachusetts, just eight miles from Scituate. She established her interest in O'Reilly with 'John Boyle O'Reilly: Prophet of progressivism', her paper to the New England regional meeting of the American Conference for Irish Studies in 1988. She was especially interested in his most considerable contribution to Irish America that he made through the pages of the Boston *Pilot*, the country's foremost Catholic newspaper of the time that he edited from 1874 to 1890 and owned part of from 1876 till his death in 1900. (Archbishop John Joseph Williams, who gave his name to the high school that Shannon attended, purchased three-quarters interest in the *Pilot*; O'Reilly owned the other quarter interest in the paper.)

While Shannon was drawn to O'Reilly's support of and promotion of Irish nationalism in the pages of the *Pilot* – land reform, home rule and Parnellism – she paid special attention to his progressive causes: his support of civil rights for African-Americans after the Civil War, his opposition to Irish-American racism, his recognition of the abuses to workers by the rapid industrial growth of the late nineteenth-century cities, and his advocacy of labour's right to organise. She would not have supported O'Reilly's view of women's suffrage!

She would return to O'Reilly to write his entry for the *Dictionary of Irish Biography* in 2009 and to give the keynote address at the opening of the John Boyle O'Reilly Exhibition in Drogheda, County Louth, in 2013. The exhibition went on to the Burns Library at Boston College later in the year. When the New Bedford Whaling Museum mounted its 2016–17 'Famine, Friends & Fenians' exhibition that celebrated the links between New Bedford and Ireland, Shannon helped organise the event, co-authored the Introduction, and contributed the essays on the Great Irish Famine, on Irish immigration to the United States, and on Irish politics to its catalogue.

While Shannon wrote about Balfour and O'Reilly, she has not compared the two figures during the period of Balfour's tenure as Ireland's chief secretary, 1887–91, a time that coincided with O'Reilly's tenure on the *Pilot* from his part-ownership in 1876 till his death in 1900. What might she have said about the two men and their work for Ireland? She might have contrasted their progressivism: O'Reilly's was urban and Balfour's was rural. Balfour had no time for Irish nationalism; however, in his effort to kill nationalism with kindness, he established the Congested Districts Board that promoted agricultural, infrastructural and some craft-based industrial development in the poor districts of the west.

Balfour's 'enlightened socialism' was admired even by those who were critical of 'Bloody Balfour's unionist politics. While he was not an admirer of Balfour, Michael Davitt praised the benefit the Congested Districts Board brought to agricultural labourers.[3] Balfour himself was proud of the board's achievements, claiming that it had done 'more good for Ireland than a hundred domestic parliaments would ever do'.[4] In his recent study of Ireland's offshore islands, Diarmaid Ferriter traced the development of the islands after the Congested Districts Board was closed down in 1923. He points out the irony that more was done for the islands by the Congested Districts Boards than by the ad hoc policy arrangements of successive Irish governments.[5]

While Shannon worked on her Balfour project, the Northern Ireland 'Troubles' began; the two were related by partition, the Balfour solution that was put in place as part of the treaty that created the Irish Free State.

Charting a course: framing scholarship and practical politics

Even before the publication of her Balfour book, Shannon recognised the work done by women on both sides of the divide in afflicted areas and began work on her project documenting women's voices across the divide, devoting her efforts to facilitating the work of those looking for peaceful ways to bridge the divide.

Shannon recognised that not only was it important for voices across the political spectrum to be heard, but also for those voices to be shared. The problem was to find a place or places away from the confines of Northern Ireland where such conversations could happen. Shannon became the principal organiser of the first symposium on Northern Ireland held at the John F. Kennedy Library, overlooking Boston Harbor, in March 1982. It was the first of a series of American-based meetings which brought the players from across the Northern Ireland political divide together for private conversations as well as for the more public but 'off the record' sessions.

In those years, Shannon's support of the work of John Hume and of his Social Democratic and Labour Party was essential for Hume to be recognised in the United States as an advocate for peaceful solutions. (When poor health limited John Hume's ability to speak for himself, Shannon continued to memorialise his contributions. Her paper 'John Hume and Boston's Irish-American Community: A case of positive diasporic intervention' was a major contribution to a Hume symposium held at Boston College on 28 April 2018.)

An Institute of Irish Studies senior research fellowship at Queen's University Belfast in 1991–2 gave Shannon the opportunity to continue her interviews and interventions with Northern Irish women and to begin her major work, a monograph on the impact of political conflict on the role and status of women living there. Her essay 'From House Rights to Civil Rights' (1993), which appeared first in Mary O'Dowd and Sabine Wichert's *Chattel, Servant or Citizen?* (1995) and was later revised and reprinted in *The Field Day Anthology of Irish Literature V* (2002), addressed the important role played by women in the campaign to reform the allocation of public housing in Northern Ireland, a system based on sectarianism. She was concerned that the Northern Irish women should receive credit for their role in addressing injustices.

In her own research, Shannon sought to correct the simplistic and stereotypical representations of Northern Irish women on both sides of the community, particularly the urban communities of Belfast and Derry and of larger towns like Dungannon and Coleraine. In her lectures and essays, Shannon argues that women were written out of the history of the protest. Their exclusion led to the founding of the Northern Ireland Civil Rights Association.

Her study of women across the Northern Ireland community led to Shannon assuming the role of an informal advisor to the Northern Ireland Women's Coalition which began formally in 1996. As usual, she sympathetically reached out to all parties and analysed their positions with rigour and compassion. A measure of the success of the coalition was their representation at the peace talks. The late Dr Marjorie 'Mo' Mowlam, who was secretary of state for Northern Ireland during the Good Friday Agreement talks, said that the coalition's two delegates and co-founders, Catholic academic Monica McWilliams and Protestant social worker Pearl Segar, were a positive influence in the peace process.

Shannon continued to use the model of off-site meetings for gatherings of women on both sides of the Northern divide that were held in the United States in the 1990s. She directed the 1994 Reaching Common Ground Conference at Boston University, working with Elizabeth Shannon, widow of William V. Shannon, the American ambassador to Ireland during the Jimmy Carter administration. Catherine Shannon further enlarged her Northern Ireland model for her Women Envisioning Peace Conference at Westfield State College that was part of the Global Women's History Project, which combined talks between women in Northern Ireland with women across the Israeli–Palestinian divide.

While she continued her work on women's voices in Northern Ireland, the Republic of Ireland observed the 150th commemoration of 1847, the worst year of the Great Irish Famine, and Shannon took on two projects linking Boston and its South Shore with the Famine. Her previous work had not focused on the Famine, but she wrote two important papers and wrote the proposal that brought the 2012 Famine commemoration to Boston.

Her earlier work had not been Famine-based, as neither John Boyle O'Reilly nor Arthur Balfour addressed the Great Irish Famine. Unlike Michael Davitt, whose family was evicted from their home in Straide, County Mayo, John Boyle O'Reilly was spared the worst of the Great Irish Famine by the wages of his parents. (When he edited his *Poetry and Songs of Ireland* (1887), he carefully avoided the most bitter and inflammatory poems like Lady Wilde's 'The Famine Year'.) As he faced the later threatened famine of 1879, Arthur Balfour certainly found resentment about the Great Irish Famine and fears about starvation and

Charting a course: framing scholarship and practical politics

eviction when he arrived in Ireland as chief secretary, but he focused his attention on the later potato crop failure and the attendant fear of eviction.

Shannon had traced the general support of the Irish through her research into the work of the Charitable Irish Society. Founded in 1737 as a relief organisation, the society is the country's oldest Irish organisation. Shannon's work for the society was recognised when she was elected its first woman president in 2015. While Shannon has been broadly interested in the Great Irish Famine and the subsequent immigration to the United States, particularly to New England, two of her biggest interests are based on her own connections with Boston and Ireland: the *Jamestown*'s mission to Ireland, which arrived in Cork on 12 April 1847 with 800 tons of food and supplies, and the voyage of the brig *St John*, which broke up off the Cohasset coast on 7 October 1849.

Boston's response to the Great Irish Famine was generous, with aid provided by the Irish Repeal Association and by Irish priests in the city. When the New England Relief Committee was formed in February 1847, Captain Robert Bennet Forbes, a veteran of the China trade, and his brother John proposed a plan which would ask the government to reassign the USS *Jamestown*, a ship of the line, to that of a relief ship bringing supplies to Ireland. Robert Forbes left on his errand of mercy to Ireland on 28 March 1847 and arrived on 12 April to a tumultuous welcome. Forbes and his officers were the guests at an elaborate banquet at which Forbes was presented with an engraved silver salver from the people of Cork. The salver was brought back to the United States in August aboard the *Macedonia*, the second warship to be refitted for relief. The salver and the wheel of the *Jamestown* are among the family heirlooms at the Forbes House in Milton, Massachusetts, a Boston suburb nine miles south of the city but not along the south shore; however, it is the *Jamestown*, not the Forbes House, that had personal associations for Shannon.

Richard Shannon was the three-term commissioner of pilots for Massachusetts's First District, which included Boston Harbor, and both Shannon and Captain Forbes served as presidents of the Boston Marine Society, a mutual maritime aid society. Appropriately, Forbes was president during the time that the *Jamestown* made its relief mission to Cork. Also, in the course of her research, Shannon discovered that a cache of food and provisions from the ship were probably delivered to the townland of Maulnarouga, west-south-west of Bandon, the place from which Shannon's ancestor David Shanahan (*sic*), a sub-tenant of the 2nd earl of Bandon, emigrated in 1864 or 1865.[6]

Shannon's second major contribution to Famine scholarship is her research on the Galway-built ship the brig *St John* that sunk off the Cohasset coast on 7 October 1849, near Shannon's own home in Scituate. The *St John* was built in the Claddagh area of Galway, where local merchant Henry Comerford bought the ship in 1848. In 1849, some 100 people signed on to the *St John* to leave famine-stricken Ireland for Boston. Shannon has discovered that it is likely that Comerford allowed passengers over the legal limit to sail on the brig. The actual number of passengers is still in dispute.

Shannon's experience sailing in Cohasset Harbor, including the seas around the Minot's Ledge Light, informs her exhaustive knowledge of the rocky shoreline along Cohasset Harbor, including the Grampus Ledge where the *St John* foundered in the heavy surf. Having navigated the hazardous harbour that leads to the mouth of Boston Harbor, Shannon would have been aware of the danger in the seas off the Scituate Light, especially under hurricane conditions. It was those conditions that led to the loss of life as the *St John* broke up on the rocks.

Shannon analysed the efforts of Cohasset residents to rescue the brig's passengers, to recover the bodies, to prepare them for their funeral and burial, to take survivors into their homes and to treat their injuries. She refers to Henry David Thoreau's account of going to Cohasset when he heard of the shipwreck, an account she describes as 'detailed if rather clinical'. At one point in his account, Thoreau might have excused himself with his description of those who came to claim the bodies of the drowned: 'I witnessed no signs of grief, but there was a sober dispatch of business which was affecting.' But Thoreau was not emotionally engaged by the victims: 'On the whole, it was not so impressive a scene as I might have expected.'[7]

Reading 'The Shipwreck' with 'Baker Field', from *Walden*, Thoreau's account of seeking shelter in the impoverished but hardworking Irish immigrant John Field's hut, Thoreau argues that Field and his family could have a better life if they were willing to forego luxuries like tea, coffee, butter and beef. Readers have read the passage as an example of Thoreau's attitude towards the Irish: an impoverished and backward people given to having large families they could not support. Laura Dassow Walls has challenged that reading in her biography *Henry David Thoreau: A life* (2018), and argues instead that Thoreau did, in fact, respect hardworking Irish families. She concentrates on the 'Baker Field' section in *Walden* and does not consider Thoreau's response to the dead in Cohasset.

Charting a course: framing scholarship and practical politics

Given her interest in local Irish-American history, Shannon devotes the second half of her brig *St John* paper to the commemorations held in Cohasset in memory of those lost. The most considerable commemorative event was the raising of a twenty-foot granite cross on 30 May 1914 by the Ancient Order of Hibernians (AOH) at the highest point of the Cohasset Cemetery. Among the organisers was the stepson of Mary Kane, one of the *St John* survivors.

The centenary of the shipwreck of the *St John* coincided with the centenary of the first mass celebrated in Cohasset, an event Shannon described in the wider contexts of the Irish and the politics of twentieth-century Boston, and the centenary of the archdiocese of Boston under Richard, Cardinal Cushing. Shannon argues that the *St John* centenary marked the success of the Irish in Boston. While the centenary celebration was moribund for some years, the AOH revived the commemoration in 1992. They planned a special commemoration for the 150th anniversary of the wreck of the *St John* in 1999, an event which included invitations to people from Lettermullan, County Galway, whose ancestors would have been among the passengers and crew of the *St John*. Shannon does not simply write about the commemorations, she has been an active participant in the events – demonstrating that link between scholarship and service that her professional life has embraced.

CHAPTER SEVENTEEN

Catherine B. Shannon: in her own words

Edited by Miriam Nyhan Grey

In the spring of 2013 Catherine B. Shannon delivered a lecture about the tragic fate of a group of Famine refugees lost in the wreck of the brig *St John* while they were bound for Massachusetts, at New York University's Glucksman Ireland House. She had been invited to NYU by her longtime friend, Professor Joe Lee, who she first met as a student in Ireland in the 1960s. During this visit to New York City Catherine recorded an in-person audio oral history for the Glucksman Ireland House Oral History Collection with historian Dr Miriam Nyhan Grey. The Glucksman collection of interviews forms part of the Archives of Irish America and is housed at NYU's renowned Tamiment Library and Robert F. Wagner Labor Archives. A follow-up phone interview took place in January 2020. The transcripts of both recordings, running to approximately three hours, have been combined and edited for flow and clarity. The interview opened with Catherine being prompted to reflect on her early life.

I was born in Hingham, Massachusetts, which is a suburban town about twenty-five miles south of Boston [in] January 1938 in the middle of a snow storm, as my mother often recalled. All of my grandparents were born in Ireland. My mother's parents came from County Mayo and my father's parents came from Newport, County Tipperary, and also from Desertserges, west Cork.

My mother's mother came over to Boston and took up work as a domestic [servant] from her home in Keelogues, not too far from Castlebar [County Mayo]. Then eventually she and my grandfather

244

Catherine B. Shannon: in her own words

17.1 Catherine B. Shannon's maternal grandparents, Bridget (neé Tonra) Cannon (1867–1942) and Thomas Cannon (1863–1940), both from County Mayo. (Image courtesy of Catherine B. Shannon)

– Thomas Cannon from Belcarra, near Westport – they took up together in Boston and married there and had ten children and stayed in the Brookline area throughout their lives.

Now my father's parents came to America via New York; his mother during the [Great Irish] Famine and his father in 1860. My paternal grandmother, Honora 'Nora' Ryan, was one of ten children and the family came over in 1850 in three different stages. The father came first with about three children; and six months later the mother came with another three kids. About a year later the youngest child – who was my grandmother – she was just an infant when her mother left her in Ireland. She came with an older sister, a cousin, and some other people, so they all made it here which was absolutely amazing and they settled down in the lower part of Manhattan; around 10th Street. My great-grandmother proved to be a very energetic woman. Within eight years of her coming [to the US] she was setting up savings accounts in the Emigrants Saving Bank for her children.[1]

And then [there was] my father's mother; this baby who came over when she was about two years old. She was trained as

17.2 Cork-born New York businessman David J. Shannon (1842–1908), paternal grandfather of Catherine B. Shannon, undated. (Image courtesy of Catherine B. Shannon)

a seamstress and worked from her young teen years until she got married at around age twenty or twenty-one to my father's father, who came from west Cork around the area east of Rosscarbery. His name was David 'Shanahan' but evidently Grandma Shannon, née Nora Ryan, thought 'Shanahan' sounded too Irish and encouraged him after their marriage to change it to 'Shannon' because she thought they'd have a better chance in America with a less Irish name. My grandfather evidently was somebody with incredible business sense and very quickly moved up the ladder. He started in the market areas as a butcher. Eventually, he owned his own meat-packing slaughterhouse. I actually have the *New York Times* clippings that indicate that he was one of the first people that went into the Metropolitan Market.[2]

They gradually had great success, David Shannon and Nora, and had ten children.[3] They gradually moved further and further up the West Side until the final residence was on West 71st, just

Catherine B. Shannon: in her own words

off Broadway, where my father grew up in a brownstone. My grandfather was a great pal of Judge Daniel Cohalan, who presented my grandfather with a silver-topped walking stick to commemorate their weekly Sunday-afternoon walks.[4] It was one of my father's cherished possessions.

The interesting thing about it is some of the people on the Shannon side of the family – particularly the aunts – had no kind of, shall I say, affection for Ireland. I mean to them it was a place that all they heard connected to it was absolute misery and they probably got this from their father – my grandfather Shannon – because he was five years old in 1847 and living in a part of Cork that was just devastated by the Famine. Exactly when his parents died I don't know. Whether they died in the Famine or survived the Famine and died later I'm not sure, but it was probably very clear that there was no future for them. I know from Griffith's Valuation they had no big land holdings or anything. It appears they were a labouring family so, given the success he had in America, you can see why his daughters didn't have a whole lot of affection [for Ireland]. And as far as my father's mother was concerned, having come here as a two-year-old baby, she grew up as an American although surrounded by a very intense Irish community.

So what was her maiden name, Catherine?
Ryan. She came from Newport, County Tipperary. I have a whole genealogy of that family. I went to Newport about eighteen months ago when I was over in Ireland with my good friend Margaret MacCurtain to see if we could find the town and house they lived in. They lived on High Street there in Newport but I'm sure the house where they lived wasn't standing. I do have a need to do some further research to find out exactly what the occupation of my great-great-grandfather Ryan was. He was George Ryan. They must have had some resources to leave when they did in 1850 and get them all over because he left with the oldest son and a couple others and the wife six months later and the last of the group about I think [came] eighteen months later.

And you have no idea, Catherine, as to how Hanora/Nora Ryan and David Shannon met?
No, no I don't. I would assume they were all living in a very Irish enclave in the lower part of Manhattan and would have met there.

So that's the Shannon side. So then just to go back to the other side, so your mother's mother married a Cannon?
Her maiden name was Tonra, which is unusual. There are a lot of Toners in Northern Ireland and Tonra isn't widely known. One of my cousins has done some research and seems to think that the Tonra family got to Mayo as part of the group that left Armagh because of the sectarian difficulties there and that they had been weavers that fled to the west in the 1790s to escape that. Now I don't actually have any documentary evidence of that and I haven't seen the notes of my cousin's research.

You said your mother's mother was from around Castlebar?
A little place called Keelogues, it's a little village now and it is right in the shadow where the National Museum has its Museum of Country Life. If you know that particular building, that 'big house' was the house of the Fitzgerald family, who were the landlords to my grandmother's family. But when she left for Boston their plot of land was up on one of the nearby mountains but when the Congested Districts Board got into the area and took some of the land and resettled people from the mountains, my grandmother's family came down and settled right down in Keelogues and thus had better land. Their descendants are still there on that small farm today.

I spent my first Christmas in Ireland at Keelogues. But what was really interesting about that is one of my cousins at the time – he would have been my first cousin once removed – took me up to the place where my grandmother, Bridget Tonra, was born on the mountainside and my reaction was, thank God she left. It was so desolate, so barren and it really gave you an understanding as to why young people left there.

She had been in school and loved school but got pulled out to go be a helpmate to an older sister who had a slew of kids. She held on for two years and realised [that it wasn't for her] and decided to emigrate and that's how she got to Boston and she worked as a domestic [servant] and then met my mother's father, Tom Cannon. They had ten children too.

And again, Catherine, do you have any idea as to how they would have met?
One of my aunts and my mother actually said they think that they knew one another in Mayo, which could have been possible. There

Catherine B. Shannon: in her own words 249

was one story that my grandfather had gotten here first and it was a tradition that they would go down to the docks and meet people coming off the boats. And supposedly my grandfather was always saying she was the prettiest girl that got off the boat, so whether he knew her beforehand or it was just as a result of some of these greeting parties that would have taken place when immigrants came I'm not entirely sure and unfortunately all the people who might have some remembrance of these early stories aren't with us any longer.

But one of the things that was kind of interesting was the memories of Ireland from my mother's family were all what a wonderful place it was. It was all stories of fairies and this kind of thing. As a young person I was totally confused about what's the real story here and I think that's probably one of the reasons why I decided (not the only one) to go to Ireland to study back in the 1960s. I've got to figure this out … There was this kind of ambivalence in the tradition that left me confused.

So then your mother grows up in Brookline and your father predominantly grows up in New York. So how did they meet?
That's a long story. After my grandfather's death in 1908 the business went into the hands of his older son, James. And it didn't prosper very well, partly I guess because James didn't have the business acumen that his father had and also at that time some of the technological advances that were coming, such as refrigerated railcars, was beginning to cut into the slaughtering and meat-packing business here on the east coast. And so it was decided that my father, who was about twenty, should go to Argentina as a representative of the firm or some other associated firm because the meat-packing business was linked with the leather business. So he was sent down to Argentina to be a representative or a buyer for the leather business.

And what year would that have been approximately?
That was about 1912 when he went down to Argentina and he stayed there for quite a while. But while he was there he got very interested in the wool business and switched from being a broker buying leather to buying wool. And he stayed in the wool business his entire life after that. He came back from Argentina in 1917, just after World War I broke out, because he had heard that his younger brother, Hubie, had enlisted in the Fighting 69th, Father Duffy's

regiment, and he decided he should also join the war effort. [When he] went to go sign up the authorities asked him [where he had been and when] he told them and they said, 'Well, you can be a lot more use to us if you go back to Argentina and collect information for us.'

So, he actually was in a government group that was a precursor to the OSS.[5] His task was to collect information about all the Germans who were down in Argentina in the Buenos Aires area. And there were many. There was a big German influence there at the time. So he went back under the cover of doing his wool business and one of his friends' associates there was Charlie Dulles, a cousin of John Foster Dulles, who served as secretary of state under President Eisenhower.

I think he came back in 1919 right after the war. And he went to England then on a trip and actually tried to go to Ireland but the British wouldn't give him a visa. They wouldn't give him the papers to go to Ireland. He had wanted to go there to look up his parents' families but for some reason they wouldn't let him, even though an older brother had gone earlier. I think it was his oldest brother had gone, probably before the war. He was in London when Terence McSwiney died on hunger strike and told me about seeing all the demonstrations about that.

So, before he got back from this trip to London he went to France as well. He settled in Boston when he returned because Boston was a huge area for the manufacture of wool fabric.

How conscious was your father about being Irish or Irish-American?
I think he had a great consciousness of it and of the terrible experience that people of the [Great Irish] Famine era encountered. He would have heard of it from his father because I can remember this from after World War II and into the Cold War [era]. My father used to get very upset if he thought American aid – particularly food aid – would ever be used or manipulated for political purposes. That was a really sensitive, really sensitive spot for him and the other way in which it showed was his hospitality to absolutely anybody who needed a bed for the night. We had a room downstairs in our house. My mother used to say, 'I never know who I'm going to see emerging from that place in the morning', because many times Dad met somebody and if the person didn't have anywhere to go or whatever he'd bring them home. And we had a lot of cousins who came and

Catherine B. Shannon: in her own words

17.3 Catherine B. Shannon with her maternal grandmother, Bridget Cannon, Hingham, Massachusetts, *c.*1941. (Image courtesy of Catherine B. Shannon)

would stay with us in the summertime because they were in the city and didn't have a whole lot of economic success so my father would say, 'Have those children come for the summer.' A couple of my cousins used to spend two or three weeks or more with us. We were in a more suburban neighbourhood, whereas they were in an area with no open fields, or accessible beaches, or things like that.

So, then, to go back to your mother's side, Catherine. You probably knew your mother's parents, did you?
I have a vague memory of my grandfather Tom, very vague. I have a much better memory of my grandmother, although she died when I was probably about four, maybe five, but I do remember her.

So, tell me a little bit about what you know of your mother's upbringing, the Cannons, what did your grandfather do, and things like that.
My grandfather was a labourer. He was a gardener for one of the very wealthy families in Boston, the name was Webster. They had two houses, two residences: they had a townhouse on Commonwealth Avenue in Boston and then they had an estate out in Brookline, which was primarily where my grandfather worked. He was with that family for decades and decades until he stopped working and I gather he had pretty fond memories of the family. They were very good to him.

So, he was Tom Cannon, and your grandmother's name was?
Bridget Tonra Cannon. As a child I remember, when we were in Boston going down Commonwealth Avenue, my mother always used

point out the Webster house. It had a kind of conservatory window of circular glass that came out into the street and my mother used to point out that it was my grandfather's responsibility, particularly in the springtime and at Easter, to make sure that place was full of flowers and plants that he had grown. That was a point of pride that they would see that window. My mother, born in 1905, was down in the lower end of the family. She had two older sisters and a brother and then herself. She was the first person to finish high school.

My mother's older sisters went out to work very early. Her oldest sister, my Aunt Helen, got work in the Bell Telephone Company – which was a great area of employment for young women at the time. The second sister, Auntie May, went to work in the Gillette factory, and then she got married and had a family.[6] Aunt Helen never married and she eventually moved up in the telephone company and was a supervisor and retired after forty or forty-five years in the telephone company. She outlived everybody else in the family, which was interesting. She lived until she was about ninety-two. My mother also started out working in the telephone company.

She did go to Catholic grammar school at St Mary's. It was a huge parish church in Brookline, almost cathedral-sized. They had a grammar school and my mother went there, I believe, through the eighth grade or at least through the sixth. One or the other, I'm not entirely sure about that one. Then she went to Brookline High School. She had wanted to go to college but didn't have the resources to do so. I'm sure Aunt Helen was helpful in getting her the job in the telephone company. She was there for a while, but took courses at night at Boston College for a while. Then she left the telephone company and went to work for a law office in Boston. And then she met my father sometime in the early 1930s.

Do you know how they met, Catherine?
They were introduced by a mutual friend, a woman my mother worked with. I gather when my father used to come around to the house in Brookline to collect my mother he was usually a half an hour late or something and the excuse always was the golf match. The golf game got in the way, so he was referred to by my grandfather as 'the golfer'.

Catherine B. Shannon: in her own words

You come along in 1938 and had two older brothers?
Richard was three and a half years older, and David was fifteen months older. My brother Christopher was born August 1941. I was [born in] January '38.

Do you have memories of the [Second World] War going on?
I remember rationing very clearly. I can remember my mother being at the kitchen table counting out the coupons and that kind of thing. I remember in Hingham, while you might have had the coupons to get certain things, they weren't available in the grocery stores. So sometimes we would go up to Jamaica Plain and my mother would give her ration tickets to her sister May and she was able to get some of that stuff from her grocer. I remember that and gas rationing, very clearly. Usually, you went up to get the rations for gas at the local fire station, and that was my treat, to go up with my father to the fire station. I remember the people next door put their car up on blocks and didn't use it at all during the war. Automobile trips for people were fairly limited. This would've been towards the end of the war, my father, when he'd come home at night, he'd always have the newspaper, and he'd go over the headlines with my brothers, and I would be there. Part of this ritual was to see a particular comic strip called Sgt Berger, I think, and the Berger fellow was one of these guys always embarrassing the officers and showing the ridiculousness of the military, so that's the first thing we would always be shown. Later, my father would begin to explain the other things going on. I recall, very clearly, the time of the Battle of the Bulge, because my father got really emotional about it, reflecting back to the First World War and his brother's participation. Hubie was gassed and never really regained his full health after that, and he died fairly young. But I do remember, the end of the war, my brother David and I, we were inside listening to one of the afternoon radio shows, the news came that the war was over and my mother took us all in to her bedroom to say prayers first, and then we all went down to the village and the place was gone wild with excitement. There was a big USO in town, and there were lots of marines around, and they used to have dances there.[7] My father was playing golf that day, and he called my mother and said, 'I'm coming home. Go down to the cellar and get that case of champagne and invite all the neighbours in. Even tell Joe Cauley

to come!' Joe was a neighbour my father didn't particularly like, but he said even he can come to this one. That's what they did.

Was there a light-bulb moment for you where you had a sense of being Irish or Irish-American, or not?
In a way it was a combination of things … the fact, for me, with that I was [Roman] Catholic. I went to an elementary school, a private school in Hingham, which was a very old school, [which] went back to the eighteenth century. When I was there, there were very few [Roman] Catholics there, it was mostly Protestant. I think in my class there were maybe three out of twenty or twenty-one.

I can remember there was one teacher, who was a wonderful English teacher, also he taught history, and I attribute my ability to write fairly well to Mr Russell, because he really taught us grammar and was very good at it. But he was certainly biased against Catholics and Irish. I remember him really giving out about how the Irish and the unions ruined industrial relations in Detroit. He was giving out about all that, and made reference to the Irish having their animals in the house with them, the usual stuff typical of nineteenth- and twentieth-century stereotypes and I got really upset and raised my hand and said to him, 'Well, I'm Irish and we don't live like that so I don't think you know what you're talking about.'

I don't remember what his exact response was. I wasn't punished or anything for it, but one of my classmates who was Catholic, and I still see her, [in] that moment, saying 'Good for you' to me.

Was St Patrick's Day a big day in your childhood life?
Yes, although there weren't great parties. My older brother Richard and his pals used to go into Boston for the parade, I never did until I was much older. There was one time that my father got all dressed up in a tuxedo and he was en route to go to the Charitable Irish Society dinner in Boston, which at that time was all-male. I was perplexed seeing him all dressed up and my mother staying home. He explained that indeed Mum was staying home and he was going in to celebrate, and ironically years and years later I was the first woman president of the Charitable Irish Society in 1990–1. It's the oldest in the Americas, [founded in] 1737. Its historic mission was, and still is, to render assistance to immigrants in distress and in need.

Catherine B. Shannon: in her own words

You were on the college track fairly early on?

I didn't consider myself one of the brighter students in Derby [Academy], I was a C student there. Then I went to Archbishop Williams [High School] and I was getting As and Bs and I was astonished, and in retrospect it's because the education at Derby was so very good. They really taught us study habits. I was well prepared.

Would you attribute the academic leaning to your parents?

My parents were great readers, there were always books on books in the house, and they were very interested in history. There was no question I was going to college. My father had a golfing friend, Father Joe Ryan, who taught at the Pontifical Institute of Medieval Studies in Toronto, and it is connected with St Michael's College. He told my father that if I was interested in history this place would be terrific. We had family friends who had children who had gone to St Michael's. I met one and was told how much she enjoyed it, so it was decided I could apply ... I'm still very close with some of my classmates from there. I majored in history.

Was there an interest in Irish history [at St Michael's]?

No, not then. It wasn't even taught. There was a big interest in British history, there wasn't much American history either in those days. The American history course was a one-semester course, and so was Canadian. It was Rome to the day before yesterday [in] European history. In second year, two semesters of British history and then the last two in third year were American and Canadian [history].

Did [St Michael's] attract [only] Catholics?

St Michael's was entirely Catholic. Most students majored in languages, English and philosophy. There were probably five or six history majors in my class, and I was the only female. I graduated in 1960. I went home for the summer and in those days there weren't an awful lot of opportunities for women. I waitressed, then came to New York, and ended up working for a publishing company ... By this time I knew I really wanted to go to Ireland, so I began my plan to go. I wrote to the people at UCD [University College Dublin] and said I wanted to come and do a master's ... and [I] left the following semester in 1961, to go to UCD ... That's when I met Joe Lee. We were graduate students together. He was doing his work on the Irish railroads and I was doing mine on local government reform and we both had Desmond Williams as a supervisor.

There you were on the boat back to Ireland almost 100 years since your grandfather set out in the opposite direction.

I remember presenting to the history faculty what I wanted to study, the 1921 treaty, for my master's and seeing all these eyes roll, not realising it was still quite taboo, and Dudley Edwards saying, 'Well, that's all very well and good, Catherine, but what about documentation? You can't get at the documentation – there's a one hundred year rule, [so] you better go find another topic.' So he suggested I travel around and get to know the country or go start doing a lot of reading or start attending some of the undergraduate lectures and I did do that, settling on the topic of Irish local government reform, which led on to my PhD, which was about Arthur Balfour and I covered eventually his entire career in Ireland from 1874 to 1922.

I had to get a job after returning from Dublin. I started as a substitute teacher in the Boston school system, and I worked there for six months and then got a job teaching history in Holbrook high school and did that for three years. During that time I made inquiries about a PhD at Harvard but even then women were few in PhD programmes and it was clear they were not going to do anything for me there. I applied to teach at Westfield State College … and they expected you'd go on to get the PhD, which I did at UMass Amherst. I did it part-time, as I was teaching. I eventually ended up teaching Irish history, as an adjunct [at UMass Amherst], from 1994 to 2000. As well as full-time teaching at Westfield State College.

Tell me about being this sort of Boston girl in Dublin [in the 1960s]. What was that like?

Oh, yes. I was rooming at the time with two other girls, one whose father was in the [US] State Department and she was finishing up an undergraduate degree at UCD probably in English, and the other was from Washington too, and she was at Trinity doing a junior year abroad. There were other Americans around. President John Fitzgerald Kennedy was coming too. Everyone was excited … We decided that we'd host a party for Americans, etc. and then go to O'Connell Street to the [presidential] parade. We barely saw him

Catherine B. Shannon: in her own words

as we were late for the parade as the party was so jolly. The next day President Kennedy was giving his speech at the Dáil, and I was on the steps of the National Library [of Ireland] so I saw him go in and out of the Dáil. I had met him briefly years before that in Toronto when he visited St Michael's.

What did you think of the Irish reaction to JFK?
The reaction was just so enthusiastic and joyous and we felt the same in America upon his election. My father had probably voted Republican through the fifties but he voted for Kennedy. Although he wasn't all that crazy about his policies but he said he had to vote for Kennedy, remembering as he did what happened to Al Smith. For him this was a real moment of ethnic and religious pride. It put such a positive message to Irish identity. There was a sense of possibility in Ireland then and a lot of that had to do with what [Seán] Lemass and T.K. Whitaker put in place [in Ireland itself]. The living standards were very different in Ireland to America, but were starting to change.

Did you ever consider moving more permanently [to Ireland]?
Yes, I did. I did consider staying there. I loved it. I did miss my family and I felt some obligation to go home at least for a while, with my parents. But the job opportunities were negligible for my kind of degree and educated women in Ireland had virtually no chance. The number of women who lectured in the universities was negligible. I thought, even if I stayed and worked and got married, the life of women there would've been quite grim compared to the US. I knew there'd be no future for me in the university at that point. I never even applied for a job in Ireland. When I got home I got into my life here and my teaching and as soon as I could I did go back. I spent a lot of summers [in Ireland] in the seventies. Then I went back a great deal in the 1980s in connection with the Northern Irish problem. I spent summers in Belfast from about 1983 to 1990. Anywhere from two to six weeks doing interviews of women to see what the impact of the conflict was on their lives. In the nineties I got into supporting Northern women's attempts to get into politics, particularly the Northern Ireland Women's Coalition.

How did you get into that? What was the hook that took you in [to engagement with Northern Ireland]?

I had to do my own re-education about the nature of the Northern [Irish] problem and move away from the traditional [idea] that the only issue was partition. Gradually, I did begin to come to a better understanding of the unionist position and [of] its historical roots and origins – [which in part I did while undertaking] research when I was on an NEH [National Endowment for the Humanities] fellowship at the University of Virginia.

As all the violence was going on, this kind of stuff affected me and I felt a sense of responsibility to get a different story out there. I began to address the issue in my classes and had people come to Westfield to talk about the roots of Northern [Irish] separatism. Also I knew people who had been badly affected by the Troubles in the North.

Tell me about your early engagement on the topic of Northern Ireland and how that came about.

It was really in the late 1970s that I began to, you know, kind of re-examine my whole view of what the reasons for the conflict were and because I had to do that in connection with the Balfour research. I was trying to find justification for his support of the unionists and so forth. So, I did an awful lot of reading [about] the North.

There certainly was an intellectual engagement. I mean, that's true. But then the other thing that bothered me was the kind of automatic response over here, and enthusiastic responses to IRA activities and, you know, support for the Noraid line. And I saw that that was pretty ... simplistic, and I began to feel an obligation to try to get people to see that the Northern Irish question was more complex and that they should try to develop more nuanced views.

I applied for some federal money and I got it to do an Irish programme at Westfield, under the Ethnic Heritage programme set up by President Carter. What that did was to enable me to have a whole lot of public lectures at Westfield, about Irish history and culture, including what was going on in the north of Ireland. Now it was getting into the time of the 'dirty protests' and the hunger strikes. These were very emotive events over here. And so that's how I got into that whole thing on Northern Ireland in a public way.

Catherine B. Shannon: in her own words

Matter of fact, I had [Professor] Tony Stewart, the prominent historian of unionism, here at Westfield to talk the day after Bobby Sands died – it had already been scheduled. And Tony wanted to cancel it. I think he was being very sensitive about it. He said, 'I don't want to be offending people.' And I said, 'Tony, now's the time when they need to hear from people like you.' There were some tensions, of course, but the audience as well as Tony learned something of each other's perspective from the encounter.

I really then became convinced that there had to be some kind of very vigorous effort to try to educate the public in the area [around Boston] about the complexity of what was going on in the North [of Ireland]. And that's how I happened to get involved in organising the Kennedy Library symposiums on Northern Ireland in 1982 and 1984.

And it was at these symposiums that I realised you've got representatives of the nationalist community and of the unionist community. But what struck me was that there was a whole perspective that was being missed and that was the voices of women; and the conflict was affecting their lives in such horrible and dramatic ways.

I think that academics, if they can, and if they've got the personality and resources to make a contribution, to the greater social good, they should. You know, I believe that firmly.

I don't regret, for a minute, the expense of my energy and time in terms of trying to change the view in Boston. I worked with Padraig O'Malley very closely on this. We did change the views in Boston and some of that led to much greater support in the area for John Hume. We also organised the 1985 closed-door Airlie House conference, which gave the opportunity for the government and diplomatic people on both sides to move forward, despite [Margaret] Thatcher's dismissal of the New Ireland Forum options with [the mantra of] 'Out! Out! Out!' And, in fact, going back to review the Airlie House sessions, what's obvious [is that] so much of what was discussed there actually became part of the 1985 Hillsborough Agreement, the Anglo-Irish Agreement. So I have no regrets about that. Even in terms of the women's activities and conferences [that I] did in 1994 and 1999, [these] enabled some women in the North [of Ireland] to have positive connections with one another across the divide for a while. I mean, [Baroness] May Blood became a great friend as a result of that. I knew her in Belfast, and then she was involved in both women's conferences and of course what happened next was

17.4 Catherine B. Shannon in November 2019, receiving a doctorate of sacred letters (*honoris causa*) from the University of St Michael's College, University of Toronto. (Image courtesy of Catherine B. Shannon)

all the support for the Women's Coalition over here in the [United] States. I got them introduced to Tip O'Neill's daughter Rosemary, who eventually got them into the White House and they connected with Hillary [Clinton]. And Hillary's involvement, I think, came out of those initiatives in an indirect way.

Catherine B. Shannon: in her own words   261

It was informed advocacy that I was involved in, both in terms of the party-political activity and what we did at the Kennedy symposiums and at Airlie House as well as the lectures at Westfield for the public. I think the work with women did make a contribution and I'm very happy for that.

I mean, we didn't know whether any of these things [would be effective] and [while] we knew they weren't going to change things overnight, at least you were moving in the right direction. And that we were trying to create some better understanding of what was going on over there, not just among people here [in the United States], but between people North and South and, you know, across the divide in Northern Ireland. Certainly by the time we got into the 1990s Monica McWilliams came over at least three, maybe four, times and got support from women in Boston and then eventually the Northern Irish Women's Coalition got plugged into the Washington dynamic. You know, I think those things were very important.

And another event that was particularly important in terms of women having their voices and demanding their voice be heard was the Washington Investment Conference that [President Bill] Clinton had originated just at the time that George Mitchell was appointed as the economic advisor to the North [of Ireland]. And then eventually Mitchell, as you know, ended up chairing the [peace] talks with such great success.

And there was a very healthy sense among the Northern women who were there at Washington at the time that they could get some encouragement and backing from American women and follow their example.

This year, it is sixty years since you graduated with your degree in history from St Michael's. You probably could never have imagined that the arc of your professional and intellectual trajectory would have engaged with Ireland so much over the decades to follow?
I was interested in Ireland and wanted to go there. And you know, fortunately, by the grace of God, I managed to be able to go and to do the MA, and it was really my time in Dublin that just changed my life and made me realise that Ireland had such a strong pull on me and that I wanted to be involved in Irish history and in teaching it.

CHAPTER EIGHTEEN

Catherine B. Shannon and the role of women in the Northern Ireland peace process

Monica McWilliams

This chapter examines the role that Catherine B. Shannon has played over the past three decades in the Northern Ireland peace process, particularly in relation to the role of women during the conflict and in the peace process that followed. Catherine recognised that women organised and led much of the movement leading up to the peace agreement but were too often written out of history. Catherine's life work has been dedicated to ensuring that women are written into, rather than out of, the historical records.

The following inscription on the wall of the Vasa Museum in Stockholm could have been put there by Catherine herself: 'In the writing of history, men are often present but where are the women? They are there ready to shoulder almost any task, to take on any responsibility. The lack of focus on women's history has been a greater problem than the lack of sources.'[1] And it is to Catherine's papers that many of us now turn for the archive material that she has collected down through the decades. Not only did Catherine work assiduously to find and publish those sources but she was also active as a participant in the process herself. As a renowned academic historian and activist for peace and justice, Catherine is frequently referred to as a reliable and credible 'scholar-activist'. There are few who have been able to work across both arenas so successfully and to stand up to that tribute.

In her published work, Catherine makes reference to the range of interventions made by women over the decades of the conflict,

262

demonstrating how the activism on the ground helped to build the strong women's movement during the years of political violence (1968–94). Her work traces the various stages from women activism in the civil rights movement to women becoming agents of change in their local communities throughout Northern Ireland. She illustrates how these movements became alternative ways to bring about policy changes in the turbulent years of the conflict. Over the decades, she travelled backwards and forwards to Belfast to highlight the changes that were taking place as women activists entered the new 'transitional space' between civil society activism and formal politics.

Catherine came to Northern Ireland long before the republican and loyalist ceasefires in 1994, and was actively involved in the peace process leading up to the peace negotiations in 1996. With the advent of British and Irish governments' proposals for 'all-party talks' in spring 1996, details of an electoral system to facilitate the representation of the smaller loyalist paramilitary-linked political parties were published. The electoral format prompted a group of women activists to explore the opportunity for direct political intervention, which Catherine greatly encouraged. Meetings were called, out of which the Northern Ireland Women's Coalition was formed as a cross-community initiative, holding to the principles of human rights, inclusion and equality. Catherine was encouraged by the decision to establish the Northern Ireland Women's Coalition as a political party in 1996 and became directly involved in helping to raise the finance for the subsequent elections.

Catherine also assisted the Women's Coalition by promoting its work in the US and organising speaking events to broaden the circle of influence. Catherine came on many occasions to Northern Ireland to help local women become actively involved in the peace process throughout the mid- to late 1990s. She assisted in the process of enabling women to grasp the opportunities to progress the aims of the Women's Coalition and to increase the representation of women at the peace table. Catherine believed in the potential of the multi-party peace talks to reach a successful outcome and was the first person the Women's Coalition reached out to following the signing of the peace agreement in Castle Buildings at 5.15 p.m. on 10 April, Good Friday, 1998.

Following the peace accord, Catherine came to Belfast to help canvass in the elections for the first Northern Ireland Legislative Assembly. The Northern Ireland Women's Coalition was running yet again, without much in the way of resources or finances, and needed every hand it could get to canvass each constituency. Catherine faced the downpours and the burned-out canvassers who had already spent weeks traipsing around Northern Ireland imploring people to vote Yes in the referendum that followed the Good Friday Agreement. When the polls finally closed and the count started in Belfast City Hall, Catherine stayed the course and was still there at midnight when the first of the Women's Coalition candidates was successfully returned to represent South Belfast. As the women from the coalition were celebrating this famous moment on the floor of the great hall, Catherine seemed to have physically shrunk through both weariness and relief. But no matter how small in stature Catherine may have appeared, she remained a giant in the eyes of the women surrounding her. Catherine had crossed the Atlantic, worked door to door for women to get elected and was there to witness that historical moment.

Catherine also knew that in terms of conflict transformation, the hard work started then. Making peace for the women involved would be a process demanding patience and persistence and, most of all, the participation from communities on the ground. Having studied other peace processes, she also knew that, where a predominantly male 'political' status quo is re/established post-conflict, women's participation could recede in both real terms as well as in institutional memory. Catherine had written extensively on how the more conservative culture impacted on the position of women, permitting a predominantly male discourse to influence the decisions taken over women's lives.[2]

Catherine documented how women throughout the 1970s and 1980s experienced increasingly oppressive conditions through a nationalist movement that had become militarised, with male privilege in the community becoming more entrenched. This state of affairs was double-sided, where the raising of 'women's issues' was often deemed a distraction from the main constitutional issues. Catherine was aware of the contradiction of women's political activism where gender issues were regarded as secondary and where women were told to wait until the 'bigger' issues were sorted out first. In addition, she was aware of the influence of international solidarity that saw women learning from transnational activism. Catherine was the organiser of the symposium on Northern Ireland at the JFK Library in March 1982, and co-organiser of the second symposium there in March 1984, and the Airlie House conference with Padraig O'Malley in January 1985. It was Catherine who later began the transatlantic meetings that were aptly titled Reaching Common Ground.

The role of women in the Northern Ireland peace process   265

The initial conference, which involved Irish and American women, was held at Boston University in November 1994. A conference was organised in 1999 at Westfield State College, where Catherine taught history. Titled 'Women Envisioning Peace: Inaugural conference of the Global Women's History Project', it involved women from Northern Ireland and the Republic of Ireland, and a delegation of Israeli and Palestinian women. Arlene Foster, later to become the first minister of Northern Ireland, was one of those attending, along with members of Sinn Féin, which created the potential for some cross-community dialogue outside the confines of Northern Ireland. Meetings had previously been held in Dublin (at the invitation of US ambassador to Ireland, Jean Kennedy Smith) to strategise around women's political participation and demands. The emphasis was on an inclusive peace process and respect for women's rights. A cross-community conference was organised following the Downing Street Declaration – seen as creating a crucial step in the negotiations between political parties and the British and Irish governments – to ensure that women would also have a role in such important decision-making.

When the peace agreement was finally concluded, the Women's Coalition was successful in having 'the right of women to full and equal participation in political life' inserted into the final proposals. It also ensured that the peace accord acknowledged issues of gender equality and non-discrimination independently of the issue of national identity. Like the Women's Coalition, Catherine was also aware that women needed to identify with the agreement by seeing themselves named in its provisions.

Catherine came to know women living in disadvantaged areas on both sides of the sectarian divide and placed an emphasis in her writing on issues of poverty and deprivation. All of the substantive issues that were close to her sense of justice also got included in the peace accord: the introduction of a new human rights body, a bill of rights and a stronger mandate for the Equality Commission, the recognition of the rights of victims and survivors of the conflict; acknowledgement of the importance of community development; and proposals to increase the provision of housing and education on a non-sectarian basis alongside a civic forum to allow for the participation of civil society representatives, in an advisory forum complementary to the Northern Ireland Assembly. By being prepared to challenge the dominant narratives, the chairperson of the peace talks, Senator Mitchell (1999), concluded, the emergence of women as a political force was a significant factor in achieving the agreement. In his book *Making Peace*, Senator Mitchell acknowledges that 'in the final stages of the negotiations, they [the Women's Coalition] were serious, important participants' and played a decisive role in both the process and the substance of the agreement.[3]

However, as Catherine might herself have predicted, the instability of the post-agreement implementation period resulted in a continuing emphasis on the predominantly male preserves of demilitarisation, decommissioning of weaponry and reconfiguring of policing and security shot through with arguments over the allocation of political power. A common experience in post-conflict situations is that women ask for, but do not get, the kind of 'hard' legal enforcement that would help to sustain gains for the long term. Catherine understood the importance of vigilance in the building of a more sustainable peace. She brings the best of academia and activism to her work, organising, lobbying and using her pen to keep a light shining on women's achievements and passing that learning to future generations.

CHAPTER NINETEEN

Safe spaces on the Falls

Margaret MacCurtain

Having been given responsibility for senior history at the Dominicans' Sion Hill in 1956, I asked permission to study for a graduate degree in Early Modern Irish History at University College Dublin. When Professor R. Dudley Edwards met me wearing my Dominican habit, he told me that I would be doing a study of an Irish bishop for my thesis. He suggested the Kerry-born Dominic O'Daly, who founded the Dominican Monastery of Corpo Santo and the Convent of Bom Successo in Lisbon. I would go on to write my thesis by candlelight because there was no electricity in the sisters' rooms in Sion Hill until the late fifties.

The other element that brought light into my graduate studies was the other students doing the MA with me: Catherine Shannon and Joe Lee. Catherine was finishing her thesis, 'The Irish Local Government Act of 1898: The politics of administration', which earned her an MA in 1963. As Catherine, Joe and I waited patiently for T. Desmond Williams to return from a late lunch with his colleagues, we forged a lifelong friendship which took us through our graduate degrees and through years of university teaching. Catherine taught at Westfield State College in western Massachusetts from 1967 to 2000. An energetic and enlightened teacher, she could have as easily taught younger children, and all her life she was the favourite aunt of young nieces and nephews and later grandnieces and grandnephews whom she entertained at her beachfront home in Scituate, Massachusetts.

While Catherine continued her interest in local history and especially in the role that Arthur Balfour played in the Ireland of the late nineteenth century, an interest that informed her book *Arthur J. Balfour and Ireland,*

267

1874–1922 (1988), when the Troubles intensified in Northern Ireland in 1969 Catherine became committed to the Northern Ireland peace process. She was the principal organiser of the symposium on Northern Ireland held at the Kennedy Library in 1982. The success of that symposium led to other North American meetings in the safe spaces where it was possible for the Northern Ireland players to meet their counterparts for constructive conversation. These symposia, particularly the one she designed called 'Reaching Common Ground: A conference of Irish and American women relating to the Northern Ireland conflict' that was held at Boston University in 1994, prompted Catherine to document women's roles in the Northern Irish conflict and subsequent peace process.

In 'The Woman Writer as Historical Witness: Northern Ireland, 1968–1994: An interdisciplinary perspective', the essay that Catherine B. Shannon wrote for *Women & Irish History: Essays in honour of Margaret MacCurtain*, Shannon speaks of Northern women's silence, a silence '… compounded by the very traditional roles ascribed to women by the region's churches and schools'.[1] While women may have been limited by the Catholic hierarchy, a hierarchy that was completely opposed to integrated schools which might enlarge gendered as well as sectarian education, according to Shannon, the religious girls' schools in west Belfast provided safe spaces on the Falls Road.

Having been awakened by gunshots as I slept in the Dominican convent on the Falls Road in the 1970s, I wondered how it was possible to create a haven of normalcy in a city that was exploding outside the walls.[2] The autobiographical writings of Northern schoolgirls like Áine da Silva's poem 'Self-Preservation' addressed the anxieties of life in the North during those years of sectarian violence:

> Children of the Troubles.
> Our bombs are close but they are not quite nuclear
> although they steal our families from us.[3]

This essay will consider how two schools on the Falls Road, the Dominicans' St Dominic's Grammar School for Girls and the Daughters of Charity's St Louise's Comprehensive School, educated girls on the Falls Road, and will examine how the administrators and faculty of the schools were able create those 'safe spaces'.[4] How did the schools protect and sustain their students during the Troubles? How did the schools prepare their students to take their place (or not) in that troubled city?

Safe spaces on the Falls

Was there a relationship between the two religious communities and their schools? What was the nature of that relationship?

Both schools operate under the auspices of the bishop of Down and Connor; however, while both schools were committed to creating safe spaces, they differed in their sizes and in their constituencies. Founded in April 1870 by the Dominicans of Cabra when Bishop Patrick Dorrian, building on Paul Cardinal Cullen's expansionism, invited Catholic teaching orders to open schools in Belfast as a step in building a Catholic infrastructure in the city, St Dominic's, the red-brick school across the Lower Falls Road from the Royal Victoria Hospital, shares its campus with St Mary's Training College that merged with the Christian Brothers' St Joseph's and became St Mary's University College. With a current enrolment of 1,000 students, 25 per cent of whom are eligible for free meals, St Dominic's was the top-performing secondary school in Northern Ireland between 2013 and 2017, with 96.5 per cent of its students achieving three or more A levels.

Before the Troubles erupted in west Belfast's Ardoyne district on 14 August 1969, when Protestants burned out the Catholic homes on the streets connecting the Catholic Falls Road with the Protestant Shankill Road, the Dominicans had worked for a century within the Northern Ireland education system to produce leaders from their cohort of girls with proven academic records based on their 11+ examination results. Later, after the free education scheme, the fact that the Dominicans provided a well-regarded grammar school education meant that St Dominic's offered an alternative to the free, integrated grammar schools when they were introduced to the Belfast area.

In addition to providing a challenging and demanding curriculum, two features of St Dominic's vision were essential elements in their success in facilitating young women's leadership skills as they worked to 'create community', a priority they shared with prayer, contemplation, study, preaching and pursuing truth through discussion and debate epitomised by their motto: *veritas*. While the Dominicans had remarkable leaders, leadership was always executed as a function of membership in a community of educators, the modern day 'Order of Preachers'.

The Dominican community produced a generation of leaders from their St Dominic's students. Early on there were women like the writer Mary Beckett, author of *A Belfast Woman* (1980) and *Give Them Stories* (1987), the maths teacher turned St Dominic's vice-principal Eileen Carragher who was a founding member in 1970 of the Social Democratic and Labour

Party (SDLP), and Geraldine Marie Smyth, OP, who served as the international prioress of the Dominican congregation between 1998 and 2004, as the director of the Irish School of Ecumenics who supervised the school's merger with Trinity College Dublin and as a founding member of an ecumenical community created at the Belfast peace line. A later cohort who attended St Dominic's with Mary Leneghan McAleese (1962–9), president of the Republic of Ireland from 1997 to 2011, demonstrated the range of leaders that St Dominic's produced, leaders who would play prominent roles during the Troubles in Northern Ireland or as a result of the Troubles in Northern Ireland. The students ranged from Dolours Price (1951–2013) – who joined the Provisional IRA and who, with her sister Marian, was sentenced to prison for trying to bomb the Old Bailey in 1973, and who was visited regularly in prison by Sister Simeon Tarpey, OP – to Anna Carragher, a television producer who became BBC Northern Ireland's first woman controller in 2000. Among the public service roles Carragher played when she retired was membership of the Commission of Equality for Northern Ireland. The women who played more centrist roles were those who attempted to develop inclusive, peaceful solutions to resolve conflict.

The best-known examples from this St Dominic's cohort were Mary Leneghan McAleese and Betty Williams. From the north Belfast Ardoyne, McAleese's father's pubs were bombed, and the family was burned out of their home during the Troubles. McAleese attended the Mercy convent on the Crumlin Road, but when she passed the 11+ examination was offered a coveted place at St Dominic's. Utilising the Dominican ethos of the search for truth through study, McAleese's decision to pursue peaceful solutions to the violence of the Troubles came from her Dominican education. She later recalled her call to peace. 'From the beginning, I set out to try to find my way through the Church and through Christ.'[5]

McAleese was not only influenced by the Dominican sisters; lay teachers at St Dominic's were also significant models. May O'Friel not only introduced McAleese to the world of art, drama and film, but she also provided practical help. When O'Friel discovered that McAleese, who was preparing for her A levels, was also trying to take care of her eight brothers and sisters after the birth of the ninth and youngest child left her mother seriously ill, she picked up McAleese every morning and drove her to school.[6]

Safe spaces on the Falls

Betty Williams also had a sick mother, but she had to drop out of St Dominic's to care for her and for a younger sister; however, she was imbued with the Dominican ideal of a reasoned peace. While she briefly joined the IRA in 1972, she founded the Community of Peace People with Mairéad Corrigan in 1976, when Corrigan's sister's children were run over and killed by an IRA fugitive. The two women shared the Nobel Prize for Peace in 1976. Later, Williams headed the World Centers of Compassion for Children.

The stability provided to St Dominic's students enabled them to pursue excellence in callings other than the peace process: the artist Rita Duffy, the artistic director of the Kabosh Theatre Paula McFetridge, the advocate for disadvantaged students Marie-Thérèse McGivern of Belfast Metropolitan College, and two high-profile politicians, the SDLP's Nichola Mallon and Órlaithí Flynn of Sinn Féin.

The second of the two religious secondary schools on the Falls Road is the Daughters of Charity's St Louise's Comprehensive College. Like the Dominicans, the Daughters of Charity of St Vincent de Paul have their own charism. They dedicate themselves annually to serving the poor. When the Daughters of Charity opened their St Vincent's School in 1900 at the invitation of Bishop Henry Henry, they provided education to the district's 'half-timers', the girls who worked in the city's linen mills and who went to school two days and worked three days each week. When the 'half-timer' system was abolished, St Vincent's became a primary school. When the Daughters of Charity opened their new school on 1 January 1958, the school that would become St Louise's Comprehensive College, it stretched along the Falls Road from Whiterock to Milltown Cemetery, the place where the IRA buried their dead.

The first principal of St Louise's was Sister Ita Polley; however, from the beginning, Sister Genevieve O'Farrell was the commanding presence in the school. She became the official head of St Louise's in 1963, a position she held for twenty-five years until her retirement in 1988. While St Dominic's has had a series of excellent heads of school, Sister Genevieve, known locally as 'the only man on the Falls Road', was St Louise's. Under her formidable leadership, and with their motto *Excellence through Caring*, the school made education a weapon in fighting unemployment in west Belfast, the evil that was responsible for the community's poverty and the girls' low self-esteem.

For Sister Genevieve, St Dominic's was both an inspiration and a challenge. The approach of the Dominicans and the Daughters of Charity towards their schools was similar in that both communities wanted to create a place of normalcy for their girls so that their students could focus on what was most important: their education. They also dedicated themselves to preparing their students for their lives after secondary school. However, the student bodies and their operation of the schools differed.

St Dominic's students wore wine-coloured uniforms, so the St Louise girls had their own uniforms of brown skirts, berets, gloves and cream shirts which were meant to be worn not only on campus but to and from school. Sister Genevieve was known to prowl along the Falls Road in her car honking her horn at miscreants who were not in full uniform. Students were expected to be punctual and ready for class. These routines meant, according to Mary O'Hara, a former St Louise head girl, that '... for at least part of the way, we were shielded from the chaos often unfolding outside the school gates'.[7] Critical to the St Louise ethos was the morning assembly, where Sister Genevieve led prayers for all who died in the Troubles, including soldiers in the British army, stressing the sameness of suffering and the need for forgiveness in the troubled North.

While she preached peace and forgiveness, Sister Genevieve was known to face down the British army and the IRA. When the British army set up roadblocks, Sister Genevieve marched up the Falls Road at the head of a line of her students and demanded that they be let pass. When the IRA wanted the school closed on the days that they buried their dead in Milltown Cemetery, except for the funeral of Bobby Sands in May 1981 she refused to close St Louise's.

Her tall, no-nonsense presence made Sister Genevieve a legend on the Falls. She was the subject of John Rae's biography *Sister Genevieve: A courageous woman's triumph in Northern Ireland* (2001) and two reminiscences of former students: the affectionate portrait by Mary O'Hara, the first St Louise graduate to attend Cambridge University, that appeared in *The Guardian* in 2002; and in the character of Sister Bonaventure in Mary Costello's coming-of-age novel *Titanic Town* (2000) set in the Belfast of the 1970s.

O'Hara described the principles that informed Sister Genevieve's leadership of St Louise's: 'Religious conviction that all people are born equal inspired her, but it was her pragmatism, radical, single-minded determination and formidable defence of our right to a top-rate education that inspired me and many others. We were trained to go out confident,

Safe spaces on the Falls

independent and accomplished and win good jobs when unemployment in some parts of the Falls was as high as 80%.'[8]

Costello's protagonist, Annie McPhelimy, a bright but poorly motivated St Catherine's (St Louise's) 'brown bomber', hopes that her school, which is 'organised along the lines of a POW camp', will sink into the bog, and she ducks into the Falls Park to eat crisps and toffee while wearing her 'hideous cocoa brown school uniform'.[9] Annie admits to admiring the 'stern, courageous and intelligent' Sister Bonaventure while being terrified of her.[10]

Sister Genevieve believed in tough girls like the fictional Annie McPhelimy. She campaigned against the 11+ system in Northern Ireland long after the examination was discontinued in the rest of the United Kingdom, because she refused to believe that a single examination could be a measure of the intellectual ability of a youngster. The Daughters of Charity believed that the 11+ examination was responsible for the low self-esteem in the west Falls. Sister Genevieve also refused to believe that a school that accepted those who failed the 11+ examination was an institution for academic failures. Over the years that she was the principal of St Louise's, Sister Genevieve presided over a school that grew from 1,000 students in 1963 to 2,400 students in 2002, and a student body that included more and more girls who stayed on beyond the required age of attendance. She took a particular pride in the numbers of students who passed their examinations and went on to post-secondary education, and she saw to it that St Louise's offered the traditional academic subjects as well as the practical courses that prepared students to go directly to work. St Louise girls rose above the Troubles through their education.

Students at the fee-paying St Dominic's Grammar School who passed the 11+ were being prepared for their O and A level examinations that brought access to post-secondary education in Northern Irish, British or Irish universities and with it subsequent economic mobility; students at St Louise's who had not passed the 11+ worked for a credential or credentials that would free them from the massive unemployment and poverty that characterised west Belfast in the 1970s. St Louise girls would not stitch shirts. By 1980, however, between 20 and 25 per cent of the girls enrolled in St Louise's had the qualifications to be admitted to a grammar school.[11]

While St Dominic's and St Louise's pursued their own visions for their schools, both were committed to increasing their students' self-esteem and to liberating them from poverty through education. For some students, the traditional curriculum was a viable option; others sought to develop their skills to take advantage of new work opportunities. These lessons were not lost on me when, at the end of the 1970s, I became the founding principal of Ballyfermot Senior College in a disadvantaged part of Dublin where enrolment in three local colleges, including those run by the Dominicans and the Daughters of Wisdom, was declining. It was an opportunity for me to make my best contribution to Irish society.

Having examined several models of post-secondary education and visiting ten community colleges in the United States, I discussed the options with the staff of the newly established Ballyfermot Senior College. We chose the community college model because it not only made further education accessible to primary school leavers who had opted out of the system, but it also provided the facilities that made it possible to establish a lively night college for the Ballyfermot adults taking Dublin Vocational Education Committee (VEC) courses.

Taking the idea of new credentials to supplement the traditional subjects, we also introduced courses in art and graphic design, animation, cinema, mixed media and music production. A moment of particular pride was the mention of Ballyfermot in the acceptance speech of those receiving an Oscar for Best Animated Film in 2016. I even questioned the usual demarcation between second and third level education in my remarks on the occasion of the formal opening of Ballyfermot Senior College in 1981, arguing instead for a seamless education system for local students. The entry point for trades like bricklaying and carpentry was an important aspect of our discussion of our mission. Ballyfermot Senior College successfully negotiated that the trade unions would accept its credentials as appropriate training models. The college also received approval for the request that its nursing courses meet the FETAC (Further Education and Training Awards Council) standards.

While it might not appear to be the case, the schools on the Falls and Ballyfermot Senior College share an important similarity. In a time of transition, the schools demonstrated to disadvantaged students that education, including education in non-traditional subjects, could be the key to economic and social mobility for people in communities plagued by poverty, unemployment and underemployment.

Notes

Preface – Catherine B. Shannon: happy recollections

1 Anna Burns, *Milkman* (London: Faber & Faber, 2018), paperback edn, esp. pp. 155–65.

Introduction

1 Charles Fanning, Editor's Introduction, *New Perspectives on the Irish Diaspora* (Carbondale and Edwardsville: Southern Illinois University Press, 2000), pp. 2–3.

2 Oscar Handlin (ed.), *Immigration as a Factor in American History* (Englewood Cliffs, NJ: Prentice-Hall, 1959), p. 1.

3 Bernard Bailyn's *The Barbarous Years: The peopling of British North America. The conflict of civilizations, 1600–1675* (New York: Alfred A. Knopf, 2012) addresses the field's evolution. Despite marginalisation as a historian, Cecil Woodham-Smith's *The Great Hunger: Ireland, 1845–9* (London: Hamish Hamilton, 1962) endures.

4 Nicholas Canny, *Kingdom and Colony: Ireland in the Atlantic world, 1560–1800* (Baltimore, MD: Johns Hopkins University Press, 1988); Nicholas Canny and Philip Morgan (eds), *The Oxford Handbook of the Atlantic World: 1450–1850* (Oxford: Oxford University Press, 2011).

5 Maurice J. Bric, 'The Irish Immigrant and the Broadening of the Polity in Philadelphia, 1790–1800', in Eliga H. Gould and Peter S. Onuf (eds), *Empire and Nation: The American revolution in the Atlantic world* (Baltimore, MD: Johns Hopkins University Press, 2005), pp. 159–77, at p. 165; Marianne Elliott, *Wolfe Tone* (Liverpool: Liverpool University Press, 2012), pp. 249–50.

6 Marion R. Casey cited the value of digitised resources in both genealogical searches and a broader history of America's Irish in 'Family, History, and Irish America', *Journal of American Ethnic History*, vol. 28, no. 4, summer 2009, pp. 110–17, particularly pp. 111–12.

7 Cian T. McMahon reminds us of 'the fledgling transatlantic network of Irish news and opinion' nurtured in newspapers such as the Boston *Pilot* and the Dublin *Nation* in *The Global Dimensions of Irish Identity: Race, nation, and the popular press, 1840–1880* (Chapel Hill, NC: The University of North Carolina Press, 2015), pp. 18, 27, 35.

8 Joseph S. Moore and Jane G.V. McGaughey, 'The Covenanter Sensibility across the Long Atlantic World', *Journal of Transatlantic Studies*, vol. 11, no. 2, 2013, pp. 125–34; quotation, p. 126. Also see David T. Gleeson's *The Irish in the Atlantic World* (Columbia, SC: University of South Carolina Press, 2010) and Rankin Sherling's *The Invisible Irish: Finding Protestants in the nineteenth-century migrations to America* (Montreal: McGill-Queen's University Press, 2016).

9 Dennis Clark, 'Portraying Irish America: Trans-Atlantic revisions', *History Ireland*, vol. 2, no. 4, winter 1994, pp. 48–52, particularly p. 49. Clark concluded: 'The history of the Irish in the United States is a subject without which modern Irish history itself simply cannot be made intelligible', p. 52.

10 David Brundage, 'Recent Directions in the History of Irish-American Nationalism', *Journal of American Ethnic History*, vol. 28, no. 4, summer 2009, pp. 82–9; transatlantic call, p. 87. See also William H. Mulligan, Jr, 'How the Irish Became American:

Reflections on the history of the Irish in the United States', in Diane Sabenacio Nititham and Rebecca Boyd (eds), *Heritage, Diaspora and the Consumption of Culture: Movements in Irish landscapes* (Surrey and Burlington, VT: Ashgate Publishing, 2014), pp. 93–111.

11 Kevin Kenny, 'Irish Emigrations in a Comparative Perspective', in Eugenio F. Biagini and Mary E. Daly (eds), *The Cambridge Social History of Modern Ireland* (Cambridge: Cambridge University Press, 2017), pp. 406–22.

12 See particularly John Killick, 'Transatlantic Steerage Fares, British and Irish Migration, and Return Migration, 1815–60', *Economic History Review*, vol. 67, no. 1, February 2014, pp. 170–91.

13 Hasia R. Diner, *Erin's Daughters in America: Irish immigrant women in the nineteenth century* (Baltimore, MD: Johns Hopkins University Press, 1983); Deirdre M. Moloney, 'A Transatlantic Reform: Boston's port protection program and Irish women immigrants', *Journal of American Ethnic History*, vol. 19, no. 1, fall 1999, pp. 50–67.

14 Bronwen Walter, '"Old Mobilities"? Transatlantic women from the west of Ireland 1880s–1920s', *Irish Journal of Sociology*, vol. 23, no. 2, November 2015, pp. 49–68; quotation, p, 49. Kevin Kenny called for attention to women in 'Diaspora and Comparison: The global Irish as a case study', *Journal of American History*, vol. 90, 2003, pp. 134–62; see also D.A.J. MacPherson and Mary J. Hickman (eds), *Women and Irish Diaspora Identities: Theories, concepts and new perspectives* (Manchester: Manchester University Press, 2014); Janet Nolan, 'Women's Place in the History of the Irish Diaspora: A snapshot', *Journal of American Ethnic History*, vol. 28, 2009, pp. 76–81; and Michèle Milan, 'Mary Anne Sadlier's Trans-Atlantic Links: Migration, religion and translation', *Atlantic Studies*, vol. 15, no. 3, 2018, pp. 365–82; quotations, p. 366. See Tyler Blethen and Curtis Wood (eds), *Ulster and North America: Transatlantic perspectives on the Scotch-Irish* (Tuscaloosa, AL: University of Alabama Press, 1997).

15 Kerby A. Miller, *Emigrants and Exiles: Ireland and the Irish exodus to North America* (Oxford and New York: Oxford University Press, 1985), and *Ireland and Irish America: Culture, class, and transatlantic migration* (Dublin: Field Day, 2008), p. 3. Patrick Ward's *Exile, Emigration and Irish Writing* (Dublin: Irish Academic Press, 2002), and Malcolm Campbell's *Ireland's New Worlds: Immigrants, politics, and society in the United States and Australia, 1815–1922* (Madison, WI: University of Wisconsin Press, 2008) remain useful.

16 See, for example, Kenneth C. Wenzer, *Henry George, the Transatlantic Irish, and Their Times: Research in the history of economic thought and methodology* (Bingley: Emerald Group Publishing Limited, 2009); and Bernadette Whelan, 'The Transatlantic World of Charles Stewart Parnell (1846–91)', *Journal of Transatlantic Studies*, vol. 14, no. 3, September 2016, pp. 293–308. Michael Doorley's *Justice Daniel Cohalan 1865–1946: American patriot and Irish-American nationalist* (Cork: Cork University Press, 2019) cites Cohalan's connections with Ireland.

17 Michael de Nie involved British sources in the Atlantic framework in '"A Medley Mob of Irish-American Plotters and Irish Dupes": The British press and transatlantic Fenianism', *Journal of British Studies*, vol. 40, no. 2, April 2001, pp. 213–40.

18 Ely M. Janis, *A Greater Ireland: The Land League and transatlantic nationalism in Gilded Age America* (Madison, WI: The University of Wisconsin Press, 2015), p. 3.

19 James H. Adams, 'The Negotiated Hibernian: Discourse on the Fenian in England and America', *American Nineteenth-Century History*, vol. 11, no. 1, March 2010, pp. 47–77.

20 Michael Mays offers insights in *Nation States: The cultures of Irish nationalism* (Lanham, MD: Rowman & Littlefield, 2007); as does David Sim in *A Union Forever: The Irish question and US foreign relations in the Victorian age* (Ithaca: Cornell University Press, 2013), p. 38.

Notes to pages 3 to 4

21 Brendan O'Leary, 'The Shackles of the State and Hereditary Animosities: Colonialism in the interpretation of Irish history', *Field Day Review*, vol. 10, 2014, pp. 148–86.

22 Marguerite Corporaal and Jason King (eds), *Irish Global Migration and Memory: Transatlantic perspectives of Ireland's famine exodus* (London: Routledge, 2018); Paul Darby, *Gaelic Games, Nationalism and the Irish Diaspora in the United States* (Dublin: UCD Press, 2009). The *Journal of Transatlantic Studies'* launch in 2003 affirms the popularity of the construct. Angela McCarthy, *Ireland in the World: Comparative, transnational, and personal perspectives* (New York: Routledge, 2015).

23 Enda Delaney, 'Directions in Historiography: Our island story? Towards a transnational history of late modern Ireland', *Irish Historical Studies*, vol. xxxvii, no. 148, November 2011, pp. 83–105; lamentation, p. 84; and Niall Whelehan (ed.), *Transnational Perspectives on Modern Irish History* (New York and London: Routledge, 2015), p. 1.

24 Sarah Roddy, 'Mass Migration's Impact on Irish Catholicism: An historical view', in Dominic Pasura and Marta Bivand Erdal (eds), *Migration, Transnationalism and Catholicism: Global perspectives* (New York: Palgrave Macmillan, 2016), pp. 51–74, at pp. 67–8; Matteo Binasco, *Rome and Irish Catholicism in the Atlantic World, 1622–1908* (Basingstoke: Palgrave Macmillan, 2019).

25 Donald H. Akenson's calls for attention to Protestants echo still; see *Small Differences: Irish Catholics and Irish Protestants, 1815–1922* (Montreal: McGill-Queen's University Press, 1988); among treatments, see Patrick Griffin's *The People with No Name: Ireland's Ulster Scots, America's Scots Irish, and the creation of a British Atlantic world, 1689–1764* (Princeton, NJ: Princeton University Press, 2001); Donald MacRaild's 'The Orange Atlantic', in Gleeson, *Irish in the Atlantic World*, pp. 307–26, and MacRaild's other work on the topic; Peter Gilmore, *Irish Presbyterians and the Shaping of Western Pennsylvania, 1770–1830* (Pittsburgh: University of Pittsburgh Press, 2018), and Lindsey Flewelling, *Two Irelands Beyond the Sea: Ulster unionism and America, 1880–1920* (Oxford: Oxford University Press, 2018).

26 From a broad field, see Timothy G. McMahon, Michael de Nie and Paul Townend (eds), *Ireland and the Imperial World: Citizenship, opportunism and subversion* (New York: Palgrave Macmillan, 2017); Ian Delahanty, 'The Transatlantic Roots of Irish-American Anti-Abolitionism, 1843–1859', *Journal of the Civil War Era*, vol. 6, no. 2, June 2016, pp. 164–92, particularly the conclusion, p. 186; Christine Kinealy's *Daniel O'Connell and the Anti-Slavery Movement* (London: Pickering & Chatto, 2011); Nini Rodgers, 'Ireland, Slavery, Antislavery, Post-slavery and Empire: An historiographical survey', *Slavery & Abolition*, vol. 37, no. 3, 2016, pp. 489–504.

27 Fiona Paisley and Pamela Scully, *Writing Transnational History* (London: Bloomsbury Academic, 2019), p. 12 – a book on 'transnational history … mostly in the Anglophone world', with nary a mention of Ireland. On the Irish, see Íde B. O'Carroll, *Irish Transatlantics 1980–2015* (Cork: Attic Press, 2018).

28 Laura R. Prieto and Stephen R. Berry (eds), *Crossings and Encounters: Race, gender, and sexuality in the Atlantic world* (Columbia, SC: University of South Carolina Press, 2020); also 'The Age of Revolution', chapter in Trevor Burnard's *The Atlantic in World History, 1490–1830* (London: Bloomsbury Academic, 2020), pp. 113–35.

29 John V. Kelleher, 'Irishness in America', in John V. Kelleher and Charles Fanning (eds), *Selected Writings of John V. Kelleher on Ireland and Irish America* (Carbondale, IL: Southern Illinois University Press, 2002), pp. 150–5; quotations, pp. 151–3 (essay previously published in *Atlantic*, vol. 208, July 1961, pp. 38–40); William J. Smyth raised analogous points in 'Irish Identity in a Transnational Context', *Acadiensis: Journal of the history of the Atlantic region / Revue d'histoire de la région atlantique*, vol. 48, no. 1, spring 2019, pp. 143–52.

278   *Notes to pages 4 to 14*

30 Smyth, 'Irish Identity', p. 152.

31 Lawrence McCaffrey, 'Ireland and Irish America: Connections and disconnections', *US Catholic Historian*, vol. 22, no. 3, summer 2004, pp. 1–18; quotations, p. 1.

32 Donald H. Akenson, *Ireland, Sweden, and the Great European Migration, 1815–1914* (Montreal: McGill-Queen's University Press, 2011), p. 7.

33 Timothy J. Meagher, 'From the World to the Village and the Beginning to the End and After: Research opportunities in Irish-American history', *Journal of American Ethnic History*, vol. 28, no. 4, summer 2009, pp. 118–35. In the same volume, William Jenkins used the term 'remap' in 'Remapping "Irish America": Circuits, places, performances', *Journal of American Ethnic History*, vol. 28, no. 4, summer 2009, pp. 90–9.

34 David Noel Doyle raised useful questions in 'Review: Cohesion and diversity in the Irish diaspora', *Irish Historical Studies*, vol. 31, no. 123, May 1999, pp. 411–34; Bronwen Walter cites debates in 'The Diaspora in Comparative and Multi-generational Perspective', in Biagini and Daly, *Cambridge Social History*, pp. 423–38.

35 T.C. Barnard, review of Niall Whelehan (ed.), *Transnational Perspectives on Modern Irish History* (New York: Routledge, 2015), in *English Historical Review*, vol. cxxxii, no. 556, June 2017, pp. 732–4; quotation, p. 733.

36 '"There is never any problem, ever, which can be confined within a single framework", from Fernand Braudel, 'On History', cited in O'Leary, 'Shackles of the State', *Field Day Review*, p. 152.

37 Timothy J. Meagher referenced 'Ireland, the source of all things authentically Irish' in 'Irish America Without Ireland: Irish-American relations with Ireland in the twentieth century', in Whelehan, *Transnational Perspectives*, pp. 189–223, especially p. 215. See also Beth O'Leary Anish, *Irish American Fiction from World War II to JFK: Anxiety, assimilation, and activism* (New York: Palgrave Macmillan, 2021).

38 Zadie Smith, 'Darryl Pinckney's Intimate Study of Black History', *The New Yorker*, 26 November 2019, https://www.newyorker.com/books/page-turner/darryl-pinckneys-intimate-study-of-black-history.

39 Canny's Irish Atlantic scholarship receives attention in Burnard's *The Atlantic in World History*, particularly p. 28.

40 Catherine B. Shannon, *Arthur J. Balfour and Ireland, 1874–1922* (Washington, DC: Catholic University of America Press, 1988). See also Francis M. Carroll's *America and the Making of an Independent Ireland: A history* (New York: New York University Press, 2021).

CHAPTER 1 – **The 'Kingdom of God' and the 'kingdom of Ireland': the life, work and politics of hymnist Cecil Frances Alexander (1818–95)**

1 Our title derives from J.M. Synge's famous account of his 'conversion' to Irish cultural nationalism in the wake of his loss of religious belief upon reading Darwin: 'Soon after I had relinquished the Kingdom of God I began to take up a real interest in the kingdom of Ireland.' J.M. Synge, 'Autobiography', *Collected Works: Prose. Volume II*, ed. Alan Price (London: Oxford University Press, 1966), p. 13.

2 John Keble, 'Notice', Mrs C.F. Alexander, *Hymns for Little Children* (London: J Masters & Co., 1887), p. 8, https://archive.org/details/HymnsForLittleChildren.

3 See *Ulster Journal of Archaeology*, vols 1–2, 1894–5, 1895–6, p. 283. 'The Siege of Derry' is praised as 'a remarkably fine balled, filled with charity, yet containing a ring of manly pride and endurance'. 'The Legend of Stumpie's Brae' is considered 'worthy to take its place beside "Eugene Aram"'. The Scotch dialect used in the narrative lends itself well

Notes to pages 14 to 16   279

to the weirdness of the tale'. The journal can be found online: https://www.jstor.org/journal/ulstjarch.

4   Gordon Lucy, 'Remembering Mrs Cecil Frances Alexander', *Church News Ireland*, 13 April 2018, http://www.churchnewsireland.org/news/irish-uk-news/faith-perspective-remembering-mrs-cecil-frances-alexander/.

5   Ernest Lovell, *A Green Hill Far Away: The life of Mrs. C.F. Alexander* (Dublin: APCK and London: SPCK, 1970), pp. 3, 65. Interestingly, Alexander had a family connection to the Rossettis, and it is notable that Christina was the author of the popular Christmas carol 'In the Bleak Midwinter' (1872), which appears in sixty-six hymnals. See https://hymnary.org/text/in_the_bleak_midwinter.

6   Kenneth W. Osbeck, *Amazing Grace: 366 inspiring hymn stories for daily devotions* (Grand Rapids, MI: Kregel, 2002), p. 112. That said, a recent article links the Rossetti circle to the Victorian valorisation of the 'Celtic'. See Emily Orlando, 'Passionate Love-Letters to a Dead Girl: Elizabeth Siddall in Oscar Wilde's *The Picture of Dorian Gray*', *Victoriographies*, vol. 17, no. 1, 2017, pp. 101–23.

7   See Lovell, *A Green Hill Far Away*, and also Valerie Wallace, *Mrs Alexander: A life of the hymn-writer Cecil Frances Alexander, 1818–1895* (Dublin: Lilliput Press, 1995). Wallace describes the Strabane of 1833 as 'a substantial centre of population' containing 'a high proportion of Protestants of every social class and denomination', quite unlike County Wicklow, 'where there were a greater number of Roman Catholics, largely among the lower-income groups', p. 40.

8   Lovell, *A Green Hill Far Away*, p. 9.

9   A 'blue plaque' is a commemorative sign installed in a public place in the United Kingdom to permanently mark a link between that location and a famous person or event.

10 https://web.archive.org/web/20150220031058/http://www.ulsterhistory.co.uk/cecilfrancesalexander.htm.

11 See Rose Novak, 'Writing Ireland's Wrongs: Nineteenth-century women, politics and violence', PhD dissertation, University of Connecticut, 2010.

12 Derry and Londonderry are used interchangeably by Lovell and others. However, the diocese, and the see, are Derry.

13 Lucy, 'Remembering Mrs Cecil Frances Alexander'; see also Lovell, *A Green Hill Far Away*, and Wallace, *Mrs Alexander*.

14 Mary Kenny, 'Fanny's Christmas Legacy: The Dublin-born hymn-writer who brought a feminine sensibility to carols', *Irish Independent*, 24 December 2017.

15 Ibid.

16 Katharine L. Brown, 'The Social and Political Thought of Cecil Frances Alexander, Hymnwriter and Poet', *Anglican and Episcopal History*, vol. lxviii, no. 1, 1999, pp. 112–16; see also Lovell, *A Green Hill Far Away*, and Wallace, *Mrs Alexander*.

17 Kenny, 'Fanny's Christmas Legacy'.

18 Wallace describes in detail the ubiquitous outpouring of sorrow after Alexander's death on 12 October 1895: 'The family were amazed at the reaction to Mrs Alexander's death among both the city's poor and its well-to-do citizens, and among Catholics as well as Protestants ... All the principal newspapers in Ireland and many in Great Britain, notably *The Times*, reported on her death.' Wallace further describes the 'Niagara of sympathetic mail' that poured into the bishop's palace, and the 'intensive pall of gloom' enveloping the city of Derry on the day of the funeral, pp. 178–9.

19 'On the night of 7 May 1856, the school was home to 18 boys and girls, sleeping in their separate dormitories. The doors were locked, as they were every night, at 9 p.m.

But some five hours later, on this night, a fire started in the kitchen and quickly took hold. There are conflicting reports of what happened next. Testimony from the time speaks of confusion about keys and access to the dormitories, which had high windows beyond the reach of small children. Local people tried frantically to break glass and knock down doors to reach those who were trapped, but despite their best efforts, six children died. The oldest was 15; the youngest, just eight years old.' Louise Cullen, 'Cecil Frances Alexander: A pioneer of deaf education', BBC Northern Ireland News, 7 May 2018, https://www.bbc.com/news/uk-northern-ireland-44018269.

20 Brown, 'The Social and Political Thought', p. 89.

21 Lovell, *A Green Hill Far Away*, p. 19.

22 Brown, 'The Social and Political Thought', p. 89.

23 Ibid., p. 88.

24 Alexander, *Hymns for Little Children*, p. 46.

25 Brown, 'The Social and Political Thought', pp. 95–6.

26 Ibid., p. 97.

27 Ibid., p. 91. Brown recounts: 'Whatever plans they may have laid for a future together ended abruptly. While visiting his sick, poor parishioners Butler contracted typhus, the principal killer in famine-era Ireland. He died in July 1848.'

28 Cecil Frances Alexander, 'The Irish Mother's Lament', in *Poems by Cecil Frances Alexander*, ed. and with a preface by William Alexander (London and New York: Macmillan, 1897), p. 291 (poem runs pp. 289–91).

29 Brown, 'The Social and Political Thought', p. 106. She is citing Sean McMahon, 'All Things Bright and Beautiful', *Éire/Ireland: A journal of Irish studies*, vol. 10, no. 4, winter 1975, p. 104 (runs pp. 101–8).

30 Alexander, *Hymns for Little Children*, p. 27.

31 Lovell, *A Green Hill Far Away*, p. 44; Brown, 'The Social and Political Thought', pp. 106–7.

32 Brown, 'The Social and Political Thought', pp. 86, 111.

33 See Lovell, *A Green Hill Far Away*, p. 11.

34 See Brown, 'The Social and Political Thought', pp. 85–6.

35 They are, by hymn number: 102, 'Once in Royal David's City' (Christmas); 167, 'There Is a Green Hill Far Away' (Easter); 180, 'He Is Risen' (Easter); 276, 'For Thy Blest Saints'; 370, 'St Patrick's Breastplate', adapted by her, originally attributed to St Patrick (372–466); 405, 'All Things Bright and Beautiful'; 549, 'Jesus Calls us O'er the Tumult' (call to missionary service; it appears twice, with different melodies).

36 Brown, 'The Social and Political Thought', p. 85.

37 Quotation from an email exchange (3 March 2021) with Frederick Roden, author of *Recovering Jewishness: Modern identities reclaimed* (Westport, CT: Praeger 2016).

38 Ireland's Anglican Church was disestablished by Gladstone's Irish Church Act of 1869. It specified that the Church of Ireland would become a voluntary body as from 1 January 1871. The legislation also provided for the disendowment of the church and its considerable landholdings (subsequently offered to tenants, many of whom availed of the offer), property and bequests. Costigan describes the act as 'the logical supplement to Catholic emancipation [in 1829 that] ended an injustice that was three centuries old'. Giovanni Costigan, *A History of Modern Ireland* (New York: Pegasus, 1970), p. 228.

39 Quoted by Lovell, *A Green Hill Far Away*, p. 48. See ibid., pp. 48–9, for a full account of Alexander's conservative objections to 'the now disestablished and disendowed church'.

40 See *The Hymnal 1982, According to the Use of The Episcopal Church* (New York: Church Hymnal Corporation, 1988), #370, https://www.poetrynook.com/poem/st-patricks-breastplate.

Notes to pages 19 to 23   281

41 For instance, a paper such as that delivered to the Royal Irish Academy in 1863 in the years immediately prior to disestablishment by the Irish Anglican bishop William Reeves considered two Irish missionaries of the seventh century and displays a knowledge of both Latin and Irish. Moreover, this trend is architecturally visible also: the building of St Mary's Anglican Cathedral in Tuam, County Galway, commenced in 1863 and concluded in 1878, the years immediately prior to and after disestablishment. Given this timing, it is striking that St Mary's incorporated a twelfth-century chancel on the site, arguably a necessary alignment of the Anglican Church in Ireland with the deep, pre-Reformation past in a town with a long ecclesiastical history and that already boasted a Catholic cathedral. William Reeves, 'On SS. Marinus and Anianus', *Proceedings of the Royal Irish Academy*, vol. 8. 1861–4, pp. 295–301, https://archive.org/details/proceedingsroya22acadgoog/page/n13; J.A. Claffey, *Irish Historic Town Atlas – Number 20: Tuam* (Dublin: Royal Irish Academy, 2009), p. 8.

42 Joseph Leerssen, 'On the Edge of Europe: Ireland in search of oriental roots, 1650–1850', *Comparative Criticism*, vol. 8, 1986, pp. 95, 102.

43 Katharine L Brown, 'An Exquisitely Beautiful Hymn', *The Living Church*, vol. 210, no. 14, 2 April 1995, pp. 12, 15. In the online *Archives of the Episcopal Church*, https://episcopalarchives.org/cgi-bin/the_living_church/TLCarticle.pl?volume=210&issue=14&article_id=2.

44 Lovell, *A Green Hill Far Away*, p. 58.

45 Ibid., p. 50.

46 Alexander provided one of the first in a line of specifically Irish touches to post-disestablishment worship. The 2004 Church of Ireland Book of Common Prayer contains a prayer in Irish and also prayers for Ireland, for the European Union, and, for use in Northern Ireland only, for Queen Elizabeth II. See https://www.ireland.anglican.org/prayer-worship/book-of-common-prayer/2004-texts.

47 The Hymnal 1982, #370. See also Alexander (ed.), *Poems by Cecil Frances Alexander*, pp. 59–62.

48 See Gregory's translations of Irish mythology, *Gods and Fighting Men* (London: Murray, 1905).

49 Philip Freeman, 'St Patrick's Breastplate', in *The World of Saint Patrick* (Oxford: Oxford University Press, 2014), pp. 49–55.

50 See Alexander, *Hymns for Little Children*, pp. 30–1.

51 Ibid., pp. 31–2; Brown, 'Social and Political Thought', p. 100.

52 https://www.tripadvisor.com/ShowUserReviews-g186482-d213983-r589999148-St_Augustine_s_Church-Derry_County_Londonderry_Northern_Ireland.html.

53 'The Grave by St Columba's Cross', in Alexander (ed.), *Poems by Cecil Frances Alexander*, pp. 356–61. See also Lovell, *A Green Hill Far Away*, pp. 13–15, and Brown, 'Social and Political Thought', pp. 99–101.

54 For full text, see Alexander (ed.), *Poems by Cecil Frances Alexander*, pp. 148–56. See also https://www.bartleby.com/297/428.html.

55 Gregory A. Schirmer, *Out of What Began: A history of Irish poetry in English* (Ithaca and London: Cornell University Press, 1998), p. 152.

56 Alexander (ed.), *Poems by Cecil Frances Alexander*, p. 153.

57 Patricia Craig, Introduction, in *Twelve Irish Ghost Stories* (Oxford: Oxford University Press, 1998), pp. ix, vii.

58 Cecil Frances Alexander, 'The Ballad of Stumpie's Brae', in *The Legend of the Golden Prayers: And other poems* (London: Bell & Daldy, 1859), p. 54.

59 Ibid., p. 48.

282   *Notes to pages 23 to 26*

60 The weaver poets were members of a self-taught and politically radical Presbyterian late eighteenth-century textile worker grouping who wrote in Ulster-Scots dialect. It may be relevant to the ballad's interpretation that members of this school who participated in the 1798 rebellion against British rule in Ireland fled to America.

61 See the discussion of the purported events upon which the legend that inspired the ballad was based, at https://www.stjohnstonandcarrigans.com/stumpysbrae.html and in Madeline McCully, *Haunted Donegal* (Dublin: History Press Ireland, 2016), p. 43.

62 Craig, Biographical Notes, *Twelve Irish Ghost Stories*, p. 143.

63 Craig includes 'The Ballad of Stumpie's Brae' in her gratifyingly idiosyncratic selection in *Twelve Irish Ghost Stories*, of course, as does Frank Ferguson in *Ulster-Scots Writing: An anthology* (Dublin: Four Courts Press, 2008), but Alexander is otherwise as good as excluded from the Irish literature canon. It may be significant in terms of where on the island of Ireland the memory of Alexander persists that both Craig and Ferguson are Northern Irish scholars.

CHAPTER 2 – **Shovelling out Ireland's permanent deadweight during the Great Famine: the Cork workhouse paupers sent to New Brunswick in 1850**

1 I wish to acknowledge the comments of Prof. Donald Akenson, Prof. Gearóid Ó Tuathaigh and Prof. Gearóid Ó hAllmhurain to an earlier draft of this paper.

2 David Fitzpatrick, 'Irish Emigration in the Late Nineteenth Century', *Irish Historical Studies*, vol. xxii, no. 86, September 1980, p. 137.

3 J.J. Lee, 'The Irish Diaspora in the Nineteenth Century', in Laurence M. Geary and Margaret Kelleher (eds), *Nineteenth-Century Ireland: A guide to recent research* (Dublin: UCD Press, 2005), pp. 182–3.

4 See Gerard Moran, *Sending Out Ireland's Poor: Assisted emigration to North America in the nineteenth century* (Dublin: Four Courts Press, 2004).

5 For accounts of these assisted emigration schemes see Wendy Cameron, 'Selecting Peter Robinson's Emigrants', *Histoire Sociale/Social History*, vol. 9, no. 17, May 1976; Gerard Moran, '"In Search of the Promised Land": The Connemara colonization scheme to Minnesota, 1880', *Éire/Ireland*, vol. 31, nos. 3 & 4, fall & winter 1996; Moran, 'James Hack Tuke and His Assisted Emigration Schemes from the West of Ireland in the 1880s', *History Ireland*, March–April 2013; Moran, '"From Poverty to Posterity": Assisted emigration from Connemara in the 1880s', in Micheál Ó hAodha and Máirtín Ó Catháin (eds), *Irish Migrants in the New Communities: Seeking the fair land?* (Plymouth: Lexington Press, 2014), pp. 93–108.

6 *Report from the Select Committee on Colonisation, together with the minutes of evidence*, HC 1890 (354), xii, p. 352, q. 5680.

7 See Gerard Moran, '"Shovelling Out the Paupers": The Irish poor law and assisted emigration during the Great Famine', in Ciarán Reilly (ed.), *The Famine Irish: Emigration and the Great Hunger* (Dublin: The History Press, 2016), pp. 22–40.

8 Gerard Moran, '"Permanent Deadweight": Female pauper emigration from Mountbellew workhouse to Canada', in Christine Kinealy, Jason King and Ciarán Reilly (eds), *Women and the Great Hunger* (Hamden: Quinnipiac University Press, 2016), pp. 109–22.

9 Ciarán Ó Murchadha, *Sable Wings Over the Land: Ennis, Co. Clare and its Wider Community during the Great Famine* (Ennis: CLASP Press, 1998), p. 123.

10 *Third Report from the Select Committee on the Poor Law (Ireland)*, HC 1849 (93), xv, pp. 152, qs. 2805–14.

11 Trevor Parkhill, 'The Famine in County Londonderry', in Christine Kinealy and Trevor Parkhill (eds), *The Famine in Ulster* (Belfast: Ulster Historical Foundation, 1997), p. 157.

Notes to pages 27 to 31   283

12 James S. Donnelly, *The Great Irish Potato Famine* (Stroud: Sutton Publishing, 2001), pp. 110–31; Donald E. Jordan, *Land and Popular Politics in Ireland: County Mayo from the plantation to the land war* (Cambridge: Cambridge University Press, 1994), pp. 110–16. The period 1847–54 was the main period of mass clearances by the landlords. Between 1849 and 1854, 48,740 families or nearly one quarter of a million people were evicted, although as Donnelly points out it does not include those families who 'voluntarily' gave up their holdings to the landowner. There are no estimates for those who were turned out between 1847 and 1848, Donnelly, *Great Irish Potato Famine*, pp. 139–40.

13 Ignatius Murphy, *A People Starved: Life and death in west Clare, 1845–1851* (Dublin: Irish Academic Press, 1996), p. 59; *Galway Vindicator*, 16 June 1849; *Limerick and Clare Examiner*, 11 March 1848.

14 *Nation*, 16 February 1850; *Dundalk Democrat*, 12 October 1850.

15 *Ninth Report from the Select Committee on the Poor Law (Ireland)*, HC 1849 (259), xv, p. 113, q. 8787; John Cunningham, 'The Famine in County Fermanagh', in Kinealy and Parkhill, *Famine in Ulster*, p. 137.

16 Ó Murchadha, *Sable Wings Over the Land*, p. 123; *Galway Vindicator*, 22 January 1848.

17 *Ninth Report from the Select Committee on the Poor Law*, p. 33, q. 7647.

18 On this point, see Gerard Moran, 'Disorderly Conduct: Riots and insubordination in the workhouses during the Great Famine', in John Cunningham and Niall Ó Ciosáin (eds), *Culture and Society in Ireland Since 1750: Tributes to Gearoid Ó Tuathaigh* (Dublin: Lilliput Press, 2015), pp. 160–80.

19 *Third Report from the Select Committee on the Poor Law*, p. 168, qs. 3043–8.

20 Moran, *Sending Out Ireland's Poor*, pp. 126–8.

21 *Galway Vindicator*, 8 April 1848.

22 *Third Report from the Select Committee on the Poor Law*, p. 64, qs. 1558–9.

23 Quoted in Murphy, *A People Starved*, p. 34; Eddie Carty, 'Wexford Workhouse in Famine Times, 1842–1849', *Journal of the Wexford Historical Society*, 1996–7, p. 108.

24 *Nation*, 18 May 1850.

25 Quoted in Trevor Parkhill, 'Convicts, Orphans, Settlers: Patterns of emigration from Ulster to Australia, 1790–1860', in John O'Brien and Pauric Travers (eds), *The Irish Emigrant Experience in Australia* (Dublin: Poolbeg Press, 1991), pp. 24–5.

26 *Ninth Report from the Select Committee on the Poor Law*, p. 54, q. 7933.

27 *Dundalk Democrat*, 1 December 1849.

28 See Kilrush poor law minute book, dated 7 February 1852 (Clare County Library); *Clare Journal*, 29 June 1854; *Leinster Express*, 26 January 1850, 6 December 1851; Moran, *Sending Out Ireland's Poor*, p. 128. See also Joseph Robins, 'The Emigration of Irish Workhouse Children to Australia in the Nineteenth Century', in O'Brien and Travers, *Irish Emigrant Experience in Australia*; *Galway Vindicator*, 8 July 1854; *Western Star*, 24 February 1855. As late as 1858 girls were entering Enniscorthy workhouse hoping their passage to North America would be paid for by the guardians, see Dympna McLoughlin, 'Workhouses and Irish Female Paupers, 1840–1870', in Maria Luddy and Cliona Murphy (eds), *Women Surviving: Studies in Irish women's history in the nineteenth and twentieth centuries* (Dublin: Poolbeg Press, 1989), pp. 120–1.

29 *Dundalk Democrat*, 17 November 1849.

30 *Seventh Report from the Select Committee on the Poor Law (Ireland)*, HC 1849 (194), xv, p. 89, q. 5674. In many unions the guardians were unable to collect the rates. In Galway and Listowel unions the rate collectors required the protection of the military when collecting the rates, see Christine Kinealy, 'The Response of the Poor Law to the Great Famine in County Galway', in Gerard Moran and Raymond Gillespie (eds), *Galway: History and society* (Dublin: Geography Publications, 1996), p. 389.

31 Matthew Potter, 'William Monsell: An Irish Catholic unionist', *North Munster Antiquarian Journal*, vol. 41, 2001, p. 70; Oliver McDonagh, 'The Poor Law, Emigration and the Irish Question, 1830–55', *Christus Rex*, vol. 12, 1958, pp. 26–37; p. 33.

32 *Ninth Report from the Select Committee on the Poor Law*, p. 108, q. 8694.

33 Ó Murchadha, *Sable Wings Over the Land*, p. 209; minutes of the Galway poor law guardians, dated 31 March 1849 (Galway County Library, Galway poor law minute book, Nov. 1848–Aug. 1849).

34 Minutes of Gort poor law guardians, dated 26 June 1850 (Galway County Library, Gort poor law minute book, Oct. 1849–Aug. 1850); minutes of Mountbellew poor law guardians, dated 29 June 1850 (Galway County Library, Mountbellew poor law minute book, May 1850–Jan. 1851).

35 See Moran, 'Shovelling Out the Paupers', pp. 28–9.

36 Thomas Reddington to Clarendon, dated 9 December 1848 (Bodleian Library, Oxford, box 24, Clarendon dept, Irish, Clarendon papers).

37 Trevor Parkhill '"Permanent Deadweight": Emigration from Ulster workhouses during the Famine', in E. Margaret Crawford (ed.), *The Hungry Stream: Essays on emigration and famine* (Belfast: Institute of Irish Studies, 1997), pp. 96–7.

38 *Third Report of the Commissioners for Administering the Laws for the Relief of the Poor in Ireland, with appendices*, HC 1850 (1243), xxii, p. 11; David Fitzpatrick, 'Emigration, 1801–70', in W.E. Vaughan (ed.), *A New History of Ireland. Vol V: Ireland under the Union, 1: 1800–70* (Oxford: Oxford University Press, 1989), p. 590; *Nation*, 13 July 1850.

39 *Tuam Herald*, 11 November 1848.

40 Between February 1849 and February 1850 Wexford workhouse sent three groups of female paupers to the Cape Colony, the final group of twenty, aged between sixteen and twenty years, leaving in early 1850, *Nation*, 9 February 1850.

41 See Moran, *Sending Out Ireland's Poor*, pp. 35–69. For example, on the Lansdowne estate, see Gerard J. Lyne, *The Lansdowne Estate in Kerry under W.S. Trench, 1849–72* (Dublin: Geography Publications, 2001), pp. 25–58.

42 *Papers Relative to Emigration to the North American Colonies*, HC 1852–3 (1650), lxviii, p. 9.

43 Emigration report for A.C. Buchanan to earl of Elgin and Kincardine, dated 31 December 1851, *Papers Relative to Emigration to the North American Colonies*, HC 1851 (1474), xxxiii, p. 21.

44 *Mayo Telegraph*, 29 January 1851; *Dundalk Democrat*, 11 January 1851. For an example for Kilkenny city, see Tony Patterson, 'Illegal Outdoor Relief in Kilkenny Workhouse', *Old Kilkenny Review*, vol. 48, 1996, p. 24; Gerard Moran, '"Suffer Little Children": Life in the workhouse during the Famine', in Christine Kinealy, Jason King and Gerard Moran, (eds), *Children and the Great Hunger in Ireland* (Hamden: Quinnipiac University Press, 2017), p. 33.

45 Ciarán Ó Murchadha, 'Limerick Union Workhouse during the Great Famine', *Old Limerick Journal*, 1995, pp. 39–42; S.C. O'Mahony, 'Emigration from the Workhouses of Limerick, 1848–1850', in Liam Irwin, Gearóid Ó Tuathaigh and Matthew Potter (eds), *Limerick: History and society* (Dublin: Geography Publications, 2009), pp. 443–4.

46 S.C. O'Mahony, 'Emigration from Limerick Workhouse, 1848–60', *Irish Ancestor*, no. 2, 1982, p. 83.

47 *Limerick Reporter and Tipperary Vindicator*, 4 August, 20 October, 2 June 1854.

48 Ibid., 17 February 1854. This was at a time when the Crimean War was taking place.

49 See Helen Burke, *The People and the Poor Law in Nineteenth-Century Ireland* (Sussex: WEB, 1987), pp. 187–81.

50 Michelle O'Mahony, *Famine in Cork City: Famine life in Cork union workhouse* (Cork: Mercier Press, 2005), pp. 46–9.

Notes to pages 34 to 42 285

51 Gerard O'Brien, 'The New Poor Law in pre-Famine Ireland: A case study', *Irish Economic and Social History*, vol. 12, 1985, p. 43.

52 Moran, *Sending Out Ireland's Poor*, p. 126.

53 O'Mahony, *Famine in Cork City*, p. 140.

54 *Nation*, 13 September 1851.

55 *Limerick Reporter and Tipperary Vindicator*, 14 February 1854; *Report from the Select Committee on the Poor Law (Ireland); together with the Proceedings of the Committee, Minutes of Evidence and Appendix*, HC 1861 (408), x, p. 326, q. 7022.

56 *Galway Vindicator*, 15 November 1848; *Clare Journal*, 16 November 1848. For an account of the riots and insubordination in the workhouses during this period, see Moran, 'Disorderly Conduct', pp. 167–9.

57 *Copies or Extracts of any Despatches Relative to Emigration to British North America*, HC 1851, p. 48

58 Ibid., pp. 53–4.

59 Thomas Jones to M.H. Perley, dated 31 December 1850, *Papers Relative to Emigration to the North American Colonies*, HC 1852 (1474), xxxiii, pp. 50–2.

60 Peter Toner (ed.), *An Index to Irish Immigrants in the New Brunswick Census of 1851* (Fredericton: Provincial Archives of New Brunswick, 1991).

61 See Moran, *Sending Out Ireland's Poor*, pp. 101–10.

62 Ibid., pp. 106–7; James M. Whalen, '"Almost as Bad as Ireland": The experience of the Irish Famine emigrants in Canada, St John, 1847', in Robert O'Driscoll and Lorna Reynolds (eds), *The Untold Story: The Irish in Canada* (Toronto: Celtic Arts of Canada, 1988); John Doran to John S. Saunders, dated 27 November 1847, *Papers Relative to Emigration to the British Provinces in North America*, HC 1847–8 (932), xlvii, pp. 53–4.

63 Jim Rees, *Surplus People: The Fitzwilliam clearances, 1847–56* (Cork: Mercier Press, 2000), pp. 82–116.

64 See Peter D. Murphy, *Poor Ignorant Children: Irish Famine orphans in St John, New Brunswick* (Halifax: D'Arcy McGee Chair of Irish Studies, 1999), p. 11. In 1847 the New Brunswick officials threatened to send the tenants sent out from Lord Palmerston's estate back to Ireland: Tyler Anbinder, 'Lord Palmerston and the Irish Famine Emigration', *Historical Journal*, vol. 44, no. 2, 2001, pp. 441–69, at p. 462.

65 Earl Grey to Sir Edmund Head, dated 19 May 1850, *Copies or Extracts of any Despatches Relative to Emigration to British North America*, HC 1851, pp. 50–2.

66 M.H. Perley to the Hon John R. Partelow, dated 16 November 1850, ibid., p. 45.

67 Ibid., p. 33; *Nation*, 19 July 1851.

68 Fitzpatrick, 'Emigration, 1801–70', p. 590; *Report for the Select Committee on the Poor Law (Ireland); together with the Proceedings of the Committee, Minutes of Evidence and Appendix*, HC 1861 (408), x, p. 215, q. 4365.

69 *Papers Relative to Emigration to the North American Colonies, 1852–3*, lxviii (1650), p. 17.

70 Minutes of Gort poor law guardians, dated 11 October 1851 (Galway County Library, Gort poor law minute book, March–October 1851).

71 *Limerick Reporter and Tipperary Vindicator*, 24 February 1852.

72 *Nation*, 15 September 1849.

73 R.A. Duncan to A.C. Buchanan, dated 28 April 1852, *Papers Relative to Emigration to the North American Colonies*, HC 1852–3 (1650), xlviii, p. 24.

74 *Ninth Report from the Select Committee on the Poor Law (Ireland)*, HC 1849 (259), xv, p. 54, q. 7933.

75 Adam Ferrie to Lord Grey, dated 1 December 1847, *Papers Relative to Emigration to the British Provinces in North America*, HC 1847–8 (932), xlvii, p. 37.

286   *Notes to pages 42 to 48*

76 See Moran, *Sending Out Ireland's Poor*, pp. 129–32.
77 *Copies of Extracts of Despatches Relative to Emigration to the North American Colonies*, HC 1860 (606), xliv, p. 5.
78 *Copies of Extracts of Despatches Relative to Emigration to the North American Colonies*, HC 1861 (186), xl, p. 7. See also Burke, *People and the Poor Law*, pp. 198–9.
79 C.S. O'Mahony, 'Emigration from Tipperary Workhouses, 1848–58', *Tipperary Historical Journal*, 1994, p. 105; *Mayo Telegraph*, 20 April 1853; *Copies of Extracts of Despatches Relative to Emigration to the North American Colonies*, HC 1854–5 (4640), xxxix, p. 19.
80 *Report from the Select Committee on the Poor Law (Ireland); together with the Proceedings of the Committee, Minutes of Evidence and Appendices*, HC 1861 (408), p. 101, q. 2085–7.

CHAPTER 3 – **Ireland, America and transnational radicalism**

1 Adrian N. Mulligan, 'A Forgotten "Greater Ireland": The transatlantic development of Irish nationalism', *Scottish Geographical Journal*, vol. 118, no. 3, 2002, pp. 219–34.
2 Ibid.
3 Leith Davis, 'Transnational Articulations in James Macpherson's Poems of Ossian and the History and Management of the East-India Company', *The Eighteenth Century*, vol. 60, no. 4, winter 2019, p. 441.
4 David Brundage, *Irish Nationalists in America: The politics of exile, 1798–1998* (New York: Oxford University Press, 2016).
5 Richard R. Weiner, 'Transnational History, Transnational Space, Transnational Law', *The European Legacy*, vol. 26, no. 1, 2021, p. 68.
6 Paul Arthur, 'Diasporan Intervention in International Affairs: Irish America as a case study', *Diaspora: A journal of transnational studies*, vol. 1, no. 2, fall 1991, pp. 143–62.
7 'In its simplest and purest form Fenianism refers to an ideology which seeks to remove the British presence from Irish affairs by force of arms. In a slightly expanded form it refers to a huge cultural empire which involves Irish language, an interpretation of Irish history, the pursuit of Irish music and … the propagation and playing of Irish games.' Joe Ambrose, *Fenian Anthology* (Cork: Mercier Press, 2008), p. 10.
8 'Scientific Warfare or the Resources of Civilization: A lecture by Glencree, 1888', file 1, envelope 8, box 6, Fenian Brotherhood Records and Jeremiah O'Donovan Rossa Personal Papers, Catholic University of America.
9 Mulligan, 'A Forgotten "Greater Ireland"'.
10 Una Ní Bhroiméil, *Building Irish Identity in America, 1890–1915: The Gaelic revival* (Dublin: Four Courts Press, 2003).
11 David Brundage, 'Matilda Tone in America: Exile, gender, and memory in the making of Irish republican nationalism', *New Hibernia Review / Iris Éireannach Nua*, vol. 14, no. 1, spring 2010, pp. 96–111.
12 Ibid.
13 Timothy J. Meagher, *The Columbia Guide to Irish-American History* (New York: Columbia University Press, 2005), p. 198.
14 John Belchem, 'Nationalism, Republicanism and Exile: Irish emigrants and the revolutions of 1848', *The Past and Present Society*, no. 146, February 1995, pp. 103–35.
15 'The name of the club was significant, for Robert Emmet, the hero of all Irish revolutionists […]. This secret society became the nucleus around which O'Mahony began to mold [US Fenianism …].' Mabel Gregory Walker, *The Fenian Movement* (Colorado Springs: Ralph Myles Publisher, 1969), p. 5.
16 David M. Doolin, *Transnational Revolutionaries: The Fenian invasion of Canada, 1866* (Bern: Peter Lang, 2016), see Chapter 7.

Notes to pages 49 to 61   287

17 R.V. Comerford, *The Fenians in Context: Irish politics and society, 1848–82* (Atlantic Highlands, NJ: Wolfhound Press, 1985).

18 Aihwa Ong, *Flexible Citizenship: The cultural logics of trasnationality* (Durham and London: Duke University Press, 1999), p. 12.

19 James Stephens, *The Birth of the Fenian Movement: American diary, Brooklyn 1859*, ed. Marta Ramon (Dublin, UCD Press, 2009).

20 *Proceedings of the Second National Congress of the Fenian Brotherhood, Held in Cincinnati, Ohio, January 1865* (Philadelphia: James Gibbons Printer, 1865), p. 10.

21 See Doolin, *Transnational Revolutionaries*.

22 Ibid.

23 Letter from 'John O'Mahony (New York) to John Mitchel (Nov. 10, 1865)', in Joseph Denieffe, *A Personal Narrative of the Irish Revolutionary Brotherhood Giving a Faithful Report of the Principal Events from 1855 to 1867 Written at the Request of Friends* (New York: The Gael Publishing Co., 1906), pp. 201–3.

24 Shane Kenna, *Jeremiah O'Donovan Rossa: Unrepentant Fenian* (Dublin: Merrion Press, 2015), p. 113.

25 Ibid.

26 Judith E. Campbell, 'The Bold Fenian Wife: Mary Jane O'Donovan Rossa', in Miriam Nyhan Grey (ed.), *Ireland's Allies: America and the 1916 Easter Rising* (New York: New York University Press, 2016), p. 66.

27 *Irish World*, 4 March 1876, quoted in Kenna, *Jeremiah O'Donovan Rossa*.

28 Kenna, *Jeremiah O'Donovan Rossa*, p. 123.

29 Ann Larabee, 'A Brief History of Terrorism in the United States', *Knowledge, Technology & Policy*, vol. 16, no. 1, spring 2003, pp. 21–38. Italics in original.

30 Kenna, *Jeremiah O'Donovan Rossa*, p. 124.

31 Jonathan Gantt, *Irish Terrorism in the Atlantic Community, 1865–1922* (Basingstoke: Palgrave Macmillan, 2010), pp. 133–4.

32 Kenna, *Jeremiah O'Donovan Rossa*, p. 130.

33 Jonathan Gantt 'Irish-American Terrorism and Anglo-American Relations', *The Journal of the Gilded Age and the Progressive Era*, vol. 5, no. 4, October 2006, p. 328.

34 See documentary, https://www.pbs.org/wnet/secrets/the-freemantle-six/131/.

35 Nyhan Grey (ed.), *Ireland's Allies*, p. 22.

36 Ibid., p. 21.

37 Gerard MacAtasney, 'Tom Clarke's New York', in Miriam Nyhan Grey (ed.), *Ireland's Allies: America and the 1916 Easter Rising* (New York: New York University Press, 2016), p. 59.

38 Patrick Ford, *The Criminal History of the British Empire: A series of open letters to Hon. Wm. E. Gladstone, prime minister of England* (New York: Irish World, 1881), p. 14.

39 John Devoy papers, ms. 18,136/ (2), NLI.

40 Desmond Ryan, 'Stephens, Devoy and Tom Clarke', *University Review*, vol. 1, no. 12, spring 1957, pp. 55.

41 Mulligan, 'A Forgotten "Greater Ireland"'.

42 Nyhan Grey (ed.), *Ireland's Allies*, p. 110.

43 Ong, *Flexible Citizenship*, p. 4.

CHAPTER 4 – **When history and hope rhymed: Fanny Parnell – nationalist, feminist and patriot poet**

1 Charles was heartbroken at Fanny's death but denied her wish to be buried in Ireland. Anna Parnell wrote *The Tale of a Great Sham* in 1904, although she failed to get it

published. It was finally published in 1986. In her history of the Land League, Anna lambasts the men for their hypocrisy, yet she ignored Fanny's crucial role in starting the Ladies' Land League.

2   For example, Marie Hughes, 'The Parnell Sisters', *Dublin Historical Record*, vol. 1, no. 1, March–May 1966, pp. 14–19; Jane Côté, 'Writing *Women Out of History: Fanny and Anna Parnell and the Irish Ladies' Land League*', *Études Irlandaises*, vol. xvii, no. 2, Décembre 1992, pp. 123–34; the sisters share a chapter in Marian Broderick, *Wild Irish Women: Extraordinary lives from history* (Madison, WI: University of Wisconsin Press, 2004), pp. 187–90; Evelyn Reesa Jenkins, 'The Marginalization of Revolutionary Sisters: The betrayal of Fanny and Anna Parnell', unpublished thesis, Drew University, NJ, 2006.

3   John Henry Parnell was born 1811 in Wicklow. He married Delia in 1835 in New York.

4   The purpose of the legislation was to clear Ireland of insolvent landowners.

5   'In Chancery', *Dublin Evening Packet and Correspondent*, 5 March 1861.

6   The house was sold to a butcher.

7   Theodosia Parnell (1853–1920). Unlike Anna and Fanny, she did marry.

8   Danae O'Regan, 'Anna and Fanny Parnell', *History Ireland* 7, no. 1, spring 1999, pp. 37–41.

9   'Fanny Parnell. Lecture by Daniel Crilly MP', The Irish Canadian, 10 May 1888.

10   'The Late Miss Fanny Parnell', Montreal Daily Witness, 22 July 1882.

11   R. Barry O'Brien, *The Life of Charles Stewart Parnell* (New York: Harper, 1898), pp. 44–5.

12   Oliver P. Rafferty, *The Church, the State and the Fenian Threat 1861–75* (New York: St Martin's Press, 1999), pp. 39–40.

13   Hughes, 'The Parnell Sisters', p. 18.

14   Masada was an ancient fortress in Israel and the site of a famous siege. The men first slew their wives and children, and then themselves, rather than yield themselves as prisoners and consequently slaves.

15   'Vice Regal Court', *Dublin Evening Mail*, 1 February 1866.

16   'The Queen's Drawing Room', *London Daily News*, 9 May 1873.

17   O'Regan, 'Anna and Fanny Parnell', pp. 37–9.

18   Delia married James Livingston Thomson in 1859, aged twenty-one. They had one child. Delia passed away in 1882, aged forty-four. Another sister, Emily, who was born in 1841, also had an unhappy marriage. She died in destitution in 1918 in the South Dublin Union. The third-born sister, Sophia, eloped to Scotland when she was aged sixteen. The marriage appears to have been happy, but Sophia died aged only thirty-three. Also see Hughes, 'The Parnell Sisters', pp. 14–15.

19   Anna published '*Notes* from the *Ladies' Cage*' in the *Celtic Monthly*.

20   Barry O'Brien, *Life of Parnell*, p. 136.

21   'Help for Farmers in the West of Ireland', *Nation*, 20 September 1879.

22   For example, at a large meeting in Faneuil Hall in 1879, Fanny donated $75; Anna and Theodosia donated $50 each. This was Fanny's second donation. 'Boston to Ireland', *Nation*, 25 October 1879; 'American and Other Subscriptions', *Nation*, 3 January 1880.

23   'Incidents in Miss Parnell's Life: Obituary', *New York Sun*, 23 July 1882, reprinted in *Nation*, 12 August 1882.

24   'American Help for the Farmers of the West of Ireland', *The Irishman* (Dublin), 20 September 1879.

25   *Dublin Weekly Nation*, 20 September 1879.

26   *Irish Canadian*, 7 January 1880.

27   Also see Christine Kinealy, *Charity and the Great Hunger: The kindness of strangers* (London: Bloomsbury, 2013).

Notes to pages 64 to 68   289

28 *Belfast Morning News*, 2 November 1880.

29 Côté, 'Writing Women Out of History', p. 125.

30 Fanny Parnell, *The Hovels of Ireland* (New York: Thomas Kelly, 1879), p. 55.

31 This point is made is Reesa Jenkins' thesis, showing that Fanny wrote many of Charles'
    key speeches, including his speech before the American Congress, although they were
    credited to him.

32 Parnell, *The Hovels of Ireland*, p. 55.

33 Ibid.

34 Ibid., p.17.

35 Ibid., p. 7.

36 Ibid., p. 21.

37 Ibid., p. 7.

38 *Dublin Weekly Nation*, 28 February 1880.

39 *Nation*, 5 June 1880.

40 Ibid.

41 Paula Bennett, *Poets in the Public Sphere: The emancipatory project of American women's
    poetry, 1800–1900* (Princeton, NJ: Princeton University Press, 2003), p. 95.

42 Michael Davitt, *The Fall of Feudalism in Ireland: Or, the story of the Land League
    revolution* (London: Harper & Brothers, 1904), p. 266.

43 The song sheet cost 1s. 6d., 'New Music', *Nation*, 23 July 1881. Maurizio G. Giannetti
    was a well-known composer, based in America. The music was criticised for its 'languid
    Italian style', 'New Music', *Nation*, 4 June 1881.

44 'The Famine Year' was published in the *Nation* in January 1847. Speranza was the pen-
    name of Jane Elgee (1821–95), also born into a Protestant family, who supported the
    union.

45 'To the Farmers of Ireland – Hold the Harvest', *Pilot*, 21 August 1880.

46 Poem 'To Irish Farmers. Hold the Harvest', *Dublin Weekly Nation*, 4 September 1880;
    'By Fanny Parnell', *Nation*, 4 September 1880; the poem was reprinted in the provincial
    press, 'Miss Fanny Parnell', *Leinster Express*, 25 September 1880. This paper chastised
    Fanny for her criticisms of the Irish poor, 'Miss Fanny Parnell', *Nenagh Guardian*, 25
    September 1880.

47 'The Parnell Family', *Waterford News and Star*, 24 December 1880; 'Literary Institute of
    New Ross', *Wexford People*, 8 January 1881; 'The Land League in Great Britain', *Nation*,
    26 March 1881.

48 Davitt, *Fall of Feudalism*, pp. 291–3.

49 'The Poetry of the Irish Land Agitation', *Edinburgh Evening News*, 22 September 1880.

50 'Blather', *Portsmouth Evening News*, 23 September 1880.

51 *Morning Post*, 8 October 1880.

52 Matthias McDonnell Bodkin, *Recollections of an Irish Judge: Press, bar and parliament*
    (New York: Dodd, Mead & Company, 1915), p. 95.

53 Davitt, *Fall of Feudalism*, pp. 291–3.

54 *Land League Songs: A collection of patriotic Irish ballads … suited to the present agitation
    – wit, sentiment and patriotism* (New York: R.F. Fox, 1880). In the WorldCat listing,
    Fanny is not mentioned, although Charles is: www.worldcat.org/title/land-league-
    songs-a-collection-of-patriotic-irish-ballads-suited-to-the-present-agitiation-wit-
    sentiment-and-patriotism/oclc/30732622&referer=brief_results#relatedsubjects.

55 Shortly after Fanny's death, Margaret Sullivan published an article about the origins of
    the Ladies' Land League, claiming that Fanny had provided her with this information.
    Sullivan, in *Dundalk Democrat*, 2 September 1882.

56 Davitt, *Fall of Feudalism*, p. 299.
57 Ibid.
58 'Ladies' Land League', *Kerry Sentinel*, 17 December 1880; *Nation*, 25 December 1880.
59 Côté, *Fanny and Anna Parnell*, p. 12.
60 *Nation*, 22 July 1881.
61 'Miss Parnell', *Sligo Champion*, 6 August 1881.
62 'Letter from Miss Fanny Parnell', *Freeman's Journal* (Sydney, Australia), 15 July 1882.
63 Quoted in Ely M. Janis, 'Petticoat Revolutionaries: Gender, ethnic nationalism, and the Irish Ladies' Land League in the United States', *Journal of American Ethnic History*, vol. 27, no. 2, winter 2008, pp. 5–27, at pp. 15, 21.
64 This comment appeared in the *Boston Globe* in May 1881. I am grateful to Dr Catherine Shannon for bringing it to my attention.
65 'Land League Lockets', *Nation*, 26 March 1881.
66 'Meeting of the Land League', *Wexford People*, 29 December 1880.
67 Anna frequently published in this journal also, see *Celtic Monthly*, March 1881.
68 *Nation*, 12 August 1882.
69 'Miss Parnell to be Buried in Ireland', *New York Times*, 8 August 1882.
70 'The Late Miss Fanny Parnell', *New York Times*, 5 August 1882.
71 *Donahoe's Magazine: An illustrated monthly journal*, vol. 8, 1882, p. 384.
72 'Obsequies of the Late Fanny Parnell', *Quebec Daily Telegraph*, 20 October 1882.
73 Anna's anger was evident in *The Tale of a Great Sham*, written over twenty years later.
74 Quoted in James Jeffrey Roche, *Life of John Boyle O'Reilly ... Together with His Complete Poems and Speeches* (London: Cassell, 1891), p. 220.
75 Ibid.
76 'Lines on the Death of Miss Fanny Parnell' (Ireland? s.n., 1882). Sung to the air of 'Exile of Erin'; signed at foot: P. Hanley. An original copy is available in the National Library of Scotland, https://digital.nls.uk/english-ballads/archive/74893081?mode=tran scription.
77 'The Late Miss Parnell', *Derry Journal*, 31 July 1882.
78 *The History of Ireland: from the earliest period to the present time, derived from native annals, and from the researches of Dr O'Donovan, Professor Eugene O'Curry, Rev. C.P. Meehan, Dr R.R. Madden, and other eminent scholars, and from all the resources of Irish history now available by Martin Haverty; together with a geography and description of the country, and of the several counties, arms and heraldic devices of ancient families of Ireland, by Martin Haverty, supplemented with Essays on* THE LAND LEAGUE MOVEMENT, BY CHARLES STEWART PARNELL, MICHAEL DAVITT, MISS FANNY PARNELL, AND J.J. CLANCY, LL.D. (New York: Kelly, 1881).
79 Ibid. (Sydney: McNeil & Coffee, 1883).
80 Davitt, *Fall of Feudalism*, p. 370.
81 Ibid., pp. 292–3.
82 Ibid., p. 256.
83 Francis Sheehy-Skeffington, *Michael Davitt: Revolutionary agitator and labour leader* (Boston: D. Estes, 1909), p. 114.
84 It was in two volumes. John O'Leary, *Recollections of Fenians and Fenianism* (London: Downey & Company, 1896).
85 Ibid., vol. 2, p. 30.
86 Ibid. (Philadelphia: Patterson & White, 1889).
87 Stopford Augustus Brooke and Thomas William Rolleston, *A Treasury of Irish Poetry in the English Tongue* (New York: Macmillan, 1900), Book III, p. vi.

Notes to pages 72 to 75   291

88 Justin McCarthy (ed.), *Irish Literature* (Washington: Catholic University of America Press, 1904), included 'Post Mortem', 'Hold the Harvest' and 'Erin My Queen'.

89 'Post Mortem by Fanny Parnell', *Sligo Nationalist and Leitrim Leader*, 16 August 1913.

90 Padraic Colum, *Anthology of Irish Verse: From ancient minstrels' songs to poems of the modern masters* (New York: Boni & Liveright, 1922).

91 This anthology was first published in 1927. Lennox Robinson (1886–1958) was born in Cork and became a leading figure in the Irish literary renaissance.

92 Brendan Kennelly, *The Penguin Book of Irish Verse* (London: Penguin, 1970).

93 Maire Tobin, 'An Irishwoman's Diary', *Irish Times*, 4 June 2001.

94 This phrase gained traction during the centenary of the 1916 Rising – the most famous example being the removal of Nurse Farrell in the photograph of Patrick Pearse's surrender.

CHAPTER 5 – 'I cannot banish the thought of home': young Irish women's responses to urban-industrial America

1 This essay has had many revisions since it was first written to provide background data for Paul Wagner's 1995 documentary film, sponsored by the National Endowment for the Humanities and titled 'Out of Ireland', which included a segment about Mary Ann Rowe, one of the emigrants featured here. In 1978 Mrs Bríd Galway of Barronsland, Thomastown, County Kilkenny, kindly provided to the author a copy of Mary Ann Rowe's 1888 letter as well as information about the Rowe family. I am very grateful to Mrs Galway and also, for their research assistance and comments on earlier drafts of this essay, to the late Dr Bruce D. Boling of the University of New Mexico; the late Dr David N. Doyle of University College Dublin; the late Professor David Fitzpatrick of Trinity College Dublin; Dr Patricia Kelleher of the University of Kutztown, Pennsylvania; and Dr Breandán Mac Suibhne of the National University of Ireland, Galway.

2 The principal book-length studies of Irish emigrant women in America are: Hasia R. Diner, *Erin's Daughters in America: Irish immigrant women in the nineteenth century* (Baltimore, MD: Johns Hopkins University Press, 1983); Janet A. Nolan, *Ourselves Alone: Women's emigration from Ireland, 1885–1920* (Lexington: University Press of Kentucky, 1989); Rita M. Rhodes, *Women and the Family in Post-Famine Ireland: Status and opportunity in a hierarchical society* (New York: Garland, 1992); and Margaret Lynch-Brennan, *The Irish Bridget: Irish immigrant women in domestic service in America* (Syracuse, NY: Syracuse University Press, 2009). Also see: Kerby A. Miller, with David N. Doyle and Patricia Kelleher, 'For "Love and Liberty": Irish women, migration and domesticity in Ireland and America, 1815–1920', in Patrick O'Sullivan (ed.), *Irish Women and Irish Migration* (Leicester: Leicester University Press, 1995), pp. 41–65; revised and expanded in Kerby A. Miller, *Ireland and Irish-America: Culture, class, and transatlantic migration* (Dublin: Field Day, 2008), pp. 300–26.

3 Quotation from historian Thomas N. Brown, cited in Kerby A. Miller, *Emigrants and Exiles: Ireland and the Irish exodus to North America* (New York: Oxford University Press, 1985), p. 4.

4 See the works by Diner, Nolan and Lynch-Brennan cited in n. 2.

5 As this author has noted in both versions of 'For "Love and Liberty"'; and also in 'Class, Culture and Ethnicity: The construction of Irish America in the nineteenth century', in Miller, *Ireland and Irish America*, pp. 273–5.

6 Margaret Lynch-Brennan, 'Ubiquitous Bridget: Irish immigrant women in domestic service in America, 1840–1930', in J.J. Lee and Marion R. Casey (eds), *Making the Irish*

292   *Notes to pages 75 to 76*

American: History and heritage of the Irish in the United States (New York: New York
University Press, 2006), pp. 339–41; Maureen Murphy (ed.), *Your Fondest Annie: Letters
from Annie O'Donnell to James P. Phelan, 1901–1904* (Dublin: UDC Press, 2005), pp. 36–
9, 44, 65.

7   According to Griffith's Valuation, in 1850 John Greene, Esq. (in partnership with a Miss
    Lucretia Greene), rented several holdings in the two townlands, including a substantial
    farmhouse in Ballylarkin, all of which had an annual valuation for tax purposes of
    over £101. In addition, Greene had property in nearby Callan town and also was a
    'middleman' who sublet seventy-one of his acres in Ballylarkin to kinsman Michael
    Dwyer. The author first viewed Griffith's Valuation books in the National Library of
    Ireland, Dublin, but they are now available online at http://www.askaboutireland.
    ie/griffith-valuation/. The relationship between the Greene and Dwyer (or Dwire)
    families is attested in Joseph Kennedy, 'Tombstones in Old Kilbride Graveyard', in
    Kennedy (ed.), *Callan 800 (1207–2007): History and heritage* (Callan: Callan Heritage
    Society, 2007), p. 508; the author is grateful for this reference to independent scholar
    Proinsias Ó Drisceoil, PhD. Traditionally, an Irish 'strong farm' was a profit-generating
    holding of at least thirty acres in size, although, in a county such as Kilkenny, where the
    farms were generally larger and more productive than in much of the island, a strong
    farm would signify a holding of perhaps fifty to one hundred or more acres.

8   It is impossible to determine Cathy Greene's precise age or year of emigration. Between
    December 1880 and October 1883, at least four women named Catherine, Cathy or
    Katy Greene (or Green) appeared in the passenger lists of ships that arrived in New
    York from Liverpool, England, via Queenstown, County Cork. The occupations of
    three were listed as 'spinster' (implying skill and experience in spinning or needle-
    work), the fourth as 'servant'; the servant's age was recorded as eighteen years, but the
    spinsters were listed as aged twenty to twenty-one years. See the passenger and crew
    lists of ships arriving in New York, available through www.ancestry.com.

9   Cathy Greene's 1884 letter is among the Greene-Norris papers, catalogued as UCD
    P2/D/6 in the Archives Department at University College Dublin. This author
    is grateful to the archivists in 1989, Kerry Holland and Seamus Heferty, for their
    research assistance and permission to publish. This text replicates the ms. letter's
    spelling, punctuation and capitalisation as closely as possible. Unfortunately, Cathy
    Greene's Brooklyn address is not known. Her mother, Catherine Greene, had been
    a widow since 1 January 1870, when her husband John Greene died aged forty-four;
    see Proinsias Ó Drisceoil, 'Pádraig Phiarais Cúndún agus Cáit Graídhin', in Pádraig
    Ó Macháin (ed.), *Ossory, Laois and Leinster*, vol. 7 (Crosspatrick, Co. Wicklow: OLL,
    2019), pp. 183–91. In addition to the land that John Greene rented (see n. 7), in 1876 his
    widow owned outright nearly six acres in Ballylarkin with an annual valuation of £2
    5s; see *Land Owners in Ireland. Return of Owners of Land … in Ireland* (Dublin, 1876;
    Baltimore: Genealogical Publishing Co., 1988), p. 37.

10 toom: tomb.

11 Johnny was Cathy Greene's brother John; in her dream last night she saw him and
    his grave – a lot of clay turned up. Her premonition belatedly proved correct: John
    Greene died on 19 November 1889, aged only twenty-three, which is why Cathy's
    sister, Honoria, eventually inherited the farm; see below and Ó Drisceoil, op. cit. The
    meaning of Cathy Greene's reference to the 'Mare is unknown.

12 nervise: nervous. swone: swoon.

13 For this reference, the author is grateful to Dr Marion Casey of the Irish Studies
    programme at New York University.

Notes to page 78   293

14 In 1901, Catherine Greene, widow, is listed in Ballylarkin with her daughter Honoria
   Tyrrell, the latter's two children, Patrick (age nine) and John (seven), Mary Clifford
   (seventy), an aunt, and John Keeffe, a farm servant. In the 1911 Irish Census, Catherine
   Greene is no longer present, and her daughter is listed as 'head of the family'. See Irish
   Census schedules, 1901 and 1911, available online through the Irish National Archives
   website, census.nationalarchives.ie.

15 Demographic data for Killaloe parish is taken from the Irish censuses of 1841, 1851
   and 1891, published in the *British Parliamentary Papers*. For all the published County
   Kilkenny census data employed in this essay, see: *Report of the Commissioners Appointed
   to Take the Census of Ireland … 1841*, HC 1843, xxiv, pp. 161–73; *Census of Ireland for …
   1851, vol. i, Province of Leinster*, HC 1852–3, xci, pp. 64–79; *Census of Ireland, 1881, vol. i,
   Province of Leinster*, HC 1881, xcvii, pp. 321–439; *Census of Ireland, 1891, pt. 1 … vol. i,
   Province of Leinster*, HC 1890–91, xcv, pp. 325–422; *Census of Ireland, 1911, pt. 1 … vol. i ,
   Province of Leinster*, HC 1912–13, cxiv, pp. 383–523.

16 On tuberculosis (or 'consumption') among the Irish in late nineteenth- and early
   twentieth-century US cities, see Miller, *Emigrants and Exiles*, p. 506.

17 Mary Ann Rowe's baptism is recorded in the Irish Catholic parish records for
   Dunnamaggan, which are available via www.ancestry.com, as are the passenger and
   crew lists of ships arriving in Boston, 1820–1963, in which Rowe's 1888 voyage aboard
   the *Pavonia* is recorded. Both her birth and emigration dates are corroborated by
   information, for which the author is very grateful, provided by the donor of Rowe's
   letter, Mrs Bríd Galway and, through her, by Mrs Robert Holden, a local descendant
   of Mary Ann Rowe's sister; Mrs Galway, letter to author, 14 February 1990. The
   Catholic parish records for Dunamaggan (note different spelling) are also available
   online through the National Library of Ireland website at https://registers.nli.ie/
   parishes/0984.

18 James Rowe died on 9 July 1892, aged sixty, from a stomach disorder; see the Irish
   Genealogical Records, Callan District: Deaths, available at www.irishgenealogy.ie.
   According to the 1901 and 1911 Irish census schedules (see n. 14), his widow Catherine
   Kennedy Rowe (sp. Roe) still lived on the Monachunna farm with her married
   daughter and the latter's husband and son. In 1901, Catherine Rowe's age was listed as
   sixty-eight, in 1911 as eighty, which suggests that she was born about 1830 and married
   James Rowe about 1860, two years before the recorded baptism of their first known
   child. However, Catherine Rowe's age was recorded as ninety-two when she died on
   24 August 1918; see Irish Genealogical Records, Callan District: Deaths (as above); the
   author thanks Dr Breandán Mac Suibhne for the data from this source.

19 According to Griffith's Valuation (see n. 7), in 1850 David Rowe of Monachunna
   (probably James Rowe's father, Mary Ann Rowe's grandfather) rented slightly over
   seventy acres from Robert C. Villiers; the land was then valued at £41 5s. per annum,
   and the Rowe farmhouse and 'offices' (farm buildings) were valued at an additional £3,
   indicating a substantial dwelling suitable for a family of strong farmer status.
       According to the updated valuations, available in the Land Valuation Office in
   Dublin, in 1876 (presumably when David Rowe died) James Rowe took control of the
   farm, which was then leased from the heirs of Rev. Cecil Russell of Drumcree, Killucan,
   County Westmeath. In 1891 James Rowe purchased his holding from the Russell estate,
   probably under the terms of one of the recent Irish Land Acts. At that time, his farm
   consisted of nearly seventy-five acres, valued (including the house and buildings) at
   £38 10s – the reduced value since 1850 reflecting the downward rent adjustments made
   under the 1881 and 1886 Land Acts.

294   *Notes to pages 79 to 80*

20 On the social history of County Kilkenny, see William Nolan and Kevin Whelan (eds), *Kilkenny: History and society* (Templeogue, Dublin: Geography Publications, 1990), especially the essays by William J. Smyth, L.M. Cullen, and P.H. Gulliver and Marilyn Silverman. Also see Silverman and Gulliver's *In the Valley of the Nore: A social history of Thomastown, County Kilkenny, 1840–1983* (Templeogue, Dublin: Geography Publications, 1986), and the essays on County Kilkenny in their edited book *Approaching the Past: Historical anthropology through Irish case studies* (New York: Columbia University Press, 1992); as well as data on rural Kilkenny in the *Agricultural Statistics for Ireland, 1851–1891*, published annually in the *British Parliamentary Papers*. Also valuable is Walter Walsh, *Kilkenny: The struggle for the land, 1850–1882* (Thomastown, Co. Kilkenny: Walsh Books, 2008); and on the Rowes' parish, see James Brennan, 'Dunamaggan Settlement History, 1650–1800', *Old Kilkenny Review: Journal of the Kilkenny Archaeological Society*, vol. 4, 1992, pp. 958–67.

21 See the Dunnamaggan and Monachunna data from the published Irish censuses of 1841, 1851, 1881 and 1891 in the *British Parliamentary Papers* (see n. 15).

22 See the published 1841, 1851, 1881 and 1911 Irish censuses (see n. 15).

23 Calculated from the data on age and conjugal status, by counties, 1851–1911, in W.E. Vaughan and A.J. Fitzpatrick (eds), *Irish Historical Statistics: Population, 1821–1971* (Dublin: Royal Irish Academy, 1978), pp. 117, 130, 149. Of course, the proportions of women *still resident in Ireland*, who were married or unmarried, would be affected by the numbers that had emigrated since the previous census.

24 Ibid.

25 Unfortunately, it is impossible to determine the precise identity and age of Mary Ann Rowe's sister. According to the Dunnamaggan Catholic parish records (see n. 17), James and Catherine Rowe had four daughters: Anna, baptised in 1862; Mary Ann, 1864; Joanna, 1866; and Elena, 1870. Family tradition states that Elena died young (as did the Rowes' two sons, both named David), which means that either Anna or Joanna should have inherited the farm after Mary Ann emigrated. However, neither appears under either of those names in subsequent records. In the 1901 and 1911 Irish censuses, the Rowes' inheriting daughter is named Alice; in 1901 she was listed as thirty-six years old, in 1911 as forty-seven, which may mean that Alice was born in 1865, a year after Mary Ann. One possibility is that Alice Rowe's baptism was not recorded in Dunnamaggan; another is that either Anna or Joanna was also known as Alice. If Anna was Alice, then the Rowes followed the rule of primogeniture and passed the farm to their eldest daughter, who in 1901 and 1911 shaved a few years off her age for the census-taker. If Joanna was Alice, then the Rowe family practised what anthropologists call ultimogeniture (not uncommon in many parts of post-Famine Ireland), and so Mary Ann's emigration enabled her younger sister to inherit and marry at home.

26 Research in Dunnamaggan's parish records (see n. 17) suggests that David Walsh was probably the son of John Walsh and Alice Comerford, and was baptised in the Dunnamaggan chapel on 5 December 1869, although according to the Irish Genealogical Records (Callan District: Marriages) David Walsh and Alice Rowe were married in the Catholic chapel of Kilmaganny, the parish adjoining Dunamaggan to the south; see www.irishgenealogy.ie. In the 1901 Irish census their only child, John, was listed as seven years of age, in 1911 as eighteen. Alice and David Walsh's ages at marriage are estimated from the census data: in 1901 Alice's age was listed as thirty-six and David's as thirty-one; in 1911 Alice was recorded as forty-seven and David as forty-one. Typically in post-Famine Irish marriages, husbands were older than wives, increasingly so by a decade or more; however, since Alice Walsh was the heir to her

Notes to pages 80 to 82   295

father's farm, a reversal of the usual age disparity between spouses was not uncommon. On James Rowe's death in July 1892, see n. 18.

27 According to Griffith's Valuation (see n. 7), in 1850 William Wallace rented a farm in Ballintee townland, adjacent to Monachunna, that contained over sixty acres valued at £53, plus a house and other buildings valued at £3 more. Comparing the valuations of the Wallace and Rowe lands at mid-century suggests that the former were richer or more productive. In addition, in 1850 William Wallace rented another fourteen-acre holding in Baunatillaun townland, also in Dunnamaggan parish. According to the 1901 Irish census, the Wallaces no longer held land in Ballintee, but if Mary Ann's correspondent was the James Wallace who in 1901 was a farmer in Baunatillaun, then he was forty-five years old in 1888 when he received her letter from Dedham.

28 little John: probably John Wallace, born in 1887 or 1888, the son of Mary Ann Rowe's correspondent, James Wallace, and his wife, Statia (i.e. Anastasia), who were married about 1881 (see n. 17). The 1901 census (see n. 14) listed John Wallace, age thirteen, living with his parents and siblings in Baunatillaun townland.

29 niecer: nicer; also see niece, for nice, below.

30 I dont [k[no[w] but they are Irish: according to Dr Proinsias Ó Drisceoil, this wording 'shows that Mary Ann's English is heavily influenced' by the Irish language, in which the phrase would be: *níl a fhios agam nach Éireannaigh iad*; email to author, 12 May 2019.

31 Collins: several Collins families, at least one of them headed by Irish emigrants, can be found in Dedham in the 1880 US census schedules, available through www.ancestry. com. However, Mary Ann Rowe's most likely employer was Mary Collins, the wife of Charles Collins, a Dedham shopkeeper and English emigrant (perhaps of Irish birth or parentage), whose address at 2 Belknap Street was so close to St Mary's Catholic church on High Street that, as Rowe testified in her letter, she could walk from work to mass in only two or three minutes.

32 Election [for] President: the 1888 US presidential election, held on 6 November, a week after Mary Ann Rowe wrote her letter, was won by Benjamin Harrison (Republican, Ohio), although the incumbent, Grover Cleveland (Democrat, New York), received more popular votes and was strongly supported by Irish Catholic voters in Boston and other US cities.

33 the night Mc Namarra was liberated: initially, the author assumed this was a reference to a local celebration of the release from prison of a Fenian or Land League leader. However, extensive research could discover no such person or incident, and the author now believes that Rowe's reference was to a concert performance, which both she and Wallace attended, perhaps in Callan or Kilkenny town, by the St Mary's Fife and Drum Band, later known as 'McNamara's Band', formed in Limerick in 1885 by four McNamara brothers, and which became famous for its performances throughout Ireland; see https:// en.wikipedia.org/wiki/McNamara%27s_Band. For research assistance, the author is grateful to: Dr William Nolan of Geography Publications, Templeogue, Dublin; Dr Proinsias Ó Drisceoil, who first suggested that Rowe's phrase was a musical title or lyric; Professor Cheryl Herr of the University of Iowa; Professor Stephen Watt of the University of Indiana; and Professors Bruce McConachie and Michelle Granshaw of the University of Pittsburgh.

34 Statia: i.e. Anastasia; probably either James Wallace's wife (see n. 28) or his sister, who was baptised in Dunnamaggan's chapel in September 1857 (see n. 17).

35 David M. Katzman, *Seven Days A Week: Women and domestic service in industrializing America* (Urbana, IL: University of Illinois Press, 1981), pp. 267–9; Faye E. Dudden,

Serving Women: Household service in nineteenth-century America (Hanover, NH: Wesleyan University Press, 1983), pp. 195–210, 222, 230–4.

36 Lynch-Brennan, 'Ubiquitous Bridget', pp. 339–40; Miller, *Emigrants and Exiles*, Table 11, p. 581.

37 Miller, 'For "Love and Liberty"' (2008 version), pp. 302–3, 323–4. Irish emigrant women's best chances of endogamous marriage were in the disproportionately male Irish communities in the midwestern and western states.

38 The classic study of late nineteenth-century metropolitan Boston is Sam Bass Warner, *Streetcar Suburbs: The process of growth in Boston, 1870–1900* (Cambridge, MA: Harvard University Press, 1978). Also see Louis A. Cook, *History of Norfolk County, Massachusetts, 1622–1918* (New York: S.J. Clarke Publishing Co., 1918), vol. 1, pp. 133, 425–7, 476–7.

39 The Norfolk County data is taken from the published US censuses for 1880 and 1890; see *Statistics of the Population of the United States at the Tenth Census … 1880* (Washington, DC: Government Printing Office, 1883), pp. 65, 210, 450–1, 494, 513; and *Report on Population of the United States at the Eleventh Census: 1890* (Washington, DC: Government Printing Office, 1895), vol. 1, pp. 24, 181, 632, 921; and vol. 9, p. 240. These volumes do not disclose the number of Dedham's Irish-born inhabitants. However, if we assume that the same proportion of Dedham's foreign-born inhabitants (1,070 in 1890) was of Irish birth as was true in Norfolk County generally (47 per cent), then at least 500 (or 7 per cent) of Dedham's town dwellers were Irish emigrants. Also see Cook, *History of Norfolk County*, as in n. 34.

40 On St Mary's church in Dedham, see Robert H. Lord, John E. Sexton and Edward T. Harrington, *History of the Archdiocese of Boston in the Various Stages of Its Development, 1604–1943* (Boston: Pilot Publishing Co., 1944), pp. 315–16, 715; and Cook, *History of Norfolk County*, p. 425.

41 Data from *Eleventh US Census, 1890* (see n. 39), vol. 9, p. 240; vol. 1, p. 921. Also see Stephen Thernstrom, *The Other Bostonians: Poverty and progress in the American metropolis, 1880–1970* (Cambridge, MA: Harvard University Press, 1973), and, on Hugh O'Brien and Boston Irish politics, Thomas H. O'Connor, *The Boston Irish: A political history* (Boston: Northeastern University Press, 1995).

42 See the works on County Kilkenny cited in n. 20.

43 Richard Lahert, *The History and Antiquities of the Parish of Dunnamaggan* (Tralee: The Kerryman, 1956), pp. i–ii, 75–125.

44 See above, n. 29, and Ó Drisceoil, 'Pádraig Phiarais Cúndún agus Cáit Graídhin'. By the early nineteenth century, if not before, literacy in Irish was rare – especially so for women. On Green's letter and family, the author is also grateful to Professor Neil Buttimer, National University of Ireland Cork, email to author, 5 June 2019.

45 Brian Ó Cuív, *Irish Dialects and Irish-Speaking Districts* (Dublin: Dublin Institute for Advanced Studies, 1971), p. 78.

46 Publications of and about Irish rural folklore are legion, and for guidance the author is grateful to Angela Bourke of University College Dublin, and Ray Cashman and Barbara Hillers of the Folklore Institute at Indiana University. See especially Bourke, 'The Virtual Reality of Irish Fairy Legends', *Éire-Ireland*, vol. 31, nos. 1–2, spring/ summer 1996, pp. 7–25; Ray Cashman, *Packy Jim: Folklore and worldview on the Irish border* (Madison, WI: University of Wisconsin Press, 2016), pp. 146–7, 259–60; Henry Glassie (ed.), *Irish Folktales* (New York: Pantheon Books, 1985), pp. 123–7, 141; Patricia Lysaght, *The Banshee: The Irish supernatural death-messenger* (Dublin: O'Brien Press, 1996); Ann Ridge, *Death Customs in Rural Ireland* (Syracuse: Syracuse University Press, 2012); Seán Ó Súilleabháin, *Folktales of Ireland* (Chicago: University of Chicago Press,

Notes to pages 84 to 85 297

1966), pp. 213–15, and *A Handbook of Irish Folklore* (Dublin: Educational Company of Ireland, 1942), pp. 249, 378; and Salvador Ryan, *Death and the Irish: A miscellany* (Dublin: Wordwell, 2016).

Many Irish emigrants, males as well as females, reported dreams or other premonitions of the deaths of loved ones in Ireland; for example: Hugh Quin, Jr, voyage journal, 1817 (T.2874, Public Record Office of Northern Ireland, Belfast); Alice McDonald, New York City, to her mother in County Monaghan, 3 February 1868 (Clogher Historical Society, Monaghan); Jennie Durkin, East Orange, NJ, to her mother in County Mayo, 1889 (John Dillon papers, ms. 6893/19–20, Trinity College, Dublin); Julia Lough, Winsted, CT, to her mother in Queen's County, 25 January 1891 (Lough Family Letters, copies in author's possession); and Hugh Daly, memoir 1870s–1940s (copy in author's possession).

47 In the early 1800s, agrarian conflict in County Kilkenny between strong farmers and the rural poor had been frequent and violent, but post-Famine mass emigration decimated the ranks of the lower classes; for example, see Paul E.W. Roberts, 'Caravats and Shanavests: Whiteboyism and Faction Fighting in East Munster, 1802–11', in Samuel Clark and James S. Donnelly, Jr (eds), *Irish Peasants: Violence and political unrest, 1780–1914* (Madison, WI: University of Wisconsin Press, 1983), pp. 73–4, 86–7, 92–8; and Lahert, *History and Antiquities of the Parish of Dennamaggan*, pp. 167–75. Even in the late 1800s and early 1900s, conflict between affluent farmers and labourers remained common; see, for instance, the works by Gulliver and Silverman cited in n. 20, as well as John W. Boyle, 'A Marginal Figure: The Irish rural laborer', in Clark and Donnelly, *Irish Peasants*, pp. 316–18.

48 Massachusetts Town and Vital Records, 1620–1988, accessed online through www.ancestry.com; thanks also to Ksenya Kiebuzinski, assistant archivist at the Boston Archdiocesan Archives, whose 1990 pre-internet research located the Rowe-Sutton marriage in the St Mary's (Dedham) parish records.

According to their marriage record, Mary A. Rowe of Dedham – recorded (incorrectly) as age twenty-eight, occupation 'domestic', and daughter of James Rowe and Catherine Kennedy – married Patrick J. Sutton of Providence, described as aged forty, occupation 'merchant', son of Patrick Sutton and Ellen Slavin, and as embarking on his second marriage.

Mary Ann Rowe's husband may have been the Patrick Sutton listed as a dealer in 'liquors' in the 1897 *Providence City Directory*. However, this author suspects that Sutton's age on the marriage record was listed incorrectly (as was Mary Ann's), and that Rowe's husband was born about 1870, the son of Patrick Sutton, an illiterate labourer, and his wife Bridget Sutton, both of whom had emigrated from County Kilkenny scarcely a year after their son's birth in Ireland. (Ellen Slavin/Sutton, whose name appears instead of Bridget Sutton's on the Rowe–Sutton marriage record, was the senior Patrick Sutton's widowed mother, who in 1890 had emigrated to join her son's family in Providence.) If these suppositions are correct, then Patrick J. Sutton was under thirty years of age when he wed Mary Ann Rowe, who therefore, like her sister in Ireland, married a man younger than herself.

The family of the elder Patrick Sutton and his wife Bridget in Providence was traced online via www.ancestry.com in the following sources: the US census schedules of 1880 (which list their Irish-born son, Patrick J. Sutton, age ten) and of 1890–1920; the Rhode Island censuses of 1885–1925; and the US Naturalization Records. The latter contain the 5 April 1880 petition for US citizenship by the elder Patrick Sutton to the Rhode Island Supreme Court in Providence. According to this petition, Sutton had been 'born in Ireland in the County Kilkenny' and had arrived in Boston on 5 April 1871. Intriguingly, the elder Sutton's petition was supported by written testimony from another Irish emigrant, Sutton's neighbour and fellow labourer Robert Ro[w]e, who in turn (according to the 1885 Rhode Island census) boarded with Irish emigrant James Kennedy, who had the same surname as Mary Ann Rowe's mother before her marriage. It seems very likely therefore that the Suttons, Rowes and Kennedys had been neighbours or kinfolk in County Kilkenny who maintained contact in New England.

49 The author is grateful to Mrs Bríd Galway and to James and Patrick Walsh of Ballintee, Dunnamaggan, the descendants of David and Alice Walsh, for providing Figs 5.1 and 5.2, the photographs of Mary Ann Rowe/Sutton, and also another photograph of her infant son (Fig. 5.3) to film-maker Paul Wagner of Charlottesville, Virginia (see n. 2). Mary Ann Rowe's altered features in the second photograph may also reflect the pregnancy that ended tragically.

50 Massachusetts Death Records, 1841–1915, accessed online via www.ancestry.com. Mary Ann Rowe's entry gives her cause of death as 'childbirth' and her burial place as Brookdale Cemetery in Dedham. In other respects, the death record is inaccurate in listing her as Mary Ellen Roe Sutton, aged thirty-one and born in 1867. Unfortunately, the author was unable to locate records of her burial and grave in church and cemetery records.

51 Mrs Bríd Galway, letter to author, 14 February 1990. Numerous Tully families, with senior members of Irish birth or descent and working-class occupations, appear in Dedham's census records in the period 1900–1920 (and earlier). However, none of the Tully households includes a young male who might have been Mary Ann Rowe Sutton's orphaned son.

52 Rhodes, *Women and the Family in Post-Famine Ireland*, pp. 257–77.

53 Horace Plunkett, *Ireland in the New Century* (London: John Murray, 1904), quoted in Miller, *Emigrants and Exiles*, p. 515.

54 For an argument similar to the one in this essay's conclusion, see Miller and Ellen Skerrett, with Bridget Kelly, 'Walking Backward to Heaven? Edmond Ronayne's pilgrimage in Famine Ireland and Gilded Age America', in Breandán Mac Suibhne and Enda Delaney (eds), *Power and Hunger: The Great Famine and Irish popular politics* (London: Routledge, 2016), pp. 80–2.

CHAPTER 6 – The Balfour war mission to America in 1917 and the Irish problem

1 The most thorough study of Balfour and his Irish connections is Catherine B. Shannon, *Arthur J. Balfour and Ireland, 1874–1922* (Washington, DC: Catholic University of America Press, 1988). For analyses of the Balfour mission in the context of American entry into the war, see G.R. Conyne, *Woodrow Wilson: The British perspective, 1912–21* (London: Macmillan, 1992), pp. 104–20; and David R. Woodward, *Trial by Friendship: Anglo-American Relations, 1917–1918* (Lexington, KY: University of Kentucky Press, 1993), pp. 44–68.

2 Cecil Spring-Rice to A.J. Balfour, 11 January 1917, vol. 58, Balfour papers, British Library. Also see Spring-Rice to Balfour, 22 January 1917, FO 371/3071, The National Archives, Kew.

3 Cecil Spring-Rice to Lord Hardinge, 23 February 1917, FO 800/242, NA.

4 Relations between the United States and Britain, 8 March 1917, E.M. House papers, Yale University Library; and W.B. Fowler, *British–American Relations, 1917–1918: The role of Sir William Wiseman* (Princeton, NJ: Princeton University Press, 1969), p. 22.

Notes to pages 89 to 96　　　　　　　　　　　　　　　　　　　　　　　　　　　299

　　Spring-Rice conveyed to the prime minister that Irish sentiment in America would
　　be satisfied by home rule with 'nothing but a united Ireland'. Sir Cecil Spring-Rice to
　　W.A.S. Adams, 29 March 1917, F63/1/15, Lloyd George papers, House of Lords Library.

5　Woodrow Wilson to Robert Lansing, 10 April 1917, 841d.00/103, *Foreign Relations of the
　　United States, The Lansing Papers, 1914–1920*, vol. 2, pp. 4–5.

6　Walter Hines Page to Secretary of State, 18 April 1917, 841d.00/106, State Department
　　papers, National Archives and Records Administration.

7　The Irish Question, No. 23, War Cabinet 116, 10 April 1917, CAB 23/1, NA.

8　Cecil Spring-Rice to [Lord Robert Cecil], 13 April 1917, Stephen Gwynn (ed.), *The
　　Letters and Friendships of Sir Cecil Spring-Rice: A record* (London: Constable & Co.,
　　1929), vol. 2, pp. 392–3; and Memo, 13 April 1917, FO 800/208 [Balfour], NA.

9　Robert Lansing, *War Memoirs of Robert Lansing* (Indianapolis: Bobbs-Merrill Company,
　　1935), pp. 272–4; Charles Seymour (ed.), *The Intimate Papers of Colonel House* (Boston:
　　Houghton Mifflin Company, 1928), vol. 3, pp. 38–41; and Charles E. Neu, *Colonel House:
　　A biography of Woodrow Wilson's silent partner* (New York: Oxford University Press,
　　2015), pp. 298–300.

10　Arthur James Balfour, *Chapters of Autobiography* (London: Cassell & Company, 1939),
　　p. 239; and A.J. Balfour to War Cabinet, 1 May 1917, F60/2/13, David Lloyd George
　　papers, HLL. House told Plunkett that Irish matters were not discussed at this
　　meeting. Plunkett Diary, 1 May 1917, MS 42,222, Horace Plunkett papers, National
　　Library of Ireland.

11　Shane Leslie Diary, 3 May 1917, box 6, folder 71, Leslie papers, Eton College Library.

12　Woodrow Wilson to Joseph Tumulty, 5 May 1917, Arthur S. Link (ed.), *Papers of
　　Woodrow Wilson* (Princeton, NJ: Princeton University Press, 1983), vol. 42, p. 223.

13　Lansing, *War Memoirs*, pp. 276–7.

14　A.J. Balfour to Prime Minister, 5 May 1917, FO 371/3070, NA.

15　A.J. Balfour to David Lloyd George, 23 June 1917, CAB 1/25(5), ibid.

16　The only specific British reference this writer has ever found to the Gunston Hall
　　meeting is in a letter by Sir Ian Malcolm quoted in Dugdale's biography of Balfour. 'In
　　the [previous] afternoon A.J.B. played tennis; he never played better; and today he has
　　motored out to the country to talk Foreign Affairs with Mr. Lansing.' No importance is
　　attributed to this meeting. See Blanche E.C. Dugdale, *Arthur James Balfour* (London:
　　Hutchinson & Co., 1936), vol. 2, pp. 205–6.

17　Shane Leslie to John Redmond, 18 May 1917, Redmond papers, NLI.

18　Joseph Brennon et al. to John Redmond, 22 April 1917, Memorandum, series I, box 330,
　　Theodore Roosevelt papers, Library of Congress.

19　*The Times*, 26 and 27 April 1917.

20　*Congressional Record, Appendix*, 65th Congress, 1st Session, vol. 55, p. 161. There had also
　　been a flurry of Irish resolutions introduced in Congress and various petitions sent by
　　constituents printed in the *Congressional Record*.

21　Plunkett Diary, 24 April 1917, MS 42,222, Horace Plunkett papers, NLI. The best study
　　of Plunkett for his American connections is Margaret Digby, *Horace Plunkett: An
　　Anglo-American Irishman* (Oxford: Basil Blackwell, 1949).

22　Plunkett Diary, 25 April 1917, MS 42,222, Horace Plunkett papers, NLI; and Horace
　　Plunkett to A.J. Balfour, 25 April 1917, FO 800 [Balfour], NA.

23　Horace Plunkett to Sir Eric [Drummond], 29 April 1917, FO 800 [Balfour], NA. For
　　Quinn's Irish nationalist activities, see Úna Ní Bhroiméil, 'An American Opinion: John
　　Quinn and the Easter Rising', in Miriam Nyhan Grey (ed.), *Ireland's Allies: America
　　and the 1916 Easter Rising* (Dublin: UCD Press, 2016).

300   *Notes to pages 96 to 106*

24 John Quinn to Sir Eric Drummond, 1 and 2 May 1917, FO 800/208 [Balfour], NA; and
   John Quinn to Theodore Roosevelt, 1 May 1917, series I, box 331, Roosevelt papers, LC.
25 Notes on Recent American Opinion and Action on the Irish Question, 2 June 1917,
   MS 1752, John Quinn papers, NLI. Quinn wrote up his notes of the meeting with
   Balfour on 2 June 1917 when he learned that George Russell would be a member of
   the Irish Convention being established in Dublin and sent him a copy. He sent a
   second copy to Maud Gonne. See John Quinn to Maud Gonne, 2 June 1917, in Janis
   and Richard Londraville (eds), *Too Long a Sacrifice: The letters of Maud Gonne and John
   Quinn* (Selinsgrove, PA: Susquehanna University Press, 1999), p. 199.
26 Transcript of Irish Deputation visit with Balfour, 4 May 1917, FO 800/208, NA. Later
   in 1917 Shane Leslie published a quite accurate summary of the meeting, obviously
   based on inside information. See Shane Leslie, *The Irish Issue in its American Aspect*
   (New York: Charles Scribner's Sons, 1917), pp. 199–201.
27 Notes of Recent American Opinion and Action on the Irish Home Rule Question, 2
   June 1917, MS 1752, John Quinn papers, NLI.
28 John Quinn to Maud Gonne, 20 May 1917, in Londraville (eds), *Too Long a Sacrifice*,
   p. 197.
29 Cecil Dormer to Theodore Russell, 6 May 1917, F60/2/17, David Lloyd George papers,
   HLL.
30 A.J. Balfour to Prime Minister, 5 May 1917, FO 371/3070, NA.
31 Shane Leslie to John Redmond, 6 May 1917, Redmond papers, NLI. A useful biography
   of Leslie is that of Otto Rauchbauer, *Shane Leslie: Sublime failure* (Dublin: Lilliput
   Press, 2009).
32 A.J. Balfour to David Lloyd George, 23 June 1917, CAB 1/25(5), NA.
33 *Congressional Record*, 65th Congress, 1st Session, vol. 55, part 12, pp. 1879–80; and
   Congressional Record, Appendix, 65th Congress, 2nd Session, vol. 56, part 12, pp. 104–6;
   Arthur Willert, *The Road to Safety: A study in Anglo-American relations* (London: Derek
   Verschoyle, 1952), pp. 75–6; and Blanche E.C. Dugdale, *Arthur James Balfour* (London:
   Hutchinson & Co., 1936), vol. 2, pp. 202–5.
34 Sir Ian Malcolm, *Lord Balfour: A memory* (London: Macmillan, 1930), p. 55.
35 A.J. Balfour to David Lloyd George, 23 June 1917, CAB 1/25(5), NA.
36 Shannon, *Arthur J. Balfour*, p. 288.
37 Ibid., p. 232. Also see Stephen Hartley, *The Irish Question as a Problem in British Foreign
   Policy, 1914–18* (New York: St Martin's Press, 1987), pp. 138–46.
38 Plunkett Diary, 23 April 1917, MS 42,222, Horace Plunkett papers, NLI.

CHAPTER 7 – 'Ireland's family re-union': The 1932 Eucharistic Congress
1 Mary E. Daly, 'Nationalism, Sentiment, and Economic Relations between Ireland and
   Irish America in the Post-War Years', in Kevin Kenny (ed.), *New Directions in Irish-
   American History* (Madison, WI: University of Wisconsin Press, 2003), p. 263.
2 Mike Cronin, 'Projecting the Nation through Sport and Culture: Ireland, Aonach
   Tailteann and the Irish Free State 1924–32', *Journal of Contemporary History*, vol. 38, no.
   3, July 2003, pp. 395–411.
3 Kevin Kenny, *The American Irish: A history* (London: Longman, 2000), p. 71.
4 *The Tablet*, 23 April 1932, p. 532.
5 John Belchem, *Irish, Catholic and Scouse: The history of the Liverpool Irish 1800–1939*
   (Liverpool: Liverpool University Press, 2007), p. 298.
6 *The Tablet*, 26 March 1932, p. 410.

Notes to pages 107 to 117 301

7 David G. Holmes, 'The Eucharistic Congress of 1932 and Irish Identity', *New Hibernia Review*, vol. 4, no. 1, spring 2000, p. 60.

8 *The Month*, January 1932.

9 *Eucharistic Congress: Advance programme*, p. 12.

10 *Irish Catholic Directory* (hereafter *ICD*), 1933, record for the year 1932, 22 June, p. 611.

11 Ibid., p. 615.

12 Ibid., p. 619.

13 A reference to the First Vatican Council held in 1869–70, where the archbishop of Dublin, Cardinal Paul Cullen, played a major role.

14 *The Tablet*, 26 March 1932, p. 408.

15 Cosgrave's claim that Ireland was largely unscathed during the international depression does not withstand scrutiny: Frank Barry and Mary E. Daly, 'Irish Perceptions of the Great Depression', in Michalie Psalidopoulus (ed.), *The Great Depression in Europe: Economic thought and policy in a national context* (Athens: Alpha Bank, 2012), pp. 395–421.

16 National Archives of Ireland, Department of the Taoiseach, S5111/4–8.

17 *Pilot*, 5 January 1929.

18 *The Tablet*, 16 February 1929, pp. 224 and 230.

19 Ibid., p. 216.

20 *Pilot*, 16 May 1931.

21 Ibid., 1 August 1931.

22 Ibid., 18 June 1932.

23 *America*, 14 May 1932, 'Ireland's Hosting for the Host'.

24 Ibid., 30 July 1932.

25 Monsignor Peter Guilday born Chester, Penn. of Irish parents; taught at Catholic University of America, editor of the *Catholic Historical Review* and co-founder of the American Catholic Historical Association.

26 *Eucharistic Congress Record* (*Irish Independent*), p. 44.

27 *Pilot*, 2 July 1932.

28 Liam Kennedy, 'Out of History: Ireland "that most distressful country"', in Liam Kennedy, *Colonialism, Religion and Nationalism in Ireland* (Belfast: Institute of Irish Studies, 1996), pp. 182–223.

29 *Pilot*, 9 July 1932.

30 *The Tablet*, 13 February 1932.

31 Ibid., p. 207.

32 *Eucharistic Congress Souvenir* (*Irish Independent*).

33 Keith Robbins, *England, Ireland, Scotland, Wales: The Christian churches 1900–2000* (Oxford: Oxford University Press, 2008), p. 198.

34 Rene Koller, 'Bourne, Francis Alphonsus', *Oxford Dictionary of National Biography*, www.oxforddnb.com.

35 'The Congress', *The Tablet*, 21 May 1932, p. 657.

36 Robbins, *England, Ireland, Scotland, Wales*, p. 43.

37 John McGreevy, *Parish Boundaries: The Catholic encounter with race in the twentieth-century urban north* (Chicago: University of Chicago Press, 1996).

38 Thomas R. Greene, 'English Roman Catholics and the Irish Free State in the 1930s', *Éire/Ireland*, vol. 19, 1984, p. 50.

39 Steven Field, *Class and Ethnicity: Irish Catholics in England, 1880–1939* (Philadelphia: Open University Press, 1993), p. 40.

40 *The Tablet*, 25 June 1932.

41 Ibid.

302   *Notes to pages 117 to 123*

42 *Irish Times*, 30 June 1932, London correspondent.
43 *America*, vol. 46, no. 19, March 1932, p. 614.
44 Seán Glynn, 'Irish Immigration to Britain, 1911–1951: Patterns and policy', *Irish Economic and Social History*, vol. 8, 1981, pp. 56–69.
45 Belchem, *Irish, Catholic and Scouse*, pp. 306–7.
46 Koller, 'Bourne, Francis Alphonsus'.
47 Greene, 'English Roman Catholics', pp. 57–8.
48 *The Month*, January 1932.
49 Ibid., August 1932.
50 G.K. Chesterton, *Christendom in Dublin: Essays in memory of the Eucharistic Congress* (London: Sheed & Ward, 1932), p. 7.

CHAPTER 8 – **Differing with the American cousins: the Irish Catholics of Canada fight the Great War, 1914–18**
1 *New Freeman*, 29 July 1916.
2 Ibid.
3 Ibid., 19 August 1916; *Northwest Review*, 5 August and 12 August 1916. The latter Catholic paper in Winnipeg, Manitoba, highlighted the common narrative McLaughlin shared with Canada's English-speaking Catholic bishops of the day.
4 National Library of Ireland, John Redmond papers, MS 15 235/2, 1897–1915, Canada. The file contains a sheaf of letters in which Redmond engages many Canadian supporters. MS 15 265/2 (1918) contains the draft of an amended proposal for home rule with an overt Canadian flavour, 'memorandum Working and History of Government of Canada', submitted by W.E. Ellis, Lord Dunraven and Lord Middleton to the Irish Convention, 1918.
5 Malcolm Campbell, *Ireland's New Worlds: Immigrants, politics and society in the United States and Australia, 1815–1922* (Madison, WI: University of Wisconsin Press, 2008), pp. 163–6; David Brundage, *Irish Nationalism in America: The politics of exile, 1798–1998* (New York: Oxford University Press, 2016), pp. 142–5.
6 Kevin Kenny, 'Diaspora and Comparison: The global Irish as a case study', *Journal of American History*, vol. 90, no. 1, June 2003, pp. 134–62.
7 See Mark G. McGowan, *The Waning of the Green: Catholics, the Irish, and identity in Toronto, 1887–1922* (Montreal and Kingston: McGill Queen's University Press, 1999); James F.E. White, 'Mobility in Place: The Irish Catholics of Victorian Halifax', *Historical Studies*, Occasional Paper, vol. 81, Canadian Catholic Historical Association, 2015, pp. 139–166; Patrick Mannion, *A Land of Dreams: Ethnicity, nationalism and the Irish in Newfoundland, Nova Scotia, and Maine, 1880–1923* (Montreal and Kingston: McGill-Queen's University Press, 2018).
8 *Debates of the House of Commons* (Hansard), 63–64 Victoria, 20 February 1900, pp. 668–9.
9 *The Morning Guardian* (Charlottetown), 24 October 1899. See Sullivan's obvious Tory connections in 'Hon. William Wilfred Sullivan', in Henry James Morgan (ed.), *The Canadian Men and Women of the Time: A hand-book of Canadian biography* (Toronto: William Briggs, 1898), p. 985.
10 *Halifax Herald*, 2 November 1899.
11 Mark G. McGowan, *The Imperial Irish: Canada's Irish Catholics fight the Great War, 1914–1918* (Montreal and Kingston: McGill-Queen's University Press, 2017), p. 55.
12 Carman Miller, 'A Preliminary Analysis of the Socio-economic Composition of Canada's South African War Contingents', *Histoire sociale / Social History*, vol. 8, November 1975, pp. 219–37. The sample of 234 English-speaking Catholics was drawn randomly from scanning over 2,496 soldiers' files documented in thirteen reels

Notes to pages 123 to 125   303

of microfilm in the RG 38 series (reels T2069, 2079, 2080–4) found in Library and Archives Canada (LAC). In total, the files of 234 non-francophone Catholics were discovered among the 2,496 files scanned. To determine Irish origin, the sample was analysed by surname, given name, religion, place of birth, address, and next of kin. Of the 234, 165 (70.5 per cent) were Irish, 49 (20.9 per cent) Scottish, 13 (5.6 per cent) English or Welsh, and 7 (3.0 per cent) other.

13 *New Freeman*, 31 October 1914; *Eganville Leader*, 13 November 1914.

14 *Northwest Review*, 8 August 1914. See also Alfred E. Burke, 'The Irishman's Place in the Empire', in J. Castell Hopkins (ed.), *Empire Club Speeches, 1909–1910* (Toronto: Warwick Bros. & Rutter, 1910), pp. 225–32.

15 Archives of the Roman Catholic Archdiocese of Toronto (ARCAT), Archbishop Neil McNeil papers, Circulars 1914; *Catholic Register*, 20 August 1914.

16 Archives of the Archdiocese of Halifax (AAH), Edward McCarthy papers, Statistics on the Church in Canada, 1916. Included in the four ecclesiastical provinces were Halifax, Antigonish, Charlottetown, Chatham, St John, Toronto, Kingston, Alexandria, Hamilton, London, Peterborough, Pembroke, Sault Ste Marie, Vancouver, Calgary and Victoria. Missing was Winnipeg. It should be clear that Irish Catholics were large minorities in the dioceses of Ottawa, Montreal and St Boniface (out of which Winnipeg was carved).

17 Examples include Bishop John T. McNally (Calgary, Alberta), *Calgary Daily Herald*, 12 September 1914; Bishop James Morrison (Antigonish, Nova Scotia), *Casket*, 13 August 1914. See Peter Ludlow, *The Canny Scot: Archbishop James Morrison of Antigonish* (Montreal and Kingston: McGill-Queen's University Press, 2015), pp. 76–7; Bishop Alexander MacDonald (Victoria, British Columbia), *Casket*, 12 November 1914 and 25 November 1914; Bishop Michael Francis Fallon (London, Ontario), Archives of the Diocese of London (ADL), Michael Francis Fallon papers, Circulars, 28 August 1914; Archbishop Timothy Casey (Vancouver, British Columbia), *New Freeman*, 19 February 1916; Archbishop Alfred A. Sinnott (Winnipeg, Manitoba), *Northwest Review*, 25 December 1915.

18 McGowan, *Imperial Irish*, pp. 89–90.

19 Some examples include Father John Burke's address to a public meeting in St John, New Brunswick, *New Freeman*, 8 January 1916; Father A. Sammut of Assinaboia, Saskatchewan, *Northwest Review*, 14 August 1915; Father John O'Reilly, Sydney, Nova Scotia, *New Freeman*, 9 January 1915; Father J.P. Cummings, Walkerton, Ontario, *Walkerton Telescope*, 10 February 1916; Father J.A. Meehan, Morrisburg, Ontario, *Canadian Freeman*, 13 July 1916; or Father John Joseph O'Gorman, Ottawa, Ontario, whose pulpit and platform presentations on the war culminated in the preparation of a pamphlet based on his lectures and sermons called *Render unto Caesar* and subsequently published as John J. O'Gorman, *Canadians to Arms!* (Toronto: Extension Print, 1916).

20 *Casket*, 12 November 1914.

21 *McKim's Directory of Canadian Publications* (Toronto: A. McKim, 1919), p. 45.

22 *Catholic Register*, 10 September 1914.

23 *Record*, 15 and 22 August 1914; 30 October 1915; the *Record* had a national circulation of about 31,000; *McKim's Directory of Canadian Publications*, p. 45. *New Freeman*, 21 November and 26 December 1914.

24 *Catholic Register*, 29 October 1914 and 21 January 1915.

25 Jonathan Vance, *Maple Leaf Empire* (Toronto: Oxford University Press, 2012), p. 44.

26 Ian Hugh MacLean Miller, *Our Glory and Our Grief: Torontonians and the Great War* (Toronto: University of Toronto Press, 2002), p. 19; Desmond Morton, *Canada and War* (Toronto: Butterworths, 1981), pp. 54–5.

27 Robert Craig Brown and Donald Loveridge, 'Unrequited Faith: Recruiting the CEF, 1914–1918', *Revue international d'histoire militaire*, vol. 51, 1982, pp. 53–79.

28 *Catholic Record*, 24 November 1917.

29 LAC, RG 9 III, vol. 4636, C-0-3, Memorandum to the Archbishops and Bishops of Ontario, October 1917, pp. 10–11; see also RG 9 III, vol. 4673, 'Religious Statistics', and RG 24, vol. 1249, HQ-593-1-77, 22 August 1916. Similar figures can be found in Sessional Paper 143-B, 1917, as cited in Elizabeth Armstrong, *Crisis in Quebec* (Toronto: McClelland & Stewart, Carleton Library Series, 1974), p. 247.

30 For a more detailed analysis, see McGowan, *Imperial Irish*, pp. 105–62 and 263–8.

31 Ibid.

32 Katherine Crooks, 'The Quest for Respectability: The charitable Irish society in Victorian Halifax', CCHA, *Historical Studies*, vol. 81, 2015, occasional paper, pp. 167–94. See also McGowan, *Imperial Irish*, Chapter 3.

33 Robin Burns, 'The Montreal Irish and the Great War', CCHA, *Historical Studies*, vol. 52, 1985, pp. 72–3.

34 *New Freeman*, 6 May 1916.

35 *The Irish Canadian*, overseas number, April 1917, p. 36.

36 *New Freeman*, 18 March 1916.

37 McGowan, *Imperial Irish*, p. 121.

38 City of Toronto Archives, Irish Regiment of Canada, fonds 70, series 340, subseries 6, file 50, The Irish Canadian: History of the 208th Overseas Battalion, 1917, privately bound, p. 2; Elizabeth Smyth, 'Developing the Powers of the Youthful Mind: The evolution of education for women at St Joseph's Academy, Toronto, 1854–1911', CCHA *Historical Studies*, vol. 60, 1993–4, p. 125.

39 LAC, RG 9 II B 3, vol. 80, '218th Battalion: Nominal roll of officers, non-commissioned officers and men, February 17, 1917'.

40 The irony here is that the chaplain of the 69th was the famous Father Francis Duffy, a native of Port Hope, Ontario, Canada, and a graduate of St Michael's College in Toronto.

41 *Northwest Review*, 18 March 1916.

42 Archives of Ontario (AO), Charles J. Foy papers, box 3, file 14, J.H. Barry to Foy, 2 October 1915.

43 *Catholic Register*, 4 May 1916.

44 *Catholic Record*, 6 May 1916. Editors continue their denunciations in the 13 and 20 May issues, referring to Sinn Féin as anti-clerical, shirkers and malcontents.

45 *New Freeman*, 6 May 1916; *Casket*, 4 May 1916.

46 Ibid.

47 *New Freeman*, 13 May 1916.

48 *Northwest Review*, 13 May 1916.

49 *Casket*, 6 July 1916; *Northwest Review*, reprinting *Casket*, 27 May 1916.

50 *Catholic Register*, 18 May 1916; *Catholic Record*, 3 June 1916.

51 *Catholic Record*, 27 May 1916. The *Northwest Review* argued that the *Record* was the most widely read Catholic newspaper in Ontario and 'it may be safely taken as an index of Catholic thought and opinion in the sister province'; *Northwest Review*, 28 July 1916. In comparison, the *Canadian Freeman* was struggling and in September was taken over by the priests of the archdiocese of Kingston. D.A. Casey remained at the helm of the paper and the new energy brought about 1,400 new subscriptions. Nevertheless, it was the smallest of Ontario's Catholic newspapers, with a readership limited to eastern Ontario, Montreal and western Quebec; *Canadian Freeman*, 15 June 1916 and 14 September 1916.

Notes to pages 130 to 135 305

52 *New Freeman*, 20 May 1916; *Northwest Review*, 13 May 1916.

53 *Canadian Freeman*, 18 May 1916.

54 Ibid.

55 *New Freeman*, 17 June 1916.

56 *Canadian Freeman*, 8 February 1917.

57 Ibid., 22 March 1917; *Catholic Record*, 24 March 1917.

58 LAC, MG 27 II D6, Charles Doherty papers, vol. 1, Michael Fallon to C.J. Doherty, Charles Murphy and T.W. McGarry, 12 March 1917. Doherty's papers contain an undated clipping (likely after 17 March 1917) from the *London Advertiser*, reporting of Fallon's St Patrick's Day speech in London in which he asserts: 'Shall less be done for Ireland than has been claimed and successfully asserted on behalf of British democracy?'

59 Cited in Simon Jolivet, *Le vert et le bleu: identité Québécoise et identité irlandaise au tournant du XXe siècle* (Montréal: Les Presses de l'Université de Montréal, 2011), p. 157.

60 *Canadian Freeman*, 22 March 1917.

61 *Ottawa Citizen*, 23 March 1917; *Canadian Freeman*, 29 March 1917; *Catholic Register*, 29 March 1917. See also LAC, MG 30 D20, vol. 1, J.J. O'Gorman papers, file 2. The document is incorrectly dated 1925.

62 Ibid.

63 Ibid.

64 *Canadian Freeman*, 29 March 1917.

65 LAC, Borden papers, vol. 219, Bruchési to Borden, 27 May 1917, pp. 123403–6, and 2 June 1917, pp. 123412–3.

66 For further details, see McGowan, *The Imperial Irish*, pp. 232–43.

67 Ibid., pp. 244–5.

68 LAC, MG 27 III B8, Charles J. Murphy papers, vol. 32, Election Returns, 1917, pp. 13295–7.

69 ADL, Fallon papers, Speeches, 'Statement of Bishop Fallon in Favour of the Union Government', 6 December 1917; *Ottawa Journal*, 7 December 1917; *Catholic Record*, 15 December 1917.

70 *New Freeman*, 2 February 1918. See Father Lancelot Minehan's comments on Sinn Féin in the *Toronto Star*, 22 January 1919.

71 *Catholic Register*, 9 January and 13 March 1919 and 4 November and 2 December 1920; *Canadian Freeman*, 12 December 1918.

72 *Catholic Record*, 25 September 1920. See also *Catholic Register*, 27 January 1921. Comparisons also appear in the *New Freeman*, 9 August 1919.

73 *Canadian Freeman*, 1 January, 3 June and 10 June 1920.

74 Ibid., 10 February 1921. The *Catholic Register* proposed the application of the war's 'principles' as early as 2 December 1920. The *Northwest Review* commented on the war principles, 29 November 1919.

75 [Diocese of Hamilton], *Cathedral Magazine*, March 1919, p. 37. See also *Catholic Register*, 20 March 1919 and 17 June 1920. The *Northwest Review* urged that the Irish issue be taken up at the Versailles conference, 5 July 1919.

76 *Canadian Freeman*, 27 January and 3 February 1921. In April 1921 $953.75 was collected on the Prairies, although a large number of the donors bore Ukrainian, not Irish, surnames, particularly in Regina and environs; *Northwest Review*, 16 April 1921.

77 *Catholic Register*, 1 July 1920. A similar meeting in Halifax also featured clergy and laymen who had been supportive of Canada's war effort. Patrick Mannion, 'Halifax Catholics' Patriotic Work: Responses to Irish nationalism, 1880–1923', CCHA,

306 *Notes to pages 135 to 139*

Historical Studies – occasional paper 81, 2015, pp. 195–223. An Ireland rally was also held in Winnipeg, *Northwest Review*, 8 November 1919. In Vancouver, the Irish National Association supported a loan appeal to Dáil Éireann, the 'parliament' held by Sinn Féin MPs, who were elected to Westminster but refused to take their seats, *Northwest Review*, 17 September 1920. Ottawa also hosted an SDIL meeting, *Northwest Review*, 30 October 1920.

78 *Northwest Review*, 16 April 1921. The Winnipeg situation is detailed, but without a national context, in Richard Davis, 'Irish Nationalism in Manitoba, 1870–1922', in Robert O'Driscoll and Lorna Reynolds (eds), *The Untold Story: The Irish in Canada*, vol. 1 (Toronto: Celtic Arts of Canada, 1988), pp. 393–416. Unfortunately, the article is the only scholarly source on Irish nationalism in Manitoba.

79 The best analysis of this local manifestation of more radical Irish nationalism is found in Jolivet, *Le vert et le bleu*, pp. 218–25 and 234–8.

80 Ibid., p. 225.

81 Pádraig Ó Siadhail, *Katherine Hughes: A life and a journey* (Ottawa: Penumbra Press, 2014), pp. 217–49. The *Canadian Freeman* was perhaps the Catholic weekly most sympathetic to the republicans; see 10 February 1921.

82 *Catholic Record*, 17 and 24 and 31 December 1921, and 2 September 1922; *Catholic Register*, 8 and 29 June, 17 and 31 August, and 5 October 1922; *Northwest Review*, 10 December 1921; Frederick J. McEvoy, 'Canadian Catholic Press Reaction to the Irish Crisis, 1916–1921', in David Wilson (ed.), *Irish Nationalism in Canada* (Montreal and Kingston: McGill-Queen's University Press, 2009), p. 137. The *Canadian Freeman* praised the Anglo-Irish treaty as not perfect, but it might have proven to be the road to something else. Although favouring Michael Collins and Arthur Griffith, it did acknowledge the right of de Valera to dissent: 5 January 1922.

CHAPTER 9 – The *Gaelic American*, 1921–8: reporting on the Anglo-Irish Treaty and the Irish Free State

1 For a study on how the American social environment has shaped Irish-American nationalism, see Michael Doorley, *Irish-American Diaspora Nationalism: The friends of Irish freedom, 1916–1935* (Dublin: Four Courts Press, 2005).

2 Francis M. Carroll, 'The Collapse of Home Rule and the UILA', in Miriam Nyhan Grey (ed.), *Ireland's Allies: America and the 1916 Rising* (Dublin: UCD Press, 2016), p. 32. For a recent study of the relationship between John Redmond and the UILA, see Tony King, *Home Rule from a Transnational Perspective: The Irish Parliamentary Party and the United Irish League of America, 1910–1918* (Wilmington, DE: Vernon Press, 2020).

3 *Gaelic American*, 12 March 1910.

4 US Bureau of the Census, *Twelfth Census of the United States 1900*; Population (Washington, 1901), vol. 1, p. clxx.

5 Kevin Kenny, *The American Irish* (London: Longman, 2000), pp. 192–9.

6 Terry Golway, *Irish Rebel: John Devoy and America's fight for Ireland's freedom* (New York: St Martin's Press, 1998), pp. 1–12.

7 F.M. Carroll, *American Opinion and the Irish Question, 1910–1923* (New York: St Martin's Press, 1978), p. 3.

8 'The story of the Clan na Gael', *Gaelic American*, 6 June 1925. For more on the first two decades of the newspaper, see M. Doorley, 'The Gaelic American and the Shaping of Irish-American Opinion, 1903–1914', in W. Everham and l. Schelbert (eds), *Probing the Past: Festschrift in honor of Leo Schelbert* (New York: Peter Lang, 2015), and M. Doorley, 'The Gaelic American 1912–1922: A case study in Irish-American transnational

Notes to pages 139 to 144 307

journalism', in D. Reddin van Tuyll, M. O'Brien and Marcel Broersma (eds), *Politics, Culture and the Irish-American Press, 1784–1963* (New York: Syracuse University Press, 2021).

9   J.P. Rodechko, *Patrick Ford and His Search for America: A case study of Irish-American journalism, 1870–1913* (New York: Arno Press, 1976), pp. 23–6. The *Gaelic American* continued publication until 1951 when it was then taken over by its main rival the *Irish World*.

10   Cohalan's chairmanship of the Clan is noted in the British government publication *Documents Relative to the Sinn Féin Movement*, PP 1921 (Cmd. 1108), pp. xxix, 429, 13.

11   A share certificate for the newspaper is available in the Joseph McGarrity papers, MS 17660, National Library of Ireland (NLI). Joseph McGarrity was a leading member of the Clan in Philadelphia and supported de Valera in his dispute with Devoy and Cohalan.

12   For more on Cohalan's role in Tammany, see M. Doorley, *Judge Daniel Cohalan: American patriot and Irish-American nationalist* (Cork: Cork University Press, 2019), pp. 42–52.

13   *New York Times*, 19 May 1911.

14   P. McCartan, *With de Valera in America* (Dublin: Fitzpatrick, 1932), p. 15.

15   'The Story of the Clan na Gael', *Gaelic American*, 6 June 1925.

16   'Kerry and Kildare Thrill Big Crowd at Croke Park, Dublin', *Gaelic American*, 19 May 1928.

17   *Gaelic American*, 3 February 1923.

18   Doorley, *Justice Daniel Cohalan*, p. 48.

19   Clan Circular, McGarrity papers, MS 17660, NLI.

20   Alison Kibler, *Censoring Racial Ridicule: Irish, Jewish and African-American struggles over race and representation, 1890–1930* (Chapel Hill, NC: University of North Carolina Press, 2015), p. 30.

21   Alison Kibler, 'The Stage Irishwoman', *Journal of American Ethnic History*, vol. 24, no. 3, spring 2005, pp. 5–30.

22   *Gaelic American*, 18 June 1904. Kibler also notes how the Gaelic League 'celebrated Celtic traits, Irish manhood and the Celtic contribution to America as a means to de-Anglicize American culture', Kibler, *Censoring Racial Ridicule*, p. 33.

23   'Political Differences Forgotten in Drive for M'Kee Ordinance to End Caricaturing of Race', *Gaelic American*, 29 October 1927.

24   *Gaelic American*, 16 June 1923.

25   *Gaelic American*, 19 July 1924. The newspaper instead campaigned for the Progressive candidate Robert M. La Follette who was well known for his isolationist views. The Republican candidate Calvin Coolidge won the presidency.

26   *Gaelic American*, 27 May 1911.

27   Doorley, *Irish-American Diaspora Nationalism*, pp. 30–1.

28   *Gaelic American*, 8 March 1924.

29   Ibid., 9 December 1911.

30   *Irish World*, 15 August 1915. For more on the decline of the UILA, see King, *Home Rule from a Transnational Perspective*.

31   *Gaelic American*, 20 May 1916.

32   Ibid., 19 May 1917.

33   Ibid., 15 March 1919.

34   Ibid., 28 June 1919.

35   Joseph McGarrity (1874–1940) from County Tyrone led the Clan in Philadelphia. Cohalan's disputes with McGarrity are explored in Sean Cronin, *The McGarrity Papers:*

Revelations of the Irish revolutionary movement in Ireland and America, 1900–1940 (Tralee, Kerry: Anvil Books, 1972).

36 For a comprehensive study of Diarmuid Lynch's role as national secretary in the FOIF, see Eileen McGough, *Diarmuid Lynch: A forgotten Irish patriot* (Cork: Mercier Press, 2013).

37 De Valera to Griffith, 9 July 1919, de Valera papers, P150/727, UCD (University College Dublin).

38 *Westminster Gazette*, 7 February 1920. See also D. McCullagh, *De Valera. Volume 1: Rise, 1882–1932* (Dublin: Gill Books, 2017), p. 175.

39 *Gaelic American*, 21 February 1920.

40 De Valera to Cohalan, 20 February 1920; Cohalan to de Valera, 22 February 1920, de Valera papers, P150/1134, UCD; See also folder 1, Box 4, Cohalan papers, American Irish Historical Society (AIHS), New York.

41 Doorley, *Justice Daniel Cohalan*, pp. 147–54.

42 *Gaelic American*, 26 June 1920.

43 Press release, 22 October 1920, McGarrity papers, MS17445, NLI.

44 Records of the National Secretary, FOIF papers, AIHS.

45 *Gaelic American*, 16 October 1920, 30 October 1920.

46 Ibid., 18 August 1920.

47 Ibid., 16 July 1921, 15 April 1922.

48 'Truce Forced by Irish Republican Army', ibid., 16 July 1921.

49 For more on interpretations of the treaty and the treaty divide, see Bill Kissane, *The Politics of the Irish Civil War* (Oxford: Oxford University Press, 2005).

50 Michael Laffin describes the divide between 'purists' and 'pragmatists'. Michael Laffin, *The Resurrection of Ireland: The Sinn Féin party, 1916–1923* (Cambridge: Cambridge University Press, 2006), pp. 350, 360.

51 Ibid., pp. 351–5.

52 The *Gaelic American* initially described the treaty as a 'surrender'. *Gaelic American*, 17 December 1921. Devoy to Collins, 16 February 1922, cited in Charles Tansill, *America and the Fight for Irish Freedom, 1866–1922* (New York: The Devin-Adair Co., 1957), pp. 438–9.

53 *Gaelic American*, 22 April 1922 and 6 May 1922.

54 *Irish World*, 6 January 1922 and 14 January 1922.

55 *Gaelic American*, 8 July 1922.

56 Francis M. Carroll, *America and the Making of an Independent Ireland: A history* (New York: New York University Press, 2021), p. 149.

57 *Gaelic American*, 2 December 1922.

58 Ibid., 3 February 1923.

59 Ibid., 30 December 1922.

60 FOIF pamphlet, *Free State Makes Bad Blunder in Applying for League Membership*, reprinted from the *Gaelic American*, 28 April 1923, FOIF papers, AIHS. See also John P. McCarthy, 'The Friends of Irish Freedom and the Founding of the Irish Free State', *The Recorder*, vol. 6, no. 2, fall 1993.

61 Cosgrave to Cohalan, 28 August 1924, Cohalan papers, Box 18, AIHS. See also Gerard Keown, 'Taking the World Stage: Creating an Irish foreign policy in the 1920s', in M. Kennedy and J. Skelly (eds), *Irish Foreign Policy 1919–1966: From independence to internationalism* (Dublin: Four Courts Press, 2000).

62 *Gaelic American*, 31 January 1925.

63 Confidential report from Timothy A. Smiddy to Desmond FitzGerald (Dublin), 5 April 1927, *Documents on Irish Foreign Policy* (DIFP), no. 76, NAI DFA EA 231/1/1929.

Notes to pages 149 to 156

The United States became even more protectionist following the introduction of the Hawley-Smoot tariff in June 1930.

64 F. Carroll, 'The Irish Free State and Public Diplomacy: The first official visit of William T. Cosgrave to the United States', *New Hibernia Review*, vol. 16, no. 2, summer 2012, p. 85; Carroll, *America and the Making of an Independent Ireland*, pp. 178–9.

65 Doorley, *Justice Daniel Cohalan*, pp. 197–8.

66 *Gaelic American*, 27 June 1925.

67 Ibid., 6 October 1928, 13 October 1928.

68 Golway, *Irish Rebel*, p. 318; *Gaelic American*, 6 October 1928. Devoy was accorded a state funeral by the Free State government on 16 June 1929.

69 *Gaelic American*, 6 October 1928.

70 Ibid., 28 August 1939.

71 Ibid., 9 September 1939, 13 December 1941.

CHAPTER 10 – **Duelling mythologies of James Michael Curley**

1 Catherine B. Shannon, email message to author, 17 July 2018.

2 William M. Bulger, *James Michael Curley: A short biography with personal reminiscences*, ed. Robert J. Allison (Boston: Commonwealth Editions, 2009), pp. 85–8, provides a useful chronology of major events in Curley's public and private life. See also the chronology in James Michael Curley, *I'd Do It Again: A record of all my uproarious years* (Englewood, NJ: Prentice-Hall, 1957), pp. 363–4. This updates the chronology in Joseph F. Dinneen, *The Purple Shamrock: The Hon. James Michael Curley of Boston* (New York: W.W. Norton & Company, 1949), pp. 323–4. The only historian to examine aspects of Curley's administration and leadership is Charles H. Trout, *Boston: The Great Depression and the New Deal* (New York: Oxford University Press, 1977), and 'Curley of Boston: The search for Irish legitimacy', in Ronald P. Formisano and Constance K. Burns (eds), *Boston, 1700–1980: The evolution of urban politics* (Westport, CT: Greenwood Press, 1984), pp. 165–95. Jack Beatty, *The Rascal King: The life and times of James Michael Curley, an epic of urban politics and Irish America* (Boston: Addison-Wesley, 1992), presents the most sweeping account of Curley's life. The information about Curley's life and career draws from these sources, especially from Beatty and Trout.

3 William V. Shannon, *The American Irish* (New York: Macmillan, 1963), p. 203, quoted in Beatty, *The Rascal King*, p. 501.

4 Beatty, *The Rascal King*, p. 45.

5 Michael P. Curran, *The Life of Patrick Collins* (Norwood, MA: The Norwood Press, 1906), p. 228, quoted in Thomas O'Connor, *The Boston Irish: A political history* (Boston: Northeastern University Press, 1995), pp. 132–3.

6 O'Connor, *Boston Irish*, pp. 123–4; Beatty, *The Rascal King*, p. 107. For more on O'Connell's power see Thomas O'Connor, 'Gangplank Bill', in *Boston A–Z* (Cambridge, MA: Harvard University Press, 2000), pp. 143–5. O'Connell earned the sobriquet 'Gangplank Bill' because he was often photographed striding down a ship's gangplank upon his return from his annual sojourn in the Bahamas.

7 William V. Shannon, 'Boston's Irish Mayors: An ethnic perspective', in Formisano and Burns (eds), *Boston, 1700–1980*, p. 208.

8 'Ireland's Contributions to America', speech given in Lowell, MA, 12 April 1915, in James Michael Curley, 'James Michael Curley Scrapbooks: Addresses 1914–1919', Book 244, http://crossworks.holycross.edu/curley_scrapbooks/244, pp. 18–21. His speech fits within the 'filiopietistic' form discussed by J.J. Lee in J.J. Lee and Marion R. Casey (eds), *Making the Irish American: History and heritage of the Irish in the United States* (New York: New York University Press, 2006), pp. 5, 25.

310   *Notes to pages 156 to 161*

9   John Gunther, *Inside USA* (New York: The Curtis Publishing Company, 1947), p. 512. He describes Curley as 'that grotesque old man' lacking in 'civic virtue', pp. 456, 478.

10   Quote from 'The Forgotten Man' speech in Bulger, *James Michael Curley*, p. 62.

11   Curley, *I'd Do It Again*, p. 7.

12   Beatty, *The Rascal King*, pp. 13–14, mentions that this event never made it into the public record. Bulger, *James Michael Curley*, pp. 41–2, presents it as fact. Thomas O'Neill, Jr, with William Novak, *Man of the House: The life and political memoirs of Speaker Tip O'Neill* (New York: Random House, 1987), p. 31, claims that he still remembers the day it happened, and the articles about it in the paper (N.B. Curley was first elected mayor in 1914 when Tip was two). James Michael Curley, 'Some Nice Things the Book Omitted', *Life*, vol. 41, no. 11, 10 September 1956, pp. 122–3, says that he did this when he became governor. This is but one small example of the challenge of sorting Curley fact from folklore.

13   Bryan Marquand, 'James Michael Curley's Ardent Defender Dies at 95', https://www.bostonglobe.com/metro/obituaries/2013/07/28/helen-mcdonough-irish-immigrant-was-maid-for-james-michael-curley-and-link-storied-era/jIahdnFowKc8XSKQlyse9K/story.html. The quote is from her son, John. See Beatty, *The Rascal King*, p. 427, for Helen McDonough's interview with a Brahmin matron for a job where she listed Curley as a reference. When told that reference was unacceptable because Curley was a crook, Mrs McDonough asserted that he was no crook and that she would not work for the matron under any circumstances. See also Mary Curran Doyle's comment about how her mother, a politically active Democrat in a city west of Boston, had no fondness for any Boston politician except the 'silver fluted Curley'. Mary Curran Doyle, *Massachusetts Review – Woman: An Issue*, winter/spring, 1972, vol. 13, nos. 1–2, pp. 147–50. See also Beatty, *The Rascal King*, pp. 198–9, on Curley's support for the unsuccessful effort in 1915 to allow women to vote in Massachusetts.

14   Gaspar G. Bacon, *Individual Rights and the Public Welfare* (Boston: privately printed, 1935), p. 318.

15   *This Man Curley* (Cambridge, MA: Citizens Security Committee, 1936); Bulger, *James Michael Curley*, p. 68, says it was written by John Hynes, who defeated Curley for mayor in 1949.

16   *This Man Curley*, p. 17.

17   Beatty, *The Rascal King*, p. 433, quoting Joseph Lee, an opponent in the election.

18   The literature on Kennedy is extensive, but a good starting point for his early years is Thomas Whalen, *Kennedy versus Lodge: The 1952 Massachusetts Senate race* (Boston: Northeastern University Press, 2000).

19   John Farrell, *Tip O'Neill and the Democratic Century: A biography* (Boston: Little Brown, 2001), pp. 127–30.

20   Dinneen, *The Purple Shamrock*, p. 322.

21   Edwin O'Connor, *The Last Hurrah* (Boston: Little Brown & Company, 1956).

22   Timothy Meagher, 'The Fireman on the Stairs: Communal loyalties in the making of Irish America', in Lee and Casey (eds), *Making the Irish American*, pp. 609–48, presents a picture of those who were less like Curley and more like Paul Dever, a leader in the Massachusetts Democratic Party from the 1940s until his death in 1958. See also Nelson Garrison's *John William McCormack: A political biography* (New York: Bloomsbury Academic, 2017) for details about the powerful congressman from South Boston from the 1930s to 1960.

23   See Whalen, *Kennedy versus Lodge*.

24   See the *Pilot*, 22 November 1958, for coverage of Cushing being named Cardinal. Ibid., 15 November 1958, p. 16, two days after Curley's death, has a brief statement by Cushing

Notes to pages 161 to 168   311

emphasising that Curley was 'ever ready to extend the warm hand of friendship and gladness to any and all ... in his long and dedicated public service'.

25 *Congressional Record*, vol. 86, first session, 4713–16 [daily edition, 25 March 1959]. Tip would later admit that there was no doubt that Curley 'was corrupt – even by the ethics of his day, which were fairly loose', but still portrays Curley as a good man by making the dubious claim that Curley gave all his ill-gotten gains to the poor: O'Neill, *Man of the House*, p. 29.

26 Farrell, *Tip O'Neill*, p. 503.

27 Sources for O'Neil include: O'Connor, *The Boston Irish*, p. 237; Brian C. Mooney, 'O'Neil, Heir to Curley Tradition, Barrels toward His Next Hurrah', *Boston Globe*, 1 October 1989, p. 29.

28 Bryan Marquand, 'Dapper O'Neil, Champion of Personal Politics, Dies at 87', *Boston Globe*, obits, 20 December 2007, http://archive.boston.com/bostonglobe/obituaries/articles/2007/12/20/dapper_oneil_champion_of_personal_politics_dies_at_87/.

29 O'Connor, *Boston Irish*, pp. 267–8, 270–2, 274–89, 297.

30 *Boston Globe*, 18 September 1980, p. 16.

31 Andrew Ryan, 'The Furniture Stops Here: Walsh goes to work at the celebrated and well-traveled Curley desk', *Boston Globe*, 13 February 2014, p. A1; Thomas M. Menino with Jack Beatty, *Mayor for a New America* (Boston: Houghton Mifflin Harcourt, 2014), pp. 163–4, on his emphasis on a city for all; Gerald F. Burke, *James Michael Curley: A lasting hurrah*, https://www.jphs.org/people/2007/3/10/james-michael-curley-a-lasting-hurrah.html. See City of Boston Trust Funds, Finance Commission report, 19 September 1996, p. 28, for a strong suggestion that the city overpaid for purchase of the house, https://archive.org/details/cityofbostontrus00bost/openlibrary.org/books/OL24992605M/City_of_Boston_trust_funds.

32 Beatty, *The Rascal King*, p. 10; E.L. Glaeser and Andrei Shleifer, 'The Curley Effect: The economics of shaping the electorate', *Journal of Law, Economics, and Organization*, vol. 21, no. 1, 2005, pp. 1–19, https://doi.org/10.1093/jleo/ewi001.

33 See *Irish Times* for many articles about Walsh. For example, Lorna Siggins and Máirtín Ó Catháin, 'Boston Mayor with Connemara Roots Promises to Visit Next Spring', *Irish Times*, 7 November 2013, https://www.irishtimes.com/news/world/us/boston-mayor-with-connemara-roots-promises-to-visit-next-spring-1.1586407; Ryan, 'The Furniture Stops Here', p. A1.

34 Trout pioneered work in this area in an effort to counter what he saw as 'having endless, albeit entertaining anecdotes, substitute for history': 'Curley of Boston', p. 168.

CHAPTER 11 – John McGahern and the historian of modern Ireland

1 *Irish Times*, 5 May 2012.

2 Ibid., 8 May 2012.

3 John McGahern, 'The Church and Its Spire', in Colm Tóibín (ed.), *Soho Square 6* (London: Bloomsbury Books, 1993), pp. 16–30.

4 John McGahern, *That They May Face the Rising Sun* (London: Faber, 2002), p. 73; John McGahern, *Memoir* (London, 2005), p. 80.

5 Hermione Lee, 'John McGahern in His Place', *Times Literary Supplement*, 2 December 2009.

6 Interview with A.T.Q. Stewart, *History Ireland*, vol. 1, no. 2, summer 1993, pp. 55–9.

7 John McGahern, 'The Christmas Rose', in John McGahern, *Love of the World: Essays* (London: Faber & Faber, 2009), pp. 152–8.

8 John Brannigan, 'Introduction: The "whole world" of John McGahern', *Irish University Review*, vol. 35, no. 1, spring/summer 2005, p. vii.

Notes to pages 168 to 177

9   *Irish Independent*, 27 September 2007.

10 Diarmaid Ferriter, *The Transformation of Ireland 1900–2000* (London: Profile Books Ltd, 2004), p. 759.

11 *Sunday Tribune*, 18 June 2000.

12 Patrick Maume, 'John McGahern', online entry to the *Dictionary of Irish Biography*, added December 2011, https://www.dib.ie/biography/mcgahern-john-a9414.

13 Patrick Crotty, '"All Toppers": Children in the fiction of John McGahern', *Irish University Review*, vol. 35, no. 1, spring/summer 2005, pp. 42–58.

14 John McGahern, *The Barracks* (London: Faber & Faber, 1963), p. 47.

15 McGahern, *Memoir*, p. 135.

16 Peter Sheridan, *44: Dublin made me* (London: Macmillan, 1999), p. 144.

17 Seán Dunne, *In My Father's House* (Meath: Gallery Press, 1991), p. 68.

18 Edith Newman Devlin, *Speaking Volumes: A Dublin childhood* (Belfast: Blackstaff Press, 2000), pp. 39–45.

19 Jamie Dockery, 'McGahern and the Influence of the Mother', *Studies: An Irish quarterly review*, vol. 99, no. 394, 2010, pp. 205–19.

20 Crotty, '"All Toppers"', p. 45.

21 McGahern, 'The Church and Its Spire'.

22 *Commission to Inquire into Child Abuse Report: Vol. 1* (Dublin, 2009).

23 www.justice.ie/en/JELR/Pages/MagdalenRpt2013; www.gov.ie/en/publication/d4b3d-final-report-of-the-commission-of-investigation-into-mother-and-baby-homes/.

24 Diarmaid Ferriter, *Occasions of Sin: Sex and society in modern Ireland* (London: Profile Books, 2009), p. 333.

25 McGahern, 'The Church and Its Spire'.

26 John McGahern, 'God and Me', in McGahern, *Love of the World*, pp. 149–52, and Peter Guy, 'Reading McGahern in Light of the Murphy Report', *Studies*, vol. 99, no. 393, 2010, pp. 91–102.

27 Daithí Ó Corráin, 'Catholicism in Ireland, 1880–2015: Rise, ascendancy and retreat', in Thomas Bartlett (ed.), *The Cambridge History of Ireland. Volume IV: 1880 to the Present* (Cambridge: Cambridge University Press, 2018), pp. 726–65.

28 Brian Fallon, *An Age of Innocence: Irish culture 1930–60* (Dublin: Gill & Macmillan, 1998).

29 Anthony Cronin, 'This Time, This Place', *The Bell*, vol. xix, no. 8, July 1954, pp. 5–7.

30 John McGahern, 'The Solitary Reader', in McGahern, *Love of the World*, p. 92.

31 Maume, 'John McGahern', *Dictionary of Irish Biography*.

32 Dublin Diocesan Archives, Papers of John Charles McQuaid, AB8/B, Censorship of Publications, Dermot O'Flynn to McQuaid, 1 March 1960.

33 National Archives of Ireland, Department of Justice, 2006/148/16: 'Publication in Newspapers of Banned Books in Serial Form', 2–4 November 1965.

34 McGahern, *Memoir*, pp. 250–1.

35 Ibid., p. 250.

36 Ferriter, *Occasions of Sin*, p. 109.

37 Brigid Brophy, *Don't Never Forget: Collected views and reviews* (New York: Holt, Rinehart & Winston, 1967).

38 *Guardian*, 19 and 20 January 1965.

39 Dublin Diocesan Archives, AB8/B Department of Justice, Estimates 1962–3: Censorship of Books.

40 National Archives of Ireland, Department of Taoiseach, 97/6/561, Censorship of Publications Act 1967, Memorandum for Government, September 1966.

41 Ibid.

Notes to pages 177 to 186   313

42 Ibid., 'Note to Minister', 28 April 1967.

43 Peter Guy, 'Reading McGahern', *Studies*, vol. 99, pp. 91–102.

44 Ferriter, *Occasions of Sin* (paperback edition, London: Profile Books, 2012), p. xii.

45 See Eamon Maher, *John McGahern: From the local to the universal* (Dublin: The Liffey Press, 2003), p. 70.

46 See David Malcolm, *Understanding John McGahern* (Columbia, SC: University of South Carolina Press, 2007), p. 134.

47 *Irish Independent*, 3 June 1965.

48 *Irish Times*, 1 April 2006.

49 McGahern, *Memoir*, p. 94.

50 John McGahern, *The Leavetaking* (London: Atlantic Little Brown, 1974), p. 65.

51 John McGahern, *Amongst Women* (London: Faber & Faber, 1991), p. 5.

52 Ibid., p. 15.

53 Catriona Crowe (ed.), *Guide to the Military Service (1916–23) Pensions Collection* (Defence Forces, Dublin, 2012), p. 10.

54 Diarmaid Ferriter, *Between Two Hells: The Irish Civil War* (London: Profile Books, 2021), pp. 131–202, and Marie Coleman, 'Compensation Claims and Women's Experience of Violence and Loss in Revolutionary Ireland, 1921–23', in Linda Connolly (ed.), *Women and the Irish Revolution* (Dublin: Irish Academic Press, 2021), pp. 129–48.

55 Diarmaid Ferriter, 'The Military Service Pension and the Battle for Material Survival, 1925–55', in Crowe (ed.), *Guide to the Military Service*, pp. 124–44.

56 McGahern, *The Barracks*, p. 109.

57 Nicholas Wroe, 'Ireland's Rural Elegist', *Guardian*, 5 January 2002.

58 McGahern, 'The Solitary Reader', in McGahern, *Love of the World*, p. 94.

59 Hermione Lee, 'John McGahern in His Place', *Times Literary Supplement*, 2 December 2009.

60 Ibid.

61 Dick Walsh, *Dick Walsh Remembered: Selected columns from the Irish Times* (Dublin: Townhouse Publishing, 2003), Foreword by John McGahern, pp. 11–19.

62 Quoted in Kolakowski's obituary in *The Economist*, 1–7 August 2009, as cited by James Kelly, *Writing Irish History Today* (Dublin: St Patrick's College, 2010), p. 27.

CHAPTER 12 – **Wild Atlantic Ways**

1 Catherine B. Shannon, *Arthur J. Balfour and Ireland, 1874–1922* (Washington: CUA Press, 1988).

2 The 'west' is beset by geographical imprecision: the Atlantic coast and islands? Connacht? The principal focus in this essay is the western districts of Mayo, Galway and Donegal.

3 Cited in C.J. Woods, *Travellers' Accounts as Source-Material for Irish Historians* (Dublin: Four Courts Press, 2009), p. 57.

4 For example, Kathleen Villiers-Tuthill, *History of Clifden 1810–1860* (Clifden: Author, 1982); Kathleen Villiers-Tuthill, *Alexander Nimmo & the Western District* (Clifden: Connemara Girl Publications, 2006).

5 William Nolan, *Tracing the Past* (Dublin: Geography Publications, 1982), pp. 81–101; Arnold Horner (ed.), *Documents Relating to the Bogs Commissioners, 1809–1813* (Dublin: Irish Manuscripts Commission, 2019); Villiers-Tuthill, *Alexander Nimmo & the Western District*.

6 Brendan Hoban, *Turbulent Diocese: The Killala troubles, 1798–1848* (Dublin: Banley House, 2011); Miriam Moffitt, *Soupers & Jumpers: The Protestant missions in Connemara 1848–1937* (Dublin: Nonsuch, 2008); Irene Whelan, *The Bible War in Ireland* (Madison, WI: University of Wisconsin Press, 2005).

314   *Notes to pages 186 to 193*

7   Cormac Ó Gráda, *Ireland: A new economic history, 1780–1939* (Oxford: Oxford University Press, 1994), pp. 24–152; Kevin Whelan, 'Introduction' to *Letters from the Irish Highlands of Connemara* (Clifden: Gibbons Publications, 1995), pp. vii–xix.

8   The definitive account is Niall Ó Ciosáin, *Ireland in Official Print Culture 1800–1850* (Oxford: Oxford University Press, 2014).

9   Patrick Knight, *Erris in the Irish Highlands and the Atlantic Railway* (Dublin: M. Keene, 1836), p. 120.

10 Rob Goodbody, *A Suitable Channel: Quaker relief in the Great Famine* (Bray: Pale Publishing, 1995); James Hake Tuke survived to advise the Congested Districts Board in the 1890s.

11 For the general economy, see Ó Gráda, *Ireland: A new economic history*; for meticulous case studies see Breandán Mac Suibhne and David Dickson (eds), *Hugh Dorian: The outer edge of Ulster* (Dublin: Lilliput Press, 2000), and Breandán Mac Suibhne, *The End of Outrage: Post-Famine adjustment in rural Ireland* (Oxford: Oxford University Press, 2017); also Donald E. Jordan on Mayo, *Land and Popular Politics in Ireland* (Cambridge: Cambridge University Press, 1994), pp. 103–69.

12 Gerard Moran, *Sending Out Ireland's Poor: Assisted emigration to North America in the nineteenth century* (Dublin: Four Courts Press, 2004).

13 James Caird, *The Plantation Scheme; or, the west of Ireland as a field for investment* (Edinburgh: Blackwood, 1850), pp. 48–59.

14 George Preston White, *A Tour in Connemara with Remarks on Its Great Physical Capabilities* (Dublin: McGlashan, 1851), pp. 8–56.

15 Katherine Haldane Grenier, *Tourism and Identity in Scotland, 1770–1914: Creating Caledonia* (Aldershot: Ashgate, 2005), p. 1.

16 Spencer to Granville, 17 September 1882. Peter Gordon (ed.), *The Red Earl: The papers of the fifth Earl Spencer 1835–1910. Volume 1: 1835–1885* (Northampton: Northamptonshire Records Society, 1981), p. 221.

17 Samuel Clark, *Social Origins of the Irish Land War* (Princeton NJ: Princeton University Press, 1979).

18 As Scottish secretary, Balfour had already shown his mettle in confronting land agitation in the Scottish Highlands during the Crofters' War. For comparison (and contrast) between the Scottish and Irish 'western' experiences, see T.M. Devine, *The Scottish Nation, 1700–2000* (London: Penguin, 2000), pp. 413–47.

19 For the politics of constructive unionism, Andrew Gailey, *Ireland and the Death of Kindness* (Cork: Cork University Press, 1987). 'Congested' districts were defined, not in simple terms of population density, but rather on population relative to the quality and ratable valuation of the land.

20 Robin Harcourt Williams (ed.), *Salisbury–Balfour Correspondence* (Ware, Herts: Hertfordshire Record Society, 1988), p. 297.

21 The album was held by the Balfour family until 1987, when it was acquired by the Hardiman Library of the National University of Ireland, Galway, where it is now housed. For Welch, see E. Estyn Evans and Brian Turner (eds), *Ireland's Eye: The photography of Robert John Welch* (Belfast: Blackstaff Press, 1977); also, Ciara Breathnach (ed.), *Framing the West: Images of rural Ireland, 1891–1920* (Dublin: Four Courts Press, 2007).

22 Ciara Breathnach, *The Congested Districts Board of Ireland, 1891–1923: Poverty and development in the west of Ireland* (Dublin: Four Courts Press, 2005), p. 154; James Morrissey (ed.), *On the Verge of Want* (Dublin: Crannóg Books, 2001), pp. xii, 1–4.

23 Breathnach, *Congested Districts*, p. 170.

24 Ibid., pp. 160–9.

25 For a perceptive analysis, see Carla King, '"Our Destitute Countrymen on the Western Coast": Relief and development strategies in the congested districts in the 1880s and

Notes to pages 193 to 207   315

'90s', in Carla King and Conor McNamara (eds), *The West of Ireland: New perspectives on the nineteenth century* (Dublin: The History Press, 2011), pp. 161–83.

26 See Fergus Campbell and Tony Varley (ed.), *Land Questions in Modern Ireland* (Manchester: Manchester University Press, 2013), for historiographically rich revisionist perspectives.

27 See Conall Mac Cuinneagáin, *Glencolmcille: A parish history* (Dublin: Four Masters Press, 2002), pp. 208–34, for an account of its impact on a south-west Donegal community.

28 P.J. Matthews, *Revival: The Abbey Theatre, Sinn Féin, the Gaelic League and the cooperative movement* (Cork: Cork University Press, 2003); Timothy G. McMahon, *Grand Opportunity: The Gaelic revival and Irish society, 1893–1910* (Syracuse: Syracuse University Press, 2008).

29 Luke Gibbons, 'Synge, Country and Western: The myth of the west in Irish and American culture', in *Transformations in Irish Culture* (Cork: Cork University Press, 1996), pp. 23–36; also, 'Introduction' to Conrad M. Arensberg and Solon T. Kimball, *Family and Community in Ireland*, 3rd edn (Ennis: CLASP Press, 2001), pp. I–CI.

30 Catherine Nash, '"Embodying the Nation": The west of Ireland landscape and Irish identity', in Barbara O'Connor and Michael Cronin (eds), *Tourism in Ireland: A critical analysis* (Cork: Cork University Press, 1993), p. 86.

31 Ibid., p. 87, and see also Anne Byrne, Ricca Edmondson and Kathleen Fahy, 'Rural Tourism and Cultural Identity in the West of Ireland', in ibid., pp. 233–57.

32 See, for example, Adele Dalsimer (ed.), *Visualizing Ireland: National identity and the pictorial tradition* (Winchester, MA: Faber & Faber, 1993).

33 Adele M. Dalsimer, '"The Irish Peasant Had All His Heart": J.M. Synge in the country shop', in Dalsimer (ed.), *Visualizing Ireland*, pp. 204–28.

34 Blanche E.C. Dugdale, *Arthur James on Balfour*, vol. 2 (London: Hutchinson, 1936), p. 288.

35 The only exception was Galway city. W.E. Vaughan and A.J. Fitzpatrick (eds), *Irish Historical Statistics: Population 1821–1971* (Dublin: RIA, 1978).

36 Tony Varley, 'Gaining Ground, Losing Ground: The politics of land reform in rural Ireland', in Fergus Campbell and Tony Varley (eds), *Land Questions in Modern Ireland* (Manchester: Manchester University Press, 2013), pp. 25–61. For a perceptive commentary on the islands, see Diarmaid Ferriter, *On the Edge: Ireland's off-shore islands. A modern history* (London: Profile, 2018).

37 In spring 2021 this precise concept was promoted, without irony, by a former taoiseach, in a commissioned television series: see *RTÉ Guide*, 1–9 April 2021.

CHAPTER 13 – **John Hume and the evolution of power-sharing in Northern Ireland**

1 *Irish Times*, 8 May 1964.
2 Roy Lilley, 'Unionism Today', *Belfast Telegraph*, 21 October 1963.
3 *Irish Times*, 8 May 1964.
4 G.B. Newe, 'The Catholics in Northern Ireland', *Christus Rex*, vol. 1, 1958.
5 *Irish News*, 12 August 1958.
6 Ibid., 19 May 1969.
7 *Derry Journal*, 21 February 1969.
8 Paper dated 3 March 1970. Copy in Linenhall Library, Belfast, P1072 ND5118.nnh.
9 *Irish Times*, 2 February 1971.
10 SDLP, *Towards a New Ireland* (Belfast: SDLP, 1972).
11 Northern Ireland Office, *The Future of Northern Ireland* (Belfast: HMSO, 1972).
12 Seán Farren, *The SDLP: The struggle for agreement in Northern Ireland* (Dublin: Four Courts Press, 2010), p. 65.

13 *Irish News* and *Newsletter*, 6 March 1973.
14 Northern Ireland Assembly, *Debates*, 24 January 1974.
15 Northern Ireland Convention, *Debates*, 19 June 1975.

CHAPTER 14 – Boston's three Irelands: busing, class and Irish ethnic identity, 1970–2015

1   'Ten O'Clock News: Bernadette Devlin', Boston TV News Digital Library, http://bostonlocaltv.org/catalog/v_mkfieibvokej4ma.
2   J. Anthony Lukas, *Common Ground: A turbulent decade in the lives of three American families* (New York: Knopf, 1985).
3   Letter to Judge W. Arthur Garrity, 25 June 1974, from Digital Collections, Joseph P. Healey Library, UMass Boston, https://openarchives.umb.edu/digital/collection/p15774coll33/id/98/rec/13.
4   Letter to Judge W. Arthur Garrity, *c.*1974, from Digital Collections, Joseph P. Healey Library, UMass Boston, https://openarchives.umb.edu/digital/collection/p15774coll33/id/100/rec/20.
5   Letter to Judge W. Arthur Garrity, including copy of letter written to local paper, 17 December 1974, from Digital Collections, Joseph P. Healey Library, UMass Boston, https://openarchives.umb.edu/digital/collection/p15774coll33/id/102/rec/22.
6   Letter to W. Arthur Garrity, Jr, 10 December 1975, from 'A White Irish American', from https://bosdesca.omeka.net/items/browse?collection=6.
7   *South Boston Tribune* (*SBT*), 27 February 1975, p. 1; *SBT*, 6 March 1975, p. 4.
8   Although South Boston was hardly unique among American cities in its working-class support for the Irish Republican Army during the 1970s, the exceptional nature of its identification showed up in these murals, https://i.redd.it/4nrxacznuy321.jpg.
9   Michael Patrick MacDonald, *All Souls: A family story from Southie* (Boston: Beacon Press, 1999), pp. 51, 84.
10 Ibid., p. 86.
11 Ibid., p. 80.
12 William A. Davis, 'The Printing of the Green: The scoop on the Irish-American newspaper war', *Boston Globe* (*BG*), 4 June 1989, p. 18.
13 'The Boston Irish News: Two major goals', *Boston Irish News* (*BIN*), vol. 1, no. 1, June 1976, p. 1.
14 Dick Sinnott, 'Why No Memorial to Curley?' *BIN*, vol. 1, no. 1, June 1976, p. 1. Rubin was one of the leaders of the upstart Youth International Party, while Groppi was a Catholic priest who had led disruptive civil rights protests in Milwaukee, Wisconsin.
15 'Irish Cultural Institute Needed in Boston', *BIN* editorial, vol. 1, no. 1, June 1976, p. 8.
16 'Time for a United Irish Society', *BIN*, vol. 1, no. 1, June 1976; Martin McGovern, 'Remembering Don Mooney, a Man with Lots of Verve', *Boston Irish Reporter* (*BIR*), vol. 1, November 2007, p. 6; Davis, 'The Printing of the Green', p. 18; *BG*, 'An Irish Challenge', 17 March 1986, p. 18.
17 John McGrath, 'Irish Language: You can learn Gaelic in Boston', *BIN*, June 1976, p. 6.
18 *BG*, 'Ask the Globe', 17 May 1980, p. 1.
19 Davis, 'The Printing of the Green', p. 18. The *Irish Echo* had published a separate Boston edition for a number of years but closed down its operations in that city in 1988. Jerry Ackerman, '*Irish Echo* Closing Boston Office: Newspaper will be consolidated with its parent in New York City', *BG*, 24 August 1988, p. 83.
20 Ed Forry, 'Celebrating Our Heritage, Staying With Our Mission', *BIR*, 1 October 2010, p. 4.
21 Ed Forry, 'The Mission Remains the Same', *25th Anniversary Dorchester Reporter Commemorative Edition* (Dorchester: Boston Neighborhood News, 2008), p. 3.

Notes to pages 221 to 247

22 William Forry, 'Boston Irish Sensibilities Guide MSNBC's O'Donnell', *BIR*, 1 December 2012, p. 8.

23 Jack Thomas, 'Rev. Richard "Doc" Conway, Shepherd of the Streets, Man for Others, Sums Up His Life: God was good to me', *BIR*, 1 November 2018, pp. 8–10.

24 William Forry, 'The Heart and Soul of Holy Family Parish: In Dorchester, Father William Francis celebrates his 40th anniversary as a priest', *BIR*, 25 June 1998, p. 8.

25 'The Reporter Story: Proudly parochial', *25th Anniversary Dorchester Reporter Edition*, p. 15.

26 Andrew Blake, 'News for Newcomers: Immigrants look to ethnic media', *BG*, 2 February 1991.

27 Colm Renehan, 'Ireland and Haiti, an Irish Observer's Account', *BIR*, 1 April 1994, p. 18.

28 Caleb DesRosiers, 'Boston Irish Influence of New Generation of Immigrants', *BIR*, 31 March 2004, p. 21.

29 Lisa Gentes, '"Black and Green" Assembly Aimed at Bridging Racial Gap', *BIR*, 31 March 2003, p. 6.

30 Eoin Cannon, 'Irishwomen Offer Hope at Boston Peace Conference', *BIR*, 1 January 2000, p. 8.

31 '*Boston Magazine*'s Brass Are the Real "April Fools"', *BIR*, 1 May 1998, p. 11.

32 William Forry, 'TV Companion Book Does "Real Injustice" to Neighborhood Folks', *BIR*, 1 December 2000, p. 10.

33 Ed Forry, 'City Has to Exorcise Demons of Busing', *BIR*, 1 July 2004, p. 6.

34 Ibid.

35 Ibid.

36 Alan Lupo, *Liberty's Chosen Home: The politics of violence in Boston* (Boston: Little, Brown & Company, 1977), p. 164.

37 Garrison Nelson, *John William McCormack: A political biography* (New York: Bloomsbury, 2017), p. 384.

CHAPTER 16 – Charting a course: framing scholarship and practical politics in the work of Catherine B. Shannon

1 John Boyle O'Reilly, 'A Man', in *Life, Poems and Speeches of John Boyle O'Reilly: The complete poems*, edited by Mrs John Boyle O'Reilly (Philadelphia: John J. McVey, 1891), p. 438.

2 *Town of Scituate. Open Space and Recreation Plan* (Sandwich, MA: Horsley Whitton Group, 2009), p. 7.

3 Catherine B, Shannon, *Arthur J. Balfour and Ireland, 1874–1922* (Washington: Catholic University of America Press, 1988), p. 55.

4 James Quinn, 'Balfour, Arthur James', *Dictionary of Irish Biography 1* (Cambridge: Cambridge University Press, 2009), p. 241.

5 Diarmaid Ferriter, *On the Edge: Ireland's off-shore islands. A modern history* (London: Profile Books, 2018), p. 61.

6 Information supplied by Catherine B. Shannon in letter of 22 January 2019.

7 Henry David Thoreau, *Cape Cod* (New York: Thomas Y. Crowell, 1961), pp. 7, 12–13.

CHAPTER 17 – Catherine B. Shannon: in her own words

1 Finding aid for the Emigrant Savings Bank, viewable at http://archives.nypl.org/mss/925.

2 *New York Times*, 27 January 1889.

3 David Shannon Company was incorporated with $100,000 in capital in 1907. See *New York Times*, 10 May 1907.

318   *Notes to pages 247 to 273*

4   Daniel Florence Cohalan (1867–1946), judge and Irish-American leader, was appointed justice of the supreme court of New York in 1911. He was active in Democratic Party politics and in Tammany Hall and was a co-founder of Friends of Irish Freedom in 1916.

5   The Office of Strategic Services (OSS) was a wartime intelligence agency of the United States during the Second World War and a predecessor to the Department of State's Bureau of Intelligence and Research (INR) and the independent Central Intelligence Agency (CIA).

6   The Gillette Company was founded by King G. Gillette in 1901 as a safety razor manufacturer.

7   The United Service Organizations Incorporated (USO) is an American nonprofit-charitable corporation that provides live entertainment, social facilities and other programmes to members of the United States armed forces and their families.

CHAPTER 18 – Catherine B. Shannon and the role of women in the Northern Ireland peace process

1   This quotation was sent to me by my son, who visited the Vasa Museum in Stockholm in 2018.

2   This democratic deficit became acutely visible over the fifty years of unionist rule, when only nine women were elected to the 52-seat Stormont parliament.

3   George J. Mitchell, *Making Peace* (New York: Alfred A. Knopf, 1999), p. 44.

CHAPTER 19 – Safe spaces on the Falls

1   Catherine B. Shannon, 'The Woman Writer as Historical Witness: Northern Ireland, 1968–1994: An interdisciplinary perspective', in Maryann Gialanella Valiulis and Mary O'Dowd (eds), *Women & Irish History: Essays in honour of Margaret MacCurtain* (Dublin: Wolfhound Press, 1997), p. 240.

2   Prior to the publication of Joe Duffy and Freya McClements' definitive *Children of the Troubles: The untold story of the children killed in the Northern Ireland conflict* (Dublin: Hachette Books Ireland, 2019), Malcolm Sutton's statistical breakdown of the ages of the fatalities due to sectarian violence in Northern Ireland estimated that some eighty-four children under the age of fourteen were killed during the Troubles. These numbers are likely to have been underestimated: Malcolm Sutton, *An index of Deaths from the Conflict in Ireland, 1969–1993* (Belfast: Beyond the Pale Publications, 1994).

3   Áine da Silva, 'Self-Preservation', in Laurel Holliday, *Children of 'The Troubles'* (New York: Pocket Books, 1997), p. 99.

4   While the author acknowledges that the Dominicans' Fortwilliam Girls' Grammar School in north Belfast, founded in 1930, has produced distinguished alumnae that include historians Marianne Elliott, OBE, and Margaret Ward and the poet Medbh McGuckian, this study will be limited to the two school on west Belfast's Falls Road.

5   Fionnuala O'Connor, *In Search of a State: Catholics in Northern Ireland* (Belfast: Blackstaff Press, 1993), p. 4.

6   Mary McAleese, 'School could make you happy or unhappy recalls Mary McAleese. It depended upon the teachers', *Irish Times*, 23 September 1977, p. 1.

7   Mary O'Hara, 'She Was the Only Man on the Falls Road', *Guardian*, 21 January 2002.

8   Ibid.

9   Mary Costello, *Titanic Town* (London: Methuen, 2000), pp. 232, 301.

10 Ibid., p. 260.

11 John Rae, *Sister Genevieve: A courageous woman's triumph in Northern Ireland* (New York: Warner Books, 2001), p. 254.

Select Bibliography

Adams, James H., 'The Negotiated Hibernian: Discourse on the Fenian in England and America', *American Nineteenth-Century History*, vol. 11, no. 1, March 2010, pp. 47–77

Akenson, Donald H., *Small Differences: Irish Catholics and Irish Protestants, 1815–1922* (Montreal: McGill-Queen's University Press, 1988)

Alexander, Cecil Frances, 'The Ballad of Stumpie's Brae', in *The Legend of the Golden Prayers: And other poems* (London: Bell & Daldy, 1859)

Ambrose, Joe, *Fenian Anthology* (Cork: Mercier Press, 2008)

Anbinder, Tyler, 'Lord Palmerston and the Irish Famine Emigration', *Historical Journal*, vol. 44, no. 2, 2001, pp. 441–69

Arensberg, Conrad M., and Solon T. Kimball, *Family and Community in Ireland*, 3rd edn (Ennis: CLASP Press, 2001)

Arthur, Paul, 'Diasporan Intervention in International Affairs: Irish America as a case study', *Diaspora: A journal of transnational studies*, vol. 1, no. 2, fall 1991, pp. 143–62

Bailyn, Bernard, *The Barbarous Years: The peopling of British North America. The conflict of civilizations, 1600–1675* (New York: Alfred A. Knopf, 2012)

Bartlett, Thomas (ed.), *The Cambridge History of Ireland. Volume IV: 1880 to the Present* (Cambridge: Cambridge University Press, 2018)

Bass Warner, Sam, *Streetcar Suburbs: The process of growth in Boston, 1870–1900* (Cambridge, MA: Harvard University Press, 1978)

Beatty, Jack, *The Rascal King: The life and times of James Michael Curley, an epic of urban politics and Irish America* (Boston: Addison-Wesley, 1992)

Belchem, John, *Irish, Catholic and Scouse: The history of the Liverpool Irish 1800–1939* (Liverpool: Liverpool University Press, 2007)

—, 'Nationalism, Republicanism and Exile: Irish emigrants and the revolutions of 1848', *The Past and Present Society*, no. 146, February 1995, pp. 103–35

Biagini, Eugenio F., and Mary E. Daly (eds), *The Cambridge Social History of Modern Ireland* (Cambridge: Cambridge University Press, 2017)

Binasco, Matteo, *Rome and Irish Catholicism in the Atlantic World, 1622–1908* (Basingstoke: Palgrave Macmillan, 2019)

Breathnach, Ciara, *The Congested Districts Board of Ireland, 1891–1923: Poverty and development in the west of Ireland* (Dublin: Four Courts Press, 2005)

Broderick, Marian, *Wild Irish Women: Extraordinary lives from history* (Madison, WI: University of Wisconsin Press, 2004)

Brundage, David, *Irish Nationalists in America: The politics of exile, 1798–1998* (New York: Oxford University Press, 2016)

—, 'Matilda Tone in America: Exile, gender, and memory in the making of Irish republican nationalism', *New Hibernia Review / Iris Éireannach Nua*, vol. 14, no. 1, spring 2010, pp. 96–111

—, 'Recent Directions in the History of Irish-American Nationalism', *Journal of American Ethnic History*, vol. 28, no. 4, summer 2009, pp. 82–9

Bulger, William M., *James Michael Curley: A short biography with personal reminiscences*, ed. Robert J. Allison (Boston: Commonwealth Editions, 2009)

Burke, Helen, *The People and the Poor Law in Nineteenth-Century Ireland* (Sussex: WEB, 1987)

Burke, Mary M., *'Tinkers': Synge and the cultural history of the Irish Traveller* (Oxford: Oxford University Press, 2009)

Burnard, Trevor, *The Atlantic in World History, 1490–1830* (London: Bloomsbury Academic, 2020)

Burns, Anna, *Milkman* (London: Faber & Faber, 2018)

Campbell, Fergus, and Tony Varley (eds), *Land Questions in Modern Ireland* (Manchester: Manchester University Press, 2013)

Campbell, Malcolm, *Ireland's New Worlds: Immigrants, politics, and society in the United States and Australia, 1815–1922* (Madison, WI: University of Wisconsin Press, 2008)

Canny, Nicholas, *Imagining Ireland's Pasts: Early modern Ireland through the centuries* (Oxford: Oxford University Press, 2021)

— and Philip Morgan (eds), *The Oxford Handbook of the Atlantic World: 1450–1850* (Oxford: Oxford University Press, 2011)

—, *Kingdom and Colony: Ireland in the Atlantic world, 1560–1800* (Baltimore, MD: Johns Hopkins University Press, 1988)

Carroll, Francis M., *America and the Making of an Independent Ireland: A history* (New York: New York University Press, 2021)

—, *American Opinion and the Irish Question, 1910–1923* (New York: St Martin's Press, 1978)

Casey, Marion R., 'Family, History, and Irish America', *Journal of American Ethnic History*, vol. 28, no. 4, summer 2009, pp. 110–17

Cashman, Ray, *Packy Jim: Folklore and worldview on the Irish border* (Madison, WI: University of Wisconsin Press, 2016)

Chesterton, G.K., *Christendom in Dublin: Essays in memory of the Eucharistic Congress* (London: Sheed & Ward, 1932)

Clark, Dennis, 'Portraying Irish America: Trans-Atlantic revisions', *History Ireland*, vol. 2, no. 4, winter 1994, pp. 48–52

Clark, Samuel, and James S. Donnelly, Jr (eds), *Irish Peasants: Violence and political unrest, 1780–1914* (Madison, WI: University of Wisconsin Press, 1983)

Comerford, R.V., *The Fenians in Context: Irish politics and society, 1848–82* (Atlantic Highlands, NJ: Wolfhound Press, 1985)

Connolly, Linda (ed.), *Women and the Irish Revolution* (Dublin: Irish Academic Press, 2021)

Select Bibliography   321

Corporaal, Marguérite, and Jason King (eds), *Irish Global Migration and Memory: Transatlantic perspectives of Ireland's famine exodus* (London: Routledge, 2018)

Costello, Mary, *Titanic Town* (London: Methuen, 2000)

Côté, Jane, 'Writing Women Out of History: Fanny and Anna Parnell and the Irish Ladies' Land League', *Études Irlandaises*, vol. xvii, no. 2, Décembre 1992, pp. 123–34

Craig, Patricia, Introduction, in *Twelve Irish Ghost Stories* (Oxford: Oxford University Press, 1998)

Crawford, E. Margaret (ed.), *The Hungry Stream: Essays on emigration and famine* (Belfast: Institute of Irish Studies, 1997

Cronin, Mike, 'Projecting the Nation through Sport and Culture: Ireland, Aonach Tailteann and the Irish Free State, 1924–32', *Journal of Contemporary History*, vol. 38, no. 3, July 2003, pp. 395–411

Cronin, Sean, *The McGarrity Papers: Revelations of the Irish revolutionary movement in Ireland and America, 1900–1940* (Tralee, Kerry: Anvil Books, 1972)

Cunningham, John, and Niall Ó Ciosáin (eds), *Culture and Society in Ireland Since 1750: Tributes to Gearoid Ó Tuathaigh* (Dublin: Lilliput Press, 2015)

Curley, James Michael, *I'd Do It Again: A record of all my uproarious years* (Englewood, NJ: Prentice-Hall, 1957)

Curtis, L.P., Jr, *Coercion and Conciliation in Ireland 1880–1892* (Princeton, NJ: Princeton University Press, 1963)

Dalsimer, Adele (ed.), *Visualizing Ireland: National identity and the pictorial tradition* (Winchester, MA: Faber & Faber, 1993)

Daly, Mary E., *Sixties Ireland: Reshaping the economy, state and society, 1957–1973* (Cambridge: Cambridge University Press, 2016)

—, *The Famine in Ireland* (Dundalk: Dundalgan Press, 1986)

Darby, Paul, *Gaelic Games, Nationalism and the Irish Diaspora in the United States* (Dublin: UCD Press, 2009)

Davitt, Michael, *The Fall of Feudalism in Ireland: Or, the story of the Land League revolution* (London: Harper & Brothers, 1904)

Delahanty, Ian, 'The Transatlantic Roots of Irish-American Anti-Abolitionism, 1843–1859', *Journal of the Civil War Era*, vol. 6, no. 2, June 2016, pp. 164–92

Delaney, Enda, 'Directions in Historiography: Our island story? Towards a transnational history of late modern Ireland', *Irish Historical Studies*, vol. xxxvii, no. 148, November 2011, pp. 83–105

de Nie, Michael, '"A Medley Mob of Irish-American Plotters and Irish Dupes": The British press and transatlantic Fenianism', *Journal of British Studies*, vol. 40, no. 2, April 2001, pp. 213–40

Denieffe, Joseph, *A Personal Narrative of the Irish Revolutionary Brotherhood Giving a Faithful Report of the Principal Events from 1855 to 1867 Written at the Request of Friends* (New York: The Gael Publishing Co., 1906)

Devine, T.M., *The Scottish Nation 1700–2000* (London: Penguin, 2000)

Diner, Hasia R., *Erin's Daughters in America: Irish immigrant women in the nineteenth century* (Baltimore, MD: Johns Hopkins University Press, 1983)

Dinneen, Joseph F., *The Purple Shamrock: The Hon. James Michael Curley of Boston* (New York: W.W. Norton & Company, 1949)

Donnelly, James S., *The Great Irish Potato Famine* (Stroud: Sutton Publishing, 2001)

Doolin, David M., *Transnational Revolutionaries: The Fenian invasion of Canada, 1866* (Bern: Peter Lang, 2016)

Doorley, Michael, *Justice Daniel Cohalan, 1865–1946: American patriot and Irish-American nationalist* (Cork: Cork University Press, 2019)

—, *Irish-American Diaspora Nationalism: The friends of Irish freedom, 1916–1935* (Dublin: Four Courts Press, 2005)

Doyle, David Noel, 'Review: Cohesion and diversity in the Irish diaspora', *Irish Historical Studies*, vol. 31, no. 123, May 1999, pp. 411–34

Duffy, Joe, and Freya McClements, *Children of the Troubles: The untold story of the children killed in the Northern Ireland conflict* (Dublin: Hachette Books Ireland, 2019)

Elliott, Marianne, *Wolfe Tone* (Liverpool: Liverpool University Press, 2012)

—, *The Catholics of Northern Ireland* (London: Allen Lane, 2000)

Evans, A.G., *Fanatic Heart: A life of John Boyle O'Reilly, 1844–1900* (Boston: Northeastern University Press, 1997)

Fanning, Charles, Editor's Introduction, *New Perspectives on the Irish Diaspora* (Carbondale and Edwardsville: Southern Illinois University Press, 2000)

Farrell, John, *Tip O'Neill and the Democratic Century: A biography* (Boston: Little Brown, 2001)

Farren, Seán, *John Hume: In his own words* (Dublin: Four Courts Press, 2018)

Ferguson, Frank, *Ulster-Scots Writing: An anthology* (Dublin: Four Courts Press, 2008)

Ferriter, Diarmaid, *Between Two Hells: The Irish Civil War* (London: Profile Books, 2021)

—, *On the Edge: Ireland's off-shore islands. A modern history* (London: Profile, 2018)

—, *Occasions of Sin: Sex and society in modern Ireland* (London: Profile Books, 2009)

—, *The Transformation of Ireland 1900–2000* (London: Profile Books Ltd, 2004)

Flewelling, Lindsey, *Two Irelands Beyond the Sea: Ulster unionism and America, 1880–1920* (Oxford: Oxford University Press, 2018)

Ford, Patrick, *The Criminal History of the British Empire: A series of open letters to Hon. Wm. E. Gladstone, prime minister of England* (New York: Irish World, 1881)

Gailey, Andrew, *Ireland and the Death of Kindness: The experience of constructive unionism, 1890–1905* (Cork: Cork University Press, 1987)

Gantt, Jonathan, *Irish Terrorism in the Atlantic Community, 1865–1922* (Basingstoke: Palgrave Macmillan, 2010)

Geary, Laurence M., and Margaret Kelleher (eds), *Nineteenth-Century Ireland: A guide to recent research* (Dublin: UCD Press, 2005)

Gibbons, Luke, 'Synge, Country and Western: The myth of the west in Irish and American culture', in Luke Gibbons, *Transformations in Irish Culture* (Cork: Cork University Press, 1996)

Select Bibliography

Gilmore, Peter, *Irish Presbyterians and the Shaping of Western Pennsylvania, 1770–1830* (Pittsburgh: University of Pittsburgh Press, 2018)

Glassie, Henry (ed.), *Irish Folktales* (New York: Pantheon Books, 1985)

Gleeson, David T., *The Irish in the Atlantic World* (Columbia, SC: University of South Carolina Press, 2010)

Golway, Terry, *Irish Rebel: John Devoy and America's fight for Ireland's freedom* (New York: St Martin's Press, 1998)

Goodbody, Rob, *A Suitable Channel: Quaker relief in the Great Famine* (Bray: Pale Publishing, 1995)

Gould, Eliga H., and Peter S. Onuf (eds), *Empire and Nation: The American revolution in the Atlantic world* (Baltimore, MD: Johns Hopkins University Press, 2005)

Griffin, Patrick, *The People with No Name: Ireland's Ulster Scots, America's Scots Irish, and the creation of a British Atlantic world, 1689–1764* (Princeton, NJ: Princeton University Press, 2001

Hachey, Thomas E., *Britain and Irish Separatism: From the Fenians to the Free State, 1867–1922* (Washington, DC: Catholic University of America Press, 1984)

Handlin, Oscar (ed.), *Immigration as a Factor in American History* (Englewood Cliffs, NJ: Prentice-Hall, 1959)

Horner, Arnold, 'Representing the Physical and Settlement Topography of County Mayo in the Early Nineteenth Century: The mapping and modelling of William Bald', in Gerard Moran and Nollaig Ó Muraíle (eds), *Mayo: History and society* (Dublin: Geography Publications, 2014)

Horsley Witten Group, *Town of Scituate: Open space and recreation plan* (Sandwich, MA: Horsley Witten Group, 2009)

Janis, Ely M., *A Greater Ireland: The Land League and transatlantic nationalism in Gilded Age America* (Madison, WI: The University of Wisconsin Press, 2015)

—, 'Petticoat Revolutionaries: Gender, ethnic nationalism, and the Irish Ladies' Land League in the United States', *Journal of American Ethnic History*, vol. 27, no. 2, winter 2008, pp. 5–27

Jenkins, William, 'Remapping "Irish America": Circuits, places, performances', *Journal of American Ethnic History*, vol. 28, no. 4, summer 2009, pp. 90–9

Jordan, Donald E., *Land and Popular Politics in Ireland* (Cambridge: Cambridge University Press, 1994)

Keble, John, 'Notice', Mrs C.F. Alexander, *Hymns for Little Children* (London: J Masters & Co., 1887)

Kelleher, John V., 'Irishness in America', in John V. Kelleher and Charles Fanning (eds), *Selected Writings of John V. Kelleher on Ireland and Irish America* (Carbondale, IL: Southern Illinois University Press, 2002), pp. 150–5

Kelly, James, *Writing Irish History Today* (Dublin: St Patrick's College, 2010)

Kelly, Mary C., 'Spiritual Heirs of the Great Protestants Who Gave Their Lives for Ireland': Expanding Irish-American nationalist landscapes, 1919–1922', *Journal of American Ethnic History*, vol. 40, no. 4, summer 2021, pp. 5–40

—, *Ireland's Great Famine in Irish-American History: Enshrining a fateful memory* (Washington, DC: Rowman & Littlefield, 2013)

—, *The Shamrock and the Lily: The New York Irish and the creation of a transatlantic identity, 1845–1921* (Lausanne: Peter Lang Inc., 2005)

Kenna, Shane, *Jeremiah O'Donovan Rossa: Unrepentant Fenian* (Dublin: Merrion Press, 2015)

Kenneally, Ian, *From the Earth, a Cry: The story of John Boyle O'Reilly* (Cork: The Collins Press, 2011)

Kennedy, Liam, *Colonialism, Religion and Nationalism in Ireland* (Belfast: Institute of Irish Studies, 1996)

Kennelly, Brendan, *The Penguin Book of Irish Verse* (London: Penguin, 1970)

Kenny, Kevin (ed.), *New Directions in Irish-American History* (Madison, WI: University of Wisconsin Press, 2003)

—, 'Diaspora and Comparison: The global Irish as a case study', *Journal of American History*, vol. 90, 2003, pp. 134–62

—, *The American Irish* (London: Longman, 2000)

Kibler, Alison, *Censoring Racial Ridicule: Irish, Jewish and African-American struggles over race and representation, 1890–1930* (Chapel Hill, NC: University of North Carolina Press, 2015)

Killick, John, 'Transatlantic Steerage Fares, British and Irish Migration, and Return Migration, 1815–60', *Economic History Review*, vol. 67, no. 1, February 2014, pp. 170–91

Kinealy, Christine, Jason King and Ciarán Reilly (eds), *Women and the Great Hunger* (Hamden: Quinnipiac University Press, 2016)

Kinealy, Christine, *Daniel O'Connell and the Anti-Slavery Movement* (London: Pickering & Chatto, 2011)

— and Trevor Parkhill (eds), *The Famine in Ulster* (Belfast: Ulster Historical Foundation, 1997)

King, Carla, and Conor McNamara (eds), *The West of Ireland: New perspectives on the nineteenth century* (Dublin: The History Press, 2011)

King, Tony, *Home Rule from a Transnational Perspective: The Irish Parliamentary Party and the United Irish League of America, 1910–1918* (Wilmington, DE: Vernon Press, 2020)

Knight, Patrick, *Erris in the Irish Highlands and the Atlantic Railway* (Dublin: M. Keene, 1836)

Laffin, Michael, *The Resurrection of Ireland: The Sinn Féin party, 1916–1923* (Cambridge: Cambridge University Press, 2006)

Lee, J.J., and Marion R. Casey (eds), *Making the Irish American: History and heritage of the Irish in the United States* (New York: New York University Press, 2006)

Leslie, Shane, *The Irish Issue in its American Aspect* (New York: Charles Scribner's Sons, 1917)

Londraville, Janis, and Richard Londraville (eds), *Too Long a Sacrifice: The letters of Maud Gonne and John Quinn* (Selinsgrove, PA: Susquehanna University Press, 1999)

Lovell, Ernest, *A Green Hill Far Away: The life of Mrs. C.F. Alexander* (Dublin: APCK and London: SPCK, 1970)

Select Bibliography　　325

Luddy, Maria, and Cliona Murphy (eds), *Women Surviving: Studies in Irish women's history in the nineteenth and twentieth centuries* (Dublin: Poolbeg Press, 1989

Lynch-Brennan, Margaret, *The Irish Bridget: Irish immigrant women in domestic service in America* (Syracuse, NY: Syracuse University Press, 2009)

Lyne, Gerard J., *The Lansdowne Estate in Kerry under W.S. Trench, 1849–72* (Dublin: Geography Publications, 2001)

Lysaght, Patricia, *The Banshee: The Irish supernatural death-messenger* (Dublin: O'Brien Press, 1996)

Mac Cuinneagáin, Conall, *Glencolmcille: A parish history* (Dublin: Four Masters Press, 2002)

MacCurtain, Margaret, *Tudor and Stuart Ireland* (Dublin: Gill & Macmillan, 1972)

MacDonald, Michael Patrick, *All Souls: A family story from Southie* (Boston: Beacon Press, 1999)

MacPherson, D.A.J., and Mary J. Hickman (eds), *Women and Irish Diaspora Identities: Theories, concepts and new perspectives* (Manchester: Manchester University Press, 2014)

Mac Suibhne, Breandán, and David Dickson (eds), *Hugh Dorian: The outer edge of Ulster* (Dublin: Lilliput Press, 2000)

Mac Suibhne, Breandán, and Enda Delaney (eds), *Power and Hunger: The Great Famine and Irish popular politics* (London: Routledge, 2016)

Mac Suibhne, Breandán, *The End of Outrage: Post-Famine adjustment in rural Ireland* (Oxford: Oxford University Press, 2017)

Matthews, P.J., *Revival: The Abbey Theatre, Sinn Féin, the Gaelic League and the cooperative movement* (Cork: Cork University Press, 2003)

Maume, Patrick, 'John McGahern', online entry to the *Dictionary of Irish Biography*, added December 2011, https://www.dib.ie/biography/mcgahern-john-a9414

McCaffrey, Lawrence, 'Ireland and Irish America: Connections and disconnections', *US Catholic Historian*, vol. 22, no. 3, summer 2004, pp. 1–18

McCarthy, Angela, *Ireland in the World: Comparative, transnational, and personal perspectives* (New York: Routledge, 2015)

McCarthy, John P., 'The Friends of Irish Freedom and the Founding of the Irish Free State', *The Recorder*, vol. 6, no. 2, fall 1993

McDonagh, Oliver, 'The Poor Law, Emigration and the Irish Question, 1830–55', *Christus Rex*, vol. 12, 1958, pp. 26–37

McGahern, John, *That They May Face the Rising Sun* (London: Faber, 2002)

McGough, Eileen, *Diarmuid Lynch: A forgotten Irish patriot* (Cork: Mercier Press, 2013)

McGowan, Mark G., *The Imperial Irish: Canada's Irish Catholics fight the Great War, 1914–1918* (Montreal and Kingston: McGill-Queen's University Press, 2017)

—, *The Waning of the Green: Catholics, the Irish, and identity in Toronto, 1887–1922* (Montreal and Kingston: McGill Queen's University Press, 1999)

McMahon, Cian T., *The Global Dimensions of Irish Identity: Race, nation, and the popular press, 1840–1880* (Chapel Hill, NC: The University of North Carolina Press, 2015)

McMahon, Timothy G., *Grand Opportunity: The Gaelic revival and Irish society, 1893–1910* (Syracuse: Syracuse University Press, 2008)

McMahon, Timothy G., Michael de Nie and Paul Townend (eds), *Ireland and the Imperial World: Citizenship, opportunism and subversion* (New York: Palgrave Macmillan, 2017)

McWilliams, Monica, *Stand Up, Speak Out: My life working for women's rights, peace and equality in Northern Ireland and beyond* (Belfast: Blackstaff Press, 2022)

Meagher, Timothy J., 'From the World to the Village and the Beginning to the End and After: Research opportunities in Irish-American history', *Journal of American Ethnic History*, vol. 28, no. 4, summer 2009, pp. 118–35

—, *The Columbia Guide to Irish-American History* (New York: Columbia University Press, 2005)

Micks, W.L., *An Account of the Constitution, Administration and Dissolution of the Congested Districts Board for Ireland from 1891 to 1923* (Dublin: Eason & Son, 1925)

Miller, Kerby A., *Ireland and Irish America: Culture, class and transatlantic migration* (Dublin: Field Day, 2008)

—, *Emigrants and Exiles: Ireland and the Irish exodus to North America* (Oxford and New York: Oxford University Press, 1985)

Mitchell, George J., *Making Peace* (New York: Alfred A. Knopf, 1999)

Moore, Joseph S., and Jane G.V. McGaughey, 'The Covenanter Sensibility across the Long Atlantic World', *Journal of Transatlantic Studies*, vol. 11, no. 2, 2013, pp. 125–34

Moore Quinn, E., *Irish American Folklore in New England* (Palo Alto, CA: Academica Press, 2009)

Moran, Gerard, *Sending Out Ireland's Poor: Assisted emigration to North America in the nineteenth century* (Dublin: Four Courts Press, 2004)

Morrissey, James (ed.), *On the Verge of Want* (Dublin: Crannóg Books, 2001)

Mulligan, Adrian N., 'A Forgotten "Greater Ireland": The transatlantic development of Irish nationalism', *Scottish Geographical Journal*, vol. 118, no. 3, 2002, pp. 219–34

Mulligan, William H., Jr, 'How the Irish Became American: Reflections on the history of the Irish in the United States', in Diane Sabenacio Nititham and Rebecca Boyd (eds), *Heritage, Diaspora and the Consumption of Culture: Movements in Irish landscapes* (Surrey and Burlington, VT: Ashgate Publishing, 2014)

Murphy, Ignatius, *A People Starved: Life and death in west Clare, 1845–1851* (Dublin: Irish Academic Press, 1996)

Newman Devlin, Edith, *Speaking Volumes: A Dublin childhood* (Belfast: Blackstaff Press, 2000)

Ní Bhroiméil, Una, *Building Irish Identity in America, 1890–1915: The Gaelic revival* (Dublin: Four Courts Press, 2003)

Select Bibliography

Nolan, Janet, 'Women's Place in the History of the Irish Diaspora: A snapshot', *Journal of American Ethnic History*, vol. 28, 2009, pp. 76–81

—, *Ourselves Alone: Women's emigration from Ireland, 1885–1920* (Lexington, KY: University Press of Kentucky, 1989)

Nyhan Grey, Miriam (ed.), *Ireland's Allies: America and the 1916 Easter Rising* (New York: New York University Press, 2016)

O'Brien, John, and Pauric Travers (eds), *The Irish Emigrant Experience in Australia* (Dublin: Poolbeg Press, 1991)

O'Carroll, Íde B., *Irish Transatlantics, 1980–2015* (Cork: Attic Press, 2018)

Ó Ciosáin, Niall, *Ireland in Official Print Culture 1800–1850* (Oxford: Oxford University Press, 2014)

O'Connor, Barbara, and Michael Cronin (eds), *Tourism in Ireland: A critical analysis* (Cork: Cork University Press, 1993)

O'Connor, Fionnuala, *In Search of a State: Catholics in Northern Ireland* (Belfast: Blackstaff Press, 1993)

O'Connor, Thomas, *The Boston Irish: A political history* (Boston: Northeastern University Press, 1995)

Ó Cuív, Brian, *Irish Dialects and Irish-Speaking Districts* (Dublin: Dublin Institute for Advanced Studies, 1971)

O'Driscoll, Robert, and Lorna Reynolds (eds), *The Untold Story: The Irish in Canada* (Toronto: Celtic Arts of Canada, 1988)

Ó Gráda, Cormac, *Ireland: A new economic history, 1780–1939* (Oxford: Oxford University Press, 1994)

Ó hAodha, Micheál, and Máirtín Ó Catháin (eds), *Irish Migrants in the New Communities: Seeking the fair land?* (Plymouth: Lexington Press, 2014)

O'Leary Anish, Beth, *Irish American Fiction from World War II to JFK: Anxiety, assimilation, and activism* (New York: Palgrave Macmillan, 2021)

O'Leary, Brendan, 'The Shackles of the State and Hereditary Animosities: Colonialism in the interpretation of Irish history', *Field Day Review*, vol. 10, 2014, pp. 148–86

O'Neill, Thomas, Jr, with William Novak, *Man of the House: The life and political memoirs of Speaker Tip O'Neill* (New York: Random House, 1987)

O'Rourke Murphy, Maureen, *Compassionate Stranger: Asenath Nicholson and the Great Irish Famine* (Syracuse, NY: Syracuse University Press, 2015)

— (ed.), *Your Fondest Annie: Letters from Annie O'Donnell to James P. Phelan, 1901–1904* (Dublin: UDC Press, 2005)

Ó Siadhail, Pádraig, *Katherine Hughes: A life and a journey* (Ottawa: Penumbra Press, 2014)

Ó Súilleabháin, Seán, *Folktales of Ireland* (Chicago: University of Chicago Press, 1966)

Ó Tuathaigh, Gearóid, *Ireland Before the Famine, 1798–1848* (Dublin: Gill Books, 2007)

Paisley, Fiona, and Pamela Scully, *Writing Transnational History* (London: Bloomsbury Academic, 2019)

Prieto, Laura R., and Stephen R. Berry (eds), *Crossings and Encounters: Race, gender, and sexuality in the Atlantic world* (Columbia, SC: University of South Carolina Press, 2020)

Quinn, James, 'Balfour, Arthur James', *Dictionary of Irish Biography* I (Cambridge: Cambridge University Press, 2009)

Rae, John, *Sister Genevieve: A courageous woman's triumph in Northern Ireland* (New York: Warner Books, 2001)

Rafferty, Oliver P., *The Church, the State and the Fenian Threat 1861–75* (New York: St Martin's Press, 1999)

Reilly, Ciarán (ed.), *The Famine Irish: Emigration and the Great Hunger* (Dublin: The History Press, 2016)

Rhodes, Rita M., *Women and the Family in Post-Famine Ireland: Status and opportunity in a hierarchical society* (New York: Garland, 1992)

Ridge, Ann, *Death Customs in Rural Ireland* (Syracuse: Syracuse University Press, 2012)

Rodechko, J.P., *Patrick Ford and His Search for America: A case study of Irish-American journalism, 1870–1913* (New York: Arno Press, 1976)

Rodgers, Nini, 'Ireland, Slavery, Antislavery, Post-slavery and Empire: An historiographical survey', *Slavery & Abolition*, vol. 37, no. 3, 2016, pp. 489–504

Rogers, James Silas, and Matthew J. O'Brien (eds), *After the Flood: Irish America, 1945–1960* (Dublin: Irish Academic Press, 2009)

Ryan, Salvador, *Death and the Irish: A miscellany* (Dublin: Wordwell, 2016)

Schirmer, Gregory A., *Out of What Began: A history of Irish poetry in English* (Ithaca and London: Cornell University Press, 1998)

Shannon, Catherine B., '"With Good Will Doing Service": The Charitable Irish Society of Boston, 1737–1857', *Journal of Massachusetts History*, vol. 43, no. 1, winter 2015

—, 'The Wreck of the Brig *St John* and its Commemoration, 1849–2008', American Conference for Irish Studies Annual Conference, National University of Ireland, Galway. Unpublished paper, 2009

—, 'The Woman Writer as Historical Witness: Northern Ireland, 1968–1994: An interdisciplinary perspective', in Maryann Gialanella Valiulis and Mary O'Dowd (eds), *Women & Irish History: Essays in honour of Margaret MacCurtain* (Dublin: Wolfhound Press, 1997)

—, *Arthur J. Balfour and Ireland, 1874–1922* (Washington: CUA Press, 1988)

Shannon, William V., *The American Irish* (New York: Macmillan, 1963)

Sherling, Rankin, *The Invisible Irish: Finding Protestants in the nineteenth-century migrations to America* (Montreal: McGill-Queen's University Press, 2016)

Sim, David, *A Union Forever: The Irish question and US foreign relations in the Victorian age* (Ithaca, NY: Cornell University Press, 2013)

Stephens, James, *The Birth of the Fenian Movement: American diary, Brooklyn 1859*, ed. Marta Ramon (Dublin, UCD Press, 2009)

Smyth, William J., 'Irish Identity in a Transnational Context', *Acadiensis: Journal of the history of the Atlantic region / Revue d'histoire de la région atlantique*, vol. 48, no. 1, spring 2019, pp. 143–52

Select Bibliography

Sutton, Malcolm, *An Index of Deaths from the Conflict in Ireland, 1969–1993* (Belfast: Beyond the Pale Publications, 1994)

Synge, J.M., 'Autobiography', *Collected Works: Prose. Volume II*, ed. Alan Price (London: Oxford University Press, 1966)

Tansill, Charles, *America and the Fight for Irish Freedom, 1866–1922* (New York: The Devin-Adair Co., 1957)

The Blake Family of Renvyle House 1823–4, *Letters from the Irish Highlands of Connemara*, introduced by Dr Kevin Whelan (Clifden: Gibbons Publications, 1995)

Tóibín, Colm (ed.), *Soho Square 6* (London: Bloomsbury Books, 1993)

Trout, Charles H., *Boston: The Great Depression and the New Deal* (New York: Oxford University Press, 1977)

Valiulis, Maryann Gialanella, and Mary O'Dowd (eds), *Women and Irish History: Essays in honour of Margaret MacCurtain* (Dublin: Wolfhound Press, 1997)

Vaughan, W.E., and A.J. Fitzpatrick (eds), *Irish Historical Statistics: Population 1821–1971* (Dublin: RIA, 1978)

Vaughan, W.E. (ed.), *A New History of Ireland. Vol V: Ireland under the Union, 1: 1800–70* (Oxford: Oxford University Press, 1989)

Walter, Bronwen, '"Old Mobilities"? Transatlantic women from the west of Ireland 1880s–1920s', *Irish Journal of Sociology*, vol. 23, no. 2, November 2015, pp. 49–68

Ward, Patrick, *Exile, Emigration and Irish Writing* (Dublin: Irish Academic Press, 2002)

Wenzer, Kenneth C., *Henry George, the Transatlantic Irish, and Their Times: Research in the history of economic thought and methodology* (Bingley: Emerald Group Publishing Limited, 2009)

Whelan, Bernadette, 'The Transatlantic World of Charles Stewart Parnell (1846–91)', *Journal of Transatlantic Studies*, vol. 14, no. 3, September 2016, pp. 293–308

Whelan, Irene, *The Bible War in Ireland* (Madison, WI: University of Wisconsin Press, 2005)

Whelan, Kevin, 'Introduction' to *Letters from the Irish Highlands of Connemara* (Clifden: Gibbons Publications, 1995)

Whelehan, Niall (ed.), *Transnational Perspectives on Modern Irish History* (New York and London: Routledge, 2015)

Wilson, David (ed.), *Irish Nationalism in Canada* (Montreal and Kingston: McGill-Queen's University Press, 2009)

Woodham-Smith, Cecil, *The Great Hunger: Ireland, 1845–9* (London: Hamish Hamilton, 1962)

Woods, C.J., *Travellers' Accounts as Source Material for Irish Historians* (Dublin: Four Courts Press, 2009)

Index

Illustrations are indicated by page numbers in **bold**.

Abbeyfeale, Co. Limerick, 28
Achill, Co. Mayo, 196
Act of Union, 185
AEolas, 38
African-Americans, 4, 5, 78, 162, 163,
    211–26, 238
'After Life' (Parnell), 72, 73
Age of Innocence (Fallon), 174
agency, 3, 6, 61, 74, 85–6
agriculture, 66–7, 75–80, 84, 95, 186–7,
    188, 192–3, 238
Airlie House conference, 259, 261, 264
Akenson, D.H., 4
Alexander, Cecil Frances, 5, 13–24
Alexander, William, 14
Alexander commemorative window, St
    Columb's, Derry, **8**
All Souls (MacDonald), 214, 226
'All Things Bright and Beautiful'
    (Alexander), 5, 17–18
Alliance Party, 208
America, 111, 114, 117
American Association for the
    Recognition of the Irish Republic
    (AARIR), 47, 146–7
American Civil War, 49–50, 238
American Conference for Irish
    Studies, 230, 231, 237
American Declaration of
    Independence, 112
American exceptionalism, 74
American Experience (PBS), 164

American Hibernian, 128
American Historical Association, 230
American Irish Historical Society
    (AIHS), 141
American Ladies' Committee, 62
American Revolutionary War, 93, 141
Amongst Women (McGahern), 168–9,
    181–3
Ancient Order of Hibernians (AOH),
    109, 112, 120–21, 128–9, 131, 135–6,
    154, 231, 243
anglicisation, 140–41
Anglo-American Arbitration Treaty,
    142
Anglo-American relations, 88–101,
    141–2, 144–5, 151
Anglo-Irish Agreement, 259
Anglo-Irish ascendancy, 13, 15, 16, 62,
    65, 73, 88–9, 98
Anglo-Irish Treaty, 6, 136, 137, 147–9,
    238, 256
Anna Maria, 34
Antigonish, Nova Scotia, 124
Anti-Partition League, 199
Apprentice Boys, 203
Aran Islands, 194
Archives of Irish America, 244
Argentina, 116, 249–50
Arthur J. Balfour and Ireland
    (Shannon), 233, 237, 267–8
Asgard, 89
assimilation, 140–41, 155

Athlone, Co. Westmeath, 112, 116
Australia, 26, 30–31, 32, 34, 36, 42, 69,
    133, 147
Avondale House, Co. Wicklow, 62, 73,
    230

Bacon, Gaspar Groswold, 158
Balfour, Arthur J., 6, 7, 88–101, **92**, 184,
    191–2, 195–6, 229–30, 233, 237–41,
    256, 258, 267–8
Balfour, Gerald, 192
Balfour war mission, 6, 88–101
ballads, 5, 18, 21–4
Ballyfermot Senior College, Dublin,
    274
Ballykeane, Co. Wicklow, 14
Ballylarkin, Co. Kilkenny, 75–8, 84
Ballymoney, Co. Antrim, 26
Baltimore, Maryland, 112, 116
Bandon, Co. Cork, 241
Banville, John, 166, 168
Barnard, T.C., 4
Barry, John H., 128–9
BBC, 270
Beckett, Mary, 269
Beckett, Samuel, 175
Bégin, Louis Nazaire, 133
Belfast, 32, 200, 209, 214, 231, 234, 240,
    257, 259, 263–4, 268–74
Belfast Agreement *see* Good Friday
    Agreement
Belcarra, Co. Mayo, 245
Belchem, John, 106, 117
Belgium, 125, 129
Bell, Sam Hanna, 23
Belmullet, Co. Mayo, 185, 186
Bill of Rights, 94
Binghamstown, Co. Mayo, 186
Birmingham, Thomas, 32
Black and Tans, 134–5, 183
Blackrock College, Dublin, 114
Blake family, 185
Blood, May, 259
Bloody Sunday, 206
Boer War, 122–3

Bogside, Derry, 203
Boland, Harry, 146
Bonds, Barry, 224
Book of Kells, 219
Borah, William, 151
Bord Fáilte, 184
Borden, Robert, 125, 131, 133–4
Bordentown, New Jersey, 62, 70
Boston, 6, 7, 9, 66, 69, 70, 78, 82–3, 96,
    109–12, 120–21, 129, 152–65, 211–26,
    231–2, 234–9, 241–5, 248–56, 259,
    261, 265, 268
Boston College, 235, 238, 239
Boston D.A. (Flynn), 223
Boston Globe, 69, 219–20
Boston Herald, 225
Boston Irish News, 213, 216–20
Boston Irish Reporter, 213, 220–25, 226
Boston Magazine, 223
Boston Marine Society, 241
Boston Peace Conference, 222
Boston School Committee, 212, 225
Boston University, 240, 265, 268
Boundary Commission, 147
Bourassa, Henri, 136
Bourne, Francis, 114–15, 116, 118
boycotting, 191
Braudel, Fernand, 4
Breathnach, Ciara, 193
Bric, Maurice, 2
British army, 56, 120–34, 143, 144, 203,
    205–6, 272
British Commonwealth, 136
British Empire, 16–17, 28–9, 50, 53–4,
    95, 115, 117, 121–36, 142, 143–4, 145
Britannia, 113–14
Brophy, Brigid, 176
Brown, Katharine, 15–18, 19–20, 22
Brown University, 233
Bruchési, Paul, 133
Brundage, David, 44–5
Buchanan, A.C., 33, 38, 39, 40–41
Buckingham Palace, 63
Buckley, Suzann, 6, 152–65
Bulger, William, 164, 215

Index

Burke, Alfred E., 124–5
Burke, Mary M., 5, 13–24
Burns, Oates & Washbourne, 114
busing, 162, 163, 211–26
Butler, Archer, 17
Butler, Nicolas Murray, 95
Byrne, Edward Joseph, 107–8

Caird, James, 189
Callahans and the Murphys (1927), 141
Canada invasion plot, 50, 52, 55, 59,
    122
Canadian Expeditionary Force (CEF),
    121, 125–34
Canadian Freeman, 125, 130–31, 133, 135
Cannon, Bridget (née Tonra), 244–5,
    245, 248–9, **251**, 251–2
Cannon, Thomas, 244–5, **245**, 248–9,
    251–2
Canny, Nicholas, 2, 5
capitalism, 74, 75, 84, 86, 194
Cardinal Secrets (RTÉ), 178
Carlow, 40
Carndonagh, Co. Donegal, 71
Carnegie Institute, 142
Carragher, Anna, 270
Carragher, Eileen, 269–70
Carrickmacross, Co. Monaghan, 27,
    29–30, 33
Carroll, Charles, 112
Carroll, Francis M., 6, 88–101, 148
Carson, Edward, 96, 130
Carter, Jimmy, 240, 258
Carter, W.H., 185
Casement, Roger, 56–7, 60
Casket, 124, 129, 130
Castlebar, Co. Mayo, 33
Castleblaney, Co. Monaghan, 30
Catalpa prison break, 56, 59
Catholic Association, 114
Catholic Church, 69, 97, 105–19, 148,
    172–6, 178, 183, 186, 199–201, 268–74
Catholic Emancipation, 109–10
Catholic Record, 125, 129, 130, 135
Catholic Register, 124, 129, 130

Catholic schools, 105, 116, 118, 252,
    268–74
Catholic Truth Society, 114
Catholic University of America, 230
Catholic University of Ireland, 97
'Catholic Women and the Northern
    Ireland Troubles' (Shannon), 233
Catholicism
    in Britain, 105–7, 109–10, 113–19
    Catholic press, 107, 109–19, 121–5,
        128–36, 237
    Catholic schools, 105, 116, 118, 252,
        268–74
    and the Eucharistic Congress, 7,
        105–19
    and the First World War, 6, 120–36
    McGahern's attitudes towards, 167,
        172–4
    in Northern Ireland, 200–202,
        268–74
    in the US and Canada, 1, 3, 6, 7, 81,
        83, 96–7, 105–13, 120–36, 141, 155,
        157, 159, 161, 164, 213, 222–3, 237,
        254, 255
Celtic Monthly, 69–70
censorship, 166, 167, 174–7
Charitable Irish Society, 9, 127, 231, 234,
    241, 254
Chesterton, G.K., 119
Chicago, 145–6, 211
Chicopee, Massachusetts, 232
child abuse, 170, 172, 178–80
Childers, Erskine, 89
childhood, 16–17, 170–73, 178–80
Choate, Joseph, 100
'Church and Its Spire, The'
    (McGahern), 167, 173
Church of Ireland, 13, 15–16, 18–21; *see
    also* Protestantism
Churchill, Randolph, 64, 231, 233
Churchill, Winston, 98
civil rights movement
    Northern Ireland, 201, 206, 240, 263
    United States, *211, 226, 238*
Civil War, 148–50, 181–2

Clan na Gael, 47, 49, 51–2, 55, 58, 59, 60, 137–41, 144, 146, 150
Clare, County, 27, 32, 214
Clark, Champ, 155
Clarke, Thomas, 56, 57, 59, 60
class, 16, 17–18, 75, 82–5, 87, 170, 212–26
Cleveland, Ohio, 69
Clifden, Co. Galway, 185, 186, 192
Clinton, Bill, 231, 233, 261
Clinton, Hillary, 260
Cobh, Co. Cork, 78, 111
Cockran, W. Bourke, 98
'Coercion – Hold the Rent' (Parnell), 66
Cohalan, Daniel, 139–41, 143–6, 149–51, 247
Cohasset, Massachusetts, 231–2, 241, 242–3
Cohasset Historical Societty, 231
Cold War, 2, 250
Coleraine, Co. Derry, 26, 202, 239
Collins, Michael, 136, 147–8
Collins, Patrick, 155
colonialism, 14, 16–18, 23–4, 141, 184
Colum, Padraic, 72
Comerford, Henry, 242
Comhaltas Ceoltóirí Éireann, 217
commemoration, 6, **8**, 15, 24, 70–71, 73, 109–10, 163–4, 181–3, 240–41, 243
Common Ground (Lukas), 212, 225–6
communications, 54, 186, 187–8
communism, 159, 214
community activism, 9, 201–2, 263
community colleges, 274
Community of Peace People, 271
'Congested Districts, The' (Synge and Yeats), 195
Congested Districts Board (CDB), 192–3, 195–6, 238, 248
Connacht, 185, 186, 188–9, 214
Connell, William, 37
Connemara, 164, 185, 189–90, 192, 195, 196
conscription, 126, 133–4
conservatism, 19, 174, 264

constitutional nationalism, 57, 121–2, 128–36, 138–9, 142–3
construction work, 83
constructive unionism, 184, 191–3
Conway, Richard 'Doc', 221
Cooper, Bob, 208
Cootehill, Co. Cavan, 39
Cork, 5, 26, 33–43, 232, 241
Cork, County, 214, 246
Corkery, John, 37
Corrigan, Mairéad, 271
corruption, 154, 156, 160
Cosgrave, W.T., 105, 109, 149, 150
Costello, Mary, 272–3
cottage industries, 79, 193
Council of Ireland, 208, 209
Country Girls, The (O'Brien), 175
Countrywomen, The (Smith), 171
Coyne, Thomas, 175
Craig, Patricia, 24
Creation, 175
credit unions, 201
Creedon, William, 37
Croagh Patrick, 109
Croke Park, 140
Cromwell, Oliver, 184–5
Cronin, Anthony, 174
Croom, Co. Limerick, 40
Crotty, Patrick, 170, 172
Crowe, Catriona, 170
Crowther Commission, 204
Cuba, 145
Cuba Five, 51
Cullen, Paul, 269
cultural nationalism, 46, 52, 139–40, 194–5
Cunard line, 109, 110, 111
Curley, James Michael, 6, 111, 152–65, 217
Curley, Michael, 112, 116
Curley, Thomas, 154
Curley Effect, The (Glaeser and Shleifer), 164
Currie, Austin, 208
Cushing, Richard, 161, 243

Index

da Silva, Áine, 268
Dáil Éireann, 147–8
Daly, Mary E., 7, 105–19
Daly, Peter, 32
dancing, 140, 217
D'Arcy, John, 185
Dark, The (McGahern), 167, 174–6, 178–80
David, Albert, 117
Davis, John W., 142
Davitt, Michael, 56, 58, 66–8, 71, 238, 240
de Valera, Éamon, 3, 106, 115, 116–17, 131, 144–8
de Vere, Audrey, 31
deafness, 15–16
'Death Bed Farewell, The' (Parnell), 62
December Bride (Bell), 23
Dedham, Massachusetts, 78, 81–3, 85
Democratic National Committee, 153, 160
Department of Agriculture and Technical Instruction, 192
Derry, 8, 15, 18–19, 22–3, 197, 201–3, 205, 206, 240
Derry and Raphoe School for the Deaf and Dumb, 16
Derry Citizens' Action Committee, 201
Derry Housing Action Committee, 201
desegregation, 7, 162, 163, 211–26
Desertserges, Co. Cork, 244
Desmond, Cornelius, 37
DesRosiers, Caleb, 222
Detroit, 164, 254
Devlin, Edith, 171
Devlin, Paddy, 208
devolution, 204, 206–8
Devoy, John, 3, 51, 52, 56–60, 89, 137–40, 143, 144–5, 147–51
Dictionary of Irish Biography, 170, 238
Dillon, John, 58, 70
diplomatic service, 105
dirty protests, 258
disestablishment, 13, 18–21

distribution networks, 187–8
Dockery, Jamie, 172
Doheny, Michael, 47–8
Doherty, Charles J., 125, 131, 134
domestic service, 33, 35, 36, 74, 78, 82–3, 85–6, 141, 244, 248
Donegal, County, 186, 188–9, 192
Donovan, Michael, 124
Don't Never Forget (Brophy), 176
Doody, Honora, 36
Doolin, David M., 5, 44–60
Doorley, Michael, 6, 137–51
Dorchester Reporter, 220–21
Dorrian, Patrick, 269
Douglass, Frederick, 4
Dowden, Richard, 35
Downey, Richard, 106, 108, 115, 116
Downing Street Declaration, 265
dowries, 79, 80
Driscoll, Mary, 37
Driscoll, Patrick, 36–8
Driscoll, Timothy, 37
Drogheda, Co. Louth, 41, 231, 238
Drummond, Eric, 96
Dublin, 14–15, 33–4, 40, 56, 60, 64, 105–19, 129, 140, 150, 171, 174, 176, 178, 219, 231, 255–7, 261, 265, 274
Dublin Castle, 32, 62, 63, 192
Dublin Historical Association, 230
Dublin Lockout, 231
Dubois, W.E.B., 211
Duffy, Rita, 271
Duggan, Honora, 36
Dukakis, Michael, 219
Dulles, Charlie, 250
Dún Laoghaire, Co. Dublin, 110, 114, 174
Duncan, Leland, 168
Duncan, R.A., 29, 41
Dungannon, Co. Tyrone, 239
Dunnamaggan, Co. Kilkenny, 78–82
Dunne, Seán, 171
Dunsany, Edward Plunkett, Lord, 95
dynamite campaign, 49, 52–6, 59
dynamite schools, 52, 54

Eagle, 237
Earl Grey, 32
Easter Rising, 51, 55, 56–60, 71, 73, 121,
  126, 129–31, 133, 143
Edmonton 'Irish Guards' battalion,
  127–8
education
  adult education, 274
  Catholic schools, 105, 116, 118, 252,
    268–74
  Catholic University, 97
  community colleges, 274
  curricula, 122, 269, 273–4
  of the deaf, 15–16
  desegregation of schools, 7, 162, 163,
    211–26
  higher education, 97, 201, 202,
    219–20, 223
  industrial schools, 172, 173, 179
  Northern Ireland, 201, 202, 265,
    268–74
  public investment in, 156, 159
  role of the state, 186
  Shannon's teaching career, 9,
    229–30, 234, 256, 267
  for women, 15–16, 252, 268–74
Edwards, Dudley, 237, 256,
  267
Éire Society, 231
electoral boundaries, 202
11+ examination, 273
Eliot, Charles W., 95
Eliza Liddell, 38
Elms Institute, 232
Emigrants and Exiles (Miller), 3
emigration
  African migration, 4
  assisted emigration schemes, 2,
    25–43, 189
  Catholic press representations,
    107–8, 115
  emigrants' letters home, 2, 75–8,
    80–82, 85
  and employment, 2, 33, 35–41, 74, 76,
    78, 82–3, 85–6, 189

Famine era, 2, 5, 17, 24, 25–43, 62, 78,
  79, 189, 231–2, 241, 242–3, 244,
  245
female emigrants, 3, 5–6, 26, 29,
  30–36, 41–3, 74–87
greeting parties for immigrants, 249
and homesickness, 75–6, 80–87
'invisible emigrants', 5, 25–43
literary representations, 17, 23–4
remittances, 25, 32, 78, 83, 86, 111
US immigration policies, 155
west of Ireland, 29, 84, 189
Emmet, Robert Temple, 96
Emmet Monument Association
  (EMA), 47–8, 49
employment
  agricultural labouring, 79, 188, 238
  construction work, 83
  cottage industries, 79, 193
  discrimination, 202
  domestic service, 33, 35, 36, 74, 78,
    82–3, 85–6, 141, 244, 248
  and emigration, 2, 33, 35–41, 74, 76,
    78, 82–3, 85–6, 189
  job creation, 156, 159
  Northern Ireland, 202, 209, 271,
    273
  railway construction, 35, 38
  seasonal migration, 188–9
  textile industry, 186–7, 193, 271
  unemployment, 127, 154, 271, 273–4
  west of Ireland, 186–7, 188–9
  for women, 16, 33, 36, 74, 78, 82–3,
    85–6, 141, 157, 193, 244, 248, 252,
    255
Encumbered Estates Acts, 62
Encumbered Estates Court, 188
Ennis, Co. Clare, 26, 27, 30, 31
Enniscorthy, Co. Wexford, 106, 116
Enniskillen, Co. Fermanagh, 27
Equality Commission, 265, 270
'Erin My Queen' (Parnell), 72
Erris, Co. Mayo, 187
ethnic politics, 155
Eucharistic Congress, 7, 105–19

Index 337

European Court for Human Rights, 206
evictions, 27, 77, 80, 241
executions, 60, 120, 129–31, 133, 143, 148
Executive Council, 105, 117, 149
exile, 1, 3, 47–8, 56, 57, 75, 107–8

Fall of Feudalism, The (Davitt), 71
Fallon, Brian, 174
Fallon, Michael Francis, 131, 134
Falls Road, Belfast, 268–74
family, 80, 84, 86, 155, 169, 170–72
'Famine, Friends & Fenians' exhibition, 238
Famine Relief Fund, 64, 65
'Famine Year, The' (Speranza), 66, 240
famines, 2, 5, 17, 24, 25–43, 61–3, 72, 78–9, 186–8, 191, 231–3, 238, 240–45, 247
farming *see* agriculture
Farren, Seán, 7, 197–210
fascism, 106
Faulkner, Brian, 205, 208–9
Female Orphan Scheme, 26, 30–31, 34, 35, 36, 42
feminism, 13–14, 15, 74, 176
Fenian Brotherhood (FB), 3, 15, 46, 47–51, 52, 53, 55, 59, 122, 138
Ferns Inquiry, 179
Ferriter, Diarmaid, 7, 166–83, 238
Fianna Fáil, 106, 149, 219
Field, John, 242
Field Day Anthology, 230, 239
'Fighting 69th' battalion, 128, 249–50
films, 141, 274
Fine Gael, 219
First Vatican Council, 108
First World War, 6, 56, 57, 60, 88–101, 120–36, 142–3, 249–50, 253
fishing, 186–7, 193, 236
Fitt, Gerry, 208
Fitzgerald, John F., 96
Fitzpatrick, Charles, 122, 125, 136
Fitzwilliam estate, Co. Wicklow, 33, 38
Flanders *see* Belgium

Flynn, Órlaithí, 271
Flynn, Raymond, 162–4
Flynn, Sean, 223
folklore, 23, 84, 184, 194
Forbes, Robert, 232, 241
Ford, Patrick, 53–4, 58
foreign relations, 3, 55–6, 88–101, 141–2, 144–5, 151
Forry, Bill, 221, 223
Forry, Ed, 215, 220–21, 224–5
Forry, Mary Casey, 220
Forster, William, 188
Forster, William Edward, 188
Foster, Arlene, 265
Foster, Vere, 26
Foy, C.J., 135
France, 47, 62, 66, 90, 93, 250
Francis, William, 221
Franco-Prussian War, 62
fraud, 152, 154, 159
Fredericton, New Brunswick, 128–9
French Canadians, 123, 125–6, 133–4, 136
French Revolution, 66
Friends of Irish Freedom (FOIF), 47, 49, 59, 143, 144, 146
'From House Rights to Civil Rights' (Shannon), 239
fundraising, 47, 53, 63–4, 135, 138, 144–5
Further Education and Training Awards Council (FETAC), 274
Future of Northern Ireland discussion paper, 207

Gaelic American, 6, 57, 137–51
Gaelic Athletic Association (GAA), 46, 139–40
Gaelic League, 139, 140, 141, 194
Gaelic revival, 46, 139–40, 193–4
Gaeltacht, 194
Gallivan, James A., 95
Galveston, Texas, 111
Galway, 27, 28, 31, 32, 33, 153, 190, 236, 242
Galway, County, 27, 185, 189, 192, 195, 214

Gannt, Jonathan, 55–6
Garrity, W. Arthur, 212–13, 215, 219, 224, 225, 116
Gates, Henry Louis, 223
Germany, 56, 57, 60, 88–90, 96, 97, 121, 123, 124, 128, 130, 132, 151, 250
Giannetti, M.G., 66
Gibbons, James Cardinal, 95
Gilmour Richard, 69
Gladstone, William E., 58, 70, 191
Glasgow, 55
Glasnevin Cemetery, 150
Global Women's History Project, 240, 265
Glucksman Ireland House Oral History Collection, 244
Godkin, Lawrence, 96
Golden Treasury of Irish Verse, 72
Golway, Terry, 56, 57
Gonne, Maud, 73
Good Friday Agreement, 198, 204, 210, 240, 263–4
Gorey, Co. Wexford, 42
Gort, Co. Galway, 31, 40
Government of Ireland Act, 147, 205, 237
governor-general of Ireland, 116–17
Grace, Thomas, 69
Graídhin, Cáit, 84
'Grave by St Columba's Cross, The' (Alexander), 22
Great Depression, 106, 108–9, 111, 117, 157
Great Famine, 2, 5, 17, 24, 25–43, 62, 78–9, 187–8, 231–3, 238, 240–45, 247
Greene, Cathy, 6, 75–8, 82–4, 85
Greene, Thomas, 116, 118
Gregory, Augusta, Lady, 20, 21
Griffith's Valuation, 185, 247
Guardian, 176, 195, 272
Guilday, Peter, 112
gun-running, 58, 60, 89
Gunston Hall, 93–4, 100
Guy, Peter, 178
Gweedore, Co. Donegal, 185

Hachey, Thomas E., 9, 229–35
Haitian-Americans, 221, 222
Hales, Seán, 148
Halifax, Nova Scotia, 91, 122, 127, 135
Handlin, Oscar, 1–2
Hanley, P., 70
Harding, Michael, 166–7
Harland & Wolff shipyard, 209
Harlem Gaelic Society, 141
Harrington, Michael, 215
Harvard University, 95, 164, 220, 223
Haughey, Charles, 176
Hayes, Patrick Joseph, 116
healthcare, 156, 159
Heaney, Seamus, 231
Heath, John, 70
Hennigan, Jim, 225
Henry, Patrick, 135–6
Henry, Paul, 195
Hicks, Louise Day, 213, 215, 225
higher education, 97, 201, 203, 219–20, 223
Highlanes Gallery, Drogheda, 231, 238
Hill, George, 185
Hingham, Massachusetts, 232, 236, 244, 253–4
Hingston, William, 127
historical sources, 7, 169–70, 181–2, 262
historiography, 7, 141, 167–70, 181–2, 262
History Ireland magazine, 234
Hoban, James, 112
Hofstra University, 231
Holbrook, Massachusetts, 229
'Hold the Harvest' (Parnell), 66–8, 72
Holmes, David, 107
Holyhead, 114
home rule, 47, 54, 58, 89–101, 121–2, 124, 131–3, 135, 138, 142–4, 147, 191–3
Home Rule Bills, 122, 124
homesickness, 75–6, 80–87
House, Edward M., 89, 91, 95–6
housing, 159, 184, 192, 201, 202, 239, 265
Hovels of Ireland, The (Parnell), 64–5, 68
Hughes, Katherine, 136

Hume, John, 7, 197–210, 235, 239, 259
199th Irish Rangers battalion, 127
hunger strikes, 250, 258–9
Hyde, Douglas, 140
Hymnal 1982, 18
hymns, 5, 13, 14, 16–22, 24
Hymns for Little Children (Alexander), 14, 16–17
Hynes, John B., 159–60

I'd Do It Again (Curley), 161
identity *see* Irish-American identity; Irish identity
immigration policies, 155
Imperial War Conference, 89
industrial schools, 172, 173, 179
inheritance, 79–80
institutionalisation, 16, 36, 37, 170, 172–3, 179
International Conference of Irish Women Historians, 230
internment, 206
Ireland 1912–85 (Lee), 168–9
Irish-American Heritage Award, 234
Irish-American identity, 4, 7, 46, 49–50, 140–41, 211–26, 257
Irish Catholic, 130
Irish Catholic Benevolent Association, 131
Irish Church Hymnal, 18, 19–20
Irish Convention, 97, 101
Irish Echo, 220
Irish Free State, 6, 7, 72, 105–7, 116–18, 136, 137, 147–9, 183, 194–6, 238
Irish Historical Society, 230
Irish Historical Studies, 233
Irish identity, 2, 3, 5, 6, 44–6, 49–50, 52, 105–6, 140–41, 166, 169, 194–5, 257
Irish Immigrant Center (IIC), 222
Irish Independent, 114–15, 179
Irish language, 46, 84, 139, 140, 185, 186, 194, 218, 220
Irish literary revival, 13, 18, 19, 20–21, 24, 72
Irish Literature series, 72

'Irish Mother's Lament, The' (Alexander), 17
Irish National Teachers' Organisation (INTO), 175
Irish News, 201, 207–8
Irish Northern Aid Society (Noraid), 216, 219, 258
Irish Parliamentary Party (IPP), 96–7, 128, 131, 134, 138–9, 142–3, 144
Irish People, 62, 72
Irish Race Conventions, 143, 144
Irish Relief Fund, 135
Irish Repeal Association, 241
Irish Republican Army (IRA), 144, 146–7, 148, 181–3, 199; *see also* Provisional IRA
Irish Republican Brotherhood (IRB), 47, 56, 59, 60, 129–30, 138, 146
Irish Times, 176, 197, 198, 201
Irish unity, 96–8, 199, 201–2, 206–7, 209
Irish Voice, 220
Irish Volunteers, 89
Irish World, 53–4, 58, 138, 141, 143, 148
Irishman, 64
isolationism, 137, 142, 150–51
Israel, 240, 265

Jamestown, 232, 241
Japan, 151
job creation, 156, 159
John L. McDonough Award, 9, 234
Joyce, James, 14, 24
Judaism, 18

Kane, Mary, 243
Keane, Patrick, 131
Keble, John, 14
Keelogues, Co. Mayo, 244, 248
Kelleher, D.J., 175
Kelleher, John V., 4
Kelly, Jim, 215, 225
Kelly, Mary C., 1–9
kelp harvesting, 186
Kenmare, Co. Kerry, 26, 27–8, 29
Kenna, Shane, 51, 55

Kennedy, John F., 159, 256–7
Kennedy, Joseph P., 159
Kennedy, Liam, 112
Kennedy, Ted, 212, 215
Kennedy Library symposiums, 239, 259, 261, 264, 268
Kennelly, Brendan, 72–3
Kenny, Kevin, 105
Kenny, Mary, 15, 16
Kerrigan, John, 225
Kerry, County, 21
Kibler, Alison, 141
Kilflyn, Co. Kerry, 40
Kilkenny, 106, 115
Kilkenny, County, 75–87
Kilmainham Gaol, 60
Kilmainham Treaty, 70
Kilmallock, Co. Limerick, 29
Kilrush, Co. Clare, 27, 28, 30
Kinealy, Christine, 6, 61–73
Kingston, Ontario, 34, 124, 125, 130–31
Kinvara, Co. Galway, 32
Knight, Patrick, 187
Knights of Columbanus, 175, 215
Knock, Co. Mayo, 109, 157
Knox, Ronald, 115
Kołakowski, Leszek, 183

Ladies' Land League, 61, 68–71, 72–3
Lamb, Charles, 195
Lancastria, 110
Land Acts, 195
land annuities, 116–17
Land League, 3, 47, 64–71, 191
Land League Songs, 68
land reform, 62, 97, 188, 191–3, 195
Land War, 54, 58, 138, 191
landing money, 39–40
landlords, 25–6, 27, 32–3, 39, 40, 62, 65, 68, 86, 185, 191
landscape, 7, 13, 16, 22, 87, 189–90, 194–5
Lansing, Robert, 90, 91–4, **92**, 100–101
Larabee, Ann, 53
Last Hurrah, The (O'Connor), 153, 160–61

Lauri, Lorenzo, 107–8
Law, Hugh, 67
League of Nations, 105, 143–5, 149, 150, 151
Leary, Ellen, 37
Leary, Hanah, 36
Leary, Johanna, 36–7
Leary, John, 36
Leary, Thomas, 36–7
Leavetaking, The (McGahern), 180–81
lecture tours, 47, 52, 64, 68–9, 121
Leddy, J.J., 131
Lee, J.J., 25
Lee, Joe, 168–9, 237, 244, 255–6, 267
Leeds, 66
'Legend of Stumpie's Brae, The' (Alexander), 5, 14, 21–2, 23–4
Leitrim, County, 168
Lemass, Seán, 257
Lenihan, Brian, 176–7
Lennon, Peter, 176
Leslie, Shane, 91, 94, 98–9, 101
Lettermullan, Co. Galway, 243
Liber Hymnorum, 19
Life magazine, 161
Limerick, 33–4, 116
literature, 7, 13, 22–4, 166–83, 230, 234, 242; *see also* poetry
Liverpool, 106, 113, 116, 117
living standards, 187, 193, 257
Lloyd George, David, 90–91, 92, 94–5, 97, 98, 101, 131
local government, 192, 229, 230, 233, 237, 256, 267
Lodge, Henry Cabot, Jr, 158
Lodge, Henry Cabot, Sr, 155
London, England, 55, 109–10, 117, 250
London, Ontario, 125, 131, 134
'Look Down, Lord of Heaven, on Our Desolation!' (Alexander), 18–19
Lough Derg, 109
Love of the World (McGahern), 168, 183
Lovell, Ernest, 14–15, 17–18, 20
Lowell, Francis Cabot, 154
loyalist paramilitaries, 208, 263

Index

Luby, Thomas Clarke, 62
Lucy, Gordon, 14
Lukas, J. Anthony, 212, 225–6
Lynch, Diarmuid, 144
Lynch, Rachael Sealy, 5, 13–24
Lynch, Sandra, 212
Lynch-Brennan, Margaret, 75, 82

Maamtrasna murders, 190
McAleese Report, 172
McAleese, Mary, 73, 270
McAliskey, Bernadette, 212
MacAtasney, Gerard, 57
McAteer, Eddie, 202
McCaffrey, Lawrence, 4
McCartan, Patrick, 139
McCarthy, Justin, 72
McCormack, John (speaker of the
    house), 226
McCormack, John (tenor), 112
McCormick, Medill, 100
MacCurtain, Margaret, 9, 229, 237, 247,
    267–74
MacDonald, Michael Patrick, 214, 226
McDonough, Helen, 157
Macedonia, 241
McFetridge, Paula, 271
McGahern, John, 7, 166–83
McGarrity, Joe, 144
McGivern, Marie-Thérèse, 271
McGowan, Mark G., 6, 120–36
McGrath, John Tracy, 218, 220
McKiernan, Eoin, 217
McLaughlin, C.J., 120–21, 129, 136
McMahon, John, 215
McMahon, Sean, 17
McNamara, Robert, 233
McNeil, Neil, 123
MacNeill, Eoin, 97
McQuaid, John Charles, 175, 176
McSwiney, Terence, 250
McWilliams, Monica, 9, 240, 261,
    262–6
Magdalen laundries, 172–3
Magee College, Derry, 202

Magherafelt, Co. Derry, 26
Magner, Eliza, 36
Mahony, Nicholas, 43
majoritarianism, 203–4
Making Peace (Mitchell), 265–6
Malcolm, Ian, 96
Malcolm X, 211
Mallon, Nicola, 271
Malone, A.E., 117
Manion, Robert J., 134
manorial system, 79, 84
marriage, 63, 74, 75, 78–80, 83, 85
Marshal, 216
Martindale, Cyril, 115
'Masada' (Parnell), 62–3, 72
Mason, George, 94
Massey, Bolton, 29
Maume, Patrick, 170
Maxwell, John, 120, 129
Mayo, County, 27, 189, 191, 192, 195,
    244–5, 248–9
Meagher, Timothy J., 4, 47
media *see* press; radio; television
Mellifont Abbey, 109
Mellows, Liam, 148
Memoir (McGahern), 168, 170, 171, 179,
    183
memoirs, 170–72
*Memorial Birthday Poem to the Poet
    Thomas Moore*, 72
memory, 46, 51, 84–5, 86–7
Menino, Thomas, 163–4
Milan Michèle, 3
Miller, Kerby A., 3, 5–6, 74–87
Military Service Act, 126
military service pensions, 181–82
Milltown Cemetery, Belfast, 271, 272
Mitchel, John, 3, 99, 138
Mitchell, George, 261, 265–6
Mitchell, John Purroy, 95, 99
Moakley, Joe, 226
model farms, 188
Monachunna, Co. Kilkenny, 78–9
Moncton, New Brunswick, 121
Monsell, William, 31

Monserrat Aspirers, 222
Month, The, 107, 110, 118
Montreal, 34, 39, 68, 125, 127, 131, 133, 135–6
Mooney, Don, 216–17, 219, 220
morality, 172–3, 176
Moran, Gerard, 5, 25–43
Morning Post, 67
mother and baby homes, 172
motherhood, 17, 69, 75, 171–3
Mountbellew, Co. Galway, 31
Mowlam, Marjorie 'Mo', 240
Muckross Abbey, 109
Mulligan, Adrian, 46
Murphy, Charles (Canadian MP), 131, 134
Murphy, Charles (Tammany Hall), 139
Murphy, James, 37
Murphy, Maureen, 75, 229
Murphy Report, 178
Museum of Country Life, Co. Mayo, 248
music, 66, 140, 217

Napier, Oliver, 208
Napoleonic wars, 187
Nash, Catherine, 194
Nation, 64, 65, 66, 73, 139
National Association for the Advancement of Colored People (NAACP), 211, 226
National Endowment for the Humanities fellowships, 233, 258
nationalism
    and Anglo-American relations, 88–101, 141–2, 144–5, 151
    constitutional nationalism, 57, 121–2, 128–36, 138–9, 142–3
    cultural nationalism, 46, 52, 139–40, 194–5
    female nationalism, 15, 46–7, 52–3, 61–73
    movements and organisations, 3, 15, 47–60, 137–51

physical force nationalism, 44–60, 122, 128–31, 136, 138–9, 144
political representation of nationalists in Northern Ireland, 197–210
and the position of women, 264
and Protestantism, 15, 73
transatlantic political activism, 2, 3, 5, 44–60, 61–73, 137–51
Nationalist Party, 200, 202–3
neoliberalism, 74
New Bedford Whaling Museum, 238
New Brunswick, 5, 26, 33, 36–43, 121, 125, 128–9, 130
New Departure, 58, 59
New England Relief Committee, 232, 241
New Freeman, 121, 125, 129, 130
New Ireland Forum, 259
New Ross, Co. Wexford, 42
New York, 47–8, 51–8, 60, 64, 68, 75–6, 99–100, 109, 116, 128, 137–43, 149, 211, 220, 244–7, 249, 255
New York Evening Post, 96
New York Times, 139, 246
New York University, 244
New York World, 95
Newcastle West, Co. Limerick, 40
Newe, G.B., 200–201
Newport, Co. Tipperary, 244, 247
Newsletter, 207–8
newspapers *see* press
Nobel, Alfred, 54
Norman settlers, 78–9, 85
Northcliffe, Alfred Harmsworth, Lord, 95
Northern Ireland
    Anglo-Irish Agreement, 259
    Bloody Sunday, 206
    Boundary Commission, 147
    civil rights movement, 201, 206, 240, 263
    commemorative plaques, 15, 24
    devolved government, *204, 206–8, 263–4, 265*

discrimination against Catholics, 202, 239

Downing Street Declaration, 265

education, 201, 202, 265, 268–74

electoral boundaries, 202

employment, 202, 209, 271, 273

Good Friday Agreement, 198, 204, 210, 240, 263–4

housing, 201, 202, 239, 265

hunger strikes, 258–9

internment, 206

partition, 13, 94, 97–9, 101, 147, 198–9, 201, 237, 238, 258

peace process, 3, 7, 8–9, 231, 233, 240, 261, 262–6, 268

political representation of nationalists, 197–210

power-sharing, 197–9, 204–10, 263–4

regional literature, 13, 22–4

role of women, 8–9, 230, 233, 234, 239–40, 259–61, 262–6, 268

Shannon's work on, 7–9, 230, 231, 233, 234, 237, 238–40, 257–66, 268

Troubles, 3, 183, 198, 205–10, 214–16, 219, 230, 233, 237, 238–9, 257–66, 268–74

Northern Ireland Assembly, 263–4, 265

Northern Ireland Civil Rights Association, 240

Northern Ireland Convention, 198

Northern Ireland Women's Coalition, 240, 257, 260–61, 263–6

Northwest Review, 123, 125, 128, 130, 135–6

Nova Scotia, 122–3, 124, 127, 130

Novak, Rose, 15

Nugent, James, 26

Nyhan Grey, Miriam, 9, 244–61

oath of allegiance, 116–17, 147

O'Brien, Cornelius, 122

O'Brien, Edna, 175

O'Brien, Hugh, 83, 155

O'Brien, Matthew, 7, 211–26

O'Brien, Michael J., 141

O'Brien, Morgan J., 96

O'Brien, William (Canadian soldier), 129

O'Brien, William (Irish Parliamentary Party), 58

O'Connell, Daniel, 4, 109–10

O'Connell, William Henry, 110–11, 112, 155

O'Connor, Andrew, 110

O'Connor, Edwin, 153, 160–61

O'Connor, Joseph, 178

O'Connor, Thomas, 155

O'Daly, Dominic, 267

O'Doherty, Eva, 15

O'Donnell, Lawrence, 221

O'Donovan Rossa, Jeremiah, 49, 51–6, 57, 59, 60, 62

O'Donovan Rossa, Mary Jane, 15, 46–7, 51–3, 60

O'Faoláin, Seán, 176, 177

O'Farrell, Sr Genevieve, 271–3

O'Flynn, Dermot, 175

O'Friel, May, 270

O'Gorman, John J., 125–6, 132–3

O'Hagan, Thomas, 135

O'Hara, Mary, 272–3

Ó hUiginn, Seán, 73

O'Leary, Ellen, 15

O'Leary, Jeremiah, 89

O'Leary, John, 72

Oliver, Marten, 231

Olympic, 91, 100

O'Mahony, John, 47–8, 50, 56

O'Malley, Ernie, 182

O'Malley, Padraig, 259, 264

On Another Man's Wound (O'Malley), 182

'Once in Royal David's City' (Alexander), 15, 18, 21

O'Neil, Albert 'Dapper', 162–3, 225

O'Neill, Rosemary, 260

O'Neill, Terence, 200, 202

O'Neill, Thomas 'Tip', 160, 161–2, 260

Ontario, 26, 34, 123–5, 127, 130–31

Ordnance Survey, 185

O'Reilly, John Boyle, 70, 213, 230, 231, 233, 236, 237–8, 240
O'Rourke Murphy, Maureen, 9, 236–43
Orpen, R.J.T., 27–8
O'Toole, Fintan, 179
Ottawa, 125, 131, 132–3, 135
Ottawa Citizen, 132–3
Ó Tuathaigh, Gearóid, 7, 184–96
Otway, C.G., 29, 41
outdoor relief, 27
Oxford University, 14, 16

Page, Walter Hines, 90–91, 97
Paisley, Ian, 208
Palestine, 240, 265
Palmerston estate, Co. Sligo, 33, 38
pamphlets, 45–6, 47, 64–5
Panama, 35
Paris, 47, 62
Paris Peace Conference, 144
Parker, Alton B., 95
Parkhill, Trevor, 32
parliamentary committees, 205
Parnell, Anna, 6, 61–2, 64, 68, 70, 71
Parnell, Charles Stewart, 3, 6, 58, 61–4, 67–71, 73, 99, 237
Parnell, Delia, 62, 63, 70
Parnell, Fanny, 6, 61–73
Parnell, Henry, 62
Parnell, Theodosia, 62
Parnell Summer School, 230
partition, 13, 94, 97–9, 101, 147, 198–9, 201, 237, 238, 258
partnership government *see* power-sharing
pastoral farming, 79, 80, 188
patriarchy, 52, 74, 172
Patrick, Saint, 106, 107, 108, 109, 114, 117, 118, 132
Patriot Ledger, 215
patriotism, 19, 48–9, 52, 61, 64, 73, 120, 123, 125, 126, 133, 136, 215
Pavonia, 78
peace process, 3, 7, 8–9, 231, 233, 240, 261, 262–6, 268

Pearl Harbor, 151
Pearse, Patrick, 51, 56, 57, 60, 130
pensions, 153, 160, 181
Permanent Court of International Justice, 150, 151
Peterborough, Ontario, 26
Petrie, George, 19
Philadelphia, 2, 72, 144, 211
philanthropy, 15–16, 68, 189
Phoenix Park, 54–5, 69, 111
Phoenix Park murders, 54–5, 69
physical force nationalism, 44–60, 122, 128–31, 136, 138–9, 144
pilgrimage, 109–15
Pilot, 66, 70, 109, 110–11, 112–13, 213, 237–8
Pim, Jonathan, 188
Pinckney, Darryl, 5
Platt Amendment, 145, 149
Plunkett, Horace, 86–7, 95–6, 98, 101
Plunkett, Joseph Mary, 56
poetry, 13–24, 61, 62–3, 65–8, 71–3, 240, 268; *see also* literature
Poetry and Songs of Ireland (O'Reilly), 240
police, 68–9, 111, 159, 178, 186, 190, 203, 221
Policy for Partnership advertisement, 207–8
political activism, 2, 3, 5–6, 7, 8–9, 44–60, 61–73, 137–51, 239–40, 257–66
Polley, Sr Ita, 271
poor law, 25–43
poor law commissioners, 29, 30–31, 34, 39–41
population decline, 78, 79, 80, 195
population growth, 185–6
Pornographer, The (McGahern), 168
post offices, 64, 186, 188
poverty, 17–18, 25–43, 64–6, 72, 73, 154–5, 162, 182, 184, 186–91, 222, 265, 271, 273–4
power, 123, 172–4, 266
Power, Charles, 134
Power, Geoffrey, 122

Index

power-sharing, 197–9, 204–10, 263–4
press
    and the Balfour war mission, 95
    Catholic press, 107, 109–19, 121–5, 128–36, 237
    and censorship, 175, 179
    coverage of the busing crisis, 213–26
    coverage of the Eucharistic Congress, 109–19
    coverage of James Michael Curley, 156–8, 160, 161
    coverage of Northern Ireland, 201, 207–8
    coverage of the path to Irish independence, 6, 52–4, 57–8, 128–36, 137–51
    and the First World War, 95, 121–5, 128–36
    nationalist press, 6, 47, 52–4, 57–8, 137–51, 201, 237–8
Price, Dolours, 270
Price, Marian, 270
Prince Edward Island, 122
Proclamation, 6, 147, 183
propaganda, 67, 142
Protestant and Catholic Encounter (PACE), 200
Protestantism
    in Britain, 105, 117
    Church of Ireland, 13, 15–16, 18–21
    evangelical societies, 186
    and the Great Famine, 186
    hymns, 5, 13, 14, 16–22, 24
    and nationalism, 15, 62, 73
    in Northern Ireland, 121, 200–203, 208, 269
    Protestant Ascendancy, 13, 15, 16, 62, 65, 73, 88–9, 98
    in the US and Canada, 2, 3–4, 96, 105, 127, 132, 134, 136, 141, 142, 144, 214, 222–3, 254
    White Anglo-Saxon Protestants (WASPs), 141, 142, 144, 214
Provisional Government, 147–8

Provisional IRA, 183, 198, 206, 208, 209, 214, 219, 258, 270, 271, 272
public opinion, 56, 57, 89, 94–101, 145, 204–5
public relief works, 27, 187
public services, 156, 158, 159, 164
Puerto Rico, 157

Quakers, 188
Quebec, 32–3, 34, 36, 38–42, 127, 133–4, 136
Quebec City, 133
Queen's University Belfast, 230, 233, 239
Queenstown *see* Cobh
Quinn, John, 89, 94–8, 101

racism, 211–26, 238
radio, 158, 217, 222, 253
Rae, John, 272
Raftery, Mary, 178, 179
railways, 35, 38, 190, 192, 196, 202
Rascal King, The (Beatty), 164
'Rascal King, The' (Mighty Mighty Bosstones), 164
rational politics, 155
Reaching Common Ground conference, 240, 264–5, 268
Reagan, Ronald, 164
Recollections of Fenians and Fenianism (O'Leary), 72
'Recruiting Officer, The' (McGahern), 178
Reddington, Thomas, 32
Redmond, John, 57, 94–5, 96–8, 121–2, 128, 129–31, 134, 138, 142–3
Redmond, Willie, 70
Reed, James, 150–51
'Reflections of a Wallflower' (Parnell), 63
Reformation, 116
regional literature, 13, 22–4
Reidy, James, 150
remittances, 25, 32, 78, 83, 86, 111
Renehan, Colm, 222

Renvyle, Co. Galway, 185
Repeal movement, 47
retail, 187–8, 193
revival *see* Gaelic revival; Irish literary
    revival
Rhodes, Rita, 86
Roberts, William Rnadall, 52, 60
Robinson, Lennox, 72
Robinson, Peter, 26
Roche, Sean, 216
Rock of Cashel, 109
Rocky Mountain Conference on
    British Studies, 230
Roddan, John T., 232
Rogers, Owen, 37
Roosevelt, Franklin D., 157, 158
Roosevelt, Theodore, 95, 97, 99–100
Rossetti, Christina, 14
Rowe, Alice, 80
Rowe, Catherine Kennedy, 78, 80
Rowe, Mary Ann, 6, **77**, 78–85, 87
Rowe, James, 78, 80
Rowe Sutton, James, **77**, 85
Royal Dublin Society, 185
Royal Historical Society, 233–4
RTÉ, 178, 179
rundale system, 186
rural–urban migration, 79
Russell, Lord John, 28
Ryan, George, 247
Ryan, Honora, 245–7
Ryan, Desmond, 59
Ryan, Joe, 255
Ryan, John, 34
Ryan, Margaret, 36
Ryan Report, 172

St Andrews, New Brunswick, 26, 33,
    36–43
St Columb's Cathedral, Derry, **8**,
    18–19
St Dominic's Grammar School for
    Girls, Belfast, 268–74
St George, New Brunswick, 37
St John, 231–2, 241, 242–3, 244

St John, New Brunswick, 39, 40, 125,
    130
St Louise's Comprehensive School,
    Belfast, 268–9, 271–4
St Mary's, Shandon, Cork, 34
St Mary's Cathedral, Kilkenny, 106,
    115
St Mary's church, Dedham, 83, 85
St Mary's University College, Belfast,
    269
St Michael's College, Toronto, 255, 257,
    261
'St Patrick's Breastplate' (Alexander),
    14, 18, 19–21
St Patrick's Day, 105, 106, 109, 127, 131,
    214, 218, 220, 226, 254
St Paul, Minnesota, 69
St Vincent's School, Belfast, 271
Salford, 54
Salisbury, Robert Gascoyne-Cecil,
    Lord, 88, 192
Saltonstall, Leverett, 158
Samaria, 111
Sands, Bobby, 259, 272
Schirmer, Gregory A., 22–3
schools *see* education
Schrembs, Joseph, 112
Scituate, Massachusetts, 236–7, 242,
    267
Scottish Highlands, 190
Scrope, George Poulett, 27
Scully, Thomas, 69
seasonal migration, 188–9
Second Boer War, 122–3
Second Vatican Council, 199–200
Second World War, 2, 151, 162, 250, 253
Segar, Pearl, 240
Select Committee on the Poor Law,
    27–8, 31, 41, 43
Self-Determination League for
    Ireland, 135–6
'Self-Preservation' (da Silva), 268
Senior, Edward, 29
sexuality, 172–3, 176, 178–81
Shanahan, David, 241

Index

Shannon, Catherine B.
  academic study, 229, 237, 255–7, 267
  awards and accolades, 9, 233–4
  early life, 236–7, 244, 253–5
  family history, 236, 244–53
  fellowships, 233–4, 239, 258
  interviewed, 244–61
  pictured, **251, 260**
  political activism, 7–9, 239–40,
    257–66
  public presentations, 230–31, 234,
    258–9, 261
  publications, 233, 268
  research on Balfour, 6, 7, 101, 184,
    229, 230, 233, 237, 238–9, 256,
    258, 267–8
  reviewing, 233
  teaching career, 9, 229–30, 234, 256,
    267
  view of James Michael Curley,
    152–3, 165
  work on Northern Ireland, 7–9, 230,
    231, 233, 234, 237, 238–40, 257–66,
    268
  work on women's studies, 8–9, 230,
    233, 234, 239–40
Shannon, Catherine Cannon, 236,
    252–5
Shannon, Christopher, 237, 253
Shannon, David (Catherine's brother),
    237, 253
Shannon, David (Catherine's father),
    236, 247, 249–51, 252–5
Shannon, David (Catherine's
    grandfather), **246**, 246–7
Shannon, Elizabeth, 240
Shannon, Hubie, 249–50, 253
Shannon, James, 249
Shannon, Richard Tonra, 237, 241, 253,
    254
Shannon, William V., 240
Shaw, George Bernard, 15
Shaw Mason, William, 185
Shawneentown, Illinois, 35
Sheehan, Patrick, Canon, 194

Sheehy-Skeffington, Francis, 71
Sheridan, Peter, 171
Shirley estate, Co. Monaghan, 27
'Siege of Derry, The' (Alexander), 14,
    22–3, 24
silent films, 141
Sinn Féin, 97, 101, 129, 131, 134–5, 136,
    139, 144, 146–8, 265, 271
Sinnott, Alfred A., 135–6
Sinnott, Dick, 217
Sion Hill College, 267
Skibbereen, Co. Cork, 27, 31
skirmishing fund, 52–5, 59
slavery, 4
Sligo, 27
Sligo Nationalist, 72
Small, Teresa Korman, 127
small nations, 91, 125, 130, 133, 135,
    144–5, 149
Smiddy, Timothy, 149
Smith, Al, 157, 257
Smith, Jean Kennedy, 265
Smith, Johanna, 36
Smith, Paul, 171
Smyth, Geraldine Marie, 270
Social Democratic and Labour Party
    (SDLP), 205–10, 239, 269–70, 271
social housing, 159, 202, 239
Sofia M'Kenzie, 36
Somme, battle of the, 120, 129
'Song' (Parnell), 62
South Africa, 32, 122–3
South Boston Information Center
    (SBIC), 216
South Boston Tribune, 213–16, 219, 220
South Dublin Union, 34, 40
Spencer, John, 5th earl, 190
Speranza *see* Wilde, Jane
sport, 3, 105, 139–40
Spratt, Michael, 124, 131
Spring-Rice, Cecil, 88–91, 96, 98
Spring-Rice, Mary, 89
stage Irishmen/women, 141
Star, 38
States of Fear (RTÉ), 179

Stephens, James, 47–8, 56
stereotyping, 65, 141, 239–40, 254
Stewart, A.T.Q., 168, 259
Strabane, Co. Tyrone, 14, 15, 16, 29
Strokestown, Co. Roscommon, 40
Sullivan, Timothy Daniel, 64
Sullivan, William Wilfred, 122
Susan, 26, 33, 36–43
Sunday Press, 175
surveying, 185
Sutton, Patrick J., 85
Swift, Johnathan, 15
Synge, J.M., 195

Tablet, 110, 113–14, 115, 116–17
Taft, William Howard, 95, 97, 99–100,
    142, 155
Tailteann Games, 105
Tammany Hall, 139, 154
Tarpey, Sr Simeon, 270
taxation, 28, 29, 31, 38, 185
television, 178, 179, 223
terrorist campaigns, 49, 52–6, 59, 199,
    270
textile industry, 186–7, 193, 271
That They May Face the Rising Sun
    (McGahern), 167, 173, 183
Thatcher, Margaret, 259
theatre, 141
'There Is a Green Hill Far Away'
    (Alexander), 18, 21, 22
This Man Curley campaign pamphlet,
    158
Thomas Cook, 109, 111, 190
Thoreau, Henry David, 242
tillage farming, 79, 188
Times, 55, 95, 99
Titanic Town (Costello), 272–3
Tobin, Maurice, 158
Todd, James H., 19
Tone, Matilda, 46
Tone, Theobald Wolfe, 2
Toronto, 123, 124, 127, 130, 135, 255,
    257
tourism, 184, 189–90, 194–5, 196

Towards a New Ireland policy
    document, 206–7
Transformation of Ireland 1900–2000
    (Ferriter), 169–70
transnationalism, 44–60
transport, 54, 83, 185, 190, 192, 196, 202
travellers' accounts, 189–90
Trinity College Dublin, 19, 256, 270
Troubles, 3, 183, 198, 205–10, 214–16,
    219, 230, 233, 237, 238–9, 257–66,
    268–74
Truce, 147
Truman, Harry S., 159, 160
Try Again, 36
tuberculosis, 78, 163
Tuke, James Hack, 26, 188
Tumulty, Joseph, 94
208th Canadian Irish battalion, 127
Tyrrell, Honoria, 78

Ulster-Scots dialect, 13, 23–4
Ulster History Circle, 15
Ulster Journal of Archaeology, 14
'Ulster Liberal Unionists and Irish
    Local Government Reform'
    (Shannon), 233
Ulster Unionist Party (UUP), 197, 202,
    205, 208
Ulster Volunteer Force (UVF), 57, 130
Ulysses (Joyce), 14, 24
unemployment, 127, 154, 271, 273–4
unionism, 22–3, 89, 97, 98, 101, 124, 130,
    143, 147, 184, 191–3, 197–210, 230,
    233, 258–9
United Irish Exiles, 47
United Irish League of America
    (UILA), 138–9, 143
United Irishmen, 2, 128
United Protestant Council, 117
University College Dublin, 229, 231,
    237, 255–7, 267
University College Galway, 233
University of Massachusetts, 229, 234,
    237, 256
University of Virginia, 233, 258

Index 349

Vancouver, 135
Vatican, 106, 107–8, 199–200
vaudeville theatre, 141
Veritas bookshop, Dublin, 114
'Verses Written on the Accession
    of Her Majesty the Queen'
    (Alexander), 17
Victoria, Queen, 17, 63, 64
Victory Fund, 144–5
violence, 170, 171, 182–3, 184, 190–91,
    198, 203, 205, 206, 211–12, 258
Vocational Education Committee
    (VEC), 274
voluntary enlistment, 125–7, 132–3,
    143

Wakefield, Edward, 185
Walden (Thoreau), 242
Wall, James, 129
Wallace, James, 80–82
Walls, Laura Dassow, 242
Walsh, David, 80
Walsh, Dick, 183
Walsh, Martin, 164–5
Walter, Bronwen, 3
War of Independence, 138, 146–7, 181–2
Ward, John William, 155
Washington, 88, 91–9, 101, 149, 261
Washington, Booker T., 211
Washington Investment Conference,
    261
Waterford, 39, 171
weaver poets, 23
Webb, Richard D., 188
Webster, Daniel, 156
Weiner, Richard, 45
Welch, Robert J., 192
welfare, 117, 159, 164
west of Ireland, 7, 29, 84, 184–96
Westfield State College, 9, 229, 232,
    234, 237, 240, 256, 258–9, 261, 265,
    267
Westminster Gazette, 145
Westport, Co. Mayo, 190
Wexford, 32

Whitaker, T.K., 257
White, George Preston, 189
White, Kevin, 163, 212
White Anglo-Saxon Protestants
    (WASPs), 141, 142, 144, 214
White House, 91, 112
White Star line, 91, 109
Whitelaw, William, 206, 207, 209
Whitman, Charles S., 100
Wicklow, County, 32
Wild Atlantic Way, 7, 184, 196
Wilde, Jane (Speranza), 15, 66, 71, 73,
    240
Wilde, Oscar, 15
Willes, Edward, Baron, 185
Williams, Betty, 270–71
Williams, Desmond, 237, 256, 267
Williams, John Joseph, 237
Wilson, Woodrow, 89–94, 97, 99,
    100–101, 143
Winnipeg, Manitoba, 123, 125, 128,
    135–6
Wiseman, William, 89, 90, 96
'Woman Writer as Historical Witness,
    The' (Shannon), 268
women
    agency, 6, 61, 74, 85–6
    critical neglect of, 14, 15
    education, 15–16, 252, 268–74
    emigration, 3, 5–6, 26, 29, 30–36,
        41–3, 74–87
    employment, 6, 16, 33, 36, 74, 78,
        82–3, 85–6, 141, 157, 193, 244, 248,
        252, 255
    feminism, 13–14, 15, 74, 176
    inheritance, 79–80
    institutionalisation of, 172–3
    literary representations of, 171–2,
        230
    literature and poetry, 15, 61, 62–3,
        65–8, 71–3
    marriage, 63, 74, 75, 78–80, 83, 85
    motherhood, 17, 69, 75, 171–3
    nationalism, 15, 46–7, 52–3, 61–73
    philanthropy, 15–16, 68

women (*continued*)
    political activism, 6, 52–3, 61–73,
        239–40, 257–66
    political participation, 265
    role in Northern Ireland, 8–9, 230,
        233, 234, 239–40, 259–61, 262–6,
        268
    and sexuality, 172–3, 180–81
    stage representations of, 141
    workhouse inmates, 26, 29,
        30–36
Women and Contemporary Ireland
    conference, 230

Women Envisioning Peace conference,
    240, 265
Woodham-Smith, Cecil, 2
workhouses, 5, 26–43, 187
World Centers of Compassion for
    Children, 271
Wyndham, George, 192

Yeats, Jack B., 195
Yeats, W.B., 13
Young Ireland movement, 15, 47–8, 52,
    73
Young Ireland rebellion, 47